ABOUT THE AUTHOR

Born in Prague, SAUL FRIEDLÄNDER spent his boyhood in
Nazi-occupied France. He is now a professor of history at
UCLA, and has written numerous books on Nazi Germany
and World War II, including the Pulitzer Prize–winning *The
Years of Extermination*.

ABOUT THE ABRIDGER

Born and raised in Tel Aviv, ORNA KENAN lives in Los Angeles.
She holds a Ph.D. in history from UCLA, and has written on
Israel and the Holocaust, including *Between Memory and History: The Evolution of Israeli Historiography of the Holocaust,
1945–1961*.

NAZI GERMANY AND THE JEWS,

1933–1945

ALSO BY SAUL FRIEDLÄNDER

The Years of Extermination:
Nazi Germany and the Jews, 1939–1945

Nazi Germany and the Jews: Volume 1:
The Years of Persecution 1933–1939

Pius XII and the Third Reich

Kurt Gerstein

Prelude to Downfall: Hitler and the United States

History and Psychoanalysis

Reflections of Nazism

When Memory Comes

Memory, History, and the Extermination of the Jews

NAZI GERMANY AND THE JEWS, 1933–1945

ABRIDGED EDITION

SAUL FRIEDLÄNDER

Abridged by Orna Kenan

HARPER  PERENNIAL

NEW YORK • LONDON • TORONTO • SYDNEY • NEW DELHI • AUCKLAND

HARPER ● PERENNIAL

NAZI GERMANY AND THE JEWS, 1933–1945. Copyright © 2009 by Saul Friedländer. Introduction copyright © 2009 by Orna Kenan. All rights reserved. Printed in the United States of America. No part of this book may be used or reproduced in any manner whatsoever without written permission except in the case of brief quotations embodied in critical articles and reviews. For information address HarperCollins Publishers, 10 East 53rd Street, New York, NY 10022.

HarperCollins books may be purchased for educational, business, or sales promotional use. For information please write: Special Markets Department, HarperCollins Publishers, 10 East 53rd Street, New York, NY 10022.

FIRST EDITION

Designed by Ellen Cipriano

Library of Congress Cataloging-in-Publication Data is available upon request.

ISBN 978-0-06-135027-6

11 12 13   OV/RRD   10 9 8 7 6 5 4

To Una

CONTENTS

PART THREE: SHOAH
(January 1942–May 1945)

FOREWORD

This abridged edition of Saul Friedländer's two volume history of *Nazi Germany and the Jews* is not meant to replace the original. Ideally it should encourage its readers to turn to the full-fledged version with its wealth of details and interpretive nuances, which of necessity could not be rendered here. Nonetheless, whatever the constraints imposed by an abridgement, the prime goal of the present work has been to render faithfully Friedländer's highly original integrative approach to the history of the persecution and extermination of European Jewry between 1933 and 1945. The policies of the perpetrators, the attitudes of surrounding society, as well as the initiatives and reactions of the victims are interwoven in a unified narrative. This type of simultaneous representation—at all levels and in all different places—enables the reader better to grasp the magnitude, depth, and multilayered evolution of the events, and to perceive correlations and comparisons hardly apparent beforehand.

The immediate impulse for writing this history, according to the author, derived from the debates of the mid-1980s known as the "historians' controversy" (*Historikerstreit*) and, more specifically, from the ensuing debate between himself and the director of the Munich-based Institute for Contemporary History, Martin Broszat, about the "historicization of National Socialism." Broszat's main criticism was directed against the traditional representation of the Third Reich as a simplistic, black-and-white rendition of "good" and "evil," whereas a full rendition (*Gesamtdarstellung*) demanded many shades of gray. Within this context the Munich scholar contended in particular that the Jewish survivors' perception of this past, as well as that of their descendants, albeit worthy of respect, represented a "mythical memory" (that is, a subjective version of their experiences) that set a "coarsening obstacle in the path of a rational German historiography," based as it were upon a scientific, dispassionate analysis of the facts.

In particular, Broszat argued, as a consequence of their biased perspective, the victims tended to set the criminality of the Nazi regime at center stage and thus saw it as defining the entire history of the Third Reich. In his view the Nazi years should be treated as any "normal" period of history. Rather than be analyzed from hindsight, from the known outcome (the implementation of the "Final Solution of the Jewish Question"), the Nazi period should be followed "in a forward direction, in keeping with historical methodology." Moreover, Broszat noted, the "Final Solution" was made possible precisely because it was systematically concealed from and thus unperceived by the German population until shortly before the end of the war; this lack of awareness of the worst crimes of the regime allowed for an ongoing normality of everyday life for the immense majority of Germans living under National Socialism.

Contrary to Broszat's interpretation, Friedländer questioned the nature of the "normality" of everyday life in the Third Reich prior to the onset of the "Final Solution" (late fall 1941) by showing the extraordinary impact of the regime's anti-Jewish propaganda on the national-racial community (*Volksgemeinschaft*), the awareness of the open persecution of the Jews and other targeted groups before the beginning of the war, and the early and rapidly spreading knowledge and generally tacit acceptance (often the complicit support) among the German population of the crimes of the regime, specifically of mass murder and, from 1942 on, of total extermination.

Also in direct contradistinction to Broszat's argument, *Nazi Germany and the Jews*, sets a major emphasis on the victims' voices in the writing and interpretation of this history. These voices, not as expressed in fallible memoirs (no more fallible of course than those of a Höss or a Speer, among any number of Nazi memorialists and witnesses), but as expressed in the immediate perception of the hundreds of diarists and correspondents whose texts have been retrieved—recorded the minutest details of their own individual world, including the initiatives and daily brutality of the perpetrators, the reactions of populations, and the life and death of their communities. These most immediate testimonies about dimensions of ongoing events, usually unperceived in other sources, do confirm intuitions, warn us against easy generalizations, and tear through the smugness of scholarly detachment. Though, at times, they do repeat the known, they do so with unmatched forcefulness.

Moreover, such personal chronicles, such individual Jewish voices, restore to these events a sharpness of focus that had been progressively lost in recent years through the emphasis in historiographical writing on interpretations essentially foregrounding abstract structures and mindless bureaucratic dynamics. They also add a crucial dimension to the understanding of previously persistent questions about the behavior of the victims and thus about the unfolding of the killing process as such: The reading of diaries and letters, for example, clearly shows that while the populations throughout Europe were becoming aware of the extermination of the Jews, the victims themselves, with the exception of a tiny minority, did not know what was ultimately in store for them. In Western and in Central Europe the Jews were somehow unable to piece the information together; in the East, the Jewish populations in their immense majority did not believe the precise details that trickled into their segregated communities. The historical significance of this inability of the Jews to grasp the fate that awaited them, or rather, their defensive refusal to do so, explains, at least in part, the notorious "passivity" of the Jewish masses and thus the smoothness of the entire process of extermination.

Some major trends in present-day historiography of the Third Reich perceive the criminal policies of the regime within a global context in which the Jewish question becomes but a secondary, almost derivative, issue: The extermination of the Jews is interpreted as the consequence of a Nazi plan to achieve economic and demographic equilibrium in occupied Europe by way of murdering surplus populations (among whom Jews were but one of the targeted groups). The "Final Solution" is also explained as a first stage in a wider ethnic reshuffling and decimation of Eastern populations in order to facilitate German colonization of Eastern spaces. It has similarly been presented as aiming at the systematic plunder of the Jews of Europe in order to alleviate the material burden of the war for the benefit of the German population.

Obversely, in Friedländer's study the extermination of the Jews, who were deemed the main enemy of Nazi Germany, was a major goal in and of itself. Robbing the victims of all their assets constituted but a secondary "benefit" deriving from the mass murder itself. Otherwise, why would the Nazi leader have personally decided in the fall of 1943 to forge ahead with the deportation of the Jews of Denmark and those of Rome, notwithstanding the serious risks involved (the possibility of unrest in Denmark and that of the pope's public protest) and the nonexistent benefits of both operations? What was the urgency and benefit, for that matter, in deporting the poor Jewish communities of the Aegean islands in July 1944, and the hundreds of Jewish children from Paris three days before the liberation of the city?

Furthermore, for Friedländer the anti-Jewish obsession that became characteristic of the regime's self-image, and that inspired the relentlessness of its murder policies to the very last moment, cannot be explained without setting Hitler at center stage: From his first letter on a political issue, sent in September 1919, up to the main exhortations of his political testament (and to its very final line), written on the eve of his suicide, the anti-Jewish struggle was at the core of the German messiah's faith and worldview. Without the obsessive anti-Semitism and the personal impact of Adolf Hitler, first as the leader of the movement, then on the national scene, the widespread German anti-Semitism of those years would probably not have coalesced into systematic anti-Jewish policies and certainly not into their murderous sequels.

Thus, according to the author, ideology as such—specifically anti-Jewish ideology—ultimately played a central role among the factors that drove Nazi policies on an ever more radical path to the most thoroughly organized genocide in modern history. "All in all," Goebbels noted after a long conversation with Hitler at the end of April 1944, "a long-term policy in this war is only possible if one considers it from the standpoint of the Jewish Question." Indeed, the logic behind this anti-Jewish passion stemmed from the ominous image of the Jew as the lethal and relentlessly active enemy of the Reich, intent on its destruction. Thus, within the same hallucinatory logic, once the Reich had to fight on both fronts, east and west, without the hope of a rapid victory and with some early intimations of defeat, Hitler opted for immediate extermination. Otherwise, as he saw it, the Jews would destroy Germany and the new Europe from within.

The lethal image of the Jew as an irreducibly destructive force did not come from nowhere. During the immediate pre-Nazi decades, the anti-Semitism of diverse national, social, and religious groups in Germany and throughout Europe expressed itself in different constructs under changing circumstances and in distinct political frameworks. Yet, whatever its manifold facets, anti-Semitism in the modern era represented but a late development of a common evolution, essentially originating in Christian anti-Judaism.

Though this Christian anti-Jewish hatred remained particularly virulent in Central-Eastern and Eastern Europe, its core myths survived throughout the continent either in their original form or in their secularized garb. Thus the accusation that the Jews were plotting to destroy Christianity became, by a series of metamorphoses, a widespread belief in Jewish attempts to achieve world domination. It found its expression, among others, in a hugely successful anti-Jewish pamphlet, "The Protocols of the Elders of Zion," a literary forgery first published in Russia in 1903, allegedly describing the path the Jews planned to follow to ensure world domination.

In the West the upsurge of anti-Semitism in those same years had a distinctly political-nationalist hue, stemming in large part from the crisis of liberalism in Continental Europe. Liberal society was attacked by revolutionary socialism (that was to become bolshevism in Russia and communism throughout the world), and by a revolutionary right that, on the morrow of World War I, turned into Fascism in Italy and elsewhere, and into Nazism in Germany. Throughout Europe the Jews were identified with liberalism and often with socialism, particularly with its revolutionary brand. In that sense antiliberal and antisocialist (or anticommunist) movements targeted the Jews as representatives of the political ideologies they fought and, more often than not, tagged them as the instigators and carriers of those beliefs. The very crisis of liberal society and its ideological underpinnings left the Jews increasingly weak and isolated throughout a Continent where the progress of liberalism had allowed and fostered their emancipation and rapid social mobility.

In the German Reich, where, from the nineteenth century on, both the traditional and the "modern" aspects of anti-Semitism, mainly in its racial aspect, mixed most radically, this new hatred found its particular expression: The Reich's new militant nationalism was suffused with racist arguments that were increasingly open to the idea of an unbridgeable opposition between the Aryan-German race and the Jewish-Semitic one. Within this context, however, one has to distinguish between two diverse trends: The "ordinary" *völkisch* brand of racial anti-Semitism aimed at the political, social, and biological segregation of the Jews from the German racial community (the *Volk*), and a new brand of racial anti-Semitism (termed "redemptive anti-Semitism" by the author), which heralded a metahistorical struggle between the forces of good and evil, between Aryan humanity and "the Jew." The redemption of the *Volk*, the race, or of Aryan humanity, would be achieved only through the elimination of the Jews.

This latter type of anti-Semitism found its ideological underpinning in late-nineteenth-century Germany, particularly in the so-called Bayreuth circle and the writings of Richard Wagner's son-in-law and ideologue of racial anti-Semitism, Houston Stewart Chamberlain. In end-of-the-century Bayreuth and later, Chamberlain's thought was indeed dominant; it strongly influenced the Munich anti-Jewish ranter and Bayreuth devotee Dietrich Eckart, who in turn became Hitler's early and most influential ideological mentor. As a result, shortly after the beginning of his political career, Hitler came to see himself as the messianic figure chosen by Providence to lead Germany in this fateful battle.

Indeed, Hitler's goals, mainly his vision of an apocalyptic final struggle against the Jews, were metapolitical, investing the core of his movement with the fervor of a crusading sect.

As we shall see, the Nazi leader knew how to "translate" his metapolitical aims into modern politics, modern organization, and modern concepts. And this peculiar fusion of seemingly distinct worlds gave the regime both its fanaticism and its deadly efficiency.

Orna Kenan

ACKNOWLEDGMENTS

I am deeply grateful to my life partner, Saul Friedländer, for his invaluable comments and support. My warm thanks go to my editor at HarperCollins, Hugh Van Dusen, to Rob Crawford, the assistant editor, and to my agent, Georges Borchardt. To Sue Llewellyn, my heartfelt thanks for her wonderful copy-editing and insights.

This work is dedicated to my first-born granddaughter, Una Mae Kenan.

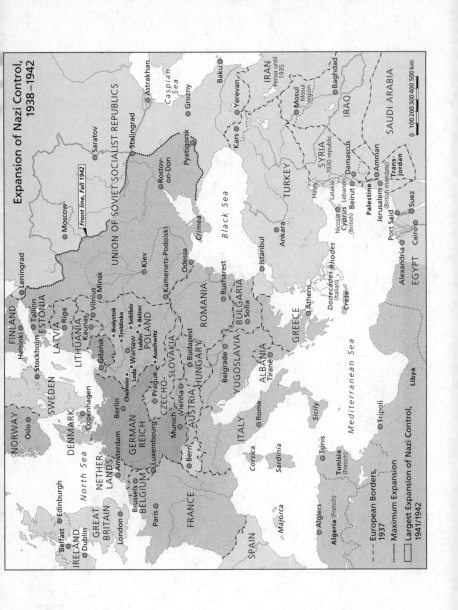

Expansion of Nazi Control, 1938–1942

NORWAY
Oslo
SWEDEN
Stockholm
DENMARK
Copenhagen
North Sea
GREAT BRITAIN
Edinburgh
Belfast
IRELAND
Dublin
London
NETHER-LANDS
Amsterdam
Brussels
BELGIUM
Luxembourg
Paris
FRANCE
SPAIN
Majorca
Corsica
Sardinia
Algiers
Algeria (French)
Tunis
Tunisia (French)
Tripoli
Libya
Mediterranean Sea
ITALY
Rome
Sicily
Bern
Munich
Berlin
GERMAN REICH
AUSTRIA
Vienna
Prague
CZECHO-SLOVAKIA
Chełmno
Łódź
Gdańsk
Białystok
Treblinka
Sobibór
Bełżec
Auschwitz
Lublin
Warsaw
POLAND
SLOVAKIA
Budapest
HUNGARY
YUGOSLAVIA
Belgrade
Tiranë
ALBANIA
GREECE
Athens
Crete
Rhodes
Dodecades (Italian)
Sofia
BULGARIA
ROMANIA
Bucharest
Istanbul
Ankara
TURKEY
Black Sea
Crimea
Odessa
Kamenets-Podolski
Kiev
Minsk
Vilnius
Kaunas
LITHUANIA
Riga
LATVIA
Tallinn
ESTONIA
Helsinki
FINLAND
Leningrad
Moscow
UNION OF SOVIET SOCIALIST REPUBLICS
Front line, Fall 1942
Saratov
Astrakhan
Caspian Sea
Grozny
Baku
Yerevan
Kars
Pyatigorsk
Rostov-on-Don
Stalingrad
IRAN
Persia until 1935
Mosul region
Mosul
Baghdad
IRAQ
SAUDI ARABIA
SYRIA
1930 republic
Hatay
Latakia
Damascus
Beirut
Lebanon
Cyprus (British)
Nicosia
Trans-Jordan
Amman
Palestine (British mandate)
Jerusalem
Port Said
Suez
Cairo
Alexandria
EGYPT

0 100 200 300 400 500 km

European Borders, 1937
Maximum Expansion
Largest Expansion of Nazi Control, 1941/1942

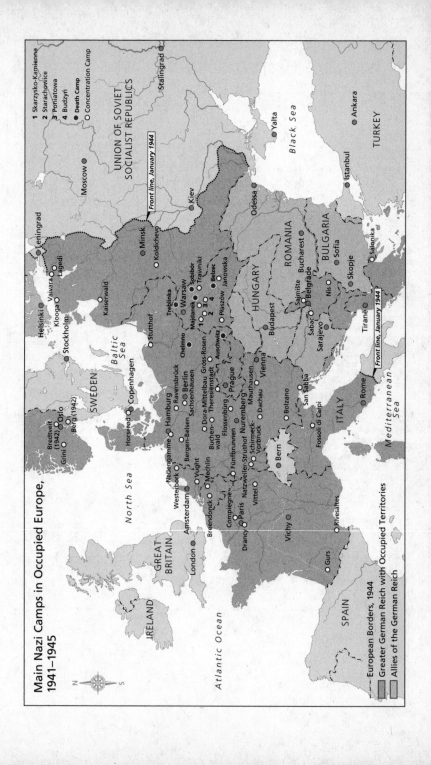

Main Nazi Camps in Occupied Europe, 1941–1945

1 Skarzysko-Kamienna
2 Starachowice
3 Poniatowa
4 Budzyń
● Death Camp
○ Concentration Camp

UNION OF SOVIET SOCIALIST REPUBLICS

Front line, January 1944

Stalingrad
Moscow
Leningrad
Helsinki
Vaivara
Klooga
Lagedi
Stockholm
Kaiserwald
Minsk
Koldichevo
Kiev
Odessa
Yalta
Black Sea
Ankara
Istanbul
TURKEY
Salonika
Sofia
Skopje
BULGARIA
Bucharest
ROMANIA
Nis
Belgrade
Sajmište
Sabac
Sarajevo
Tirane
Budapest
HUNGARY
Vienna
Bolzano
San Sabba
Fossoli di Carpi
Rome
ITALY
Mediterranean Sea
Front line, January 1944
Treblinka
Warsaw
Sobibor
Trawniki
Belzec
Janowska
Chelmno
Majdanek
Plaszow
Auschwitz
Stutthof
Gross-Rosen
Dora-Mittelbau
Buchenwald
Theresienstadt
Prague ?
Flossenburg
Mauthausen
Dachau
Nuremberg
Natzweiler-Struthof
Schirmeck-Vorbruck
Innsbruck
Funfbrunnen
Mechlin
Vught
Breendonk
Compiegne
Drancy
Paris
Vittel
Vichy
Rivesaltes
Gurs
SPAIN
Amsterdam
Westerbork
Neuengamme
Hamburg
Ravensbruck
Berlin
Sachsenhausen
Bergen-Belsen
Horserod
Copenhagen
Bern
Baltic Sea
SWEDEN
Bredtveit (1942)
Oslo
Berg (1942)
Grini
North Sea
GREAT BRITAIN
London
IRELAND
Atlantic Ocean

N

European Borders, 1944
Greater German Reich with Occupied Territories
Allies of the German Reich

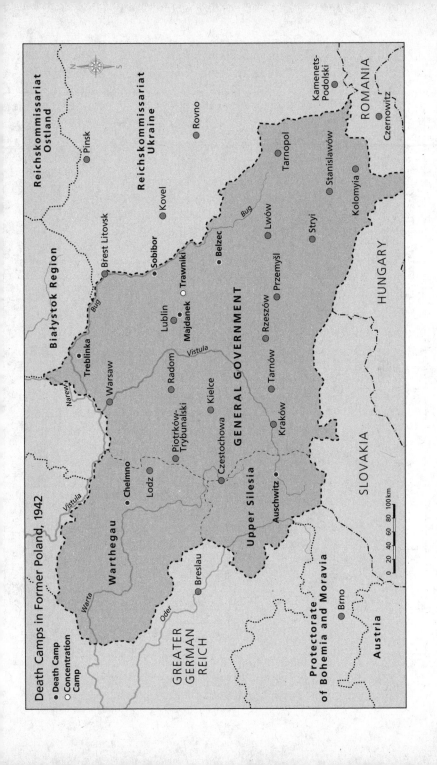

Death Camps in Former Poland, 1942

- ● Death Camp
- ○ Concentration Camp

Reichskommissariat Ostland

Reichskommissariat Ukraine

Białystok Region

GENERAL GOVERNMENT

Warthegau

Upper Silesia

GREATER GERMAN REICH

Protectorate of Bohemia and Moravia

SLOVAKIA

HUNGARY

ROMANIA

Austria

Pinsk

Rovno

Kovel

Kamenets-Podolski

Czernowitz

Tarnopol

Stanislawów

Kolomyia

Stryi

Lwów

Przemyśl

Rzeszów

Brest Litovsk

Sobibor

Trawniki

Belzec

Lublin

Majdanek

Tarnów

Kraków

Treblinka

Warsaw

Radom

Piotrków-Trybunalski

Kielce

Czestochowa

Auschwitz

Chelmno

Lodz

Breslau

Brno

Narew

Vistula

Bug

Bug

Vistula

Warta

Oder

0 20 40 60 80 100 km

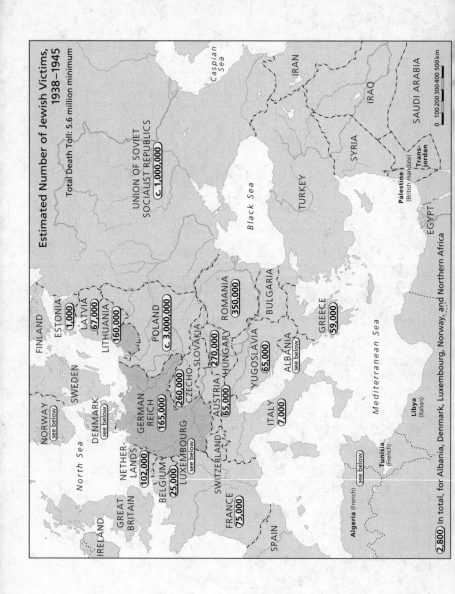

Estimated Number of Jewish Victims, 1938–1945

Total Death Toll: 5.6 million minimum

UNION OF SOVIET SOCIALIST REPUBLICS c. 1,000,000

FINLAND

ESTONIA 1,000

LATVIA 67,000

LITHUANIA 160,000

POLAND c. 3,000,000

ROMANIA 350,000

BULGARIA

GREECE 59,000

SWEDEN

NORWAY see below

DENMARK see below

GERMAN REICH 165,000

CZECHO-SLOVAKIA 260,000

AUSTRIA 65,000

HUNGARY 270,000

YUGOSLAVIA 65,000

ALBANIA see below

ITALY 7,000

NETHER-LANDS 102,000

BELGIUM 25,000

LUXEMBOURG see below

SWITZERLAND

FRANCE 75,000

GREAT BRITAIN

IRELAND

SPAIN

TURKEY

IRAN

IRAQ

SYRIA

SAUDI ARABIA

Palestine (British mandate)

Trans-Jordan

EGYPT

Libya (Italian)

Tunisia (French)

Algeria (French) see below

North Sea

Caspian Sea

Black Sea

Mediterranean Sea

2,800 In total, for Albania, Denmark, Luxembourg, Norway, and Northern Africa

0 100 200 300 400 500 km

PART I

PERSECUTION

January 1933–August 1939

I would not wish to be a Jew in Germany.

—HERMANN GÖRING,
NOVEMBER 12, 1938

CHAPTER 1

Into the Third Reich

January 1933–December 1933

T<small>HE EXODUS FROM</small> G<small>ERMANY</small> of Jewish and left-wing artists and intellectuals began during the early months of 1933, almost immediately after Adolf Hitler's accession to power on January 30. As among thousands, the conductors Otto Klemperer and Bruno Walter were compelled to flee, Hans Hinkel, the new Nazi president of the Prussian Theater Commission and the official in charge of the "de-Judaization" of cultural life in Prussia, explained in the *Frankfurter Zeitung* of April 6 that Klemperer and Walter had disappeared from the musical scene because there was no way to protect them from the "mood" of a German public long provoked by "Jewish artistic liquidators."[1]

Prominence and fame shielded no one. On January 30, 1933, Albert Einstein, on a visit to the United States, described what was happening in Germany as a "psychic illness of the masses." He ended his return journey in Ostend (Belgium) and never again set foot on German soil. The Kaiser Wilhelm Society dismissed him from his position; the Prussian Academy of Sciences expelled him; his citizenship was rescinded. Einstein was no longer a German. Max Reinhardt was expelled from the directorship of the German Theater and fled the Reich. Max Liebermann, possibly the best-known German painter of the time, was too old to emigrate when Hitler came to power. Formerly president of the Prussian Academy of Arts, and in 1933 its honorary president, he held the highest German decoration, the Pour le Mérite. On May 7 Liebermann resigned from the academy; none of his colleagues deemed it necessary to express a word of recognition or sympathy. Isolated and ostracized, Liebermann died in 1935; only three "Aryan" artists attended his funeral.[2]

By and large there was no apparent sense of panic or even of urgency among the great majority of the approximately 525,000 Jews living in Germany in January 1933. The board of the Central Association of German Citizens of the Jewish Faith (Zentralverein, or CV) announced, on January 30: "In general, today more than ever we must follow the directive: wait calmly."[3] An editorial in the association's newspaper for January 30, written by the organization's chairman, Ludwig Holländer, was slightly more worried in tone, but reflected basically the same stance: "The German Jews will not lose the calm they derive from their tie to all that is truly German. Less than ever will they allow external attacks to influence their inner attitude toward Germany."[4]

As the weeks went by, Max Naumann's Association of National German Jews and the Reich Association of Jewish War Veterans hoped for no less than integration into the new order of things. On April 4 the veterans' association chairman, Leo Löwenstein, addressed a petition to Hitler including a list of nationalistically oriented suggestions regarding the Jews of Germany, as well as a copy of the memorial book containing the names of the twelve thousand German soldiers of Jewish origin who had died for Germany during World War I. Ministerial Councillor Wienstein answered on April 14 that the chancellor acknowledged receipt of the letter and the book with "sincerest feelings."[5] The head of the Chancellery, Hans

Heinrich Lammers, received a delegation of the veterans on April 28, but with that the contacts ceased. Soon Hitler's office stopped acknowledging petitions from the Jewish organization. Like the Central Association, the Zionists continued to believe that the initial upheavals could be overcome by a reassertion of Jewish identity or simply by patience; the Jews reasoned that the responsibilities of power, the influence of conservative members of the government, and a watchful outside world would exercise a moderating influence on any Nazi tendency to excess.

For some Jews the continuing presence of the aged, respected President Paul von Hindenburg as head of state was a source of confidence; they occasionally wrote to him about their distress. "I was engaged to be married in 1914," Frieda Friedmann, a Berlin woman, wrote to Hindenburg on February 23: "My fiancé was killed in action in 1914. My brothers Max and Julius Cohn were killed in 1916 and 1918. My remaining brother, Willy, came back blind. . . . All three received the Iron Cross for their service to the country. But now it has gone so far that in our country pamphlets saying, 'Jews, get out!' are being distributed on the streets, and there are open calls for pogroms and acts of violence against Jews. . . . Is incitement against Jews a sign of courage or one of cowardice when Jews comprise only one percent of the German people?" Hindenburg's office promptly acknowledged receipt of the letter, and the president let Frieda Friedmann know that he was decidedly opposed to excesses perpetrated against Jews. The letter was then transmitted to Hitler, who wrote in the margin: "This lady's claims are a swindle! Obviously there has been no incitement to a pogrom!"[6] The Jews finally, like a considerable part of German society, were not sure—particularly before the March 5, 1933, Reichstag elections—whether the Nazis were in power to stay or whether a conservative military coup against them was still possible.

The primary political targets of the new regime, at least during the first months after the Nazi accession to power, were not Jews but Communists. On February 27, the Reichstag was set on fire. The Communists were accused of the arson, and the manhunt that followed led to the arrest of almost ten thousand party members and sympathizers and to their imprisonment in newly created concentration camps. Dachau had been established on March 20 and was officially inaugurated by SS chief Heinrich Himmler on April 1 (the Schutzstaffel, or SS, was the Nazi party's elite force). In June SS Group Leader Theodor Eicke became the camp's commander, and a year later he was appointed "inspector of concentration camps": Under Himmler's aegis he had become the architect of the life-and-death routine of the camp inmates in Hitler's new Germany.

On February 28, the morning after the Reichstag fire, a presidential decree had already given Hitler emergency powers. Although the Nazis failed to gain an absolute majority in the March 5 elections, their coalition with the ultraconservative German National People's Party obtained it. A few days later, on March 23, the Reichstag divested itself of its functions by passing the Enabling Act, which gave full legislative and executive powers to the chancellor. The rapidity of the changes that followed was stunning: The states were brought into line; in May the trade unions were abolished and replaced by the German Labor Front; in July all political parties formally ceased to exist with the sole exception of the National Socialist German Workers Party (NSDAP). Popular support for this surge of activity and constant demonstration of power snowballed. In the eyes of a rapidly growing number of Germans, a "national revival" was under way.

Anti-Jewish violence spread after the March elections. On March 9 Storm Troopers (the Sturmabteilung, or SA—the original paramilitary formation of the NSDAP) seized dozens of Eastern European Jews in the Scheunenviertel, one of Berlin's Jewish quarters. Traditionally the first targets of German Jew-hatred, these *Ostjuden* were also the first Jews to be sent off to concentration camps. On March 13 forcible closing of Jewish shops was imposed by the local SA in Mannheim; in Breslau, Jewish lawyers and judges were assaulted in the court building; and in Gedern, in Hesse, the SA broke into Jewish homes and beat up the inhabitants "with the acclamation of a rapidly growing crowd." The list of similar incidents is a long one.[7]

There were also killings. According to the late March report of the governing president of Bavaria, "On the 15th of this month, around 6 in the morning, several men in dark uniforms arrived by truck at the home of the Israelite businessman Otto Selz in Straubing. Selz was dragged from his house in his night-clothes and taken away. Around 9:30 Selz was shot to death in a forest near Wang, in the Landshut district. . . . Several people claim to have noticed that the truck's occupants wore red arm-bands with a swastika."[8] On March 31 Interior Minister Wilhelm Frick wired all local police stations to warn them that communist agitators disguised in SA uniforms and using SA license plates would smash Jewish shopwindows and exploit the occasion to create disturbances. This could have been standard Nazi disinformation or some remaining belief in possible communist subversion. On April 1 the Göttingen police station investigating the damage to Jewish stores and the local synagogue on March 28 reported having caught two members of the Communist Party and one Social Democrat in possession of parts of Nazi uniforms; headquarters in Hildesheim was informed that the men arrested were the perpetrators of the anti-Jewish action.

Much of the foreign press gave wide coverage to the Nazi violence. American newspapers, in particular, did not mince words about the anti-Jewish persecution. Jewish and non-Jewish protests grew. These very protests became the Nazis' pretext for the notorious April 1, 1933, boycott of Jewish businesses. In mid-March, Hitler had already allowed a committee headed by Julius Streicher, party chief of Franconia and editor of the party's most vicious anti-Jewish newspaper, *Der Stürmer*, to proceed with preparatory work for it.

Among the Nazis much of the agitation for anti-Jewish economic measures was initiated by a motley coalition of "radicals." Their common denominator was what former number two party leader Gregor Strasser once called an "anti-capitalist nostalgia";[9] their easiest way of expressing it: virulent anti-Semitism. Such party radicals will be encountered at each major stage of anti-Jewish policy up to and including the Kristallnacht pogrom of November 1938. In April 1933 they can be identified as members of the party's various economic interest groups. But specifically, as a pressure group, the radicals consisted mainly of "old fighters"—SA members and rank-and-file party activists dissatisfied with the pace of the National Socialist revolution, with the meagerness of the spoils that had accrued to them, and with the often privileged status of comrades occupying key administrative positions in the state bureaucracy. Their influence should not be overrated, however. They never compelled Hitler to take steps he did not want to take. When their demands were deemed excessive, their initiatives were dismissed. But in the spring of 1933 the anti-Jewish agitation helped the regime channel SA violence into state-controlled measures; to the Nazis, of course, these measures were also welcome for their own sake.

Hitler informed the cabinet of the planned boycott of Jewish-owned businesses on March 29, telling the ministers that he himself had called for it. He described the alternative as spontaneous popular violence. An approved boycott, he added, would avoid dangerous unrest. The German National ministers objected, and President Hindenburg tried to intervene. Hitler, however, rejected any possible cancellation.

In the meantime Jewish leaders, mainly in the United States and Palestine, were in a quandary: Should they support mass protests and a counterboycott of German goods, or should confrontation be avoided for fear of further "reprisals" against the Jews of Germany? Hermann Göring, since January the number two man in the Nazi Party's hierarchy, had summoned several leaders of German Jewry and sent them to London to intervene against planned anti-German demonstrations and initiatives. Simultaneously, on March 26, Kurt Blumenfeld, president of the Zionist Federation for Germany, and Julius Brodnitz, president of the Central Association, cabled the American Jewish Committee in New York, demanding that efforts be made TO OBTAIN AN END TO DEMONSTRATIONS HOSTILE TO GERMANY.[10] By appeasing the Nazis the fearful German-Jewish leaders were hoping to avoid the boycott.

The leaders of the Jewish community in Palestine also opted for caution, whereas American Jewish leaders remained divided; most of the Jewish organizations in the United States were opposed to mass demonstrations and economic action, mainly for fear of embarrassing President Roosevelt and the State Department. Reluctantly, and under pressure from such groups as the Jewish War Veterans, the American Jewish Congress finally decided otherwise. In March protest meetings took place in several American cities, with the participation of church and labor leaders. As for the boycott of German goods, it spread as an emotional grass-roots movement that, over the months, received an increasing measure of institutional support, at least outside Palestine.

Joseph Goebbels, the propaganda minister, was elated. In his diary entry for March 27 he wrote: "I've dictated a sharp article against the Jews' atrocity propaganda. At its mere announcement the whole *mischpoke* [*sic*; Yiddish for "family"] broke down."[11] And on April 1: "The boycott against the international atrocities propaganda broke out in the fullest intensity in Berlin and all over the Reich. The public," Goebbels added, "has everywhere shown its solidarity."[12]

In reality, however, the Nazi action ran into immediate problems. The population proved rather indifferent to the boycott and sometimes even intent on buying in "Jewish" stores. In Munich, for example, repeated announcements concerning the forthcoming boycott resulted in such brisk business in Jewish-owned stores during the last days of March (the public did not yet know how long the boycott would last) that the *Völkischer Beobachter* bemoaned "the lack of sense among that part of the population which forced its hard-earned money into the hands of enemies of the people and cunning slanderers."[13] On the day of the boycott many Jewish businesses remained shut or closed early. Vast throngs of onlookers blocked the streets in the commercial districts of major city centers to watch the unfolding event: They were passive but in no way showed the hostility to the "enemies of the people" the party agitators had expected.

The lack of popular enthusiasm was compounded by a host of unforeseen questions: How was a "Jewish" enterprise to be defined? By its name, by the Jewishness of its managers, or by Jewish control of all or part of its capital? If the enterprise was hurt, what, in a time of economic crisis, would happen to its Aryan employees? What would be the overall consequences, in terms of possible foreign retaliation, for the German economy?

Although impending for some time, the April boycott was clearly an improvised action. It may have aimed at channeling the anti-Jewish initiatives of the SA and of other radicals; at indicating that, in the long run, the basis of Jewish existence in Germany would be destroyed; or, more immediately, at responding in an appropriately Nazi way to foreign protests against the treatment of German Jews. Whatever the various motivations may have been, Hitler displayed a form of leadership that was to become characteristic of his anti-Jewish actions over the next several years: He usually set an *apparent* compromise course between the demands of the party radicals and the pragmatic reservations of the conservatives, giving the public the impression that he himself was above operational details. Such restraint was obviously tactical; in the case of the boycott, it was dictated by the state of the economy and wariness of international reactions.

The possibility of further boycotts remained open. Nonetheless it was becoming increasingly clear to Hitler that Jewish economic life was not to be openly interfered with, at least as long as the German economy was still in a precarious situation. A fear of foreign economic retaliation was shared by Nazis and their conservative allies alike and dictated temporary moderation. And, once the conservative Hjalmar Schacht moved from the presidency of the Reichsbank to become minister of the economy in the summer of 1934, noninterference with Jewish business was quasi-officially agreed upon.

The failed boycott was quickly overshadowed by the laws of April 1933. The first of them—the most fundamental one because of its definition of the Jew—was the April 7 Law for the Restoration of the Professional Civil Service. In its most general intent, the law aimed at reshaping the entire government bureaucracy in order to ensure its loyalty to the new regime. Applying to more than two million state and municipal employees, its exclusionary measures were directed against the politically unreliable, mainly communists and other opponents of the Nazis, and against Jews. Paragraph 3, which came to be called the "Aryan paragraph," announced: "Civil servants of non-Aryan origin are to retire. . . ." On April 11 the law's first supplementary decree defined "non-Aryan" as "anyone descended from non-Aryan, particularly Jewish, parents or grandparents. It suffices if one parent or grandparent is non-Aryan."[14]

Up to this point the Nazis had unleashed the most extreme anti-Jewish propaganda and brutalized, boycotted, or killed Jews on the assumption that they could somehow be identified as Jews, but no formal disenfranchisement based on an exclusionary definition had yet been initiated. The definition as such—whatever its precise terms were to be in the future—was the necessary initial basis of all the persecutions that were to follow.

The definition of Jewish origin in the civil service law was the broadest and most comprehensive, and the provisions for assessment of each doubtful case the harshest possible. But in 1933 the overall number of Jews in the civil service was small. Moreover, as a result of Hindenburg's intervention, combat veterans and civil servants whose fathers or sons had been killed in action in World War I were exempted from the law. Civil servants, moreover, who had been in state service by August 1, 1914, were also exempt. All others were forced into retirement.

Legislation regarding Jewish lawyers illustrates, even more clearly than the economic boycott, how Hitler maneuvered between contradictory demands from Nazi radicals on the one hand and from his conservative allies on the other. By the end of March physical molestation of Jewish jurists had spread throughout the Reich. In several cities Jewish judges and lawyers were dragged out of their offices and even out of courtrooms during proceedings, and, more often than not, beaten up. At the same time local Nazi leaders such as the Bavarian justice minister, Hans Frank, and the Prussian justice minister, Hanns Kerrl, on their own initiative, announced measures for the immediate dismissal of all Jewish lawyers and civil servants. Franz Schlegelberger, state secretary of the Ministry of Justice, reported to Hitler that these local initiatives created an entirely new situation and demanded rapid legislation to impose a new, unified legal framework. The Justice Ministry had prepared a decree excluding Jewish lawyers from the bar on the same basis—but also with the same exemptions regarding combat veterans and their relatives, and longevity in practice, as under the civil service law. At the April 7 cabinet meeting the decree was confirmed; it was made public on April 11.

Because of the exemptions, the initial application of the law was relatively mild. Of the 4,585 Jewish lawyers practicing in Germany, 3,167 were allowed to continue their work; 336 Jewish judges and state prosecutors, out of a total of 717, were also kept in office. In June 1933 Jews still made up more than 16 percent of all practicing lawyers in Germany. However, these statistics should not be misinterpreted. Though still allowed to practice, Jewish lawyers were excluded from the national association of lawyers and listed not in its annual directory but in a separate guide; all in all, notwithstanding the support of some Aryan institutions and individuals, they worked under a "boycott by fear."

Nazi rank-and-file agitation against Jewish physicians did not lag far behind the attacks on Jewish jurists. Hitler, nonetheless, was even more careful with physicians than with lawyers. At this stage Jewish doctors were merely barred de facto from clinics and hospitals run by the national health insurance organization, with some even allowed to continue to practice there. Thus, in mid-1933, nearly 11 percent of all practicing German physicians were Jews. Here is another example of Hitler's pragmatism in action: Thousands of Jewish physicians meant tens of thousands of German patients. Disrupting the ties between these physicians and a vast number of patients could have caused unnecessary discontent. Hitler preferred to wait.

On April 25 the Law Against the Overcrowding of German Schools and Universities was passed. It was aimed exclusively at non-Aryan students. The law limited the enrollment of new Jewish students in any German school or university to 1.5 percent of the total of new applicants, with the overall number of

Jewish students in any institution not to exceed 5 percent. Children of World War I veterans and those born of mixed marriages contracted before the passage of the law were exempted from the quota.

For Jewish children the new atmosphere was possibly more significant than the laws as such. Young Hilma Geffen-Ludomer, the only Jewish child in the Berlin suburb of Rangsdorf, recalled the sudden change: The "nice, neighborly atmosphere ended abruptly. . . . Suddenly, I didn't have any friends. I had no more girlfriends, and many neighbors were afraid to talk to us. Some of the neighbors that we visited told me: 'Don't come anymore because I'm scared. We should not have any contact with Jews.'" Lore Gang-Salheimer, eleven in 1933 and living in Nuremberg, could remain in her school as her father had fought at Verdun. Nonetheless "it began to happen that non-Jewish children would say, 'No, I can't walk home from school with you anymore. I can't be seen with you anymore.'"[15]

The April laws and the supplementary decrees that followed compelled at least two million state employees and tens of thousands of lawyers, physicians, students and many others to look for adequate proof of Aryan ancestry; the same process turned tens of thousands of priests, pastors, town clerks, and archivists into investigators and suppliers of vital attestations of impeccable blood purity; willingly or not they were becoming part of a racial bureaucratic machine that had begun to search, probe, and exclude.

In September 1933 Jews were forbidden to own farms or engage in agriculture. That same month, the establishment, under the control of the Propaganda Ministry, of the Reich Chamber of Culture, enabled Goebbels to limit the participation of Jews in the new Germany's cultural life. Also under the aegis of Goebbels's Propaganda Ministry, Jews were barred from belonging to the Journalists' Association and, on October 4, from being newspaper editors. The German press had been cleansed.

In Nazi racial thinking the German national community drew its strength from the purity of its blood and from its root-edness in the sacred German earth. Such racial purity was a condition of superior cultural creation and of the construction of a powerful state, the guarantor of victory in the struggle for racial survival and domination. From the outset, therefore, the 1933 laws pointed to the exclusion of the Jews from all key areas of this utopian vision: the state structure itself (the civil service law), the biological health of the national community (the physicians' law), the social fabric of the community (the disbarring of Jewish lawyers), culture (the laws regarding schools, universities, the press, the cultural professions), and, finally, the sacred earth (the farm law). The civil service law was the only one of these to be fully implemented at this early stage, but the symbolic statements the laws expressed and the ideological message they carried were unmistakable.

Very few German Jews sensed the implications of the Nazi edicts in terms of sheer long-range terror. One who did was Georg Solmssen, spokesman for the board of directors of the Deutsche Bank and son of an Orthodox Jew. In an April 9, 1933, letter addressed to the bank's chairman of the board, Solmssen wrote: "I am afraid that we are merely at the beginning of a process aiming, purposefully and according to a well-prepared plan, at the economic and moral annihilation of all members, without any distinctions, of the Jewish race living in Germany. The total passivity not only of those classes of the population that belong to the National Socialist Party, the absence of all feelings of solidarity becoming apparent among those who until now worked shoulder to shoulder with Jewish colleagues, the increasingly more obvious desire to take personal advan-tage of vacated positions, the hushing up of the disgrace and the shame disastrously inflicted upon people who, although

innocent, witness the destruction of their honor and their existence from one day to the next—all of this indicates a situation so hopeless that it would be wrong not to face it squarely
without any attempt at prettification."[16]

Another group targeted by the Nazi regime from the outset
included a segment of the Aryan population itself. The Law
for the Prevention of Genetically Diseased Offspring, adopted
on July 14, 1933, allowed for the sterilization of anyone recognized as suffering from supposedly hereditary diseases, such as
feeble-mindedness, schizophrenia, manic-depressive disorder,
genetic epilepsy, blindness, deafness, or severe alcoholism.

The evolution leading to the July 1933 law was already no-
ticeable during the Weimar period. Among eugenicists, the
promoters of "positive eugenics" were losing ground, and
"negative eugenics"—with its emphasis on the exclusion, that
is, mainly the sterilization, of carriers of incapacitating hereditary diseases—was gaining the upper hand even within official institutions: A trend that had appeared on a wide scale
in the West before World War I was increasingly dominating
the German scene. As in so many other domains, the war was
of decisive importance: Weren't the young and the physically
fit being slaughtered on the battlefield while the incapacitated
and the unfit were being shielded? Wasn't the reestablishment
of genetic equilibrium a major national-racial imperative? Economic thinking added its own logic: The social cost of maintaining mentally and physically handicapped individuals whose
reproduction would only increase the burden was considered
prohibitive. This way of thinking was widespread and by no
means a preserve of the radical Right. Although the draft of a
sterilization law submitted to the Prussian government in July
1932 still emphasized *voluntary* sterilization in case of hereditary defects, the idea of *compulsory* sterilization seems to have
been spreading. It was nonetheless with the Nazi accession to

power that the decisive change took place. About two hundred thousand people were sterilized between mid-1933 and the end of 1937. By the end of the war, the number had reached four hundred thousand.

From the outset of the sterilization policies to the apparent ending of euthanasia in August 1941—and to the beginning of the "Final Solution" close to that same date—policies regarding the handicapped and the mentally ill on the one hand and those regarding the Jews on the other followed a simultaneous and parallel development. These two categories of policies, however, had different origins and different aims. Whereas sterilization and euthanasia were exclusively aimed at enhancing the purity of the German racial community itself and were bolstered by cost-benefit computations, the segregation and the extermination of the Jews—though also a racial purification process—was mainly a struggle against an active, formidable enemy that was perceived as endangering the very survival of Germany and of the Aryan world. Thus, in addition to the goal of racial cleansing, identical to that pursued in the sterilization and euthanasia campaign and in contrast to it, the struggle against the Jews was seen as a confrontation of apocalyptic dimensions.

The boycott of Jewish businesses was the first major test on a national scale of the attitude of the Christian churches toward the situation of the Jews under the new government. In the historian Klaus Scholder's words, "during the decisive days . . . , no bishop, no church dignitary, no synod made any open declaration against the persecution of the Jews in Germany."[17]

In a radio address broadcast to the United States on April 4, 1933, the most prominent German Protestant clergyman, Berlin Bishop Otto Dibelius, justified the new regime's actions, denying that there was any brutality even in the concentration camps and asserting that the boycott—which he called a reasonable defensive measure—took its course amid "calm and order."[18] His broadcast was no momentary aberration. A few days later Dibelius sent a confidential Easter message to all the pastors of his province: "My dear Brethren! We all not only understand but are fully sympathetic to the recent motivations out of which the *völkisch* movement has emerged. Notwithstanding the evil sound that the term has frequently acquired, I have always considered myself an anti-Semite. One cannot ignore that Jewry has played a leading role in all the destructive manifestations of modern civilization."[19]

The Catholic Church's reaction to the boycott was not fundamentally different. On March 31, at the suggestion of the Berlin cleric Bernhard Lichtenberg, the director of the Deutsche Bank in Berlin and president of the Committee for Interconfessional Peace, Oskar Wassermann, asked Adolf Johannes Cardinal Bertram, chairman of the German Conference of Bishops, to intervene against the boycott. Nothing was done.

The main debate within the churches focused on the status of converted Jews and the links between Judaism and Christianity. It had become particularly acute within Protestantism, when, in 1932, the pro-Nazi German Christian Faith Movement published its "Guidelines." The relevant theme was a sort of race-conscious belief in Christ; race, people and nation as part of a God-given ordering of life. Point 9 of "Guidelines," for example, reads: "In the mission to the Jews we see a serious threat to our people. That mission is the entry way for foreign blood into the body of our *Volk*. . . . Marriage between Germans and Jews particularly is to be forbidden."[20] In the 1932 church elections the German-Christian movement received a third of the vote; and, on September 27, 1933, Ludwig Müller, a fervent Nazi, was elected Reich bishop—that is, as some sort of führer's coordinator for all major issues pertaining to the Protestant churches.

But precisely this election and a growing controversy regarding pastors and church members of Jewish origin caused a widening rift within the Evangelical Church. In an implementation of the civil service law, the synod governing the Prussian Evangelical Church demanded the forced retirement of pastors of Jewish origin or married to Jews. This initiative was quickly followed by most other synods throughout the Reich. Simultaneously, however, a contrary trend made its appearance; it was supported by a group of leading theologians who issued a statement on "The New Testament and the Race Question" that rejected any theological justification for adoption of the Aryan paragraph. And, on Christmas 1933, Pastors Dietrich Bonhoeffer and Martin Niemöller founded an oppositional organization, the Pastors' Emergency League, which, within a few months, grew to six thousand members. One of the league's first initiatives was to issue a protest against the Aryan paragraph: "As a matter of duty, I bear witness that with the use of 'Aryan laws' within the Church of Christ an injury is done to our common confession of faith."[21] The Confessing Church was born. The steadfastness of the Confessing Church regarding the Jewish issue was limited, however, to support of the rights of non-Aryan Christians. From the Church's viewpoint, the real debate was about principle and dogma, which excluded unconverted Jews.

On the face of it the Catholic Church's attitude toward the new regime should have been firmer than that of the Protestants. The Catholic hierarchy had expressed a measure of hostility to Hitler's movement during the last years of the republic, but this stance was uniquely determined by church interests and by the varying political fortunes of the Catholic Center Party. The attitude of many German Catholics toward Nazism before 1933 was fundamentally ambiguous: Many Catholic publicists pointed to the anti-Christian elements in the Nazi program and declared these incompatible with Catholic teaching. But they went on to speak of the healthy core of Nazism—its reassertion of the values of religion and love of fatherland, its standing as a strong bulwark against atheistic bolshevism. In general the attitude of the Catholic Church regarding the Jewish issue in Germany and elsewhere can be defined as a "moderate anti-Semitism" that supported the struggle against "undue Jewish influence" in the economy and in cultural life. As Vicar-General Mayer of Mainz expressed it, "Hitler in *Mein Kampf* had 'appropriately described' the bad influence of the Jews in press, theater and literature. Still, it was un-Christian to hate other races and to subject the Jews and foreigners to disabilities through discriminatory legislation that would merely bring about reprisals from other countries."[22]

On the occasion of the ratification of a Concordat between the Nazi regime and the Vatican, in September 1933, Cardinal Secretary of State Eugenio Pacelli sent a note to the German chargé d'affaires that affirmed the Catholic Church's position: "The Holy See takes this occasion to add a word on behalf of those German Catholics who themselves have gone over from Judaism to the Christian religion . . . , and who for reasons known to the Reich government are likewise suffering from social and economic difficulties."[23] In principle this was to be the consistent position of the Catholic and the Protestant churches, although in practice both submitted to the Nazi measures against converted Jews when they were racially defined as Jews.

The dogmatic confrontation the Catholic hierarchy took up was mainly related to the religious link between Judaism and Christianity. This position found an early expression in five Advent sermons preached by Michael Cardinal Faulhaber of Munich in 1933. Faulhaber rose above the division between Catholics and Protestants when he declared: "We extend our hand to our separated brethren to defend together with them the holy books of the Old Testament." Clearly Faulhaber's sermons were not directed against the political anti-Semitism of the time, but against the racial anti-Semitism that was invading the church. To avoid any misunderstanding, Faulhaber declared: "Let me begin by making three distinctions. We must first distinguish between the people of Israel before and after the death of Christ. Before the death of Christ . . . , the people of Israel were the vehicle of Divine Redemption. . . . It is only with this Israel and the early biblical period that I shall deal in my Advent sermons." The cardinal then described God's dismissal of Israel after Israel had not recognized Christ. Finally, the cardinal continued, "we must distinguish in the Old Testament Bible itself between what had only transitory value and what had permanent value. . . . For the purpose of our subject, we are concerned only with those religious, ethical and social values of the Old Testament which remain as values also for Christianity."[24] Cardinal Faulhaber himself later stressed that in his Advent sermons he had wished only to defend the Old Testament and not to comment on contemporary aspects of the Jewish issue.

A comparison between the attitudes of the churches and those of the universities toward the regime's anti-Jewish measures of 1933 reveals basic similarities along with some minor differences. Although outright supporters of National Socialism as a whole were a small minority both in the churches and in the universities, those in favor of the national revival heralded by the new regime were definitely a majority. That majority shared a conservative-nationalist credo that easily converged with the main ideals proclaimed by the regime at its beginning. But what distinguished the churches' attitude was the need to preserve some basic tenets of Christian dogma. The Jews as Jews were abandoned to their fate, but both the Protestant and Catholic churches attempted to maintain the preeminence of such fundamental beliefs as the supersession of race by baptism and the sanctity of the Old Testament. Nothing of the kind hampered acceptance by university professors of the regime's anti-Jewish acts. Thus, when Jewish colleagues were dismissed, no German professor publicly protested; when the number of Jewish students was drastically reduced, no university committee or faculty member expressed any opposition; when books were burned throughout the Reich, no intellectual in Germany, or for that matter anyone else within the country, openly expressed any shame.

Whereas the attitude of the majority of "Aryan" university professors could be defined as "cultured Judeophobia," among the students a radical brand of Judeophobia had taken hold. Already in the early years of the Weimar Republic the majority of German student fraternities joined the German University League, an organization with openly *völkisch* and anti-Semitic aims, which soon came to control student politics. Membership in the league was conditional on fully Aryan origin, with racial Germans from Austria or the Sudetenland accepted despite their not being German citizens. The league dominated the universities until the mid-1920s, when it was replaced by the National Socialist Students Association. In 1931 Nazis gained a majority in the German Student Association; within a short time a whole cohort of young intellectuals would put its energy and ability at the disposal of the party and its policies.

After January 1933 student groups took matters into their own hands, not unlike the SA. The national leader of the Nazi student organization, Oskar Stabel, announced shortly before the April 1 boycott that student pickets would be posted that day at the entrances to Jewish professors' lecture halls and seminar rooms in order to "dissuade" anyone from entering. Later on Nazi students with cameras positioned themselves on the podiums of lecture halls so as to take pictures of students attending classes taught by Jews. In early April 1933 the National Socialist Student Association established a press and propaganda section. Its very first measure, decided on April 8, was to be "the public burning of destructive Jewish writing" by university students as a reaction to world Jewry's "shameless incitement" against Germany.[25] An "information" campaign was to be undertaken between April 12 and May 10; the public burnings were scheduled to start on university campuses at 6:00 p.m. on the last day of the campaign.

The notorious twelve theses the students prepared for ritual declamation during the burnings were not exclusively directed against Jews and the "Jewish spirit": Among the other targets were Marxism, pacifism, and the "overstressing of the instinctual life" (that is, "the Freudian School and its journal *Imago*"). It was a rebellion of the German against the "un-German spirit." But the main thrust of the action remained essentially anti-Jewish; in the eyes of the organizers it was meant to extend anti-Jewish action from the economic domain to the entire field of German culture.

On the evening of May 10 rituals of exorcism took place in most of the university cities and towns of Germany. More than twenty thousand books were burned in Berlin, and from two to three thousand in every other major German city. In Berlin a huge bonfire was lit in front of the Kroll Opera House, and Goebbels was one of the speakers. After the speeches, in the capital as in the other cities, slogans against the banned authors were chanted by the throng as the poisonous books were hurled, batch after batch, into the flames.

While Germany's intellectual and spiritual elites were granting their explicit or tacit support to the new regime, the leading figures of the Jewish community were trying to hide their distress behind a facade of confidence: Despite all difficulties, the future of Jewish life in Germany was not being irretrievably endangered. Ismar Elbogen, one of the most prominent Jewish historians of the time, expressed a common attitude when he wrote: "They can condemn us to hunger but they cannot condemn us to starvation."[26] This was the spirit that presided over the establishment of the National Representation of German Jews (Reichsvertretung Deutscher Juden), formally launched in 1933. It would remain the umbrella organization of local and national Jewish associations until 1938, headed throughout by the Berlin rabbi Leo Baeck, the respected chairman of the Association of German Rabbis and a scholar of repute, and by the lay leader Otto Hirsch. Despite opposition from "national German Jews," ultra-Orthodox religious groups, and, sporadically, from the Zionist movement, the National Representation played a significant role in the affairs of German Jewry until its transformation, after a transition period in 1938–39, into the National Association of Jews in Germany, an organization closely controlled by the Gestapo.

There was not any greater sense of urgency at the National Representation than there was among most individual Jews in Germany. In early 1934 Otto Hirsch would still be speaking out against "hasty" emigration: He believed in the possibility of maintaining a dignified Jewish life in the new Germany. That Alfred Hirschberg, the most prominent personality of the assimilationist Central Association, denied "any need at all to enlarge upon the utopia of resettlement [in Palestine]" was true to type, but that a publication of the Zionist Pioneer organization defined *unprepared immigration* to Palestine as "a crime against Zionism" comes as a surprise, perhaps because of the vehemence of its tone.[27]

Not all German Jewish leaders displayed such nonchalance. One who insistently demanded immediate emigration was Georg Kareski, head of the right-wing [Revisionist] Zionist Organization. A vocal but marginal personality even within German Zionism, Kareski was ready to organize the exodus of the Jews from Germany by cooperating, if need be, with the Gestapo and the Propaganda Ministry.

Even as the months went by, the leaders of German Jewry did not, in general, gain much insight into the uncompromisingly anti-Jewish stance of the Nazis. Thus, in August 1933, Werner Senator, who had returned to Germany from Palestine in order to become a director of the newly established Central Committee for Help and Reconstruction, suggested, in a memorandum sent to the American Joint Distribution Committee, that a dialogue be established between the Jews and the Nazis. In his opinion such a dialogue "should lead to a kind of Concordat, like the arrangements between the Roman Curia and European States."[28]

No Roman Curia and no Concordat were mentioned as examples in the "Memorandum on the Jewish Question" that the representatives of Orthodox Jewry sent to Hitler on October 4. The signatories brought to the Reich chancellor's attention the injustice of the identification of Jewry with Marxist materialism, the unfairness of the attribution to an entire community of the mistakes of some of its members, and the tenuousness of the connection between the ancient Jewish race and the modern, uprooted, ultra-rationalistic Jewish writers and journalists. Orthodox Jewry disavowed the atrocity propaganda being directed against Germany, and its delegates reminded Hitler of the Jewish sacrifices during World War I. The authors of the letter were convinced that the new government did not have in mind the annihilation of German Jewry, but in case they were wrong on this point, they demanded to be told so. On the assumption that such was not the aim of the regime, the representatives of Orthodox Jewry demanded that the Jews of Germany be granted a living space within the living space of the German people, where they could practice their religion and follow their professions "without being endangered and insulted."[29] The memorandum was filed before it even reached Hitler's desk.

Thirty-seven thousand of the approximately 525,000 Jews in Germany left the country in 1933; during the four following years, the annual number of emigrants remained much lower than that. In 1933 about 73 percent of the emigrants left for other countries in Western Europe, 19 percent for Palestine, and 8 percent chose to go overseas. Such seeming lack of enthusiasm for leaving a country where segregation, humiliation, and a whole array of persecutory measures were becoming steadily worse, was due, first of all, to the inability of most of the Jewish leadership and mainly of ordinary German Jews to grasp an essentially unpredictable course of events. Most expected to weather the storm in Germany. In addition the material difficulty of emigrating was considerable, especially in a period of economic uncertainty; it entailed an immediate and heavy material loss: Jewish-owned property was sold at ever lower prices, and the emigration tax was prohibitive. Although the Nazis wanted to get rid of the Jews of Germany, they were intent on dispossessing them first by increasingly harsh methods.

In one instance only were the economic conditions of emigration somewhat facilitated. Not only did the regime encourage Zionist activities on the territory of the Reich, but concrete economic measures were taken to ease the departure of Jews for Palestine. The so-called Haavarah (Hebrew: Transfer) Agreement, concluded on August 27, 1933, between the German Ministry of the Economy and Zionist representatives from Germany and Palestine, allowed indirect transfer by Jewish emigrants of part of their assets and facilitated exports of goods from Nazi Germany to Palestine. As a result some one hundred million reichsmarks were transferred to Palestine, and most of the sixty thousand German Jews who arrived in that country during 1933–39 could thereby ensure a minimal basis for their material existence.

Economic agreement and some measure of cooperation in easing Jewish emigration from Germany to Palestine were of course purely instrumental. The Zionists had no doubts about the Nazis' evil designs on the Jews, and the Nazis considered the Zionists first and foremost as Jews. About Zionism itself, moreover, Nazi ideology and Nazi policies were divided from the outset: while favoring Zionism as a means of enticing the Jews to leave Europe, they also considered the Zionist Organization established in Basel in 1897 as a key element of the Jewish world conspiracy—a Jewish state in Palestine would be a kind of Vatican coordinating Jewish scheming all over the world. Such necessary but unholy contacts between Zionists and Nazis nonetheless continued up to the beginning of (and into) the war.

Some leaders of German Jewry still believed in 1933 that the Nazis would be duly impressed by an objective presentation of Jewish contributions to German culture. A few months after the change of regime, Leopold Ullstein, a younger member of the publishing family, launched the preparation of a wide-ranging study to that effect. Within a year a hefty volume was ready, but in December 1934 its publication was prohibited. "The naïve reader of this study," the Gestapo report pronounced, "would get the impression that the whole of German culture up to the National Socialist revolution was carried by Jews."[30] Jewish culture for Jews, however, was another matter, and whereas Ullstein had set his sights on an untimely enterprise, another Berlin Jew, Kurt Singer, the former deputy director of the Berlin City Opera, came up with a different kind of idea: the establishment of an autonomous Jewish cultural association.

Singer's Kulturbund fitted Nazi needs. When Singer's project of cultural activities by Jews and for Jews (only) was submitted to the new Prussian authorities, it received Göring's approval. On the face of it the Kulturbund appeared to be a perfectly functional initiative to solve the problems created both for the regime and for the Jews by the expulsion from German cultural life of thousands of Jewish writers, artists, musicians, and performers of all kinds, as well as their coworkers and agents. Apart from the work it provided and the soothing psychological function it filled for part of the Jewish community, the Kulturbund also offered the surrounding society an easy way to dismiss any potential sense of embarrassment: "Aryans who found the regime's anti-Semitic measures distasteful could reassure themselves that Jewish artists were at least permitted to remain active in their chosen professions."[31] The Kulturbund also played another role, unseen but no less real, which pointed to the future: As the first Jewish organization under the direct supervision of a Nazi overlord, it foreshadowed the Nazi ghetto, in which a pretense of internal autonomy camouflaged the total subordination of an appointed Jewish leadership to the dictates of its masters.

Sporadically the Nazis informed the Kulturbund of works Jews were no longer allowed to perform. In theater, the performance of Germanic legends, of works from the German Middle Ages and German romanticism, were prohibited. For a time the classical period was allowed, but Schiller was forbidden in 1934 and Goethe in 1936. Among foreign writers Shakespeare was allowed, but Hamlet's "To be or not to be" soliloquy was forbidden: In a Jewish theater in the Third Reich, "the oppressor's wrong, the proud man's contumely" could have sounded subversive, hence that line led to the exclusion of the entire speech. Needless to say, despite the attachment of German Jews to the works of Richard Wagner and Richard Strauss, these composers were not to be performed by Jews. Beethoven was forbidden in 1937, but Mozart had to wait until the next year, after the Anschluss.

Notwithstanding such growing constraints, the activity of the Kulturbund in all major German cities was remarkable. More than 180,000 Jews from all parts of Germany became active members of the association. In its first year the Kulturbund staged 69 opera performances and 117 concerts, and, from mid-1934 to mid-1935, 57 opera performances and 358 concerts.

It is hard to evaluate how much importance German society at its various levels granted the Jewish issue in 1933. Political stabilization, the dismantling of the Left, economic improvement, national revival, and international uncertainties were undoubtedly more present in the minds of many than the hazy outlines of the Jewish issue; for most Germans the challenges of daily life in times of political change and of economic turmoil were the paramount focus of interest. It is against this background that Hitler's own obsession with the Jewish issue must be considered.

In a remarkable dispatch sent to Foreign Minister Sir John Simon on May 11, 1933, the British ambassador in Berlin, Sir Horace Rumbold, described the course taken by an interview with Hitler once he had alluded to the persecution of the Jews: "The allusion to the treatment of the Jews resulted in the Chancellor working himself up into a state of great excitement. 'I will never agree,' he shouted, as if he were addressing an open-air meeting, 'to the existence of two kinds of law for German nationals. There is an immense amount of unemployment in Germany, and I have, for instance, to turn away youths of pure German stock from higher education. There are not enough posts for the pure-bred Germans, and the Jews must suffer with the rest. If the Jews engineer a boycott of German goods from abroad, I will take care that this hits the Jews in Germany.' These remarks were delivered with great ferocity. Only his excitement, to which I did not wish to add, prevented me from pointing out that there were, in fact, two standards of treatment of German nationals, inasmuch as those of Jewish race were being discriminated against." At the end of the dispatch Rumbold returned to the issue: "My comment on the foregoing is that Herr Hitler is himself responsible for the anti-Jewish policy of the German government and that it would be a mistake to believe that it is the policy of his wilder men whom he has difficulty in controlling. Anybody who has had the opportunity of listening to his remarks on the subject of Jews could not have failed, like myself, to realize that he is a fanatic on the subject."[32] The American consul general in Berlin reached the same conclusion. "One of the most unfortunate features of the situation," George S. Messersmith wrote to Secretary of State Cordell Hull on November 1, 1933, "is that . . . Mr. Hitler himself is implacable and *unconvinced* and is the real head of the anti-Jewish movement. He can be reasonable on a number of subjects, but on this he can only be passionate and prejudiced."[33]

Hitler did not express his obsession with the Jewish peril in major public utterances during 1933. As he put it in his meeting with the Reich district governors, on July 6, 1933, for Germany the most dangerous front at the time was the external one: "One should not irritate it, when it is not necessary to deal with it. To reopen the Jewish question would mean to start a world-wide uproar again."[34] Clearly the shaky economic circumstances of the Reich were also a major factor in his decisions. And, as mentioned, on some matters such as the issue of Jewish physicians, Hitler certainly took into account German public opinion: In other words he understood the need for tactical pragmatism regarding immediate anti-Jewish measures, and thus his policy had to remain, for a time at least, close to the preexisting anti-Jewish agenda of the conservatives.

But although the Nazi leader avoided public statements on the Jewish issue and his "worldview," he could not restrain himself entirely. In his closing speech at the September 1933 Nuremberg party rally, he launched into disparaging comments about the Jews in his expostulations on the racial foundations of art: "It is a sign of the horrible spiritual decadence of the past epoch that one spoke of styles without recognizing their racial determinants. . . . Each clearly formed race has its own handwriting in the book of art, insofar as it is not, like Jewry, devoid of any creative artistic ability." As for the func-

tion of a worldview, Hitler defined it in his address: "World-
views," he declared, "consider the achievement of political
power only as the precondition for the beginning of the fulfill-
ment of their true mission. In the very term 'worldview' there
lies the solemn commitment to make all enterprise dependent
upon a specific initial conception and a visible direction. Such
a conception can be right or wrong; it is the starting point for
the attitude to be taken toward all manifestations and occurrences of life and thereby a compelling and obligatory rule for
all action."[35] In other words a worldview as defined by Hitler
was a quasi-religious framework encompassing immediate political goals. Nazism was no mere ideological discourse; it was
a political religion commanding the total commitment owed
to a religious faith.

CHAPTER 2

The Spirit of the Laws

January 1934–February 1936

Cell 6: approximately 5 m. high, window approx. 40 x 70 cm. at a height of 4 meters, which gives the feeling of a cellar. . . . Wooden plank with straw mat and two blankets, a wooden bucket, a jug, a basin, soap, a towel, no mirror, no toothbrush, no comb, no brush, no table, no book from January 12 [1935] until my departure on September 18; no newspaper from January 12 to August 17; no bath and no shower from January 12 to August 10; no leaving of the cell, except for interrogations, from January 12 to July 1. Incarceration in an unlighted cell from April 16 to May 1, then from May 15 to August 27, a total of 119 days."[1]

This was the Würzburg wine merchant Leopold Obermayer's writing about the first of his imprisonments in Dachau, in a seventeen-page report, dated October 10, 1935, which he managed to smuggle out to his lawyer. It was seized by the Gestapo and found after the war in their Würzburg files. Obermayer had a doctorate in law and he was a practicing Jew, a Swiss citizen, and a gay man. October 29, 1934, he had complained to the Würzburg police that his mail was being opened. Two days later, having been ordered to report to headquarters, he was arrested. From then on he became a special case for the local

Gestapo chief, Josef Gerum, a Nazi "old fighter" with a bad reputation even among his colleagues. Gerum accused Obermayer of spreading accusations about the new regime. Shortly afterward nude photographs of Obermayer's male lovers were found in his bank safe. Both a Jew and a homosexual: For Gerum this was indeed a rewarding catch. Why didn't Obermayer's tormentors kill him? It may be that murdering a Swiss citizen, albeit a Jewish one, was not yet undertaken lightly in 1935, all the more so since the Swiss consulate in Munich and later the legation in Berlin were aware of his incarceration; the Ministry of Justice in particular was worried about the possibility of Swiss intervention.

In mid-September 1935 Obermayer was transferred from Dachau to an ordinary prison in Ochsenfurt, pending court interrogation. At Gerum's insistence, however, the Jewish homosexual was taken back to Dachau on October 12, 1935.

At this time Germany and the world were witnessing a dramatic consolidation of Hitler's internal and international power. The murder of Ernst Röhm and other SA leaders on the notorious "Night of the Long Knives" in June 1934 eliminated even the faintest possibility of an alternative source of power within the party. Immediately following Hindenburg's death, the naming of Hitler as führer and chancellor on August 2 made him the sole source of legitimacy in Germany. Furthermore Hitler's popularity reached new heights in 1935: On January 13 an overwhelming majority of the Saar population voted for return of the territory to the Reich. On March 16 general conscription and establishment of the Wehrmacht were announced. No foreign power dared to respond to these massive breaches of the Versailles treaty; the common front against Germany formed at Stresa by Britain, France, and Italy in April 1935, in order to defend Austria's independence against any German annexation attempt and preserve the status quo in Europe, had crumbled by June, when the British signed a separate naval agreement with Germany.

On March 17 of that year, Hitler had been in Munich, and a report for the clandestine Socialist Party vividly captured the overall mood: "Enthusiasm on 17 March enormous. The whole of Munich was on its feet. People can be forced to sing, but they can't be forced to sing with such enthusiasm. I experienced the days of 1914 and can only say that the declaration of war did not make the same impact on me as the reception of Hitler on 17 March. . . . Trust in Hitler's political talent and honest intentions is getting ever greater. . . . He is loved by many."[2]

Between 1933 and 1936 a balance of sorts was kept between the revolutionary-charismatic impulse of Nazism and the authoritarian-conservative tendencies of the pre-1933 German state. Within this temporary alliance Hitler's role was decisive. For the traditional elites the new "belief in the führer" became associated with the authority of the monarch. Basic elements of the imperial state and of the National Socialist regime were linked in the person of the new leader.

Such "belief in the führer" led quite naturally to an urge for action on the part of state and party agencies according to the general guidelines set by Hitler, without the constant necessity of specific orders from him. The dynamics of this interaction between base and summit was, as the British historian Ian Kershaw pointed out, "neatly captured in the sentiments of a routine speech of a Nazi functionary in 1934: 'Everyone who has the opportunity to observe it knows that the Führer can hardly dictate from above everything which he intends to realize sooner or later. On the contrary, up till now everyone with a post in the new Germany has worked best when he has, so to speak, worked towards the Führer. Very often and in many spheres it has been the case—in previous years as well—that individuals have simply waited for orders and instructions. Unfortunately, the same will be true in the future; but in fact it is the duty of everybody to try to work towards the Führer along the lines he would wish. Anyone who makes mistakes will notice it soon enough. But anyone who really works towards the Führer along his lines and towards his goal will certainly both now and in the future . . . have the finest reward in the form of the sudden legal confirmation of his work.' "[3]

Thus the majority of a society barely emerging from years of crisis believed that the new regime offered solutions that, in diverse but related ways, would give answers to the aspirations, resentments, and interests of its various sectors. This belief survived the difficulties of the early phase (such as a still-sluggish economy) as a result of a new sense of purpose, of a series of successes on the international scene, and, above all, of unshaken faith in the führer. As one of its corollaries, however, that very faith brought with it widespread acceptance, passive or not, of the measures against the Jews: Sympathy for the Jews would have meant some distrust of the rightness of Hitler's way, and many Germans had definitely established their individual and collective priorities in this regard. The same is true in relation to the other central myth of the regime, that of the "racial community." The racial community explicitly excluded the Jews. Belonging to the racial community implied acceptance of the exclusions it imposed.

Yet biological criteria for defining the Jew remained elusive, and it was on the basis of the religious affiliation of parents and grandparents that the Nazis had to launch their crusade for racial purification of the *Volk*. Officials increasingly referred to the Law for the Restoration of the Professional Civil Service in order to refuse, on the basis of the law's "general national principles," to perform marriage ceremonies between Jews and "those of German blood."[4] The pressure grew to such a point that on July 26, 1935, Interior Minister Frick announced that, since the legal validity of "marriages between Aryans and non-

Aryans" would be officially addressed in the near future, such marriages should be "postponed until further notice."[5]

The refusal to perform marriages was an easy matter compared to the other "logical" corollary stemming from the situation: the dissolution of existing mixed marriages. The Civil Code allowed for divorce on the basis of wrongdoing by one of the partners, but it was difficult to equate belonging to a particular race with the notion of wrongdoing. Paragraph 1333 of the Civil Code did however stipulate that a marriage could be challenged if a spouse had been unaware, on contracting the marriage, of "personal qualities" or circumstances that would have precluded the union. But it could only be invoked within six months of the wedding, and racial identity could hardly be defined as a personal quality; finally it is unlikely that partners to a marriage were unaware of such racial identity at the time of their decision. Nevertheless, paragraph 1333 increasingly became the prop of Nazi legal interpretation, on the grounds that "Jewishness" was indeed a personal quality whose significance had become clear only as a result of the new political circumstances. Consequently the six-month period could be counted from the date when the significance of Jewishness became a major element in public consciousness, that is, from January 30 (Hitler's accession to the chancellorship) or even April 7, 1933 (the civil service law's promulgation). It was only with the law of July 6, 1938, that "racially" mixed marriages could in fact be legally annulled.

In the meantime the judges, lawyers and registrars who were intent on the dissolution of mixed marriages went beyond the immediate instructions of the Nazi leadership. The anti-Jewish zeal of the courts regarding mixed marriages was reinforced by police initiatives and even by mob demonstrations against any form of sexual relations between Jews and Aryans: "Race defilement" was the obsession of the day. Thus on August 19, 1935, a Jewish businessman was arrested on that charge in Stuttgart. As he was brought to the police station, a crowd gathered and demonstrated against the accused. Shortly afterward, according to the city chronicle, a Jewish woman merchant who had had a stall in the market hall since 1923 lost her permit because she allowed her son to have a relationship with a non-Jewish German girl.

The presence of Jews in public swimming pools was a major theme, second only to outright race defilement, in the Nazis' pornographic imagination: It expressed a "healthy" Aryan revulsion at the sight of the Jewish body, the fear of possible contamination resulting from sharing the water or mingling in the pool area and, most explicitly, the sexual threat of Jewish nakedness, often alluded to as the impudent behavior of Jewish women and outright sexual harassment of German women by Jewish men.

Among the newspapers spewing a constant stream of anti-Jewish abuse, Streicher's *Der Stürmer* was the most vicious; its ongoing campaign and the wide distribution it achieved by means of public display may have been abhorrent to the educated middle class or even to educated party members, but its appeal among the general population, school youngsters, and the Hitler Youth, possibly because of its pornographic and sadistic streak, seems to have been quite widespread. On May 1, 1934, *Der Stürmer* published its notorious special issue on Jewish ritual murder. The front-page headline, THE JEWISH MURDER PLOT AGAINST NON-JEWISH HUMANITY IS UNCOVERED, was graced by a half-page drawing of two particularly hideous-looking Jews holding a vessel to collect the blood streaming from the naked bodies of angelic Christian children they have just murdered. In the background stands a cross. The next day the National Representation of German Jews wired Reich Bishop Ludwig Müller: "We feel obliged to draw your attention to the special issue of the *Der Stürmer* of May 1. We have sent the following telegram to the Reich chancellor: '*Der Stürmer* has come out

with a special issue which, using incredible insults and horri-
fying descriptions, accuses Jewry of ritual murder. Before God
and humanity, we raise our voice in solemn protest against this
unheard-of profanation of our faith.' We are convinced that the
deep outrage that we are feeling is shared by every Christian."⁶
Neither Hitler nor Reich Bishop Müller replied.

In the summer of 1935, as Jews were forbidden access to
swimming pools and other bathing facilities in numerous
German cities and the very presence of Jews was not allowed
in many small towns and villages, a surrealistic situation developed in some of the Baltic seaside resorts. It seems that a
number of popular guesthouses in these resorts belonged to
Jews. In Binz, for instance, a Hungarian Jew owned the most
prominent guesthouse, which, according to a Gestapo report,
the local population was boycotting, when who should choose
to stay there at Whitsuntide but Gauleiter and Reich Governor
Wilhelm Friedrich Löper! And, adding insult to injury, a month
later, in July, it was the Hungarian Jew's guesthouse that was
favored by officers and men from the *Köln* on the cruiser's visit
to Binz. This paradoxical situation lasted for three more years,
coming to an end in the spring of 1938, when the director of the
Binz office of Baltic Sea resorts announced that "the efforts of
recent months have been successful": All the formerly Jewish-
owned guesthouses were now in Aryan hands.⁷

The clash between party propaganda against business
relations with Jews and the economic advantages brought
by such relations was only a reflection of the contradictory nature of the orders from above: On the one hand,
no contacts between Jews and Germans; on the other, no
interference with Jewish economic activities. This contradiction, which stemmed from two momentarily irreconcilable
priorities—the ongoing struggle against the Jews and the
need to further Germany's economic recovery—found repeated expression in reports from local authorities. It was

often particularly visible at the small-town level. On July 2, 1935, a report was sent by Laupheim town officials to the Württemberg Ministry of the Interior. "Under present circumstances, the Jewish question has increasingly become a source of uncertainty for the Laupheim authorities. . . . If the fight against the Jews . . . continues, one has to take into account that the local Jewish businesspeople will emigrate as fast as possible. The municipality of Laupheim will thereby have to expect a further acute loss of income and will have to raise taxes in order to meet its obligations." The author of the report believed that the dying out of the older Jews and the emigration of the younger ones would cause the Jewish question to resolve itself within thirty years. Meanwhile, he suggested, let the Jews stay as they were, the more so since, apart from a few exceptions, they were a community of well-established families. If Jewish tax revenues were to disappear with no replacement, "the decline of Laupheim into a big village would be unavoidable."[8]

This tension between party initiatives and economic imperatives was illustrated at length in a report devoted entirely to the Jews, sent on April 3, 1935, by the SD "major region Rhine" to SS-Gruppenführer (the SS Group Leader) August Heissmeyer in Koblenz (the Sicherheitsdienst, or SD, was the intelligence service of the SS). A "quiet boycott" against the Jews is described as having been mainly initiated by the party and its organizations repeatedly asking members in "closed meetings" not to patronize Jewish stores. The report then points to the fact that, "despite more limited possibilities of control in the cities, the boycott is more strictly adhered to there than in rural areas. In Catholic regions in particular, the peasants buy as they did before, mainly from Jews, and this turns in part into an antiboycott movement, which gets its support from the Catholic clergy."[9]

Sometimes genuine sympathy for the plight of the Jews and

even offers of help found direct or indirect ways of expression. Thus, in a letter to the *Jüdische Rundschau*, the granddaughter of the poet Hoffmann von Fallersleben, author of the lyrics of the national anthem, offered to put a house on the Baltic shore at the disposal of Jewish children. The undercurrent of sympathy for the persecuted Jews must have been significant enough for Goebbels to address it in a speech he gave in mid-June. Goebbels "attacked those of his countrymen who . . . 'shamelessly,' argued that the Jew, after all, was a human being too." According to Robert Weltsch, who at the time was the editor of the *Jüdische Rundschau*, Goebbels's wrath reveals that a whispering campaign was still going on, indicating some measure of indignation on the part of people whom Goebbels called bourgeois intellectuals. It was these Germans whom the Gauleiter [of Berlin, Goebbels] wanted to warn."[10]

It may be difficult to prove how effective Goebbels's speech was in intimidating the "bourgeois intellectuals," but it surely had other consequences. In its July 2, 1935, issue, the *Jüdische Rundschau* published an article by Weltsch entitled "The Jew Is Human Too: An Argument Put Forward by Friends of the Jews."[11] It was a subtly ironic comment on the minister's tirade, and it did lead to the banning of the paper. After a few weeks and some negotiating, a letter written in Goebbels's name (but signed "Jahnke") was sent to Weltsch: "The *Jüdische Rundschau* No. 53, dated July 2, 1935, published an article 'The Jew Is Human Too.' . . . Your paper has been banned because of this article. The ban on the paper will be lifted, but in view of the polemic nature of the article I have to reprimand you most severely and expect to have no further cause to object to your publications."[12]

Why would Goebbels have taken the trouble to engage in these maneuvers regarding a periodical written by Jews for Jews? As Weltsch explains it, "One has to keep in mind that the Jewish papers were at that time sold in public. The pretentious main thoroughfare of Berlin's West End, the Kurfürstendamm, was literally plastered with the *Jüdische Rundschau*—all kiosks displayed it every Tuesday and Friday in many copies, as it was one of their best-sellers, especially as foreign papers were banned."[13] This, too, could not last for long. On October 1, 1935, the public display and sale of Jewish newspapers was prohibited.

The regime's efforts to physically segregate the Jews from German society was accompanied by a vigorous campaign to cleanse German cultural life of its Jewish presence and spirit. During the first months of 1933, this campaign was further complicated by a bitter competition waged between Goebbels and Alfred Rosenberg, the party's ideologue, for control of culture in the new Reich. Hitler had at first given the preference to Goebbels, mainly by allowing him to establish the Reich Chamber of Culture. Not long afterward, however, an equilibrium of sorts was reestablished by Rosenberg's appointment, in January 1934, as the "Führer's Representative for the Supervision of the General Intellectual and Ideological Education of the NSDAP."

From August 1934 to June 1935 Goebbels's diaries repeatedly record his determination to achieve the goal of complete Aryanization, mainly in regard to the cleansing of the Reich Music Chamber of its Jewish members. The battle was waged on two fronts: against individuals and against melodies. Most Jewish musicians emigrated during the first three years of Hitler's regime, but to the Nazis' chagrin, it was more difficult to get rid of Jewish tunes—that is, mainly "light" music. "[Arguments] that audiences often asked for such music," writes the historian Michael Kater, "were refuted on the grounds that it was the duty of 'Aryan' musicians to educate their listeners by consistently presenting non-Jewish programs."[14] Moreover, as far as light music was concerned, intricate commercial relations between Jewish émigré music publishers and partners who were still in Germany enabled a steady flow of undesirable music scores and records into the Reich. Music arrived from Vienna, London, and New York, and it was only in late 1937, when "alien" music was officially prohibited, that Jew hunters could feel more at ease.

All in all, however, the initial confusion of the new regime's culture masters did not stop the de-Judaization of music in the Reich. Jewish performers such as Artur Schnabel, Jascha Heifetz, and Yehudi Menuhin were no longer heard either in concert or on the radio; Jewish conductors had fled, as had the composers Arnold Schoenberg, Kurt Weill, and Franz Schreker. After some early hesitations, Mendelssohn, Meyerbeer, Offenbach, and Mahler were no longer performed. Mendelssohn's statue, which had stood in front of the Leipzig Gewandhaus, was removed. But that was far from the end of it: Pieces with Jewish connotations, such as Händel's Old Testament oratorios, lost their original titles and were Aryanized so that *Judas Maccabeus* turned into *The Field Marshal: A War Drama* or, alternatively, into *Freedom Oratorio: William of Nassau*. Certain operas, such as Mozart's *Don Giovanni, Le Nozze di Figaro*, and *Così fan tutte*, had to be translated into German, as their librettist, Lorenzo Da Ponte, was of Jewish origin.

In 1935 Hans Hinkel moved to Goebbels's ministry to become one of the three supervisors of the Reichskulturkammer (RKK). Soon afterward an unusual title was added to those he already bore: "Special Commissioner for the Supervision and Monitoring of the Cultural and Intellectual Activity of All Non-Aryans Living in the Territory of the German Reich." In a 1936 speech Hinkel restated the immediate aim of Nazi cultural policy regarding the Jews: They were entitled to the development of their own cultural heritage in Germany, but only in total isolation from the general culture. Jewish artists "may work unhindered as long as they restrict themselves to the cultivation of Jewish artistic and cultural life and as long as they do not attempt—openly, secretly, or deceitfully—to influ-ence our culture."[15]

From the beginning of 1935 intense anti-Jewish incitement had newly surfaced among party radicals. Lingering economic difficulties, as well as the absence of material and ideological compensation for the great number of party members unable to find positions and rewards either on the local or the national level, were leading to increasing agitation.

A first wave of anti-Jewish incidents started at the end of March 1935; during the following weeks, Goebbels's *Der Angriff* fanned the pogromlike atmosphere. An announcement by the Ministry of the Interior of forthcoming anti-Jewish legisla-tion and the exclusion of Jews from the new Wehrmacht did not calm the growing unrest.

The first city to witness large-scale anti-Jewish disturbances was Munich. In March and April, Jewish stores were sprayed nightly with acid or smeared with such inscriptions as JEW, STINKING JEW, OUT WITH THE JEWS. In May the smashing of win-dowpanes of Jewish shops began. The police report indicates involvement by Hitler Youth groups in one of these early in-cidents. By mid-May the perpetrators were not only attacking Jewish stores in broad daylight but also assaulting their owners, their customers, and sometimes even their Aryan employees. On Saturday, May 25, the disturbances took on a new dimen-sion. By midafternoon the attacks had spread to every identifi-ably Jewish business in the city. According to the police the perpetrators were "not only members of the Party and its or-ganizations but also comprised various groups of a very ques-tionable nature."[16] It was not until about nine in the evening that some measure of order was reestablished in the Bavarian capital.

A second major outbreak occurred in mid-July in Berlin, mainly on the Kurfürstendamm, where elegant stores owned by Jews were still relatively active. Jochen Klepper, a deeply religious Protestant writer whose wife was Jewish, wrote in his diary on July 13: "Anti-Semitic excesses on the Kurfürstendamm. . . . The cleansing of Berlin of Jews threateningly announced."[17] A week later Klepper again wrote of what had happened on the Kurfürstendamm: Jewish women had been struck in the face; Jewish men had behaved courageously. "Nobody came to their help, because everyone is afraid of being arrested."[18] On September 7 Klepper, who in 1933 had lost his position with the radio because of his Jewish wife, was fired from the recently Aryanized Ullstein publishing house, where he had found some employment. That day he noticed that signs forbidding Jews access to the local swimming pool were up, and that even the small street in which he took walks with his wife had the same warning on one of its fences.

Most party leaders opposed the spreading of anti-Jewish attacks, not because of potential negative reactions among the populace, but mainly because the regime could ill afford to give the impression inside and outside Germany that it was losing control of its own forces by allowing the spread of unbridled violence, particularly in view of the forthcoming Olympic Games. Repeated orders to abstain from unauthorized anti-Jewish actions were issued in Hitler's name by the deputy führer, Rudolf Hess, and others, but without complete success.

For Schacht the spread of anti-Jewish violence was particularly unwelcome. In the United States the economic boycott of German goods had flared up again. On May 3 the minister of the economy sent a memorandum to Hitler regarding "the imponderable factors influencing German exports,"[19] in which he warned of the economic consequences of the new anti-Jewish campaign. On the face of it at least, Hitler fully agreed with Schacht: At that stage the violence had to stop.

On the afternoon of September 15, 1935, the final parade of the annual Nuremberg party congress marched past Hitler and the top leadership of the NSDAP. At 8 P.M. that evening an unusual meeting of the Reichstag opened in the hall of the Nuremberg Cultural Association. It was the first and only time during Hitler's regime that the Reichstag was convened outside Berlin.

In his speech Hitler briefly addressed foreign affairs; then he turned to the main topic of his address—the Jews. The Jews were behind the growing tension among peoples: In New York harbor, they had insulted the German flag on the passenger ship *Bremen*, and they were again launching an economic boycott against Germany. In Germany itself their provocative behavior increasingly caused complaints from all sides. Hitler thus set the background. Then he came to his main point: "To prevent this behavior from leading to quite determined defensive action on the part of the outraged population, the extent of which cannot be foreseen, the only alternative would be a legislative solution to the problem. . . . However, should this hope prove false and intra-German and international Jewish agitation proceed, a new evaluation of the situation would have to take place."[20] He then asked the Reichstag to adopt the three laws that Göring was about to read.

The first law, the Reich flag law, proclaimed that henceforth black, red, and white were the national colors and that the swastika flag was the national flag. The second, the citizenship law, established the fundamental distinction between "citizens of the Reich," who were entitled to full political and civil rights, and "subjects," who were now deprived of those rights. Only those of German or related blood could be citizens. Thus, from that moment on, in terms of their civil rights, the Jews had in fact a status similar to that of foreigners. The third, the Law for the Defense of German Blood and Honor, forbade marriages and extramarital relations between Jews and citizens of German or kindred blood. Marriages contracted in disregard of the law, even those contracted outside Germany, were considered invalid. Jews were not allowed to employ in their households female German citizens under forty-five years of age. Finally Jews were forbidden to hoist the German flag (an offense against German honor) but were allowed to fly their own colors.

The preamble to the third law revealed all its implications: "Fully aware that the purity of German blood is the condition for the survival of the German *Volk*, and animated by the unwavering will to secure the German nation forever, the Reichstag has unanimously decided upon the following, which is thereby proclaimed."[21] This was immediately followed by paragraph one: "Marriages between Jews and citizens of German and related blood are forbidden." The relation of the preamble to the text of the law reflected the extent of the racial peril represented by the Jew.

Much debate has arisen regarding the origins of the Nuremberg laws: Were they the result of a haphazard decision or of a general plan aiming at the step-by-step exclusion of the Jews from German society and ultimately from the territory of the Reich? Depending on the view one takes, Hitler's mode of decision making, in both Jewish and other matters, can be interpreted in different ways.

The idea of a new citizenship law had been on Hitler's mind from the outset of his regime. In July 1933 an Advisory Committee for Population and Race Policy at the Ministry of the Interior started work on draft proposals for a law designed to exclude the Jews from full citizenship rights. From the beginning of 1935 the signs pointing to such forthcoming changes multiplied. Allusions to them were made by various German leaders—Frick, Goebbels, and Schacht—during the spring and summer months of that year; the foreign press, particularly the London *Jewish Chronicle* and the *New York Times*, published similar information, and, according to Gestapo reports, German Jewish leaders such as Rabbi Joachim Prinz were openly speaking about a new citizenship law that would turn the Jews into "subjects"; their information was precise indeed.

Simultaneously, as has also been seen, mixed marriages were encountering increasing obstruction in the courts, to such an extent that, in July, Frick announced the formulation of new laws in this domain as well. In the same month the Justice Ministry submitted a proposal for the interdiction of marriages between Jews and Germans. From then on the issue was the object of ongoing interministerial consultations. Thus, whatever the immediate reason for Hitler's decision may have been, both the issue of citizenship and that of mixed marriages were being discussed in great detail at the civil service level and within the party, and various signs indicated that new legislation was imminent.

In his opening address of September 11 at the Nuremberg party congress, Hitler warned that the struggle against the internal enemies of the nation would not be thwarted by failings of the bureaucracy: The will of the nation—that is, the party—would, if necessary, take over in case of bureaucratic deficiency. It was in these very terms that Hitler ended his September 15 closing speech by addressing the solution of the Jewish problem. Thus it seems that the basic motive for pressing forward with anti-Jewish legislation was to deal with the specific internal political climate already alluded to.

In the precarious balance that existed between the party on the one hand and the state administration and the Reichswehr on the other, Hitler had in 1934 favored the state apparatus by decapitating the SA. Moreover, at the beginning of 1935, when tension arose between the Reichswehr and the SS, Hitler "warned the party against encroachments on the army and called the Reichswehr 'the sole bearer of arms.'"[22] In the fall of 1935, however, it was time to lean the other way, especially since discontent was growing within the lower party ranks. In short the Nuremberg laws were to serve notice to all that the role of the party was far from over—quite the contrary. Thus, the mass of party members would be assuaged, individual acts of violence against Jews would be stopped by the establishment of clear "legal" guidelines, and political activism would be channeled toward well-defined goals. The summoning of the Reichstag and the diplomatic corps to the party congress was meant as an homage to the party on the occasion of its most important yearly celebration, irrespective of whether the major declaration was to be on foreign policy, on the German flag, or on the Jewish issue. The preliminary work on the Jewish legislation had been completed, and Hitler could easily switch to preparation of the final decrees at the very last moment.

On the evening of September 13 Hitler summoned from Berlin to Nuremberg two "race specialists" from the Interior Ministry. There the two were ordered to prepare a law dealing with marriage and extramarital relations between Jews and Aryans, and with the employment of Aryan female help in Jewish families. The next day Hitler demanded a citizenship law broad enough to underpin the more specifically racial-biological anti-Jewish legislation. The party and particularly such individuals as Gerhardt Wagner, the Reich physicians' leader, insisted on the most comprehensive definition of the Jew, one that would have equated even "quarter Jews" with full Jews. The Nazi leader himself demanded four versions of the law, ranging from the least (version D) to the most inclusive (version A). Hitler chose version D. But in a typical move that canceled this apparent "moderation" and left the door open for further extensions in the scope of the laws, he crossed out a decisive sentence introduced into the text by the two specialists: "These laws are applicable to full Jews only."[23] That sentence was meant to exclude *Mischlinge* (mixed breeds) from the legislation; now their fate also hung in the balance.

There is a plausible reason why, if Hitler was planning to

announce the laws at the Nuremberg party congress, he waited until the very last moment to have the final versions drafted: His method was one of sudden blows meant to keep his opponents off balance, to confront them with faits accomplis that made forceful reactions almost impossible if a major crisis was to be avoided. Had the anti-Jewish legislation been drafted weeks before the congress, technical objections from the state bureaucracy could have hampered the process. Surprise was of the essence.

During the days and weeks following Nuremberg, party radicals close to the Wagner line exerted considerable pressure to reintroduce their demands regarding the status of *Mischlinge* into the supplementary decrees to the two main Nuremberg laws. Hitler himself was to announce the ruling on *"Mischlinge of the first degree"* at a closed party meeting scheduled for September 29 in Munich. The meeting did take place, but Hitler postponed the announcement of his decision. Early in the debate both sides agreed that three-quarter Jews were to be considered Jews, and that one-quarter Jews were *Mischlinge*. The entire confrontation focused on the status of the half-Jews (two Jewish grandparents). Whereas the party wanted to include the half-Jews in the category of Jews, the ministry insisted on integrating them into the *Mischlinge* category. The final decision, made by Hitler, was much closer to the demands of the ministry than to that of the party. Half-Jews were *Mischlinge*: Only as a result of their personal choice, either by selecting a Jewish spouse or joining the Jewish religious community, did they become Jews.

The supplementary decrees were finally published on November 14. The first defined as Jewish all persons who had at least three full Jewish grandparents, or who had two Jewish grandparents and were married to a Jewish spouse or belonged to the Jewish religion at the time of the law's publication, or who entered into such commitments at a later date.

From November 14 on, the civil rights of Jews were canceled, their voting rights abolished; Jewish civil servants who had kept their positions owing to their veteran or veteran-related status were forced into retirement. On December 21 a second supplementary decree ordered the dismissal of Jewish professors, teachers, physicians, lawyers, and notaries who were state employees and had been granted exemptions.

The various categories of forbidden marriages were spelled out in the first supplementary decree to the Law for the Defense of German Blood and Honor: between a Jew and a *Mischling* with one Jewish grandparent; between a *Mischling* and another, each with one Jewish grandparent; and between a *Mischling* with two Jewish grandparents and a German. *Mischlinge* of the first degree (two Jewish grandparents) could marry Jews—and thereby become Jews —or marry one another, on the assumption that such couples usually chose to remain childless, as indicated by the empirical material collected by Hans F. K. Günther. Finally, female citizens of German blood employed in a Jewish household at the time of the law's publication could continue their work only if they had turned forty-five by December 31, 1935.

In a circular addressed to all relevant party agencies on December 2, Hess restated the main instructions of the November 14 supplementary decree to explain the intention behind the marriage regulations that applied to both kinds of *Mischlinge*: "The Jewish *Mischlinge*, that is, the quarter and half-Jews, are treated differently in the marriage legislation. The regulations are based on the fact that the mixed race of the German-Jewish *Mischlinge* is undesirable under any circumstances—both in terms of blood and politically—and that it must disappear as soon as possible." According to Hess the law ensured that "either in the present or in the next generation, the German-Jewish *Mischlinge* would belong either to the Jewish group or to that of the German citizens." By being allowed to marry only full-blooded German spouses, the quarter Jews would become Germans and, as Hess put it, "the hereditary racial potential of a nation of 65 million would not be changed or damaged by the absorption of 100,000 quarter Jews." The deputy führer's explanations regarding the half-Jews were somewhat more convoluted, as there was no absolute prohibition of their marrying Germans or quarter Jews, if they received the approval of the deputy führer. Hess recognized that this aspect of the legislation went against the wishes of the party, declaring laconically that the decision had been taken "for political reasons."[24]

To how many people did the Nuremberg laws apply? According to statistics produced by the Ministry of the Interior on April 3, 1935, living in Germany at the time were some 750,000 *Mischlinge* of the first and second degree. Apart from the *Mischlinge*, the document also listed 475,000 full Jews belonging to the Jewish religion and 300,000 full Jews not belonging to it, which made a total of approximately 1.5 million, or 2.3 percent of the population of Germany. In his circular Rudolf Hess estimated the overall number of *Mischlinge* at 300,000. This number was also an exaggeration. Recent studies have set the number of *Mischlinge* at the time of the decrees at about 200,000.

Two laws directed against individuals and groups other than Jews followed the September laws. The first of these was the October 18, 1935, Law for the Protection of the Hereditary Health of the German People, which aimed at registering "alien races" or racially "less valuable" groups and imposed the obligation of a marriage license certifying that the partners were (racially) "fit to marry."[25] This law was reinforced by the first supplementary decree to the Law for the Protection of German Blood and Honor of November 14, which also forbade Germans to marry or have sexual relations with persons of "alien blood" other than Jews. Twelve days later a circular from the Ministry of the Interior was more specific: Those referred to were "Gypsies, Negroes, and their bastards."[26]

Proof that one was not of Jewish origin or did not belong to any "less valuable" group became essential for a normal existence in the Third Reich. And the requirements were especially stringent for anyone aspiring to join or to remain in a state or party agency. Even the higher strata of the civil service, the party, and the army could not escape racial investigation.

Did public opinion fall further into step with the anti-Jewish policies of the regime after the passage of the Nuremberg Laws? According to the Israeli historian David Bankier, a majority of Germans acquiesced in the laws; people in various cities and areas of the Reich seemed to have been particularly satisfied with the Law for the Protection of German Blood and Honor, on the assumption that enforcement of the law would put an end to the anti-Jewish terror of the previous months. Tranquillity would return, and with it the good name of Germany in the eyes of the world. People believed that under the new laws the relation to Jewry in Germany was now clearly defined: "Jewry is converted into a national minority and gets through state protection the possibility to develop its own cultural and national life."[27]

For the party radicals the laws were a clear victory of the party over the state bureaucracy, but many considered the new decrees to be "too mild." The Dortmund Nazis, for instance, regarded the fact that the Jews could still use their own symbols as too much of a concession. Some activists hoped that the Jews would offer new pretexts for action, others simply demanded that the scope of some of the measures be extended: that, for example, no German female of any age should be allowed to work in a Jewish (or mixed-marriage) family—or even in the household of a single Jewish woman.

The laws were sharply criticized in opposition circles, mainly among the (now underground) Communists. Some Communist leaflets denounced the Nazis' demagogic use of anti-Semitism and demanded a united opposition front; others demanded the freeing of political prisoners and the cessation of anti-Jewish measures. According to Bankier, however, Communist material at the time, despite its protests against the Nuremberg laws, continued to reiterate such longtime standard assertions as: "Only poor workers were arrested for race defilement, while rich Jews were not touched by the Nazis," and, "There were no racial principles behind the ban on keeping maids under forty-five years of age; rather, the clause was simply an excuse for firing thousands of women from their jobs."[28]

The churches kept their distance, except for the strongly Catholic district of Aachen and some protests by Evangelical pastors, for instance in Speyer. The Evangelical Church was put to the test when the Prussian Confessing Synod met in Berlin at the end of September 1935: A declaration expressing concern for both baptized and unbaptized Jews was discussed and rejected, but so was too explicit an expression of support for the state. The declaration that was finally agreed on merely reaffirmed the sanctity of baptism, which led Niemöller to express his misgivings about its failure to take any account of the postbaptismal fate of baptized Jews.

The Jews reacted to growing persecution and segregation by intensifying all possible aspects of internal Jewish life, which explains both the number and the diversity of meetings, lectures, dances, and so on; these offered some measure of sanity and dignity, but meant more trouble for the Gestapo. As early as 1934 the State Police complained that many Jewish meetings, particularly those of the Central Association of German Jews, took place in private homes, which made control almost impossible; then, at the end of 1935, Jewish events were allegedly often moved from Saturdays to Sundays and to the Christian holidays, "obviously," according to the Gestapo, "on the assumption that on those days the events would not be controlled. It was difficult to forbid meetings in private homes, but events taking place on Sundays or Christian holidays were from then on to be authorized in exceptional cases only."[29] The last straw came in April 1936: Gestapo stations reported an increasing use of the Hebrew language in public Jewish political meetings. "Orderly control of these meetings and the prevention of hostile propaganda have thereby become impossible," wrote Reinhard Heydrich, head of the SD and chief of the main Gestapo office.[30] The use of Hebrew in public Jewish meetings was therewith forbidden, but the language could continue to be used in closed events, for study purposes, and to prepare for emigration to Palestine. Incidentally, the reports on the use of Hebrew remain somewhat mysterious unless (and this is very unlikely) only meetings of the small minority of East European, Orthodox (though not ultra-Orthodox), and ardent Zionist Jews are being referred to. Any sort of fluency in Hebrew among the immense majority of German Jews was nil.

Many German Jews still hoped that the crisis could be weathered *in* Germany and that the new laws would create a recognized framework for a segregated but nonetheless manageable Jewish life. The official reaction of the Reichsvertretung (which was now obliged to change its name from National Representation of German Jews to Representation of Jews in Germany) took at face value Hitler's declaration regarding the new basis created by the laws for relations between the German people and the Jews living in Germany, and thus demanded the right to free exercise of its activities in the educational and cultural domains. Even at the individual level many Jews believed that the new situation offered an acceptable basis for the future. According to a study of Gestapo and SD reports on Jewish reactions to the laws, in a significant number of communities "the Jews were relieved precisely because the laws, even if they established a permanent framework of discrimination, ended the reign of arbitrary terror." There was a measure of similarity in the way average Germans and average Jews reacted. The

Germans expressed satisfaction while the Jews saw ground for hope. As the author of the report put it: "the laws finally defined the relation between Jews and Germans. Jewry becomes a *de facto* national minority, enjoying the possibility of ensuring its own cultural and national life under state protection."[31]

The ultrareligious part of the community even greeted the new situation. On September 19, 1935, *Der Israelit*, the organ of Orthodox German Jewry, after expressing its support for the idea of cultural autonomy and separate education, explicitly welcomed the interdiction of mixed marriages. As for the German Zionists, although they stepped up their activities, they seemed in no particular hurry, the mainstream group Hechalutz wishing to negotiate with the German government about the ways and means of a gradual emigration of the German Jews to Palestine over a period of fifteen to twenty years. Like other sectors of German Jewry, it expressed the hope that, in the meantime, an autonomous Jewish life in Germany would be possible.

The Jews of Germany were in fact still confronted with what appeared to be an ambiguous situation. They were well aware of their increasing segregation within German society and of the constant stream of new government decisions designed to make their life in Germany more painful. Some aspects of their daily existence, however, bolstered the illusion that segregation was the Nazis' ultimate aim and that the basic means of economic existence would remain available. For instance, despite the 1933 law on "the overcrowding of German schools" and the constant slurs and attacks against Jewish children, in early 1937 almost 39 percent of Jewish pupils were still in German schools. In the spring of the following year, the percentage had decreased to 25 percent. As will be seen, many Jewish professionals, benefiting from various exemptions, were still active outside the Jewish community. But it remains difficult to assess accurately the economic situation of the average Jewish family with a retail business or making its living from any of the various trades.

In 1935 the *Jüdische Rundschau*, which, one would have thought, should have aimed at showing how bad the situation was, quoted statistics published by the *Frankfurter Zeitung* indicating that half the ladies' garment industry was still owned by Jews, the figure rising to 80 percent in Berlin. Whether or not these numbers are accurate, the Jews of the Reich still thought they would be able to continue to make a living; they did not, for the most part, foresee any impending material catastrophe.

Yet, even though most German Jews still hoped to survive this dire period in Germany, and even though emigration was slow, the very idea of leaving the country, previously unthinkable for many, was now accepted by all German-Jewish organizations. Not an immediate emergency flight, but an orderly exodus was contemplated. Overseas (the American continent or Australia, for instance) was higher on the list of concrete possibilities than Palestine, but all German Jewish papers could wholeheartedly have adopted the headline of a *Jüdische Rundschau* lead article addressed to the League of Nations: "Open the Gates!"[32]

For the many Jews who were considering the possibility of emigration but still hoped to stay in Germany, the gap between public and private behavior was widening: "We must avoid doing anything that will attract attention to us and possibly arouse hostility." Jewish women's organizations warned, "Adhere to the highest standards of taste and decorum in speaking manner and tone, dress and appearance."[33] Jewish pride was to be maintained, but without any public display. Within the enclosed space of the synagogue or the secular Jewish assemblies, this pride and of the pent-up anger against the regime and the surrounding society found occasional expression. Religious texts were chosen for symbolic meaning and obvious allusion. A selection of psalms entitled *Out of the Depths Have I Called Thee,* published by Martin Buber in 1936, included verses that could not be misunderstood: "Be Thou my judge, O God, and plead my cause against an ungodly nation; O deliver me from the deceitful and unjust man." A new type of religious commentary, conveyed mainly in sermons—the "New Midrash," as the scholar of Judaism Ernst Simon called it—interwove religious themes with expressions of practical wisdom that were meant to have a soothing, therapeutic effect on the audience.[34]

The Zionist leadership in Palestine showed no greater sense of urgency regarding emigration than did the German Jewish community itself. Indeed, the Palestine leadership refused to extend any help to emigrants whose goal was not Eretz Israel. Its list of priorities was increasingly shifting: The economic situation of the *Yishuv* (as the Jewish community in Palestine was called in Hebrew) worsened from 1936 on, while the Arab Revolt of that year increased Britain's resistance to any growth in Jewish immigration to Palestine. Some local Zionist leaders even considered the easier-to-integrate immigrants from Poland by and large preferable to those from Germany, with an exception for German Jews who could transfer substantial amounts of money or property within the framework of the 1933 Haavarah Agreement. Thus, after 1935, the number of immigration certificates demanded for German Jews out of the total number of certificates allocated by the British remained the same as before.

"In Bad Gastein. Hitler leads me in animated conversation down an open stairway. We are visible from afar and at the bottom of the stairs a concert is taking place and there is a large crowd of people. I think proudly and happily: now everyone can see that our Führer does not mind being seen with me in public, despite my grandmother Recha."[35] Such was a dream reported by a young girl whom the Nuremberg laws had just turned into a *Mischling* of the second degree.

Here is the dream of a woman who had become a *Mischling* of the first degree: "I am on a boat with Hitler. The first thing I tell him is: 'In fact, I am not allowed to be here. I have some Jewish blood.' He looks very nice, not at all as usual: a round pleasant kindly face. I whisper into his ear: 'You [the familiar *Du*] could have become very great if you had acted like Mussolini, without this stupid Jewish business. It is true that among the Jews there are some really bad ones, but not all of them are criminals, that can't honestly be said.' Hitler listens to me quietly, listens to it all in a very friendly way. Then suddenly I am in another room of the ship, where there are a lot of black-clad SS men. They nudge each other, point at me and say to each other with the greatest respect: 'Look there, it's the lady who gave the chief a piece of her mind.' "[36]

The dream world of full Jews was often quite different from that of the *Mischlinge*. A Berlin Jewish lawyer of about sixty dreamed that he was in the Tiergarten: "There are two benches, one painted green, the other yellow, and between the two there is a wastepaper basket. I sit on the wastepaper basket and around my neck fasten a sign like the ones blind beggars wear and also like the ones the authorities hang from the necks of race defilers. It reads: WHEN NECESSARY, I WILL MAKE ROOM FOR THE WASTEPAPER."[37]

Some of the daydreams of well-known Jewish intellectuals living beyond the borders of the Reich were at times no less fantastic than the nighttime fantasies of the trapped victims. "I don't like to make political prophecies," Lion Feuchtwanger wrote to Arnold Zweig on September 20, 1935, "but through the intensive study of history I have reached the, if I may say so, scientific conviction that, in the end, reason must triumph over madness and that we cannot consider an eruption of madness such as the one in Germany as something that can last more than a generation. Superstitious as I am, I hope in silence that this time too the German madness won't last longer than the [1914–18] war madness did. And we are already at the end of the third year."[38]

Some prominent non-Jewish voices had a very different sound. Carl Gustav Jung, the famous Swiss psychologist, tried to delve "deeper" in his search for the characteristics of the Germanic psyche—and for those of the Jewish one as well. Writing in 1934, his evaluation was quite different for each of the two groups: "The Jew, who is something of a nomad, has never yet created a cultural form of his own and as far as we can see never will, since all his instincts and talents require a more or less civilized nation to act as host for their development. . . . The 'Aryan' consciousness has a higher potential than the Jewish; that is both the advantage and the disadvantage of a youthfulness not yet fully weaned from barbarism. In my opinion it has been a grave error in medical psychology up to now to apply Jewish categories . . . indiscriminately to German and Slavic Christendom. Because of this the most precious secret of the Germanic peoples—their creative and intuitive depth of soul—has been explained as a morass of banal infantilism, while my own warning voice has for decades been suspected of anti-Semitism. This suspicion emanated from Freud. He did not understand the Germanic psyche any more than did his Germanic followers. Has the formidable phenomenon of National Socialism, on which the whole world gazes with astonished eyes, taught them better?"[39]

The "formidable phenomenon of National Socialism" did not, apparently, impress Sigmund Freud. On September 29, 1935, he wrote to Arnold Zweig: "We all thought it was the war and not the people, but other nations went through the war as well and nevertheless behaved differently. We did not want to believe it at the time, but it was true what the others said about the Boches." [40]

As for Kurt Tucholsky, possibly the most brilliant antination-
alist satirist of the Weimar period, now trapped in his Swedish
exile, his anger was different from that of Freud, and his despair
was total: "I left Judaism in 1911," he wrote to Arnold Zweig on
December 15, 1935, but he immediately added: "I know that this
is in fact impossible." In many ways Tucholsky's helplessness
and rage were turned against the Jews. The unavoidable fate
could be faced with courage or with cowardice. For Tucholsky
the Jews had always behaved like cowards, now more than
ever before. Even the Jews in the medieval ghettos *could* have
behaved differently: "But let us leave the medieval Jews—and
let us turn to those of today, those of Germany. There you see
that the same people who in many domains played first violin
accept the ghetto—the idea of the ghetto and its realization. . . .
They are being locked up; they are crammed into a theater for
Jews, with four yellow badges on their front and back and they
have . . . only one ambition: 'Now for once we will show them
that we have a better theater.' For every ten German Jews, one
has left, nine are staying; but after March 1933, one should have
stayed and nine should have gone, ought to, should have. . . .
The political emigration has changed nothing; it is business
as usual: everything goes on as if nothing had happened. Forever on and on and on—they write the same books, hold the
same speeches, make the same gestures. . . ." Tucholsky knew
that he and his generation would not see the new freedom:
"What is needed . . . is a youthful strength that most emigrants
do not have. New men will come, after us. As they are now,
things cannot work anymore. The game is up."[41] Six days later
Tucholsky committed suicide.

CHAPTER 3

Ideology and Card Index

March 1936–March 1938

I N EARLY 1937, during a meeting on church affairs, Hitler once more gave free rein to his world-historical vision: "The Führer," Goebbels wrote in his diary, "explains Christianity and Christ. He [Christ] also wanted to act against the Jewish world domination. Jewry had him crucified. But Paul falsified his doctrine and undermined ancient Rome. Marx did the same with the German community spirit, with socialism."[1] On November 30 of the same year, the remarks Goebbels inscribed in his diary were much more ominous: "Long discussion [with Hitler] over the Jewish question. . . . The Jews must get out of Germany, in fact out of the whole of Europe. It will still take some time but it must happen, and it will happen. The Führer is absolutely determined about it."[2] Indeed, Hitler's prophecy of 1937 implicitly indicated the possibility of war: The expulsion of the Jews could be fulfilled only in a situation of war.

On March 7, 1936, the Wehrmacht had marched into the Rhineland, and a new phase in European history had begun. It would unfold under the sign of successive German aggressions and, in three years, lead to the outbreak of a new conflagration.

The demilitarization of the left bank of the Rhine had been

guaranteed by the Versailles and Locarno treaties. The guarantors of the status quo were Great Britain and Italy, whereas France was the country directly endangered by the German move. Although the French government threatened to act, it did nothing. As for the British, they did not even threaten; after all, Hitler was merely taking possession of his own "backyard," as the saying went. The French and British policy of appeasement was gaining momentum.

In France the 1936 elections brought the center-left Popular Front to power, and for a large segment of French society the threat of revolution and a Communist takeover became an obsessive nightmare. A few months earlier the Spanish electorate had also brought a left-wing government to power. It was a short-lived victory. In July 1936 units of the Spanish army in North Africa, led by Gen. Francisco Franco, rebelled against the new Republican government and crossed over into Spain. The Spanish civil war—which was to become a murderous struggle of two political mystiques, backed on both sides by a massive supply of foreign weapons and regular troops as well as volunteers—had started. Between the summer of 1936 and the spring of 1939, the battle lines drawn in Spain were the explicit and tacit points of reference for the ideological confrontations of the time.

On the global scene the anti-Comintern pact signed between Germany and Japan on November 25, 1936, and joined by Italy a year later, became, at least symbolically, an expression of the struggle that was to unfold between the anticommunist regimes and bolshevism. In the countries of East-Central Europe (with the exception of Czechoslovakia) and the Balkans, right-wing governments had come to power. Their ideological commitments included three basic tenets: authoritarianism, extreme nationalism, and extreme anticommunism. From the Atlantic to the Soviet border, right-wing movements and regimes had generally one more element in common: anti-Semitism. For the European Right, anti-Semitism and antibolshevism were often identical.

The year 1936 also clearly marks the beginning of a new phase on the internal German scene. During the previous period (1933–36), the need to stabilize the regime, to ward off preemptive foreign initiatives, and to sustain economic growth and the return to full employment had demanded relative moderation in some domains. By 1936 full employment had been achieved and the weakness of the anti-German front sized up. Further political radicalization and the mobilization of internal resources were now possible: Himmler, already Reich leader of the SS, was named, in addition, chief of all German police forces, and Göring overlord of a new four-year economic plan, whose secret objective was to prepare the country for war. The impetus for and the timing of both external and internal radicalization also may have been linked to yet unresolved tensions within German society itself, or may have resulted from the fundamental needs of a regime that could only thrive on ever more hectic action and ever more spectacular success. And radicalization as such meant new anti-Jewish steps.

Most immediately three main lines of action dominated the new phase of the anti-Jewish drive: accelerated Aryanization, increasingly coordinated efforts to compel the Jews to leave Germany, and furious propaganda activity to project on a world scale the theme of Jewish conspiracy and threat.

Accelerated Aryanization resulted in part from the new economic situation and the spreading confidence in German business and industrial circles that the risks of retaliation or its effects no longer had to be taken into account. Economic growth led to gradual coordination of the contradictory measures that, of necessity, had earlier hindered the course of anti-Jewish policy: By 1936 ideology and policy could progress along a single track. Himmler's and Göring's appointments to their new positions created two power bases essential for the effective implementation of the new anti-Jewish drive. And yet, although the framework of the new phase was clearly perceptible, the economic expropriation of the Jews of Germany could not be radically enforced before the beginning of 1938, after the expulsion of the conservative ministers from the government in February 1938 (mainly after Schacht's dismissal as minister of the economy in late 1937). During 1938 worse than total expropriation was to follow: Economic harassment and even violence would henceforward be used to force the Jews to flee the Reich or the newly annexed Austria. Thus, within the second phase, 1938 was another fateful turning point.

The anti-Jewish rhetoric suffusing Hitler's speeches and statements from 1936 on took several forms. Foremost was its relation to the general ideological confrontation with bolshevism. The world peril as presented by Hitler was not bolshevism as such but the Jews: the ultimate threat behind bolshevism. But Hitler's anti-Jewish harangues were not only ideological in a concrete sense; often the Jew was described as the world enemy per se, as the peril that had to be destroyed lest Germany (or Aryan humanity) be exterminated by it. The "redemptive" anti-Semitism that had dominated Hitler's early ideological statements now resurfaced. With the conservative agenda crumbling, a new atmosphere of murderous brutality was spreading.

It is at the start of this darkening path that the Nazis achieved one of their greatest propaganda victories: the successful unfolding of the 1936 Olympic Games. Foreign visitors discovered a Reich that looked powerful, orderly, and content. As the American liberal periodical the *Nation* expressed it on August 1, 1936: "[One] sees no Jewish heads being chopped off, or even roundly cudgeled. . . . The people smile, are polite and sing with gusto in beer gardens. Board and lodging are good, cheap, and abundant, and no one is swindled by grasping hotel and shop proprietors. Everything is terrifyingly clean and the visitor likes it all."[3] Even the president of the United States was deceived. In October of that year, Rabbi Stephen Wise, president of the World Jewish Congress, was invited to meet with Roosevelt at Hyde Park. When the conversation turned to Germany, the president cited two people who had recently "toured" Germany and reported to him that "the synagogues were crowded and apparently there is nothing very wrong in the situation at present." Wise tried to explain to his host the impact of the Olympic Games on Nazi behavior, but felt that Roosevelt still regarded accounts of persecution of the Jews as exaggerated.[4]

Signs forbidding access to Jews were removed from Olympic areas and from other sites likely to be visited by tourists, but only very minor ideological concessions were made. The Jewish high-jump finalist Gretel Bergmann, from Stuttgart, was excluded from the German team on a technical pretext; the fencing champion Helene Mayer was included because she was a *Mischling* and thus a German citizen according to the Nuremberg laws. Only one German full Jew, the hockey player Rudi Ball, was allowed to compete for Germany. But the Winter Games in those days were far less visible than the summer ones. The negotiations that had preceded the Olympics showed that Hitler's tactical moderation emanated only from the immense propaganda asset the games represented. When, on August 24, 1935, the führer received Gen. Charles Sherrill, an American member of the International Olympic Committee, he was still adamant: The Jews were perfectly entitled to their separate life in Germany, but they could not be members of the national team. As for the foreign teams, they were free to include whomever they wanted. Finally, because of the threat of an American boycott of the Olympics, very minor concessions were adopted, as mentioned, which allowed Germany to reap all the expected advantages, the recent passage of the Nuremberg laws notwithstanding.

The Winter Games had opened on February 6 in Garmisch-Partenkirchen. The day before, Wilhelm Gustloff, the Nazi Party representative in Switzerland, had been assassinated by the Jewish medical student David Frankfurter. Within a few hours a strict order was issued: Because of the Olympic Games all anti-Jewish actions were prohibited. And indeed no outbursts of "popular anger" occurred.

The anti-Jewish campaign, mainly in its perceived Judeo-bolshevik connection, resumed following the games and reached its full scope at the "Party Congress of Labor," in September 1937. On September 11 Goebbels set the tone. In a speech devoted to the situation in Spain, the propaganda minister launched into a hysterical attack against the Jews, whom he held responsible for bolshevist terror. "Who are those responsible for this catastrophe?" Goebbels asked. His answer: "Without fear, we want to point the finger at the Jew as the inspirer, the author, and the beneficiary of this terrible catastrophe: look, this is the enemy of the world, the destroyer of cultures, the parasite among the nations, the son of chaos, the incarnation of evil, the ferment of decomposition, the visible demon of the decay of humanity."[5]

On the evening of September 13, it was Hitler's turn. All restraint was now gone. For the first time since his accession to the chancellorship, he used the platform of a party congress, with the global attention it commanded, to launch a general historical and political attack on world Jewry as the wire puller behind bolshevism and the enemy of humanity from the time of early Christianity on. Never since the fall of the ancient world order, Hitler declared, never since the rise of Christianity, the spread of Islam, and the Reformation had the world been in such turmoil. This was no ordinary confrontation but a fight for the very essence of human culture and civilization. "What others profess not to see because they simply do not want to see it, is something we must unfortunately state as a bitter truth: the world is presently in the midst of an increasing upheaval, whose spiritual and factual preparation and whose leadership undoubtedly proceed from the rulers of Jewish Bolshevism in Moscow."[6] Hitler repeated his main themes in an ever-changing variety of formulas all bearing the same message. And, although in the Ministry of Foreign Affairs and in the army efforts were made to maintain a more realistic assessment of Soviet affairs, the equation of Jewry and bolshevism and the theme of Jewish world conspiracy remained the fundamental slogans for most party and state agencies.

How did the churches react to the growing attacks on German Jewry? In July 1936 a memorandum was submitted to Hitler by the Provisional Directorate of the Confessing Church. It was a forceful document mentioning the concentration camps, the Gestapo's methods, and even the misuse of religious terms and images in worship of the führer. In an unusually bold departure from previous practice, the memorandum prophesied disaster for Germany if "there were persistence in totalitarian presumption and might contrary to the will of God."

The document was leaked and received extraordinary coverage abroad. Such a courageous statement, one could assume, must have given pride of place to the persecution of the Jews. "Yet," in the words of the historian Richard Gutteridge, "all that was devoted to this subject was the rather awkward observation that, when in the framework of the National Socialist *Weltanschauung* a form of anti-Semitism was forced upon the Christian which imposed an obligation of hatred towards the Jews, he had to counter it by the Christian command of love towards one's neighbor. Here was no disavowal of anti-Semitism as such, but merely of the militant Nazi version without even an oblique reference to the plight of the Jews themselves. The emphasis was upon the severe conflict of conscience experienced by the devout German Church people."[7] When a declaration of the Confessing Church referring indirectly to the memorandum was read in church by many pastors on August 23, not a single word was directed toward anti-Semitism or hatred of the Jews. A few months later, in March 1937, Pius XI's sharp critique of the Nazi regime, the encyclical *Mit brennender Sorge*, was read from all Catholic pulpits in Germany. Nazi pseudo-religion and the regime's racial theories were strongly condemned in general terms, but no direct reference was made to the fate of the Jews.

For the converted "full Jew" Friedrich Weissler, the memorandum of the Confessing Church was to have fateful consequences. A lawyer by profession, Weissler was employed by the Confessing Church as a legal adviser and was secretly in charge of informing the outside world about its activities. It was probably he who leaked the memorandum to the foreign press. Pretending outrage, the leadership of the Confessing Church asked the Gestapo to find the culprit. Weissler and two Aryan assistants were arrested. Whereas the Aryans were ultimately released, Weissler, for whom the church did not intervene, succumbed in the Sachsenhausen concentration camp on February 19, 1937. Thus a "full Jew" became "the first martyr of the Confessing Church."[8]

As mentioned, on June 17, 1936, Himmler was appointed head of all German police forces, thus becoming Reichsführer SS and Chief of the German Police. This decisive reorganization signaled an unmistakable step toward the ever-increasing intervention of the party in the state's sphere of competence and a shift of power from the traditional state structure to the party. On June 26, 1936, Himmler divided the police forces into two separate commands: the Order Police, under Kurt Daluege, was to comprise all uniformed police units; whereas the Security Police (SIPO) under Heydrich's command, integrated the Criminal Police and the Gestapo into a single organization.

Heydrich now had control of both the new SIPO and the Security Service of the SS, the SD.

Although Heydrich's own anti-Jewish initiatives and proposals had been increasingly influential, and while the Gestapo already played a central role in the implementation of anti-Jewish decisions, until 1938 the activities of those sections of the SD that dealt with the Jewish question (II 112) were limited to three main domains: gathering information on Jews, Jewish organizations, and Jewish activities; drafting policy recommendations; and participating in surveillance operations and interrogations of Jews in coordination with the Gestapo. Moreover, as II 112 unabashedly considered itself the top group of "Jew experts" in Germany, it systematically organized conferences in which, several times a year, the most updated information was imparted to delegates of other SD sections from the main office and from various parts of Germany. The largest of such conferences, convened on November 1, 1937, brought together sixty-six mostly middle-ranking members of the SD.

One of II 112's pet projects was the compilation of a card index of Jews, intended to identify every Jew living in the Reich. It also started to compile another card index of the most important Jews in foreign countries and their mutual connections. In the words of SS-Hauptsturmführer Erich Ehrlinger at the November conference, the aim of this listing was "(1) to establish the number of Jews and of people of Jewish origin according to the Nuremberg Laws living today in the Reich; (2) to establish the direct influence of Jewry and eventually the influence it exercises through its connections on the cultural life, the community life, and the material life of the German people."[9]

The general population census of May 1939 was to provide the opportunity for the complete registration of all the Jews in Germany (including half- and quarter-Jews): In each town or village the local police made sure that the census cards of Jews and *Mischlinge* carried the letter *J* as a distinctive mark; copies of all local census registration lists were to be sent to the SD. The card files would fulfill their function when the deportations began.

A second information-gathering effort was aimed at every Jewish organization in Germany and throughout the world, from the ORT (an organization for vocational training and guidance) to the Agudath Yisrael (ultra-Orthodox Jewry). For the men of II 112 and the SD in general, no detail was too minute, no Jewish organization too insignificant. As the organized enemy they were fighting was nonexistent as such, their own enterprise had to create it. Jewish organizations were identified, analyzed, and studied as parts of an ever more complex system; the anti-German activities of that system had to be discovered, its internal workings decoded, its very essence unveiled.

The most astonishing aspect of this system was its delusional concreteness. Very precise—and totally imaginary—Jewish plots were uncovered, names and addresses provided, countermeasures taken. Thus, in his lecture, "World Jewry," at the November 1 conference, Adolf Eichmann, an increasingly important official of the Jewish "desk" of the SD, listed a whole series of sinister Jewish endeavors: An attempt on the life of the Sudeten German Nazi leader Konrad Henlein had been planned at the Paris Asyle de Jour et de Nuit (a shelter for destitute Jews). It had failed only because Henlein had been warned and the murderer's·weapon had not functioned. Worse still, Nathan Landsmann, the president of the Paris-based Alliance Israélite Universelle (a Jewish educational organization), was in charge of planning attempts on the führer's life—and also on Julius Streicher's. To that effect Landsmann was in touch with a Dutch Jewish organization, the Komitee voor Bizondere Joodsche Belange in Amsterdam, which in turn worked in close cooperation with the Dutch (Jewish) Unilever Trust, including its branches in Germany. This is a mere sample of Eichmann's revelations.

In its policy recommendations, II 112 backed any action to accelerate Jewish emigration, including the potentially positive effects of instigated violence. As early as May 1934, an SD memorandum addressed to Heydrich had opened with the unambiguous statement that "the aim of the Jewish policy must be the complete emigration of the Jews." In the context of 1934 the lines that followed were unusual: "The life opportunities of the Jews have to be restricted, not only in economic terms. To them Germany must become a country without a future, in which the old generation may die off with what still remains for it, but in which the young generation should find it impossible to live, so that the incentive to emigrate is constantly in force. Violent mob anti-Semitism must be avoided. One does not fight rats with guns but with poison and gas. . . ."[10] It was within the overall shifting of Nazi goals in 1936 that the policy of the SD became an active element in a general drive of all Nazi agencies involved in Jewish matters: For all of them emigration was the first priority.

Palestine was considered one of the more promising outlets for Jewish emigration, as it had been since 1933. Like the Foreign Ministry and the Rosenberg office (which was mainly in charge of ideological matters, including contacts with foreign Nazi sympathizers), the SD was confronted with the dilemma entailed by the need to encourage Jewish emigration to Palestine on the one hand, and, on the other, the danger that such emigration could lead to the creation of a strategic center for the machinations of world Jewry: a Jewish state. It was in relation to such policy considerations that Heydrich allowed Herbert Hagen (soon to become head of II 112) and Eichmann to visit Palestine in the fall of 1937 and to meet with their contact at the Haganah (the main Jewish paramilitary organization in Palestine), Feivel Polkes.

The mission failed miserably: The British did not allow the two SD men to stay in Palestine more than a day, and their conversations with Polkes—who came to meet them in Cairo—produced no valuable information whatsoever. But the favorable SD view of Palestine as a destination for German Jews did not change. Later on it was with the SD that Zionist emissaries organized the departure of convoys of emigrants to Romanian ports, from which they attempted to sail for Palestine in defiance of the British blockade.

In the thirties the Nazi regime used two different but complementary methods to achieve the complete exclusion of racially dangerous groups from the *Volksgemeinschaft*: segregation and expulsion on the one hand, sterilization on the other. The first method was used in its various aspects against the Jews, Gypsies, and homosexuals; the second method was applied to the carriers of hereditary diseases (physical or mental) and to persons showing dangerous characteristics deemed hereditary, as well as to "racially contaminated individuals" who could not be expelled or put into camps.

When the health argument could not easily be used for racial purposes, other methods were found. Thus the new regime had barely been established when the attention of the authorities was directed to a group probably numbering no more than five to seven hundred, the young offspring of German women and colonial African soldiers serving in the French military occupation of the Rhineland during the early postwar years. In Nazi jargon these were the "Rhineland bastards."[11] Hitler had already described this "black pollution of German blood" in *Mein Kampf* as one more method used by the Jews to undermine the racial fiber of the *Volk*.

As early as April 1933, Göring as Prussian minister of the interior requested the registration of these "bastards," and a few weeks later the ministry ordered that they undergo a racial-anthropological evaluation. In July the evaluation of thirty-eight of these schoolchildren was undertaken and, as expected, determined that the subjects showed various defects in intellectual ability and behavior. The Prussian ministry reported the findings on March 28, 1934, warning of dire racial consequences if, despite their very small number, these "bastards" were allowed to reproduce. The upshot of the argument was that, since the presence in France of half a million mixed breeds would lead within four or five generations to the bastardization of half the French population, the similar presence of mixed breeds on the German side of the border would lead to local miscegenation and the consequent disappearance of any racial difference between the French and the population of the adjacent western parts of the Reich.[12]

That the matter was not taken lightly is shown by a meeting of the Advisory Committee for Population and Racial Policy of the Ministry of the Interior, which on March 11, 1935, convened representatives of the Ministries of the Interior, Health, Justice, Labor, and Foreign Affairs, as well as eugenicists from the academic world. Walter Gross, head of the racial policy office of the Nazi Party, did not hide the difficulties in handling the problem of what he called the "Negro bastards." Their rapid expulsion was impossible; thus, Gross left no doubt about the need for sterilization.

But sterilization of a healthy population, if carried out openly, could cause serious internal and external reactions. As the reliability of ordinary practitioners was not to be depended on, Gross saw no other way but to demand the secret intervention of physicians who were also seasoned party members and would understand the imperatives of the higher good of the *Volk*. In the course of 1937, these hundreds of boys and girls were identified, picked up by the Gestapo, and sterilized.

In contrast, the decision to sterilize carriers of hereditary diseases and the so-called feeble-minded was based on medical

examinations and specially devised intelligence tests. The results were submitted to hereditary health courts, whose decisions were in turn forwarded for review to hereditary health
appellate courts: their final verdicts were mandatory.

For mental patients sterilization was often but a first stage.
Organized tours of mental institutions were meant to demonstrate both the freakish appearance of mental patients and
the unnecessary costs entailed by their upkeep. A crop of propaganda films aimed at indoctrinating the wider public were
produced and shown during the same years, and in schools,
appropriate exercises in arithmetic demonstrated the financial
toll such inmates imposed on the nation's economy. According
to the head of the Reich Chancellery, State Secretary Hans
Heinrich Lammers, Hitler had already mentioned the possibility of euthanasia in 1933, and according to his personal physician, Karl Brandt, the Nazi leader had discussed the subject
with the Reich physicians' leader Wagner in 1935, indicating
that such a project would be easier to carry out in wartime.

Nonetheless, starting in 1936, mental patients were gradually
being concentrated in large state-run institutions, and reliable SS
personnel were placed on the staffs of some private institutions.
The privately run institutions [mainly by Protestant religious
groups] were well aware of the ominous aspect of these developments. In fact, what is chilling about the documentation of the
years 1936–38 is that "the associations established for the care of
the handicapped often . . . denounced those left to their care and
thereby helped to bring about their persecution and extermination."[13] Many of the religious institutions that were losing some
of their inmates as a result of the regrouping of patients into state
institutions did complain—but only about the economic difficulties such transfers were causing them.

The first concrete step toward a euthanasia policy was
taken in the fall of 1938. The father of an infant born blind,
retarded, and with no arms and legs petitioned Hitler for

the right to a "mercy death" for his son. Karl Brandt, Hitler's personal physician, was sent to Leipzig, where the baby was hospitalized, to consult with the doctors in charge and perform the euthanasia. At this stage Hitler acted with prudence. He was aware that the killing of mentally ill adults or of infants with grave defects could encounter staunch opposition from the Churches, the Catholic Church in particular. This potential obstacle was all the more significant as the largely Catholic population and the ecclesiastical hierarchy of Austria had just given their enthusiastic endorsement to the Anschluss. But an "opinion" about the Church's attitude toward euthanasia, prepared by Albert Hartl, head of SD desk II 113 (political churches), revealed that despite the Catholic pronouncements on the subject, the door was open for exceptions. Through indirect channels the memorandum was sent to Bishop Wilhelm Berning and to the papal nuncio, Monsignor Cesare Orsenigo. On the Protestant side it was submitted to Pastors Paul Braune and Friedrich von Bodelschwingh. It seems that no opposition was voiced by any of the German clerics—Catholic or Protestant—contacted by Hitler's Chancellery. The pope's delegate, too, remained silent.

On September 29, 1936, the state secretary in the German Ministry of the Interior, Wilhelm Stuckart, convened a conference of high officials from his agency, from the Ministry of the Economy, and from the Office of the Deputy Führer in order to prepare recommendations for a meeting of ministers about further steps to be taken in regard to the Jews at this post-Nuremberg stage. The Office of the Deputy Führer represented the party line, the Ministry of the Interior (though headed by the Nazi Wilhelm Frick) often represented middle-of-the-road positions between the party and the conservative state bureaucracy, and the Ministry of the Economy (still headed by Schacht) was decidedly conservative. It is remarkable that, at this conference, the highest officials of the three agencies were entirely in agreement.

All those present recognized that the fundamental aim now was the "complete emigration" of the Jews and that all other measures had to be taken with this aim in mind. After restating this postulate, Stuckart added a sentence that was soon to find its dramatic implementation: "Ultimately one would have to consider carrying out compulsory emigration."[14] Most of the discussion was concentrated on dilemmas that were to bedevil German choices until the fall of 1938: First, what measure of social and economic activity should be left to Jews in the Reich so as to prevent their becoming a burden to the state and yet not diminish their incentive to emigrate? Second, toward which countries was Jewish emigration to be channeled without it leading to the creation of new centers of anti-German activity? The participants agreed that all emigration options should be left open, but that German means should be used only to help the emigration to Palestine. No decision was made regarding the problem of the identification of Jewish businesses.

The September 1936 conference was the first high level policy-planning meeting devoted to the regime's future anti-Jewish measures in which the priority of total emigration (that is, expulsion if need be) was clearly formulated. Before the passage of the Nuremberg laws, segregation had been the main goal. The move to new objectives tallied, as has been seen, with the new radicalization in both the internal and the external domains.

Simultaneously the "cleansing" process was relentlessly going forward: The major initiatives stemmed from Hitler; yet, when other initiatives were submitted to him by cabinet ministers or high party leaders, his approval was far from automatic.

On April 1, 1933, some 8,000 to 9,000 Jewish physicians

were practicing in Germany. By the end of 1934, approximately 2,200 had either emigrated or abandoned their profession; but despite a steady decline during 1935, at the beginning of 1936, 5,000 Jewish physicians (among them 2,800 in the Public Health Service) were still working in the Reich. The official listing of the country's physicians for 1937 identified Jewish physicians as Jews according to the Nuremberg criteria; by then their total number was about 4,200, approximately half of those listed in 1933, yet in Nazi eyes still far too many.

On December 13, 1935, the minister of the interior, Wilhelm Frick, submitted the draft of a law regulating the medical profession. But although the proposal was accepted, for an unspecified reason the final drafting of the law was postponed for more than a year. On June 14, 1937, Wagner met with Hitler in the presence of Martin Bormann, Hess's deputy: "As I submitted to the Führer that it was necessary to free the medical profession of the Jews," Wagner wrote, "the Führer declared that he considered such cleansing exceptionally necessary and urgent. Nor did he consider it right that Jewish physicians should be allowed to continue to practice [in numbers] corresponding to the percentage of the Jewish population. In any case, these doctors had also to be excluded in case of war. The Führer considered the cleansing of the medical profession more important than for example that of the civil service, as the task of the physician was in his opinion one of leadership. . . . The Führer demanded that we inform State Secretary Lammers of his order to prepare the legal basis for the exclusion of the Jewish physicians still practicing (cancellation of licenses)."[15]

Interior Minister Frick, a party stalwart if ever there was one, nevertheless seemed to have underestimated the stepped-up pace of radicalization. It appears, from a November 25, 1936, Education Ministry memorandum, that at the beginning of the year, Frick had decided that there was no legal basis for the dismissal of Aryan civil servants with Jewish wives. In the words of the memorandum, "[Frick's] position has not received the approval of the Führer and Reich Chancellor." The corollary was simple: Frick's initiative was invalid.[16]

A few months later Frick made up for his initial lack of creative legalism. On April 19, 1937, he issued the following ordinance: "My memorandum of December 7, 1936, which forbids the raising of the national colors over the house of a German living in a German-Jewish mixed marriage, also applies to civil servants. As a situation in which a civil servant cannot raise the national flag at home is not tenable in the long run, civil servants married to a Jewish wife are usually to be pensioned off."[17] Some exceptions were allowed, but the legal basis for dismissing civil servants with Jewish spouses had been found. On July 21, 1937, Frick solved another major problem: safety measures to be taken regarding the presence of Jews in health resorts and related establishments. Jews were to be housed only in Jewish-owned hotels and guesthouses, on condition that no German female employees under forty-five worked on the premises. The general facilities (for bathing, drinking spa waters, and the like) were to be accessible to Jews, but there was to be as much separation from the other guests as possible. As for facilities with no immediate health function (gardens, sports grounds), these could be prohibited to Jews.

But as in previous years, Hitler hesitated when a measure could create unnecessary political complications. Thus, on November 17, 1936, he ordered further postponement of a law on Jewish schooling, a draft of which had been submitted to him by the minister of education. It seems that at the time Hitler was still wary of implementing the segregation of Jewish students along racial lines, as it would have entailed the transfer of Jewish children of Christian faith into Jewish schools and added further tension to relations with the Catholic Church.

At times the cleansing measures turned into a totally surrealistic imbroglio. The issue of doctoral degrees for Jewish students was one such instance. The problem was apparently raised at the end of 1935 and discussed by the minister of the interior: Any restrictions on the right to obtain a doctoral degree were not to apply to foreign Jewish students; for German Jews the issue remained unresolved. At the beginning of 1936, it was brought up again by Wilhelm Grau, who was about to become head of the Jewish Section in Walter Frank's Institute for the History of the New Germany, whose goal was to create a new Nazi historiography. On February 10, Grau wrote to the secretary of state for education that he had been asked to evaluate a dissertation on the history of the Jews of Ulm in the Middle Ages, submitted by a Jew at the faculty of philosophy of Berlin University. "Whereas in the above-mentioned case," wrote Grau, "the dissertation is already inadequate from a scientific viewpoint, a general question also arises, namely whether Jews should be allowed to obtain a doctorate at all in a German university on such historical subjects. As our university professors unfortunately have little knowledge and even less instinct regarding the Jewish question, the most incredible things happen in this area." Grau continued with a story mentioned in his first contribution to the *Historische Zeitschrift*: "Last October, an Orthodox Jew called Heller obtained his doctorate at the University of Berlin with a dissertation on Jews in Soviet Russia, in which he attempted to deny entirely the Jewish contribution to Bolshevism by using a method that should raise extreme indignation in the National Socialist racial state. Heller simply does not consider those Jews he finds unpleasant, such as Trotsky and company, to be Jews but anti-Jewish 'internationalists.' With reference to this, I merely want to raise the question of the right of Jews to obtain a doctorate."[18]

The discussion on this topic, which developed throughout 1936 and early 1937, involved the Ministry of Education, the deans of the philosophy faculties at both Berlin and Leipzig Universities, the rectors of these universities, the Reichstatthalter of Saxony, and the Office of the Deputy Führer. The attitude of the Ministry of Education was to adhere to the law regarding Jewish attendance at German universities: As long as Jewish students were allowed to study in German universities, their right to acquire a doctoral degree could not be abrogated. The best way of handling the situation was to appeal to the national feelings of the professors and prevail upon them not to accept Jews as doctoral students.

On October 15, 1936, Bormann intervened. For him, appealing to "the national consciousness of the professors" was not the right way to handle the matter. "In particular," Bormann wrote to Frick, "I would not want the implementation of basic racial tenets that derive from the worldview of National Socialism to be dependent upon the goodwill of university professors." Bormann did not hesitate: A law prohibiting the award of doctoral degrees to Jewish students was necessary, and it was to be aimed at the professors, not the students. As for foreign reactions, Bormann thought that the impact of the law would be beneficial; in justifying this claim he used an argument whose significance extended well beyond the issue at hand: "I believe that the decree will fall on favorable ground, particularly in racially alien countries, which feel slighted by our racial policy, as thereby Jewry will once more be consciously set apart from other foreign races." There was no objection to granting the doctoral degree to Jewish students who had already fulfilled all the necessary requirements.[19]

A decree reflecting Bormann's view was drafted by the minister of education on April 15, 1937: The universities were ordered not to allow Jewish students of German citizenship to sit for doctoral exams. Exemptions were granted to *Mischlinge* under various conditions, and the rights of foreign Jews remained as before.

The purification process also duly progressed at the local level. Thus, the Munich city fathers, who had excluded the Jews

from public swimming pools in 1935, took a further bold step
in 1937. Now the Jews were to be forbidden access to municipal
baths and showers. But as the matter was weighty, Bormann's
authorization was requested. It was refused, although it is not
clear what Bormann's reasons were. Slowed down in one area,
the Munich authorities pushed ahead in another. Since 1933
the city streets that bore Jewish names had gradually been renamed. At the end of 1936, however, Mayor Karl Fiehler discovered that eleven Jewish street names still remained. During
1937, therefore, with assistance from the municipal archive,
the names that were undoubtedly Jewish were changed. But
as an archive official put it, there was always the possibility
that "as a result of more thorough research, one or more street
names might be identified as being Jew-related."[20]

In Frankfurt the problems created by Jewish street names
were worse. It seems that the first person to raise the issue publicly was a woman party member, who on December 17, 1933,
wrote an open letter to the *Frankfurter Volksblatt*: "Please do
me the great favor of seeing whether you could not use your
influence to change the name of our street, which is that of the
Jew Jakob Schiff. Our street is mainly inhabited by people who
are National Socialist–minded, and when flags are flown, the
swastika flutters from every house. The 'Jakob Schiff' always
gives one a stab to the heart."[21] The letter was sent to the municipal chancellery, which forwarded it to the city commission
for street names. In March 1934 the commission advised the
mayor of all the donations made by the Jewish-American finan-
cier Jacob Schiff to various Frankfurt institutions, including
the university, and therefore suggested rejecting the proposed
name change, especially since, given the importance of the
Jacob Schiff private banking house in the United States, such a
change would be widely reported and could lead to a demand
for restitution of the moneys that had been given to the city.
The letter in the *Volksblatt* had, however, triggered a

number of similar initiatives, and on February 3, 1935, after a lengthy correspondence, the city commission for street names requested the mayor's agreement to the following proposal: The names of fourteen streets or squares were to be changed immediately, starting with Börne Square, which was to become Dominicans' Square. When Nazi propaganda "discovered" that Schiff had heavily financed the bolsheviks, Jakob-Schiff-Strasse became Mumm-Strasse (in honor of a former Frankfurt mayor). Twelve more streets were to be renamed in 1936, and twenty-nine others whose renaming had been suggested were to keep their names, either because their real meaning could be explained away (Mathilden-Strasse, Sophien-Strasse, Luisen-Strasse, and Luisen-Platz, all in fact named after women of the Rothschild family, would now be regarded as merely named for generic women) or because no sufficient or valid reason could be found for the change.

In Stuttgart the exclusion of Jews from public swimming pools was postponed until after the Olympic Games; anti-Jewish initiatives did not, however, lag behind those in other German cities. The local party leaders were infuriated by the fact that, at least until 1937, the Jewish population of the city was growing rather than declining. Jews from the small towns and villages of surrounding Württemberg were fleeing to the city in the hope of finding both the protection of anonymity and the support of a larger community. Thus, whereas during the first seven months of 1936, 582 Jews left Stuttgart, 592 moved in. It was only at the end of 1937 that the four-thousand-strong Jewish population started to decline.

The city council decided to take Jewish matters in hand. At its September 21, 1936, meeting, the council announced that old people's homes, nursery schools, and (finally) swimming pools belonging to the city were henceforth forbidden to Jews; in hospitals Jews were to be separated from other patients; city employees were forbidden to patronize Jewish shops and consult Jewish physicians; Jewish businessmen were forbidden to attend markets and fairs; and the city canceled all its own real estate and other business transactions with Jews.

For Jews and Germans alike, the fundamental criterion for measuring the success of the anti-Jewish segregation policies was the level of Jewish economic presence in Germany. Some local occurrences seemed, on occasion, to point to unexpected resilience. Thus, on February 2, 1937, the Stuttgart *NS-Kurier* published a lengthy article on a particular instance of "wretchedness and lack of character."[22] The wife of the director of a city enterprise had been seen buying laundry soap in the Jewish department store Schocken. Still worse, on March 20 that same year, the *NS-Kurier* must have deeply angered its readers when it reported that the Munich Jewish-owned fashion house Rothschild had presented its designs at the Marquardt Hotel, and that "some German women, rich and accordingly devoid of convictions," had accepted the Jewish invitation to attend.[23]

Sometimes silence was a safer option for the local party press. No Munich newspaper published anything about the four-hour visit paid in 1936 by Göring, accompanied by his adjutant, Prince Philipp von Hessen, to Otto Bernheimer's carpet and tapestry store. Although Bernheimer's was well known as a Jewish-owned business, Göring paid 36,000 reichsmarks for two rare carpets, which were duly sent to their lofty destination in Berlin. Indeed, Göring was no exception, nor were the Stuttgart society ladies. Gestapo reports from various parts of the Reich indicate that at the end of 1935 and in 1936, many Germans were still not hesitating to do business with Jews.

In the cities the annual late-winter sales at Jewish stores were big occasions. Thus in February 1936, the Munich police directorate reported that the sale at the Jewish-owned textile house Sally Eichengrün had drawn "large crowds." At times as many as three hundred eager female customers stood in line on the street outside the store. And various SD reports indicate that even in 1937 economic relations between Germans and Jews still remained active in several domains, with, for example, members of the aristocracy, of the officer corps, and of the high bourgeoisie still keeping their assets in Jewish banks.

It is difficult to assess what was paid—as an average percentage of value—to the tens of thousands of Jewish owners of small businesses during this early phase of Aryanization. Recent research indicates that the considerable scope of Aryanization at the medium—and small—business level was not indicative of the situation at the higher levels of the economy: There the competition was more limited, and the attitude toward extortion still negative because the enterprises involved had higher international visibility. The Nazis decided, therefore, to avoid any head-on clash. Thus, dozens of Jews remained on boards of directors and in other important managerial positions at companies such as Mannesmann, IG Farben, Gesellschaft für Elektrische Unternehmungen, and so on. The Dresdner Bank, for instance, "still had 100 to 150 Jewish employees in Berlin in 1936, and five directors retained their posts until the period 1938 to 1940." [24]

When Aryanization did take place at the big-business level, there are indications in some very significant instances that fair prices were being offered to the owners until the end of 1937, when the situation was to change drastically. Self-interest was obviously part of the motivation for this kind of seeming restraint and fairness: As the economic recovery remained uncertain, some of the largest German firms, eager to avoid additional taxation on their new profits or to escape the effects of eventual devaluation, used the costly acquisition of tested yet depreciable enterprises to improve their accountable benefits.

In general, however, the overall economic situation of the Jews in Germany was steadily worsening. In villages and small cities, harassment was often the easiest way to compel Jews to sell their businesses at a fraction of their value and move away or emigrate. In the larger cities and for more important businesses, credit restrictions and other boycott measures devised by Aryan firms led to the same result. Those Jews who clung to their economic activity were increasingly confined to the rapidly shrinking Jewish market. Excluded from their occupations, Jewish professionals became peddlers, either selling wares out of their homes or traveling from place to place—a reversal of the historic course of Jewish social mobility.

Soon the ever weaker and ever more ambiguous protection offered by the conservatives against radicalization of the regime's anti-Jewish policies disappeared. Once Hitler had taken concrete steps to launch the Reich on the course of a major military confrontation, the fate of the conservatives was sealed. At the end of 1937 Schacht would be on his way out, replaced by the Nazi Walther Funk. At the beginning of 1938, other conservative ministers, including Foreign Minister Neurath and Defense Minister Blomberg, would follow. At the same time, the army chief of staff, Gen. Werner von Fritsch, left in disgrace on trumped-up charges of homosexuality. Hitler himself became the commander of the armed forces, which henceforward were led de facto by a new Supreme Command of the Wehrmacht (Oberkommando der Wehrmacht, or OKW), under Gen. Wilhelm Keitel.

In the directive establishing the Four-Year Plan, Hitler demanded passage of a law that "would make the whole of Jewry responsible for all damage some individual members of this gang of criminals caused the German economy and thereby the German people."[25] In order to punish the Jews for the death of Gustloff (the Nazi representative in Switzerland who was murdered by a Jewish student in early February 1936), the decree concerning the collective fine was to be ready by the end of the assassin's trial in Switzerland. The deadline was missed because discussions between the Ministries of Finance and the Interior on technicalities regarding the fine continued throughout 1937 and the first half of 1938. But the postponement really resulted from Göring's hesitations about the potential effects of such a decree on the Reich's foreign currency and raw materials situation.

On November 5, 1937, Hitler convened a wide array of military, economic, and foreign affairs experts to inform them of his strategic plans for the next four to five years. In the near future Hitler envisioned taking action against Czechoslovakia and against Austria, given the Western democracies' glaring weakness of purpose. In fact Austria came first, due to an unforeseen set of circumstances cleverly exploited by the Nazi leader.

In the German-Austrian treaty of 1936, the Austrian chancellor Kurt von Schuschnigg had promised to include some Nazi ministers in his cabinet. As, in Hitler's view, Schuschnigg was going neither far nor fast enough, he was summoned to Berchtesgaden in February 1938. Under threat of military action, the Austrian chancellor accepted the German dictator's demands. Yet, once back in Vienna, he tried to outwit Hitler by announcing a plebiscite on Austrian independence. Hitler responded by threatening an immediate invasion of Austria if the plebiscite was not canceled. Berlin's further demands—including Schuschnigg's resignation and his replacement by an Austrian Nazi, Arthur Seyss-Inquart—were all accepted. Nonetheless Hitler's course was now set: On March 12, 1938, the Wehrmacht crossed the Austrian border; the next day Austria was annexed to the Reich.

On March 15 Hitler spoke from the balcony of the Hofburg to hundreds of thousands of ecstatic Viennese assembled on the Heldenplatz. His closing words could hardly have been surpassed: "As Führer and Chancellor of the German nation and Reich, I now report to history that my homeland has joined the German Reich."[26]

CHAPTER 4

Radicalization

March 1938–November 1938

O<small>N</small> J<small>UNE</small> 4, 1938, Sigmund Freud, aged eighty-two, was allowed to depart from Vienna, the city that had been his home since he was four years old. His apartment had twice been searched by the Gestapo, and his daughter Anna summoned for interrogation. Finally, after the Nazis had impounded part of his possessions and imposed the emigration tax, they demanded his signature on a declaration that he had not been ill treated. Freud dutifully signed, and added: "I can most highly recommend the Gestapo to everyone. . . ."[1]

As a result of the Anschluss, an additional 190,000 Jews had fallen into Nazi hands. The persecution in Austria, particularly in Vienna, outpaced that in the Reich. Public humiliation was more blatant and sadistic; expropriation better organized; forced emigration more rapid. The Austrians—their country renamed Ostmark and placed under the authority of Gauleiter Josef Bürckel, who received the title Reich Commissar for the Reunification of Austria with the Reich—seemed more avid for anti-Jewish action than the citizens of what now became the Old Reich (*Altreich*). Violence had already started before the Wehrmacht crossed the border; despite official efforts to curb its most chaotic and moblike aspects, it lasted for several weeks. The populace relished the public shows of degradation; countless crooks from all walks of life, either wearing party uniforms or merely displaying improvised swastika armbands, applied threats and extortion on the grandest scale: money, jewelry, furniture, cars, apartments, and businesses were grabbed from their terrified Jewish owners.

In Austria in the early 1930s, the Jewish issue had become an even more potent tool for right-wing rabble-rousing than had been the case in Germany during the last years of the republic. When the Nazi campaign against Engelbert Dollfuss reached its climax in early 1934, it harped unceasingly on the domination of the chancellor by the Jews. The incitement intensified after Dollfuss's assassination, on July 25, and during the entire chancellorship of his successor, Kurt von Schuschnigg, which ended with the German invasion of March 1938. "The most dangerous breach in the Austrian line of defense [against Nazism] was caused by anti-Semitism," wrote the ultraconservative Prince Ernst Rüdiger Starhemberg, the commander of the Heimwehr and head of the Patriotic Front, in his postwar memoirs. "Everywhere people sniffed Jewish influence and although there was not a single Jew in any leadership position in the whole Patriotic Front, the Viennese were telling each other . . . of the Judaization of this organization, that after all the Nazis were right and that one should clean out the Jews."[2]

The anti-Jewish violence following the Anschluss quickly reached such proportions that by March 17 Heydrich was informing Bürckel that he would order the Gestapo to arrest "those National Socialists who in the last few days allowed themselves to launch large-scale assaults in a totally undisciplined way [against Jews]."[3] In the overall chaos, such threats had no immediate effect, nor did the fact that the violence was officially attributed to the Communists change the situation. It was only on April 29, when Bürckel announced that the leaders of SA units whose men took part in the excesses would lose their rank and could be dismissed from the SA and the party, that the violence started to ebb.

In the meantime the official share of the takeover of Jewish property was rapidly growing. On March 28 Göring had issued orders "to take quiet measures for the appropriate redirecting of the Jewish economy in Austria."[4] By mid-May a Property Transfer Office with nearly five hundred employees was actively promoting the Aryanization of Jewish economic assets. Within a few months, 83 percent of the handicrafts, 26 percent of the industry, 82 percent of the economic services, and 50 percent of the individual businesses owned by Jews were taken over in Vienna alone; of the eighty-six Jewish-owned banks in Austria's capital, only eight remained after this first sweep.

The overall Aryanization process continued to unfold with extraordinary speed. By mid-August 1939 Walter Rafelsberger, the head of the Property Transfer Office, could announce to Himmler that within less than a year his agency "had practically completed the task of de-Judaizing the Ostmark economy."[5] All Jewish-owned businesses had disappeared from Vienna. Simultaneously Jewish dwellings began to be confiscated throughout the country, particularly in Vienna. By the end of 1938, out of a total of approximately 70,000 apartments owned by Jews, about 44,000 had been Aryanized. After the beginning of the war the rate of occupancy in the remaining Jewish apartments was approximately five to six families per apartment. Often there were neither plumbing nor cooking facilities, and only one telephone was available in every building.

Herbert Hagen, the head of the Jewish desk of the SD, arrived in Vienna on March 12 with the first units of the Wehrmacht; a few days later Eichmann, who had just been promoted to second lieutenant in the SS, joined him. On the basis of lists that had been prepared by the SD, employees of Jewish organizations were arrested and documents impounded. After this first sweep, some measure of "normalization," allowing for the implementation of farther-reaching plans, took place.

Soon after being appointed adviser on Jewish affairs to the inspector of the Security Police and SD, Franz Stahlecker, Eichmann established in Vienna a Central Office for Jewish Emigration. The idea apparently came from the new head of the Jewish community, Josef Löwenherz. The community services, assisting would-be emigrants, had been overwhelmed by the tens of thousands of requests for departure authorizations; a lack of coordination among the various German agencies involved in the emigration process turned the obtaining of these documents into a grueling ordeal. Löwenherz approached Eichmann, who transmitted the suggestion to Bürckel. Berlin gave its agreement, and on August 20, 1938, the central office was established under the formal responsibility of Stahlecker and the de facto responsibility of Eichmann himself. The procedure used, according to Eichmann, the "conveyor belt" method: "You put the first documents followed by the other papers in at one end and out comes the passport at the other."[6] One more principle was implemented: Through levies imposed on the richer members of the Jewish community, the necessary sums were confiscated to finance the emigration of the poorer Jews.

Aside from hastening legal emigration by all available means, the new masters of Austria started to push Jews over the borders, mainly those with Czechoslovakia, Hungary, and Switzerland. What had been a sporadic Nazi initiative in some individual cases until March 1938 became a systematic policy after the Anschluss. According to Göring and Heydrich, some five thousand Austrian Jews were expelled in that way between March and November 1938. And even tighter control was imposed on those Jews who had not left. Sometime in October 1938, Himmler gave the order to concentrate all Jews from the Austrian provinces in Vienna. Within six months of the Anschluss, 45,000 Austrian Jews had emigrated, and by May 1939, approximately 100,000, or more than 50 percent, had left.

Another idea—not directly related to anti-Jewish policies, but deadlier in the immediate future—was also quickly implemented. A few days after the Anschluss, in March 1938, Himmler, accompanied by Oswald Pohl, chief of the administrative office of the SS-Hauptamt, made a visit to Mauthausen, a small town, located in an area rich in granite, on the north bank of the Danube, just fourteen miles downriver from Linz. The intention was clear: excavation of the granite would bring considerable financial benefits to an SS-operated enterprise, the German Earth and Stoneworks Corporation (DEST), which was about to be established in April; a concentration camp on location would provide the necessary workforce. The first 300 inmates, Austrian and German criminals from Dachau, arrived on August 8, 1938. By September 1939 Mauthausen held 2,995 inmates, among them 958 criminals, 1,087 Gypsies, and 739 German political prisoners: "The first Jewish inmate was a Viennese-born man arrested as a homosexual, who was registered at Mauthausen in September 1939 and recorded as having died in March 1940. During 1940 an additional 90 Jews arrived; all but 10 of them were listed as dead by the year's end."[7]

It was in Austria that, according to historians Götz Aly and Susanne Heim, the Nazis inaugurated their "rational," economically motivated anti-Jewish measures, which from then on became part of their initiatives in this domain, from the "model" established in Vienna to the "Final Solution." According to this view, the Viennese model was basically characterized by a drastic restructuring of the economy as a result of the liquidation of virtually all the unproductive Jewish businesses on the basis of a thorough assessment of their profitability prepared by the Reich Board for Economic Management; by a systematic effort to get rid of the newly created Jewish proletariat by way of accelerated emigration whereby wealthy

Jews contributed to the emigration fund for the destitute part of the Jewish population; by establishing labor camps, where the upkeep of the Jews would be maintained at a minimum and financed by the labor of the inmates themselves.

In essence those in charge of the Jewish question in annexed Austria were supposedly motivated by economic logic and not by any Nazi anti-Semitic ideology. The argument seems bolstered by the fact that not only was the entire Aryanization process in Austria masterminded by Göring's Four-Year Plan administration and its technocrats, but the same technocrats also planned the solution of the problem of impoverished Jewish masses by way of forced-labor concentration camps that appeared to be early models of the future ghettos and eventually of the future extermination camps. But, in fact, as has been seen, the liquidation of Jewish economic life in Nazi Germany had started at an accelerated pace in 1936 and, by late 1937, with the elimination of all conservative influence, the enforced Aryanization drive had become the main thrust of the anti-Jewish policies, mainly in order to compel the Jews to emigrate. Thus what happened in Austria after the Anschluss was simply the better organized part of a general policy adopted throughout the Reich. The link between economic expropriation and expulsion of the Jews from Germany and German-controlled territories did continue to characterize that stage of Nazi policies until the outbreak of the war.

After the Anschluss the Jewish refugee problem became a major international issue. By convening a conference of thirty-two countries in the French resort town of Evian from July 6 to 14, 1938, President Roosevelt publicly demonstrated his hope of finding a solution to it. Roosevelt's initiative was surprising, because "he chose to intrude into a situation in which he was virtually powerless to act, bound as he was by a highly restrictive immigration law."[8] Indeed, the outcome of Evian was decided before it even convened: The invitation to the conference clearly stated that "no country would be expected to receive a greater number of emigrants than is permitted by its existing legislation."[9]

The conference and its main theme, the fate of the Jews, found a wide and diverse echo in the world press. "There can be little prospect," wrote the *London Daily Telegraph* on July 7, "that room will be found within any reasonable time."[10] According to the *Gazette de Lausanne* of July 11: "Some think that they [the Jews] have got too strong a position for such a small minority. Hence the opposition to them, which in certain places has turned into a general attack." "Wasn't it said before the World War that one-tenth of the world's gold belonged to the Jews?" queried *Libre Belgique* on July 7.[11]

Not all of the press was so hostile. "It is an outrage to the Christian conscience especially," wrote the London *Spectator* on July 29, "that the modern world with all its immense wealth and resources cannot get these exiles a home and food and drink and a secure status."[12] For the future postwar French Prime Minister and Foreign Minister Georges Bidault, writing in the left-wing Catholic paper *L'Aube* on July 7, "One thing is clearly understood: the enlightened nations must not let the refugees be driven to despair."[13] The mainstream French Catholic newspaper *La Croix* urged compassion: "We cannot stand aside," it pleaded on July 14, " . . . We cannot be partners to a solution of the Jewish question by means of their extinction, by means of the complete extermination of a whole people."[14] But no doors opened at Evian, and no hope was offered to the refugees. An Intergovernmental Committee for Refugees was established under the chairmanship of the American George Rublee: Ultimately it achieved nothing.

Nazi sarcasm had a field day. For the SD, Evian's net result was "to show the whole world that the Jewish problem was in no way provoked only by Germany, but was a question of the most immediate world political significance. Despite the general rejection by the Evian states of the way in which the Jewish question has been dealt with in Germany, no country, America not excepted, declared itself ready to accept unconditionally any number of Jews. It was remarkable that the Australian delegate even mentioned that Jewish emigration would endanger his own race."[15] There was no fundamental difference between the German assessment and the biting summary of Evian by the *Newsweek* correspondent there: "Chairman Myron C. Taylor, former U.S. Steel head, opened the proceedings: 'The time has come when governments . . . must act and act promptly.' Most governments represented acted promptly by slamming their doors against Jewish refugees."[16] The *Völkischer Beobachter* headlined triumphantly: "Nobody wants them."[17]

For Hitler too, this was an opportunity not to be missed. He chose to insert his comments into the closing speech of the party rally on September 12. Its main theme, the Sudeten crisis, riveted the attention of the world. Never since 1918 had the danger of war seemed closer, but the Jews could not be left unmentioned: "They complain in these democracies about the unfathomable cruelty that Germany—and now also Italy—uses in trying to get rid of their Jews. In general, all these great democratic empires have only a few people per square kilometer, whereas Germany, for decades past, has admitted hundreds and hundreds of thousands of these Jews, without even batting an eye. "But now, . . . as the nation is not willing anymore to let itself be sucked dry by these parasites, cries of pain arise all over. But it does not mean that these democratic countries have now become ready to replace their hypocritical remarks with acts of help; on the contrary, they affirm with complete coolness that over there, evidently, there is no room! Thus, they expect that Germany with its 140 inhabitants per square kilometer will go on keeping its Jews without any problem, whereas the democratic world empires with only a few people per square kilometer can in no way take such a burden upon themselves. In short, no help, but preaching, certainly!"[18]

The Evian debacle acquires its full significance from its wider context. The growing strength of Nazi Germany impelled some of the countries that had aligned themselves with Hitler's general policies to take steps that, whether demanded by Germany or not, were meant to be demonstrations of political and ideological solidarity with the Reich. The most notorious among such initiatives were the Italian racial laws, which were approved by the Fascist Grand Council on October 6, 1938, and took effect on November 17.

In Italy the Jewish community numbered barely thirty-five to forty thousand and was fully integrated into the general society. Anti-Semitism had become rare with the waning of the church's influence, and even the army—and the Fascist Party—included prominent Jewish members. Finally Mussolini himself had not, in the past, expressed much regard for Nazi racial ideology. Modeled on the Nuremberg pattern, the new anti-Jewish laws caused widespread consternation among Italian Jews and many non-Jews alike.

The October laws had been preceded, in mid-July, by the Racial Manifesto, a declaration setting forth Mussolini's concoction of racial anti-Semitism and intended as the theoretical foundation of the forthcoming legislation. Hitler could not but graciously acknowledge so much goodwill. He duly did so on September 6, in the first of his speeches to the Nuremberg party rally: "I think that I must at this point announce . . . our deep and heartfelt happiness in the fact that another European world power has, through its own experiences, by its own decision and along its own paths arrived at the same conception as ourselves and with a resolution worthy of admiration has drawn from this conception the most far-reaching consequences."[19] In Hungary two anti-Jewish laws, introduced in 1938, were greeted with less fanfare than Mussolini's decision, but they pointed to the same basic evidence: The shadow of Hitler's anti-Jewish policy was lengthening over Europe.

While the Jews were becoming targets of legal discrimination in a growing number of European countries, and while international efforts to solve the problem of Jewish refugees came to naught, an unusual step was being taken in complete secrecy. In the early summer of 1938, Pope Pius XI, who over the years had become an increasingly staunch critic of the Nazi regime, requested the American Jesuit John LaFarge to prepare the text of an encyclical against Nazi racism and Nazi anti-Semitism in particular. LaFarge had probably been chosen because of his continuous antiracist activities in the United States and his book *Interracial Justice*, which Pius XI had read.

LaFarge completed the draft of *Humani Generis Unitas* (The Unity of Humankind) by the autumn of 1938 and delivered it to the general of the Jesuit order in Rome, the Pole Wladimir Ledochowski, for submission to the pope. In the meantime Pius XI had yet again criticized racism on several other occasions. On September 6, 1938, speaking in private to a group of Belgian pilgrims, he went further. With great emotion, apparently in tears, the pope, after commenting on the sacrifice of Abraham, declared: "It is impossible for Christians to participate in anti-Semitism. We recognize that everyone has the right to self-defense and may take the necessary means for protecting legitimate interests. But anti-Semitism is inadmissible. Spiritually, we are all Semites."[20] In this declaration, made in private and thus not mentioned in the press, the pope's condemnation of anti-Semitism remained on theological grounds: He did not criticize the ongoing persecution of the Jews, and he included a reference to the right of self-defense (against undue Jewish influence). Nonetheless his statement was clear: Christians could not condone anti-Semitism of the Nazi kind (or, for that matter, as it was shaping up in Italy at the very same time).

The message of the encyclical was similar: a condemnation of racism in general and the condemnation of anti-Semitism on theological grounds, from the viewpoint of Christian revelation and the teachings of the church regarding the Jews. Even so, the encyclical would have been the first solemn denunciation by the supreme Catholic authority of the anti-Semitic attitudes, teachings, and persecutions in Germany, in Fascist Italy, and in the entire Christian world. But Ledochowski, a fanatical anti-Communist who moreover hoped for some political arrangement with Nazi Germany, procrastinated. The draft of *Humani Generis Unitas* was sent by him for further comment to the editor in chief of the notoriously anti-Semitic organ of the Roman Jesuits, *Civiltà Cattolica*. It was only a few days before his death that Pius XI received the text. The pontiff died on February 9, 1939. His successor, Pius XII, probably took the decision to shelve *Humani Generis Unitas*.

Small islands of purely symbolic opposition to the anti-Jewish measures existed inside Germany, even in 1938. Four years earlier the Reich Ministry of Education had ordered the German Association for Art History to expel its Jewish members. The association did not comply but merely reshuffled its board of directors. Education Minister Bernhard Rust repeated his demand in 1935, again apparently to no avail. In March 1938 State Secretary Werner Zschintsch sent a reminder to his chief: All funds for the association were to be eliminated, and, if the order was not obeyed, it would no longer be allowed to call itself "German." We do not know what the association then decided to do; in any case its Jewish members were certainly not retained after the November 1938 pogrom.

There were some other—equally unexpected—signs of independence. Such was to be the case at the 1938 Salzburg Festival. After the Anschluss, Arturo Toscanini, who had refused to conduct at Bayreuth in 1933, turned Salzburg down as well. He was replaced by Wilhelm Furtwängler. Throughout his career in Nazi Germany, Furtwängler showed himself to be a political opportunist who had moments of courage. In Salzburg he agreed to conduct Wagner's *Meistersinger* on condition that the Jew Walter Grossmann be kept as the understudy in the role of Hans Sachs. As it happened, on opening night Karl Kammann, the scheduled Hans Sachs, fell ill and Walter Grossmann sang. "A glittering crowd headed by Joseph Goebbels and his entourage sat dutifully enthralled through the Führer's favorite opera, while Grossmann brought Nuremberg's most German hero to life."[21] But neither the actions of the art historians' association nor Walter Grossmann's performance could stem the ever growing tide—and impact—of Nazi anti-Jewish propaganda.

"The Eternal Jew," the largest anti-Jewish exhibition of the prewar years, opened on November 8, 1937, in Munich's Deutsches Museum. Streicher and Goebbels spoke. On the same evening the director of the Bavarian State Theater organized a cultural event in the Residenz Theater, which, according to the *Deutsche Allgemeine Zeitung*, expressed "the basic themes of the exhibition." The first part of the program offered a staged rendition of excerpts from Luther's notorious pamphlet "Against the Jews and their Lies"; the second part presented readings from other anti-Jewish texts, and the third, the Shylock scenes from Shakespeare's *The Merchant of Venice*.

An exhibition such as The Eternal Jew was merely the most extreme expression of the ongoing effort to assemble any kind of damning material about the Jews. Diverse forms of this endeavor were encountered during the first years of the regime. Now, at the end of 1937 and throughout 1938, the search went on with renewed inventiveness. The extent of the gathered material was in fact so large that on February 24, 1938, the minister of justice informed all prosecutors that it was no longer necessary to forward a copy of every indictment against a Jew to the ministry's press division, as it had already acquired a sufficient perspective on the criminality of the Jews.

By the beginning of 1938 all German Jews had had to turn in their passports (new ones were issued only to those Jews who were about to emigrate). In July the Ministry of the Interior decreed that before the end of the year all Jews had to apply to the police for an identity card, which was to be carried at all times and shown on demand. In August another decree announced that from January 1, 1939, Jews who did not bear the first names indicated on an appended list were to add the first name Israel or Sara to their names. The appended list of men's names started with Abel, Abieser, Abimelech, Abner, Absalom, Ahab, Ahasja, Ahaser, and so on; the list of women's names was of the same ilk.

The anti-Jewish economic campaign started at full throttle in early 1938; laws and decrees followed one another throughout the year, shattering all remaining Jewish economic existence in Germany. As the year began, some 360,000 Jews still lived in the *Altreich*, most of them in several large cities, mainly in Berlin. Jewish assets, estimated at some ten to twelve billion Reichsmarks in 1933, had been reduced to half that sum by the spring of 1938, indicating nonetheless that Aryanization was a gradual process leading to the measures that were to descend on the Jews of Germany throughout 1938.

On April 26 all Jews were ordered to register their property. On June 14 the problem that had defeated the boycott committee on April 1, 1933, was solved. According to the third supplementary decree to the Reich citizenship law, "a business was Jewish if the proprietor was a Jew, if a partner was a Jew, or if, on January 1, 1938, a member of the board of directors was a Jew. Also considered Jewish was a business in which Jews owned more than one-quarter of the shares or more than one-half of the votes, or which was factually under predominantly

Jewish influence. A branch of a Jewish business was considered Jewish if the manager of the branch was a Jew."[22]

On July 6, 1938, a law established a detailed list of commercial services henceforth forbidden to Jews, including credit information, real estate brokerage, and so on. On July 25 the fourth supplementary decree to the Reich citizenship law put an end to Jewish medical practice in Germany: The licenses of Jewish physicians were withdrawn as of September 30, 1938. The last line of the decree was entirely in the spirit of the new Germany: "Those [physicians] who receive an authorization [to give medical services to Jewish patients] are not authorized to use the appellation 'physician,' but only the appellation 'caretakers of the sick.' "[23] Incidentally the decree was signed and promulgated in Bayreuth: Hitler was attending the festival.

On September 27, 1938, on the eve of the Munich conference, Hitler signed the fifth supplementary decree, forbidding Jews to practice law. The decree was not immediately made public because of the international tension. Finally, on October 13, he allowed the announcement to be made the next day.

The final blow that destroyed all Jewish economic life in Germany came on November 12, when, just after the Kristallnacht pogrom, Göring issued a ban on all Jewish business activity in the Reich. Meanwhile, however, National Socialist physicians and lawyers were still not satisfied with having definitively driven the Jews out of their professions. As was usual in the world of Nazi anti-Jewish measures, concrete destruction had to find a symbolic expression as well. On October 3, 1938, the Reich Physicians' Chamber had demanded of the minister of education that Jewish physicians, now forbidden to practice, should also suffer further deprivation: "I am therefore requesting," Reich physicians' leader Wagner concluded his letter to Rust, "that the title 'Doctor' should be taken away from these Jews as soon as possible."[24] The minister of education and the minister of justice consulted on the matter: Their common proposal to the Ministry of the Interior was not to cancel the title of doctor in medicine and law only, but rather to consider drafting a law that would strip Jews of all titles, academic degrees, and similar distinctions. On the morrow of the November 9–10 pogrom, the matter was postponed.

The atmosphere permeating German business circles as the forced Aryanization—or more precisely, confiscation of all Jewish property progressed—is revealed in a letter from a Munich businessman who had been asked by the authorities to serve as a consultant in the Aryanization transactions. The author of the letter described himself as a National Socialist, a member of the SA, and an admirer of Hitler. He then added: "I was so disgusted by the brutal . . . and extraordinary methods employed against the Jews that, from now on, I refuse to be involved in any way with Aryanizations, although this means losing a handsome fee. . . . As an old, honest and upstanding businessman, I [can] no longer stand by and countenance the way many 'Aryan' businessmen, entrepreneurs and the like . . . are shamelessly attempting to grab up Jewish shops and factories, etc., as cheaply as possible and for a ridiculous price. These people are like vultures swarming down, their eyes bleary, their tongues hanging out with greed, to feed upon the Jewish carcass."[25]

The wave of forced Aryanization swept away the relatively moderate behavior that, as we have seen, major corporations had adhered to until then. The new economic incentives, the pressure from the party, the absence of any conservative ministerial countervailing forces put an end to the difference between low-grade grabbing and high-level mannerliness.

The Nazis were well aware of the dilemma exacerbated by accelerated Aryanization: The rapid pauperization of the Jewish population and the growing difficulties in the way of emigration were creating a new Jewish social and economic problem of massive proportions. At the outset men like Frick still had very traditional views of what could be done. According to a report of June 14, 1938, entitled "Jews in the Economy," presented in a discussion held in April of that year, Frick had apparently summed up his views as follows: "Insofar as Jews in Germany are able to live off the proceeds of their commercial and other assets, they require strict state supervision. Insofar as they are in need of financial assistance, the question of the public support must be solved. Greater use of the various organizations for social welfare appears to be unavoidable."[26]

In the early fall of 1938, another measure, this time involving locally planned economic extortion, was initiated in Berlin. One of the largest low-rent housing companies, the Gemeinnützige Siedlungs- und Wohnungsbaugesellschaft (GSW) Berlin, ordered the registration of all its Jewish tenants and canceled most of their leases. Some of the Jewish tenants left, but others sued the GSW. Not only did the Charlottenburg district court back the housing company, it indicated that similar measures could be more generally applied. The court would probably have reached the same decision without external pressure, but it so happened that pressure was brought to bear upon the Ministry of Justice by Albert Speer, whom, in early 1937, Hitler had appointed general inspector for the construction of Berlin. The eager general inspector was simultaneously negotiating with the capital's mayor for the construction of 2,500 small apartments to which to transfer other Jews from their living quarters. These details seem to have escaped Speer's highly selective postwar memory.

In June 1938, on Heydrich's orders, some ten thousand "asocials" were arrested and sent to concentration camps: Fifteen hundred Jews with prior sentences were included and shipped off to Buchenwald (which had been set up in 1937). A few weeks before, at the end of April, the propaganda minister had asked the Berlin police chief, Count Wolf Heinrich Helldorf, for a proposal for new forms of segregation and harassment of the city's Jews. The result was a lengthy memorandum prepared by the Gestapo and handed to Helldorf on May 17. At the last moment the document was hastily reworked by the SD's Jewish Section, which was critical of the fact that the maximal segregation measures proposed by the Gestapo would make the first priority, emigration, even more difficult than it already was. The final version of the proposal was passed on to Goebbels and possibly discussed with Hitler at a meeting on July 24. Some of the measures envisaged were already in preparation, others were to be applied after the November pogrom, and others still after the beginning of the war.

Goebbels simultaneously moved to direct incitement. Party organizations were brought into action. Now that Jewish businesses had been defined by the decree of June 14, their marking could finally begin. "Starting late Saturday afternoon," the American ambassador to Germany, Hugh R. Wilson, cabled Secretary of State Hull on June 22, 1938, "Civilian groups, consisting usually of two or three men, were to be observed painting on the windows of Jewish shops the word 'JUDE' in large red letters, the star of David and caricatures of Jews. . . . The painters in each case were followed by large groups of spectators who seemed to enjoy the proceedings thoroughly. . . . Reports are received that several incidents took place in this region leading to the looting of shops and the beating up of their owners; a dozen or so broken or empty showcases and windows have been seen which lend credence to these reports."[27]

Bella Fromm, a Berlin social reporter of Jewish background, described in her diary the action of a Hitler Youth group against Jewish retail shops in graphic details. "We were about to enter a tiny jewelry shop when a gang of ten youngsters in Hitler Youth uniforms smashed the shop window and stormed into the shop, brandishing butcher knives and yelling, 'To hell with the Jewish rabble! Room for the Sudeten Germans!'" She continued: "The smallest boy of the mob climbed inside the window and started his work of destruction by flinging everything he could grab right into the streets. Inside, the other boys broke glass shelves and counters, hurling alarm clocks, cheap silverware, and trifles to accomplices outside. A tiny shrimp of a boy crouched in a corner of the window, putting dozens of rings on his fingers and stuffing his pockets with wristwatches and bracelets. His uniform bulging with loot, he turned around, spat squarely into the shopkeeper's face, and dashed off."[28]

The situation soon got out of hand, however, and as the American ambassador was sending his cable, an order emanated from Berchtesgaden: The führer wished the Berlin action to stop. Wide-scale anti-Jewish violence was not what Hitler needed as the international crisis over the fate of the Sudetenland was reaching its climax.

If Goebbels's diary faithfully reproduced the gist of the views Hitler expressed during their July 24 meeting, then he must have been considering several options regarding the Jewish question. "The Führer approves my action in Berlin. What the foreign press writes is unimportant. The main thing is that the Jews be pushed out. Within ten years they must be removed from Germany. But for the time being we still want to keep the Jews here as pawns. . . ."[29] Soon, however, the Sudeten crisis would be over and an unforeseen occurrence would offer the pretext for anti-Jewish violence on a yet unseen level. The Berlin events had merely been a small-scale rehearsal.

At the beginning of 1938, Werner Best, Heydrich's deputy as head of the Security Police Main Office, had signed an expulsion decree for approximately five hundred Jews of Soviet nationality living in the Reich. This was a measure requested by the Wilhelmstrasse (which dealt with all Jewish issues related to diplomatic relations) in retaliation for the expulsion of some German citizens from the Soviet Union. As these Soviet Jews were not granted entry permits into the USSR, the expulsion order was twice extended—without any result. On May 28, 1938, Heydrich ordered the incarceration of the male Soviet Jews in concentration camps until they could provide proof of immediately forthcoming emigration. In May expulsion orders were also issued to Romanian Jews living in Germany. All of this was but a prologue to the new expulsion drive that was to start in the fall.

During the months immediately following the Anschluss, however, there was a development that threatened to hamper these Nazi plans for rapid forced emigration: the measures taken by Switzerland. In its meeting of March 28, 1938, the Swiss Federal Council (the country's executive branch) decided that all bearers of Austrian passports would be obliged to obtain visas for entry into Switzerland. According to the meeting's minutes: "In view of the measures already taken and being prepared by other countries against the influx of Austrian refugees, we find ourselves in a difficult situation. It is clear that Switzerland can only be a transit country for the refugees from Germany and from Austria. Apart from the situation of our labor market, the present excessive degree of foreign presence imposes the strictest defense measures against a longer stay of such elements. If we do not want to create a basis for an anti-Semitic movement that would be unworthy of our country, we must defend ourselves with all our strength and, if need be, with ruthlessness against the immigration of foreign Jews, mostly those from the East."[30] This was to remain the basic position of the Swiss authorities during the coming seven years, with one additional point sometimes being added in the various internal memoranda: The Swiss Jews certainly did not want to see their own position threatened by an influx of foreign Jews into the country.

Once all Austrian passports were replaced by German ones, the visa requirement was applied to all bearers of German travel documents. The Swiss knew that their visa requirement would have to be reciprocal, that from then on Swiss citizens traveling to Germany would also have to obtain visas. On both sides the dilemma seemed insoluble. For Germany to avoid having visa requirements imposed on its Aryan nationals traveling to Switzerland would mean inserting some distinctive sign into the passports of Jews, which would make their emigration far more difficult. Various technical solutions were considered throughout the summer of that year. At the end of September 1938, undeterred by the Sudeten crisis, a Swiss delegation traveled to Berlin for negotiations. As a result of a Swiss demand, the Germans finally agreed to stamp the passports of Jews with a J, which would allow the Swiss police "to check at the border whether the carrier of the passport was Aryan or not Aryan."

The Swiss authorities had not yet solved all their problems: Jews who had received an entrance permit before the stamping of their passports might attempt to make early use of it. On October 4, therefore, all border stations were informed that if "there was uncertainty whether a person traveling with a German passport was Aryan or non-Aryan, an attestation to his being Aryan should be produced. In doubtful cases, the traveler should be sent back to the Swiss consulate of his place of origin for further ascertainment."[31]

While this was going on, Hitler turned to Czechoslovakia: Prague must allow the Sudetenland, its mainly German-populated province, to secede and join the German Reich. In May the Wehrmacht had received the order to invade Czechoslovakia on October 1. A general war appeared probable when, formally at least, the French declared their readiness to stand by their Czech ally. After a British mediation effort had come to nought, and after the failure of two meetings between British prime minister Neville Chamberlain and Hitler, European armies were mobilized. Then, two days before the scheduled

German attack, Mussolini suggested a conference of the main powers involved in the crisis (but without the presence of the Czechs—and of the Soviet Union). On September 29 Britain, France, Germany, and Italy signed an agreement in Munich: By October 10 the Sudetenland was to become part of the German Reich. Peace had been saved; Czecho-Slovakia (the newly introduced hyphen came from a Slovak demand) had been abandoned; its new borders, though, were "guaranteed."

As soon as the Wehrmacht occupied the Sudetenland, Hitler informed Joachim von Ribbentrop, since February, Germany's foreign minister, that, in addition to the expulsion of those Sudeten Jews who had not yet managed to flee into truncated Czecho-Slovakia, the expulsion of the 27,000 Czech Jews living in Austria should be considered. But the immediate expulsion measures mainly affected the Jews of the Sudetenland: The Germans sent them over the Czech border; the Czechs refused to take them in. Göring was to describe it with glee a month after the event: "During the night, the Jews were expelled to Czecho-Slovakia. In the morning, the Czechs got hold of them and sent them to Hungary. From Hungary back to Germany, then back to Czecho-Slovakia. Thus, they turned round and round. Finally, they ended up on a riverboat on the Danube. There they camped. As soon as they set foot on the river bank they were pushed back."[32] In fact several thousand of these Jews were finally forced, in freezing weather, into improvised camps of tents situated in the no-man's land between Hungary and Czecho-Slovakia, such as Mischdorf, some twenty kilometers from Bratislava.

Throughout the summer and autumn, Austrian Jews attempted to flee illegally to various neighboring countries and farther on, to England. The Gestapo had shipped some groups to Finland, to Lithuania, and to Holland or pushed them over the borders into Switzerland, Luxembourg, and France. Yet, as foreign protests grew, illegal entry or expulsion westward became increasingly difficult. Within days, however, it was the Jews of Polish nationality living in Germany who became the overriding issue.

The census of June 1933 had indicated that among the 98,747 foreign Jews still residing in Germany, 56,480 were Polish citizens. The Polish Republic showed no inclination to add any newcomers to its Jewish population of 3.1 million, and various administrative measures aimed at hindering the return of Polish Jews living in Germany were utilized between 1933 and 1938. The Anschluss triggered even sharper initiatives. On March 31, 1938, the Polish parliament passed a law establishing a wide array of conditions under which Polish citizenship could be taken away from any citizen living abroad. The Germans immediately perceived the implications of the new law for their forcible emigration plans. German-Polish negotiations led nowhere, and, in October 1938, a further Polish decree announced the cancellation of the passports of residents abroad who did not obtain a special authorization for entry into Poland before the end of the month. As more than 40 percent of the Polish Jews living in the Reich had been born in Germany, they could hardly hope to liquidate their businesses and homes within less than two weeks. Most of them would therefore lose their Polish nationality on November 1. The Nazis decided to preempt the Polish measure.

Whether or not Hitler was consulted about the expulsion of the Polish Jews is unclear. The general instructions were given by the Wilhelmstrasse, and the Gestapo was asked to take over the actual implementation of the measure. Ribbentrop, Himmler, and Heydrich must have sensed, like everyone else, that given the international circumstances after the Munich agreement—the craving for peace and its consequence, appeasement—no one would lift a finger in defense of the hapless Jews. Poland itself was ultimately dependent on German goodwill; had it not just grabbed the Teschen region of northeastern Czecho-Slovakia in the wake of Germany's annexation of the Sudetenland? The timing of the expulsion could not have been more propitious. Thus, according to Himmler's orders, by October 29 all male Polish Jews residing in Germany were to be forcibly deported over the border to Poland.

The Reichsführer knew that the women and children, deprived of all support, would have to follow. On October 27 and 28, the police and the SS assembled and transported Jews to the vicinity of the Polish town of Zbaszyn, where they sent them over the river marking the border between the two countries. The Polish border guards dutifully sent them back. For days, in pouring rain and without food or shelter, the deportees wandered between the two lines; most of them ended up in a Polish concentration camp near Zbaszyn. The rest were allowed to return to Germany. About 16,000 Polish Jews were thus expelled.

The Grynszpans, a family from Hannover, were among the Jews transported to the border on October 27. Herschel (Yiddish version of Hermann), their seventeen-year-old son, was not with them; at the time he was living clandestinely in Paris, barely subsisting on odd jobs and on some help from relatives. It was to him that his sister Berta wrote on November 3: "We were permitted to return to our home to get at least a few essential things. So I left with a 'Schupo' [the German gendarmerie] accompanying me and I packed a valise with the most necessary clothes. That is all I could save. We don't have a cent. To be continued when next I write. Warm greetings and kisses from us all. Berta."[33]

Young Herschel Grynszpan did not know the details of what was happening to his family near Zbaszyn, but he could well imagine it. On November 7 he wrote a note to his uncle in Paris: "With God's help [written in Hebrew] . . . I couldn't do otherwise. My heart bleeds when I think of our tragedy and that of the 12,000 Jews. I have to protest in a way that the whole world hears my protest, and this I intend to do. I beg your forgiveness. Hermann."[34] Grynszpan purchased a pistol, went to the German Embassy, and asked to see an official. He was sent to the office of First Secretary Ernst vom Rath; there he shot and fatally wounded the German diplomat.

CHAPTER 5

A Broken Remnant

November 1938–September 1939

ON THE MORNING of November 10, 1938, at eight a.m., the farmer and local SA leader of Eberstadt, Adolf Heinrich Frey, accompanied by several of his cronies, set out for the house of the eighty-one-year-old Jewish widow Susannah Stern. According to Frey, the widow Stern took her time before opening the door, and when she saw him she smiled "provocatively" and said: "Quite an important visit this morning." Frey ordered her to dress and come with them. She sat down on her sofa and declared that she would not dress or leave her house; they could do with her whatever they wanted. Frey reported that the same exchange was repeated five or six times, and when she again said that they could do whatever they wanted, Frey took his pistol and shot Stern through the chest. "At the first shot, Stern collapsed on the sofa. She leaned backward and put her hands on her chest. I immediately fired the second shot, this time aiming at the head. Stern fell from the sofa and turned. She was lying close to the sofa, with her head turned to the left, toward the window. At that moment Stern still gave signs of life. From time to time she gave a rattle, then stopped. Stern did not shout or speak. My comrade C.D. turned Stern's head to see where she had been hit. I told him that I didn't see why we should be standing around; the right thing to do was to lock the door and surrender the keys. But to be sure that Stern was dead I shot her in the middle of the brow from a distance of approximately ten centimeters. Thereupon we locked the house and I called Kreisleiter Ullmer from the public telephone office in Eberstadt and reported what had happened." Proceedings against Frey were dismissed on October 10, 1940, as the result of a decision of the Ministry of Justice.[1]

In the course of the prewar anti-Jewish persecutions, the pogrom of November 9 and 10, the so-called Kristallnacht, was in many ways another major turning point. The publication in 1992 of Goebbels's hitherto missing diary accounts of the event added important insights about the interaction between Hitler, his closest chieftains, the party organizations, and the wider reaches of society in the initiation and management of this major outburst of anti-Jewish violence. As for the reactions of German and international opinion to the events, they raise a host of questions, not least as an intimation of responses yet to come.

On November 8 the *Völkischer Beobachter* published a threatening editorial against the Jews, closing with the warning that the shots fired in Paris would herald a new German attitude regarding the Jewish question. In some places local anti-Jewish riots had started even before the Nazi press brandished its first threats. An SD report of November 9 described events that had taken place in the Kassel and Rotenburg/Fulda districts during the night of November 7–8, presumably as an immediate reaction to the news. In some places Jewish house and shop windows had been smashed. In Bebra a number of Jewish apartments had been "demolished," and in Rotenburg the synagogue's furniture was "significantly damaged" and "objects [were] taken away and destroyed on the street."[2]

One of the most telling aspects of the events of November 7–8 was Hitler's and Goebbels's public and even "private" silence.

In his November 9 diary entry (relating events of November 8), Goebbels did not devote a single word to the shots fired in Paris, although he had spent the late evening in discussion with Hitler. Clearly both had agreed to act, but had probably decided to wait for the seriously wounded Rath's death. Their unusual silence was the surest indication of plans that aimed at a "spontaneous outburst of popular anger," which was to take place without any sign of Hitler's involvement. And, on that same evening of November 8, in his speech commemorating the 1923 putsch attempt, Hitler refrained from any allusion whatsoever to the Paris event.

Rath died on November 9 at 5:30 in the afternoon. The news of the German diplomat's death was officially brought to Hitler during the traditional "old fighters" dinner held at the Altes Rathaus in Munich, at around nine o'clock that evening. An "intense conversation" then took place between Hitler and Goebbels, who was seated next to him. Hitler left the assembly immediately thereafter, without giving the usual address. Goebbels spoke instead. After announcing Rath's death, he added, alluding to the anti-Jewish violence that had already taken place in Magdeburg-Anhalt and Kurhessen, that "the Führer had decided that such demonstrations should not be prepared or organized by the party, but insofar as they erupted spontaneously, they were not to be hampered."[3] The message was clear.

For Goebbels there had been no such occasion to display his leadership talents in action since the boycott of April 1933. "I report the matter to the Führer," wrote Goebbels on the tenth, alluding to the conversation at the dinner the evening before. "He [Hitler] decides: demonstrations should be allowed to continue. The police should be withdrawn. For once the Jews should get the feel of popular anger. That is right. I immediately give the necessary instructions to the police and the Party. Then I briefly speak in that vein to the Party leadership. Stormy applause. All are instantly at the phones. Now the people will act."

Goebbels then described the destruction of synagogues in Munich. He gave orders to make sure that the main synagogue in Berlin, on Fasanenstrasse, be destroyed. He continued: "I want to get back to the hotel and I see a blood-red [glare] in the sky. The synagogue burns. . . . We extinguish only insofar as is necessary for the neighboring buildings. Otherwise, should burn down. . . . From all over the Reich information is now flowing in: 50, then 70 synagogues are burning. The Führer has ordered that 20–30,000 Jews should immediately be arrested. . . . In Berlin, 5, then 15 synagogues burn down. Now popular anger rages. . . . It should be given free rein." Goebbels went on: "As I am driven to the hotel, windowpanes shatter. Bravo! Bravo! The synagogues burn like big old cabins."[4]

At approximately the same time as the propaganda minister was gleefully contemplating a good day's work, Hitler informed Himmler that Goebbels was in overall charge of the operation. On that same night Himmler summed up his immediate reaction in writing: "I suppose that it is Goebbels's megalomania—something I have long been aware of—and his stupidity which are responsible for starting this operation now, in a particularly difficult diplomatic situation."[5] The Reichsführer was certainly not opposed to the staging of a pogrom; what must have stung Himmler was the fact that Goebbels had been the first to exploit the shots fired at Rath to organize the action and obtain Hitler's blessing. But he may indeed also have thought that the timing was not opportune.

Still in Munich on the eleventh, Goebbels kept writing about the previous day: "Yesterday: Berlin. There, all proceeded fantastically. One fire after another. It is good that way. I prepare an order to put an end to the actions. It is just enough by now. . . . Danger that the mob may appear on the scene. In the whole country the synagogues have burned down. I report to the Führer at the Osteria [a Munich restaurant]. He agrees with everything. His views are totally radical and aggressive. The action itself took place without the least hitch. 100 dead. But no German property damaged."[6]

Heydrich's orders to the Gestapo and the SD included a warning to his men: Jewish businesses or apartments could be destroyed but not looted (looters would be arrested); foreigners (even when identified as Jews) were not to be molested. Finally he commanded, ". . . in all districts as many Jews, especially rich ones, are to be arrested as can be accommodated in the existing jails. For the time being only healthy men not too old should be arrested. Upon their arrest, the appropriate concentration camps should be contacted immediately, in order to confine them in these camps as fast as possible. Special care should be taken that the Jews arrested in accordance with these instructions are not mistreated."[7]

Heydrich's report of November 11 indicated that thirty-six Jews had been killed and the same number seriously injured throughout the Reich. "One Jew is still missing, and among the dead there is one Jew of Polish nationality and two others among those injured."[8] The real situation was worse. Apart from the 267 synagogues destroyed and the 7,500 businesses vandalized, some ninety-one Jews had been killed all over Germany, and hundreds more had committed suicide or died as a result of mistreatment in the camps. "The action against the Jews was terminated quickly and without any particular tensions," the mayor of Ingolstadt wrote in his monthly report on December 1. "As a result of this measure a local Jewish couple drowned themselves in the Danube."[9]

An uncontrollable lust for destruction and humiliation of the victims drove the squads roaming the cities. "Organized parties moved through Cologne from one Jewish apartment to another," the Swiss consul reported. "The families were either ordered to leave the apartment or they had to stand in a corner of a room while the contents were hurled from the windows. Gramophones, sewing machines, and typewriters tumbled down into the streets. One of my colleagues even saw a piano being thrown out of a second-floor window."[10] Even worse was reported from Leipzig: "Having demolished dwellings and hurled most of the movable effects to the streets," the American consul in Leipzig reported, "the insatiably sadistic perpetrators threw away many of the trembling inmates into a small stream that flows through the Zoological Park, commanding the horrified spectators to spit at them, defile them with mud and jeer at their plight. . . . The slightest manifestation of sympathy evoked a positive fury on the part of the perpetrators, and the crowd was powerless to do anything but turn horror-stricken eyes from the scene of abuse, or leave the vicinity. These tactics were carried out the entire morning of November 10 without police intervention and they were applied to men, women and children." The same scenes were repeated all over the country: sadistic brutality of the perpetrators, shamefaced reactions of some of the onlookers, grins of others, silence of the immense majority, helplessness of the victims.[11]

Once again Hitler had followed the by-now-familiar pattern he had displayed throughout the 1930s. Secretly he gave the orders or confirmed them; openly his name was in no way to be linked with the brutality. Having refrained from any open remark about the events on November 7–8, Hitler also avoided any reference to them in his midnight address to SS recruits in front of the Feldherrnhalle on November 9. At the time of his address, synagogues were already burning, shops being demolished, and Jews wounded and killed throughout the Reich. A day later, in his secret speech to representatives of the German press, Hitler maintained the same rule of silence regarding events that could not but be on the mind of every member of the audience; he did not even speak at Rath's funeral. The fiction of a spontaneous outburst of popular anger imposed silence. Any expression of Hitler's wish or even any positive comment would have been a "Führer order." Of Hitler's involvement the outside world—including trustworthy party members—was, at least in principle, to know nothing.

However, knowledge of Hitler's direct responsibility quickly trickled out from the innermost circle. According to the diaries of Ulrich von Hassell, the former German ambassador to Rome and an early opponent of the regime, many conservatives were outraged by the events, and the minister of finance of Prussia, Johannes Popitz, protested to Göring and demanded the punishment of those responsible for the action. "My dear Popitz, do you want to punish the Führer?" was Göring's answer.[12]

On the morning of November 12, Goebbels summed up the events of the previous days in the *Völkischer Beobachter*: "The Jew Grynszpan," so the last paragraph ran, "was the representative of Jewry. The German vom Rath was the representative of the German people. Thus in Paris Jewry has fired on the German people. The German government will answer legally but harshly."[13]

The German government's legal answers were hurled at the Jews throughout the remaining weeks of 1938; they were accompanied by three major policy guidelines: the first on November 12, at the top-echelon conference convened by Göring; the second on December 6, in Göring's address to the Gauleiter; the third on December 28, in a set of new rules also announced by Göring. All of Göring's initiatives and interpretations were issued on Hitler's explicit instructions.

The conference of high-ranking officials that Göring convened on November 12 at the Air Transport Ministry has become notorious. "Gentlemen," Göring began, "today's meeting is of decisive importance. I received a letter that Bormann, the Führer's Deputy's chief of staff, wrote to me on instruction from the Führer, according to which the Jewish question should now be dealt with in a centralized way and settled in one form or another. In a telephone call which I received from the Führer yesterday, I was once again instructed to centralize the decisive steps to be taken now."[14]

The concrete discussions that took place on November 12 at Göring's headquarters dealt not only with various additional ways of harassing the Jews and further economic steps to be taken against the Jews but also, and at length, with the immediate problem of insurance compensation for the damages inflicted on Jewish property during the pogrom. Göring issued the orders secretly given by Hitler two days before: The Jews would bear all the costs of repairing their businesses; the Reich would confiscate all payments made by German insurance companies. "The Jews of German citizenship will have to pay as a whole a contribution of 1,000,000,000 RM to the German Reich."[15]

On the same day Göring ordered the cessation of all Jewish business activity as of January 1, 1939. The Jews had "to sell their enterprises, as well as any land, stocks, jewels, and art works. They could use the services of 'trustees' to complete these transactions within the time limit. Registration and deposit of all shares was compulsory."[16] Göring's main policy statement, again delivered after consultation with Hitler, was yet to come, in a meeting with the Gauleiter on December 6. But more than for its major executive decisions, the November 12 conference remains significant for its sadistic inventiveness and for the spirit and tone of the exchanges.

Still carried away by the flurry of his activities during the previous days, the propaganda minister had a whole list of proposals: The Jews should be compelled to demolish the damaged synagogues at their own expense; they should be forbidden public entertainments. At that point a notorious debate arose between Goebbels and Göring on how to segregate Jews on trains. Both agreed on the necessity of separate compartments for Jews but, Goebbels declared, there should be a law forbidding them to claim a seat even in a Jewish compartment before all Germans had secured one. The mere existence of a separate compartment would have the undesirable effect of allowing some Jews to sit at their ease in an overcrowded train. Göring had no patience for such formalities: "Should a case such as you mention arise and the train be overcrowded, believe me, we won't need a law. We will kick him [the Jew] out and he will have to sit all alone in the toilet all the way!" Goebbels insisted on a law, to no avail.[17]

This minor setback did not paralyze Goebbels's brainstorming: the Jews, he demanded, should absolutely be forbidden to stay in German resorts. The propaganda minister also wondered whether German forests should not be made out of bounds for them. This gave Göring an idea of his own: Some sections of the forests should be open to Jews, and animals that resembled Jews—"the elk has a crooked nose like theirs"—should be gathered in those sections. Goebbels continued; he demanded that parks should also be forbidden to Jews, as Jewish women, for instance, might sit down with German mothers and engage in hostile propaganda. There should also be separate benches for Jews, with special signs: For Jews Only! Finally, Jewish children should be excluded from German schools.

At the end of the debate on the economic issues, Heydrich reminded those present that the main problem was to get the Jews out of Germany. The idea of setting up a central emigration agency in Berlin on the Viennese model was broached. But in Heydrich's opinion at the current rate it would take some eight to ten years to achieve a solution of the problem. How, then, should the Jews be isolated in the meantime from the German population? Heydrich was in favor of a special badge to be worn by all those defined as Jews by the Nuremberg laws. Göring was skeptical: He was in favor of establishing ghettos in the major cities. The difference of opinion remained unresolved, and, three weeks later, Hitler was to reject both badges and ghettos.

Like Goebbels earlier, Heydrich had more suggestions on his list: no driver's licenses, no car ownership, no access to areas of national significance in the various cities, no access to cultural institutions—along the lines of Goebbels's suggestion—none to resorts and not even to hospitals. When the discussion moved to what the Jews could do to counter the financial measures about to be taken against them, Göring was sure that they would do nothing whatsoever. Goebbels concurred: "At the moment, the Jew is small and ugly and he will remain at home."[18] Shortly before the last exchange Göring commented, as if an afterthought: "I would not like to be a Jew in Germany."

The Generalfeldmarschall then mentioned that on November 9 Hitler had told him of his intention to turn to the democracies that were raising the Jewish issue and to challenge them to take the Jews; the Madagascar possibility would also be brought up, as well as that of "some other territory in North America, in Canada or anywhere else the rich Jews could buy for their brethren." Göring added: "If in some foreseeable future an external conflict were to happen, it is obvious that we in Germany would also think first and foremost of carrying out a big settling of accounts with the Jews."[19]

On the same day that Goebbels forbade Jews access to cultural institutions, he also banned the Jewish press in Germany. Shortly afterward, Erich Liepmann, director of the *Jüdische Rundschau*, which by then had been closed down, was summoned to the propaganda minister's office: ' "Is the Jew here?' Goebbels yelled by way of greeting," Liepmann recalled. "He was sitting at his desk; I had to stand some eight meters away. He yelled: 'An informational paper must be published within two days. Each issue will be submitted to me. Woe to you if even one article is published without my having seen it. That's it!'"[20] Thus the *Jüdisches Nachrichtenblatt* was born: It was designed to inform the Jews of all the official measures taken to seal their fate.

But sometimes, it seems, even Goebbels's eye wasn't sharp enough. In early December, some six weeks after Kristallnacht, the *Nachrichtenblatt* reviewed the American film *Chicago*: "A city goes up in flames and the firefighters stand by without taking any action. All the hoses are poised, the ladders have been prepared . . . but no hand moves to use them. The men wait for the command, but no command is heard. Only when the city has burned down and is lying in cinders and ashes, an order arrives; but the firefighters are already driving away. A malicious invention? An ugly tale? No. The truth. And it was revealed in Hollywood."[21]

The law of November 12 compelling the Jews to sell all their enterprises and valuables, such as jewels and works of art, inaugurated the wholesale confiscation of art objects belonging to them. The robbery that had already taken place in Austria now became common practice in the Reich. In Munich, for example, the procedure was coordinated by Gauleiter Wagner himself who, in the presence of the directors of state collections, gave the orders for "the safekeeping of works of art belonging to Jews."[22] This "safekeeping" was implemented by the Gestapo: An inventory was duly taken in the presence of the owners and a receipt issued to them.

On November 15 all Jewish children still remaining in German schools were expelled. They were henceforth allowed to attend only Jewish schools. On November 19 Jews were excluded from the general welfare system. On November 28 the minister of the interior informed all the state presidents that some areas could be forbidden to Jews and that their right of access to public places could also be limited to a few hours a day. It did not take long for the Berlin police chief to move ahead. On December 6 the city's Jews were banned from all theaters, cinemas, cabarets, concert and conference halls, museums, fairs, exhibition halls, and sports facilities (including ice-skating rinks), as well as from public and private bathing facilities. Moreover Jews were banned from the city districts where most government offices and major monuments and cultural institutions were located.

On December 3, on Himmler's orders, the Jews were deprived of their driver's licenses. The access of Jewish scholars who possessed a special authorization to university libraries was canceled on December 8. On December 20 Jews were no longer allowed to train as pharmacists, and a day later they were excluded from midwifery. On the twenty-eighth, the first indications of a potential physical concentration of the Jews appeared (to be discussed later on). On November 29 the minister of the interior forbade Jews to keep carrier pigeons.

Göring's main policy statement was delivered on December 6 at a Gauleiter conference. What is striking in Göring's address is his constant reference to the fact that these were Hitler's orders, that all the steps mentioned had been discussed with Hitler and had his complete backing. The most likely reason for this repeated emphasis was that some of the measures announced would not be popular with the assembly, since they would put an end to the profits party members of all ranks, including some Gauleiter, had derived from their seizure of Jewish assets. It seems that this was why Göring repeatedly linked the Jewish issue to the general economic needs of the Reich. Party members were to be fully aware that any transgression of the new orders was harmful to the Reich's economy and an outright violation of the führer's orders. In concrete terms, after stressing the fact that the party and the *Gaue* (party districts) had taken Jewish assets, Göring made it clear that, on Hitler's orders, such unlawfully acquired property would have to be transferred to the state. It was not the fate of the Jews that mattered, Göring emphasized, but the reputation of the party inside and outside Germany.

The other internal party issue dealt with at some length was that of punishment for deeds committed on November 9 and 10: Whatever was undertaken on purely ideological grounds, out of a justified "hatred for the Jews," should go unpunished; purely criminal acts of various kinds were to be prosecuted as they would be prosecuted under any other circumstances, but all publicity liable to cause scandal was to be strictly avoided.[23]

As for the main policy matters regarding the Jews, the recurring two issues reappeared once again: measures intended to further Jewish emigration, and those dealing with the Jews remaining in the Reich. In essence the life of the Jews of Germany was to be made so unpleasant that they would make every effort to leave by any means. Forced emigration was to have top priority. Apparently Göring was even willing to refrain from stamping Jewish passports with a recognizable sign (the letter J) if a Jew had the means to emigrate but would be hindered from doing so by such identification. Göring informed the Gauleiter that the money needed to finance the emigration would be raised by an international loan; Hitler, Göring stated, was very much in favor of this idea. The guarantee for the loan, presumably to be raised by "world Jewry" and by the Western democracies, was to consist of the entire assets still belonging to the Jews in Germany—one reason why Jewish houses were not to be forcibly Aryanized at that stage, even though many party members were particularly tempted by that prospect.

From world Jewry Göring demanded the bulk not only of the loan but also the cessation of any economic boycott of Germany, so that the Reich could obtain the foreign currency needed to repay the principal and the interest on the international loan. In the midst of these practical explanations, Göring mentioned Hitler's rejection of any special identifying signs, and of excessively drastic travel and shopping restrictions.

Hitler's reasons were unexpected: Given the state of mind of the populace in many *Gaue*, if Jews wore identifying signs they would be beaten up or refused any food. The other limitations would make their daily life so difficult that they would become a burden on the state. In other words, the Gauleiter were in-directly warned not to launch any new actions of their own against the Jews in their *Gaue*. Jewish-owned houses, as has been seen, were the last Jewish assets to be Aryanized. Indeed, while discussing the measures that would induce the Jews to leave Germany, Göring assured his listeners he would make sure that the rich Jews would not be allowed to depart first, leaving the mass of poor Jews behind.

One additional conference took place on December 16. Convened by Frick, that meeting was held in the presence of Funk, Lammers, Heydrich, Gauleiter, and various other party and state representatives. In the main Frick and Funk took up Göring's explanations, exhortations, and orders. Yet it also became apparent that throughout the Reich, party organiza-tions such as the German Labor Front had put pressure on shopkeepers not to sell to Jews. And, mainly in the Ostmark, *Mischlinge* were being treated as Jews, both in terms of their employment and of their business activities. Such initiatives were unacceptable in Hitler's eyes. Soon no Jewish businesses would be left, and the Jews would have to be allowed to buy in German stores. As for the *Mischlinge*, the policy, according to Frick, was to absorb them gradually into the nation (strangely enough Frick did not distinguish the half- from the quarter-Jews), and the current discrimination against them contra-vened the distinctions established by the Nuremberg laws. On the whole, however, the main policy goal was emphasized over and over again: Everything had to contribute to expedite the emigration of the Jews.

Yet another set of measures descended on the Jews toward the end of December. On the twenty-eighth Göring, again referring to orders explicitly given by Hitler, established the rules for dealing with dwellings belonging to Jews (they should not be Aryanized at this stage, but Jewish occupants should gradually move to houses owned and inhabited only by Jews) and defined the distinction between two categories of "mixed marriages." Marriages in which the husband was Aryan were to be treated more or less as regular German families, whether or not they had children. The fate of mixed marriages in which the husband was Jewish depended on whether there were children. The childless couples were eventually to be transferred to houses occupied by Jewish tenants and were to be treated as full Jewish couples. Couples with children were temporarily shielded from persecution.

On January 17, 1939, the eighth supplementary decree to the Reich citizenship law forbade Jews to exercise any paramedical and health-related activities, particularly pharmacy, dentistry, and veterinary medicine. On February 15 members of the Wehrmacht, the Labor Service, party functionaries, and members of the SD were forbidden to marry "*Mischlinge* of the second degree," and on March 7, in answer to a query from the justice minister, Hess decided that Germans who were considered as such under the Nuremberg laws but who had some Jewish blood were not to be hired as state employees.

During the crucial weeks from November 1938 to January 1939, the measures decided upon by Hitler, Göring, and their associates entirely destroyed any remaining possibility for Jewish life in Germany or for the life of Jews in Germany. The demolition of the synagogues' burned-out remains symbolized an end; the herding of the Jews into "Jewish houses" intimated a yet unperceived beginning.

The regime's anti-Jewish fury, culminating in the Kristallnacht pogrom, was not shared by the majority of Germans. On November 10 a clear difference emerged from the outset between activists and onlookers on the streets of the large cities. SD reports show widespread popular criticism of the violence and the damage caused during the pogrom. Some of the criticism, expressed even by people usually favorable to the regime, was motivated by practical considerations: the wanton destruction of property and the losses thus incurred not only by all Germans but also by the state. When news of the billion-mark fine imposed on the Jews was announced, and when official propaganda stressed the immense wealth still possessed by the Jews, the general mood improved. Sometimes, however, the reactions of the population were not negative at all. Thus, according to a Sozialdemokratische Partei, Deutschlands (SOPADE) report of December 1938, "the broad mass of people has not condoned the destruction, but we should nevertheless not overlook the fact that there are people among the working class who do not defend the Jews. There are certain circles where you are not very popular if you speak disparagingly about the recent incidents. The anger was not, therefore, as unanimous as all that."[24]

No criticism of the pogrom was publicly expressed by the churches. Only a month after the events, in a message to the congregations, did the Confessing Church make an oblique reference to the most recent persecutions: "We exhort all members of our congregations to concern themselves with the material and spiritual distress of our Christian brothers and sisters of the Jewish race, and to intercede for them in their prayers to God." The Jews as such were excluded from the message of compassion.

The overall attitude of the Catholic Church was no different. Apart from Provost Bernhard Lichtenberg of Berlin's Saint Hedwig Cathedral, who declared on November 10 that "the temple which was burnt down outside is also the House of God," and who later was to pay with his life for his public prayers for the Jews deported to the East,[25] no powerful voice was raised.

No open criticism (or even indirect protest) came from the universities. Some strong condemnations of the pogrom were committed to private correspondence and, probably, to the privacy of diaries. On November 24, 1938, the historian Gerhard Ritter wrote to his mother: "What we have experienced over the last two weeks all over the country is the most shameful and the most dreadful thing that has happened for a long time."[26] Ritter's indignation, however, and the initiative that followed, paradoxically shed some light on the anti-Semitism that underlay the attitudes of the churches and the universities.

Following the pogrom, and certainly in part as a result of it, an opposition group was formed at Freiburg University. The Freiburg Circle was composed mainly of university members close to the Confessing Church. The group's discussions resulted in the drafting of the "Great Memorandum," which offered a social, political, and moral basis for a post–National Socialist Germany. The fifth and last appendix to the memorandum, completed in late 1942 when the group members were fully aware of the extermination of the Jews, listed "Proposals for a Solution of the Jewish Question in Germany."[27] The group suggested that after the war the Jews be internationally subjected to a special status. Moreover, although the "Proposals" rejected the Nazis' racial theories, they recommended caution regarding close contacts and intermarriage between German Christians and other races—the allusion to the Jews is clear. It seems that even in one of the most articulate groups of anti-Nazi academics, there was explicit and deep-seated anti-Jewish prejudice. The logical corollary is obvious: If a university resistance group, consisting mostly of members of the Confessing Church or the Catholic Church, could come up with such proposals even though they had knowledge of the extermination, the evidence of prevalent anti-Semitism among Germany's elites must be taken into account as a major explanation of their attitudes during the Third Reich.

In an indirect way, however, the pogrom created further tension between the German Catholic Church and the state. On November 10 the National Socialist Association of Teachers decided not only to expel all remaining Jewish students from German schools but also to stop providing (Christian) religious education—as had been the rule until then—under the pretext that "a glorification of the Jewish murderers' nation could no longer be tolerated in German schools." Cardinal Bertram sent a vigorous protest to Rust in which he stated that "whoever has the least familiarity with the Catholic faith and certainly every believing teacher knows that this assertion is false and that the contrary is true."[28]

"The foreign press is very bad," Goebbels noted on November 12. "Mainly the American."[29] Indeed, "in the weeks following Kristallnacht, close to 1,000 different editorials were published on the topic. . . ."[30] Moreover President Roosevelt recalled Ambassador Hugh Wilson for consultation.

But despite such emotional outpourings, basic attitudes and policies did not change. In the spring of 1939 Great Britain, increasingly worried by the pro-Axis shift in the Arab world—a trend with possibly dire consequences for Britain in case of war—reneged on its commitments and for all practical purposes closed the doors of Palestine to Jewish immigration. And, after slightly liberalizing its immigration policy in 1937, the United States did not even fill the quotas for Germany and Austria in 1938. In July 1939 the Wagner-Rogers Child Refugee Bill, which would have allowed twenty thousand Jewish refugee children to enter the country, was not passed by the Senate, and, at the same time, despite all entreaties, the 936 hapless Jewish emigrants from Germany who had sailed on the soon-to-become-notorious *St. Louis*, after being denied entry to Cuba, their destination, were not admitted into the United States. Their voyage back to Europe became a vivid illustration of the overall situation of Jewish refugees from Germany. After Belgium, France, and England finally agreed to give asylum to the passengers, the *London Daily Express* echoed the prevalent opinion in no uncertain terms: "This example must not set a precedent. There is no room for any more refugees in this country. . . . They become a burden and a grievance."[31]

France was neither more nor less inhospitable than other countries, but it did not volunteer even a symbolic gesture of protest against the anti-Jewish pogrom. It was the only major democratic country that did not react. Most newspapers expressed their outrage, but neither Prime Minister Édouard Daladier nor Foreign Minister Georges Bonnet did so. On the contrary, Bonnet continued with the planning for Ribbentrop's visit to Paris, which was to lead to a Franco-German agreement.

In a way the official French attitude demonstrated that Hitler did not have to worry too much about international reactions when he unleashed the pogrom. But the outcry that immediately followed the events of November and the criticism now directed at the French attitude confirmed that the Munich atmosphere was quickly dissipating. No less a supporter of appeasement than the London *Times* was taken aback by Bonnet's eagerness to go ahead with the agreement, the pogrom notwithstanding. Even the Italian government expressed surprise that "the recrudescence of anti-Semitic persecutions in Germany did not lead to the ruin of the project of Franco-German declaration."[32]

Yet another sequel to the events of November took place in the French capital: preparations for the trial of Herschel Grynszpan. The forthcoming event attracted worldwide attention. Hitler dispatched international law professor Friedrich Grimm to Paris in order to follow the work of the prosecution, while an international committee headed by the American journalist Dorothy Thompson collected money to pay for Grynszpan's defense. The beginning of the war interrupted the preparations of both prosecution and defense. When the Germans occupied France, the Vichy government duly delivered to them the young Jew they were searching for.

During these early months of 1939, the expulsion of the Jews from the Reich continued to follow the pattern inaugurated in 1938; the Jews were sent over the borders, but usually to no avail. On December 23, 1938, very strict orders had been issued by Gestapo headquarters to all stations on the western borders of the Reich to prevent illegal crossings of Jews into neighboring countries, due to increasing complaints. However, as a further Gestapo order of March 15, 1939, confirms, such illegal crossings continued well into the spring of that year.

One escape route was still open, but only for a very short time. An interministerial conference held in Tokyo on December 6, 1938, decided on a lenient policy toward Jewish refugees, making Japanese-occupied Shanghai accessible to them and even permitting prolonged transit stays in Japan itself. The Japanese seem to have been moved by their distrust of Germany and possibly by humane considerations, but undoubtedly too, as accounts of the conference show, by their belief in Jewish power—a belief reinforced by Nazi propaganda and by study of the "Protocols of the Elders of Zion"—and its possible impact on Japanese interests in Great Britain and the United States. Be that as it may, Shanghai, where no visa was required, became an asylum for desperate German and Austrian Jews. On the eve of the war, around eighteen thousand Jews had reached the safe shores of the China Sea, mainly via Lithuania and the USSR.

Thus some tens of thousands of Jews managed to leave Germany for neighboring European countries, North, Central, and South America, and remote Shanghai. Tiny groups were driven over Germany's borders. And finally, despite British policy, Jewish emigrants managed to reach Palestine by way of illegal transports organized secretly both by the majority Zionist leadership and by its right-wing rivals, the Revisionists. These illegal operations were backed by Heydrich and all branches of the SD and the Gestapo, with the full knowledge of the Wilhelmstrasse. The illegal road first led through Yugoslavia, then down the Danube to the Romanian port of Constantaţa. The main problem was not for the emigrants to leave the Greater Reich, but for the Zionist organizations to find the money to bribe officials and buy ships, and then to avoid the British patrols along the Palestine coast. Some seventeen thousand illegal immigrants reached Palestine from early 1939 to the outbreak of the war.

On March 15, 1939, the Wehrmacht occupied Prague; Czecho-Slovakia ceased to exist. Slovakia became a German satellite; Bohemia-Moravia was turned into a protectorate of the Reich. The crisis had started in the early days of the month. Enticed and supported by the Germans, the Slovaks seceded from the already truncated Czecho-Slovakia. The elderly Czech president, Emil Hacha, was summoned to Berlin, threatened with the bombing of Prague and bullied into acceptance of all German demands. But before he even signed the document of his country's submission, the first German units had crossed the border.

Some 118,000 more Jews were now under German domination. Stahlecker was transferred from Vienna to Prague to become inspector of the Security Police and the SD in the new protectorate, and Eichmann soon followed; imitating the Viennese model, he set up a Central Office for Jewish Emigration in Prague.

"At home for breakfast, I found that I myself had a refugee, a Jewish acquaintance who had worked many years for American interests," the American diplomat George F. Kennan, who had been posted to the Prague legation a few months earlier, wrote in a March 15 memorandum. "I told him that I could not give him asylum, but that as long as he was not demanded by the authorities he was welcome to stay here and to make himself at home. For twenty-four hours he haunted the house, a pitiful figure of horror and despair, moving uneasily around the drawing room, smoking one cigarette after another, too unstrung to eat or think of anything but his plight. His brother and sister-in-law had committed suicide together after Munich, and he had a strong inclination to follow suit. Annelise [Kennan's wife] pleaded with him at intervals throughout the coming hours not to choose this way out, not because she or I had any great optimism with respect to his chances for future happiness but partly on general Anglo-Saxon principles and partly to preserve our home from this sort of unpleasantness."[33]

As in every year since 1933, the Reichstag was convened in festive session on January 30, 1939, to mark the anniversary of Hitler's accession to power. Hitler's speech started at 8:15 in the evening and lasted for more than two and a half hours. The first part of the speech dealt with the history of the Nazi movement and the development of the Reich. Hitler then castigated some of the main British critics of appeasement, whom he accused of calling for a war against Germany. Behind the British opponents of Munich, the führer pointed to "the Jewish and non-Jewish instigators" of that campaign. He promised that when National Socialist propaganda went on the offensive, it would be as successful as it had been within Germany, where "we knocked down the Jewish world enemy . . . with the compelling strength of our propaganda."[34]

After referring to the American intervention against Germany during the Great War, which, according to him, had been determined by purely capitalistic motives, Hitler—probably infuriated by the American reactions to the November pogrom and to other Nazi measures against the Jews—thundered that nobody would be able to influence Germany in its solution of the Jewish problem. He sarcastically pointed to the pity expressed for the Jews by the democracies, but also to the refusal of those same democracies to help and to their unwillingness to take in the Jews to whom they were so sympathetic. Hitler then abruptly turned to the principle of absolute national sovereignty: "France to the French, England to the English, America to the Americans, and Germany to the Germans." This allowed for a renewed anti-Jewish tirade: The Jews had attempted to control all dominant positions within Germany, particularly in culture. In foreign countries there was criticism of the harsh treatment of such highly cultured people. Why then weren't the others grateful for the gift Germany was giving to the world? Why didn't they take in these "magnificent people"?

After rehashing an array of anti-Jewish themes that had become a known part of his repertory, Hitler's tone changed, and threats as yet unheard in the public pronouncements of a head of state resonated in the Reichstag: "In my life I have often been a prophet, and I have mostly been laughed at. At the time of my struggle for power, it was mostly the Jewish people who laughed at the prophecy that one day I would attain in Germany the leadership of the state and therewith of the entire nation, and that among other problems I would also solve the Jewish one. I think that the uproarious laughter of that time has in the meantime remained stuck in German Jewry's throat." Then came the explicit menace: "Today I want to be a prophet again: If international finance Jewry inside and outside Europe again succeeds in precipitating the nations into a world war, the result will not be the Bolshevization of the earth and with it the victory of Jewry, but the annihilation of the Jewish race in Europe."[35]

Over the preceding weeks and months Hitler had mentioned any number of possibilities regarding the ultimate fate of the German Jews. On September 20, 1938, he had told the Polish ambassador to Berlin, Jósef Lipski, that he was considering sending the Jews to some colony in cooperation with Poland and Romania. The same idea, specifying Madagascar, had come up in the Bonnet-Ribbentrop talks and, earlier, in Göring's addresses of November 12 and December 6. To South African defense minister Oswald Pirow, Hitler declared on November 24, 1938, that "some day, the Jews will disappear from Europe." On January 5, 1939, Hitler stated to Polish foreign minister Jozef Beck that had the Western democracies had a better understanding of his colonial aims, he would have allocated an African territory for the settlement of the Jews; in any case, he made it clear once more that he was in favor of sending the Jews to some distant country. Finally, on January 21, a few days before his speech, Hitler told Czech foreign minister František Chvalkovsky that the Jews of Germany would be "annihilated," which in the context of his declaration seemed to mean their disappearance as a community; he added again that the Jews should be shipped off to some distant place. A more ominous tone appeared in this conversation when Hitler mentioned to Chvalkovsky that if the Anglo-Saxon countries did not cooperate in shipping out the Jews and taking care of them, they would have their deaths on their consciences.[36] If Hitler was mainly thinking in terms of deporting the Jews from Europe to some distant colony, which at this stage was clearly a vague plan, then the threats of extermination uttered in the January 30 speech at first appear unrelated. But the background needs to be considered once more.

On the face of it Hitler's speech seems to have had a twofold context. First—as mentioned—British opposition to the appeasement policy and the strong American reactions to Kristallnacht would have sufficed to explain his multiple references to Jewish-capitalist warmongering. Second, it is highly probable that in view of his project of dismembering what remained of Czecho-Slovakia, and of the demands he was now making on Poland, Hitler was aware of the possibility that the new international crisis could lead to war. Thus Hitler's threats of extermination, accompanied by the argument that his past record proved that his prophecies were not to be made light of, may have been aimed in general terms at weakening anti-Nazi reactions at a time when he was preparing for his most risky military-diplomatic gamble. More precisely he may have expected that these murderous threats would impress the Jews active in European and American public life sufficiently to reduce what he considered to be their warmongering propaganda.

It was precisely because Hitler believed in Jewish influence in the capitalist world that, in its immediate context, his speech may be considered as yet another exercise in blackmail. The Jews of Germany were to be held hostage in case their warmongering brethren and assorted governments were to instigate a general war. The idea of holding the Jews hostage did not necessarily contradict the urgent desire to expel them from Germany. As has been seen, Hitler himself evoked this idea in his conversation with Goebbels on July 24, 1938. In his December 6 address to the Gauleiter, Göring returned to it as part of his emigration plan. Moreover, during the negotiations between Schacht and Rublee, which will be discussed below, the plan submitted by the Reichsbank president foresaw the departure of 150,000 Jews with their dependents over the following three years, whereas some 200,000 Jews, mainly the elderly, would stay behind in order to ensure international Jewry's positive behavior toward the Reich.

It would be a mistake, however, to consider Hitler's January 30 speech merely in its short-term, tactical context. The wider vistas may have been part calculated pressure, part uncontrolled fury, but they may well have reflected a process consistent with his other projects regarding the Jews, such as their transfer to some remote African territory. This was, in fact, tantamount to a search for radical solutions, a scanning of extreme possibilities. Perceived in such a framework, the prophecy about extermination becomes one possibility among others, neither more nor less real than others.

Throughout the weeks during which Hitler was hinting at the dire fate in store for the Jews and publicly threatening them with extermination, he was kept informed of the negotiations taking place between German representatives and the Intergovernmental Committee for Refugees set up at Evian to formulate an overall plan for the emigration of the Jews from Germany. An agreement in principle had been achieved on February 2. As has been seen, it envisaged that some 200,000 Jews over the age of forty-five would be allowed to stay in the Greater German Reich, whereas some 125,000 Jews belonging to the younger male population would emigrate, with their dependents. The emigration process was to be spread over a period of three to five years, with its financing to be ensured by an international loan mainly taken out by Jews all over the world and secured by the assets still belonging to the Jews of Germany. As in the Haavarah Agreement, the Germans made sure that various arrangements included in the plan would enhance the export of German goods and thus ensure a steady flow of foreign currency into the Reich. The agreement was nothing less than Germany's use of hostages in order to extort financial advantages in return for their release.

The concrete significance of the agreement depended on the successful floating of the loan and, in particular on the designation of the countries or areas to which the Jews leaving Germany were to emigrate. Each of the Western powers involved had its preferred territorial solution, usually involving some other country's colony or semicolony: Angola, Abyssinia, Haiti, the Guianas, Madagascar, and so on. In each case some obstacle arose or, more precisely, was raised as a pretext; even on paper no refuge zone was agreed upon before the outbreak of the war put an end to all such pseudoplanning.

According to the German census of May 1939, 213,000 full Jews were living in the *Altreich* at the time of the census. By the end of 1939, the number had been reduced to 190,000. Strangely enough, a June 15, 1939, SD report indicated that at the end of December 1938, 320,000 full Jews were still living in the *Altreich*. Whatever the reasons for these discrepancies, the demographic data provided by the Jewish Section of the SD are nonetheless significant. Only 16 percent of the Jewish population were under age twenty; 25.93 percent were between twenty and forty-five, and 57.97 percent over forty-five. These indications correspond to other known estimates: The Jewish population in Germany was rapidly becoming a community of elderly people. And it was also becoming hopelessly impoverished.

For some time the Nazis had been aware that, in order to expedite the emigration of the Jews, they had to hold them in an even tighter organizational grip than before, and that they themselves also needed to set up a centralized emigration agency on the Viennese model, so as to coordinate all the emigration measures in the Reich. Heydrich appointed the head of the Gestapo, SS-Standartenführer Heinrich Müller, chief of the new Reich Central Office. To further that aim it was necessary to bring together in one single organization for the whole Reich the means dispersed among the various Jewish organizations. "To further that aim," a Gestapo memorandum explained, "the Reichsvertretung has therefore been given the task of building a so-called Reich Association of the Jews in Germany (Reichsvereinigung) and of ensuring that all existing Jewish organizations disappear and put all their installations at the disposal of the Reichsvereinigung."[37]

The association was finally established on July 4, 1939, by the tenth supplementary decree to the Reich citizenship law. Its main function was clearly defined in Article 2: "The purpose of the Association is to further the emigration of the Jews."[38] But despite the Nazis' clear priorities, the bulk of the decree dealt with the other functions, such as education, health, and especially welfare. Thus the structure of the decree conveyed the impression that the Nazis themselves did not believe in the success of the emigration drive. For all practical purposes the association was becoming the first of the "Jewish Councils," the Nazi-controlled Jewish organizations that in most parts of occupied Europe were to carry out the orders of their German masters regarding life and death in their respective communities.

The Jews of Germany who had not managed to flee were increasingly dependent on public welfare. As noted before, from November 19, 1938, on, Jews were excluded from the general welfare system: They had to apply to special offices, and they were subjected to different and far more stringent assessment criteria than was the general population. The German welfare authorities attempted to shift the burden onto the Jewish welfare services, but there too the available means were overstrained by the increasing need. The solution to the problem soon became evident, and on December 20, 1938, the Reich Labor Exchange and Unemployment Insurance issued a decree ordering all unemployed Jews who were fit for work to register for compulsory labor. "It was obvious that only carefully chosen hard and difficult work was to be assigned to the Jews. Building sites, road and motorway work, rubbish disposal, public toilets and sewage plants, quarries and gravel pits, coal merchants and rag and bone works were regarded as suitable."[39]

As a whole, German society did not oppose the regime's anti-Jewish initiatives. Hitler's identification with the anti-Jewish drive may have reinforced the inertia or perhaps the passive complicity of the vast majority about a matter that most, in any event, considered peripheral to their main interests. It has been seen that economic and religious interests triggered some measure of dissent. Such dissent did not, however, except in some individual instances, lead to open questioning of the policies. Yet, during the thirties, the German population, the great majority of which espoused traditional anti-Semitism in one form or another, did not demand anti-Jewish measures, nor did it clamor for their most extreme implementation. Among most "ordinary Germans" there was acquiescence regarding the segregation and dismissal from civil and public service of the Jews; there were individual initiatives to benefit from their expropriation; and there was some glee in witnessing their degradation. But outside party ranks there was no massive popular agitation to expel them from Germany or to unleash violence against them. The majority of Germans simply chose to look the other way. Moreover, Hitler's accession to power would be remembered by a majority of Germans as the beginning of a period of "good times."

"People experienced the breakneck speed of the economic and foreign resurgence of Germany as a sort of frenzy—as the common expression has it," writes the German historian Norbert Frei. "With astonishing rapidity, many identified themselves with the social will to construct a *Volksgemeinschaft* that kept any thoughtful or critical stance at arm's length. . . . They were beguiled by the esthetics of the Nuremberg rallies and enraptured by the victories of German athletes at the Berlin Olympic Games. Hitler's achievements in foreign affairs triggered storms of enthusiasm. . . . In the brief moments left between the demands of a profession and those of the ever-growing jungle of Nazi organizations, they enjoyed modest well-being and private happiness."[40]

The Polish crisis had unfolded throughout the spring and summer of 1939. This time, however, the German demands were met by an adamant Polish stand and, after the occupation of Bohemia and Moravia, by new British resolve. On March 17, in Birmingham, Chamberlain publicly vowed that his government would not allow any further German conquests. On March 31 Great Britain guaranteed the borders of Poland, as well as those of a series of other European countries. On April 11 Hitler gave orders to the Wehrmacht to be ready for "Operation White," the code name for the attack on Poland.

On May 22 Germany and Italy signed a defense treaty. Simultaneously, while Great Britain and France were conducting hesitant and noncommittal negotiations with the Soviet Union, Hitler made an astounding political move and opened negotiations of his own with Stalin. The German-Soviet Nonaggression Pact was signed on August 23; an attached secret protocol divided a great part of Eastern Europe into areas to be eventually occupied and controlled by the two countries in case of war. Hitler was now convinced that, as a result of this coup, Great Britain and France would be deterred from any military intervention. On September 1 the German attack on Poland started. After some hesitation the two democracies decided to stand by their ally, and on September 3, France and Great Britain were at war with Germany. World War II had begun.

PART II

TERROR

September 1939–December 1941

---

*The proportions of life and death have radically changed. Times
were, when life occupied the primary place, when it was the
main and central concern, while death was a side phenomenon,
secondary to life, its termination. Nowadays, death rules in all
its majesty; while life hardly glows under a thick layer of ashes.
Even this faint glow of life is feeble, miserable and weak, poor,
devoid of any free breath, deprived of any spark of spiritual
content. The very soul, both in the individual and in the
community, seems to have starved and perished, to have dulled
and atrophied. There remain only the needs of the body; and it
leads merely an organic-physiological existence.*

—ABRAHAM LEWIN,
"EULOGY IN HONOR OF YITSHAK MEIR WEISSENBERG,
SEPTEMBER 13, 1941," IN *A CUP OF TEARS:
A DIARY OF THE WARSAW GHETTO*

CHAPTER 6

Poland Under German Rule

September 1939–April 1940

O N FRIDAY MORNING, September 1, the young butcher's lad came and told us: There has been a radio announcement, we already held Danzig and the Corridor, the war with Poland was under way, England and France remained neutral," Victor Klemperer wrote in his diary, on September 3. "I said to Eva [that] a morphine injection or something similar was the best thing for us; our life was over."[1]

Klemperer was of Jewish origin; in his youth he converted to Protestantism and later on married Eva, a Protestant "Aryan." On April 30, 1935, he was dismissed from the Technical University in Dresden, where he taught Romance languages and literature; yet he went on living in the city with his Protestant wife, painstakingly recording what happened to him and around him. The British and French responses to the German attack remained uncertain for two days. "Annemarie brought two bottles of sparkling wine for Eva's birthday," Klemperer reported on September 4. "We drank one and decided to save the other for the day of the English declaration of war. So today it's the turn of the second one."[2]

In Warsaw, Chaim Kaplan, the director of a Hebrew school, was confident that this time Britain and France would not betray their ally as they had betrayed Czechoslovakia in 1938. On day one of the war Kaplan also sensed the apocalyptic nature of the new conflict: "We are witnessing the dawn of a new era in the history of the world. This war will indeed bring destruction upon human civilization but this is a civilization that merits annihilation and destruction." The Hebrew school director also grasped the peculiar threat that the outbreak of the war represented for the Jews. "As for the Jews, their danger is seven times greater. Wherever Hitler's foot treads there is no hope for the Jewish people."[3]

On September 8, the Wehrmacht occupied Lodz, the second largest Polish city: "All of a sudden the terrifying news: Lodz has been surrendered!" Dawid Sierakowiak, a Jewish youngster, barely fifteen, recorded. "All conversation stops; the streets grow deserted; faces and hearts are covered with gloom, cold severity and hostility. Mr. Grabinski comes back from downtown and tells how the local Germans greeted their countrymen. The Grand Hotel where the General Staff is expected to stay is bedecked with garlands of flowers: [ethnic German] civilians—boys, girls—jump into the passing military cars with happy cries of Heil Hitler! . . . Everything patriotically and nationalistically [German] that was hidden in the past now shows its true face. . . ."[4]

And, in Warsaw again, Adam Czerniaków, an employee of the Polish foreign-trade clearing house and an active member of the Jewish community, was organizing a Jewish Citizens Committee to work with the Polish authorities: "The Jewish Citizens Committee of the capital city of Warsaw," he wrote on September 13, "received legal recognition and was established in the Community building." On September 23 he further noted: "Mayor Starzynski named me Chairman of the Jewish Community in Warsaw. A historic role in a besieged city. I will try to live up to it."[5] Four days later Poland surrendered.

On the edge of destruction, European Jewry was characterized mainly by its extraordinary diversity. After a steady decline of religious observance and the uncertainties of cultural-ethnic Jewishness, no obvious common denominator fitted a maze of parties, associations, groups, and some nine million individuals, spread all over the Continent, who nonetheless considered themselves as Jews (or were considered as such). This diversity resulted from the impact of distinct national histories, the dynamics of large-scale migrations, a predominantly urban-centered life, a constant economic and social mobility driven by any number of individual strategies in the face of surrounding hostility and prejudice or, obversely, by the opportunities offered in liberal surroundings. These constant changes contributed to ever greater fragmentation within "the dispersion," mainly during the chaotic decades that separated the late nineteenth century from the eve of World War II.

Some basic distinctions nonetheless structured the European Jewish scene between the two world wars. The main dividing line ran between Eastern European and Western Jewries; it was geographic to a point, but its manifest expression was cultural. Eastern European Jewry (excluding after 1918 the Jews of Soviet Russia, who were developing according to the rules and opportunities offered by the new regime) encompassed in principle the communities of the Baltic countries, Poland, the eastern part of Czechoslovakia, Hungary (except for the large cities) and the eastern provinces of post-1918 Romania. The largely "Spanish" (Sephardi) Jews of Bulgaria, Greece, and parts of Yugoslavia represented a distinct world of their own. Eastern European Jewry was less integrated into surrounding society, more religiously observant—at times still strictly Orthodox—often Yiddish-speaking, occasionally fluent in Hebrew. In short, it was more traditionally "Jewish" than its Western counterpart (although many Jews in Vilna, Warsaw, Lodz, and Iasi were no less "Western" than those of Vienna, Berlin, Prague, and Paris). Economically the majority of Eastern Jewry often hovered on the edge of poverty, but, nonetheless it nurtured a distinct, vibrant, and multifaceted Jewish life.

Despite growing difficulties, mainly from the early 1930s onward, Jewish emigration from Eastern and Central Europe to the West went on. By dint of deep-seated cultural and social differences, estrangement between Western and Eastern Jews grew—both ways. For Eastern Jews, the Westerners lacked *Yiddishkeit* (Jewishness), while for the Westerners, notwithstanding some idealization of an "authentic" Jewish life, the Eastern European Jews appeared "backward," "primitive," and increasingly a source of embarrassment and shame.

Whatever the degree of estrangement between Western and Eastern Jews may have been on the eve of the war in various Western European countries, there is little doubt that the stream of Jewish immigrants and refugees contributed to the surge of anti-Semitism. But as we shall see, Jewish immigration was but one aspect of the darkening scene. In most general terms the crisis of Jewry in the Western world was the direct outcome and expression of the crisis of liberal society as such and the rise of antidemocratic forces throughout the West. Needless to say, Nazi propaganda had found an ideal terrain for its anti-Semitic invectives: The Jews were profiteers, plutocrats, and mainly warmongers intent on dragging the European nations into another world conflict to further their own interests and, eventually, to achieve world domination.

Notwithstanding the political, economic, or cultural achievement of some individuals, however, European Jews were devoid of any significant collective political influence. This powerlessness was not recognized by the environment and individual success was often interpreted as a collective Jewish drive to undermine and dominate surrounding society. No less blatant than their powerlessness was the inability of most European Jews to assess the seriousness of the threats that they faced; notwithstanding all warning signals, notwithstanding Hitler's furious anti-Jewish threats and the steep increase of local hostility, the trickle of Jewish emigration from Eastern and Central Europe did not grow significantly nor did almost any Jews leave Western Europe before the German onslaught. In the West the misperception was more extreme, as we shall see. Moreover, mainly in Western Europe, the Jews believed in the validity of abstract principles and universal values; in other words they believed in the rule of law. Law offered a stable framework for facing ordeals, planning everyday life, and long-term survival.

Hitler's views about the newly conquered populations and territories in the East were tentatively outlined on September 29 in a conversation with Rosenberg: "The Poles," the Nazi leader declared, "a thin Germanic layer, underneath frightful material. The Jews, the most appalling people one can imagine. . . . What was needed now was a determined and masterful hand to rule. He [Hitler] wanted to split the territory into three strips: (1) Between the [river] Vistula and the [river] Bug: this would be for the whole of Jewry, as well as all other unreliable elements. . . . (2) Create a broad cordon of territory along the previous frontier to be Germanized and colonized. . . . (3) In between, a form of Polish state. The future would show whether after a few decades the cordon of settlement would have to be pushed further forward."[6]

At this stage Hitler's plans included only half of former Poland, as the eastern part of the country had been invaded by the Soviet Union on September 17, in accordance with the secret protocol added to the German-Soviet pact of August 23, 1939. Moreover, the Germans had recognized Soviet "special interests" in the Baltic countries, in Finland, in Bulgaria, and in regard to two Romanian provinces. For both sides the August treaty and a further secret arrangement signed on September 27 were tactical moves. Both Hitler and Stalin knew that a confrontation would ultimately come.

In a festive Reichstag speech on October 6, in a so-called peace offer, Hitler indeed spoke of a territorial reorganization of those areas of Eastern Europe lying between the German border and the Soviet-German demarcation line. His settlement idea was to be based on the principle of nationalities and to solve the problem of national minorities, including the Jewish problem. Reestablishing a Polish state was mentioned as a possibility. By then, however, Great Britain and France had become familiar with Hitler's tactics; the "peace offer" was rejected.

As the idea of some form of Polish sovereignty disappeared, German-occupied Poland was further divided. The Reich annexed several areas along its eastern borders: A large region along the Warta River (Warthegau), Eastern Upper Silesia, the Polish corridor with the city of Danzig, and a small stretch of territory south of East Prussia. A population of 10 million people was thus added to Germany, around 750,000 of whom were Germans. The remaining Polish territory, which included the cities of Warsaw, Kraków, and Lublin, became the "General Government," an administrative unit of around 12 million people, governed by German officials and occupied by German troops. The General Government itself was subdivided into four districts: Warsaw, Radom, Kraków, and Lublin. The district of Galicia would be added in August 1941, after the German attack against the Soviet Union.

On October 17, freed from the peace proposal gimmick, the Nazi leader was back on track. In a meeting with a group of military commanders and some high-ranking party members, Hitler remarked about what was to be achieved in Poland: "The hard struggle of nationalities does not allow for any legal constraints." Two groups in particular would be targeted: Jews and "Polish elites."[7] The murder of Jews was haphazard at this stage, that of Polish elites more systematic.

Some sixty thousand Poles whose names had been collected over the prewar years were to be eliminated; the operation was partly camouflaged under directives for ensuring the security of the troops and, more generally, of the occupied territory. SS Chief Heinrich Himmler chose the code name "Tannenberg" for the terror campaign; it evoked the victory of the German armies against the Russian forces at Tannenberg in East Prussia in 1914, and a symbolic retaliation against the Poles for the resounding defeat they had inflicted upon the Teutonic Knights at that same place in the early fifteenth century.

On-the-spot executions were the most common practice, in retaliation against Polish civilians for attacks against German troops and as revenge for Polish murders of ethnic Germans in the initial stages of the war. For the elimination of the local elites, however, other methods were also used. Thus, on November 3, 1939, 183 faculty members of the Jagiellonian University in Kraków were summoned by the Gestapo, arrested, and deported to the Sachsenhausen concentration camp near Berlin. A few months later the older scholars were released and the younger ones sent to Dachau. By that time thirteen of the imprisoned scholars had already died; none of the Jews was set free.

Although in Hitler's view the Jews were first and foremost an active (eventually deadly) threat, in the wake of the Polish campaign, primary German reactions to the sight of the *Ostjuden* were more immediately dominated by disgust and utter contempt. On September 10, Hitler toured the Jewish quarter of Kielce; his press chief, Otto Dietrich, described the impression of the visit in a pamphlet published at the end of that year: "If we had once believed we knew the Jews, we were quickly taught otherwise here.... The appearance of these human beings is unimaginable.... Physical repulsion hindered us from carrying out our journalistic research. . . . The Jews in Poland are in no way poor, but they live in such inconceivable dirt, in huts in which no vagrant in Germany would spend the night."[8]

On October 7, referring to Hitler's description of his impressions from Poland, Goebbels added: "The Jewish problem will be the most difficult to solve. These Jews are not human beings anymore. [They are] predators equipped with a cold intellect which has to be rendered harmless."[9] In Nazi parlance "to render harmless" meant to kill. There was no such concrete plan in the fall of 1939, but murderous thoughts regarding the Jews were certainly swirling around.

Victory in the racial struggle would be attained not only through unbridled ruthlessness against non-Germanic races but, simultaneously, by an equally ruthless cleansing of the German racial community inside the Germanic space. In line for eradication were the mentally ill, the Gypsies, and various "racially foreign" elements still mingling with the *Volk* (homosexuals, "asocials," criminals, and the like) although many of them had already been shipped to concentration camps.

Thousands of mental patients from asylums in Pomerania, East Prussia, and the Posen region in the Warthegau were eliminated soon after the German attack in Poland. They were murdered without any medical cover-up, independently of the "euthanasia" operation. On orders from Himmler these patients were to be killed so that the buildings they lived in could be used for billeting Waffen SS soldiers and accommodating military casualties, possibly also in order to help in the resettlement of ethnic Germans from neighboring Eastern countries. As we have seen, newborn children with serious defects had already been targeted on the eve of the war. The "euthanasia" program as such (identified by its code name, T4), which also extended to the adult population, did secretly start in October 1939 on Hitler's order. It was established under the direct authority of "the Chancellory of the Führer of the National Socialist Party," headed by Philipp Bouhler. In the framework of T4, some seventy thousand mental patients were assembled and murdered in six mental institutions between the beginning of the war and August 1941, when the framework of the extermination system changed. In each of the medical institutions turned into killing centers, physicians and police officers were jointly in charge. The exterminations followed a standardized routine: The chief physician checked the paperwork; photos of the victims were taken; the inmates were then led to a gas chamber fed by containers of carbon monoxide and asphyxiated. Gold teeth were torn out and the bodies cremated.

The killing of Jewish patients started in June 1940; they had previously been moved to a few institutions destined only for them. They were killed without any formalities; their medical record was of no interest. Their death was camouflaged nonetheless: the Reichsvereinigung had to pay the costs of the victims' hospitalization in a fictitious institution: the "Cholm State Hospital," near Lublin. In August 1940 identical letters were sent from Cholm to the families of the patients, informing them of the sudden death of their relatives, all on the same date. The cause of death was left unspecified.

While in his conversations with Goebbels, Rosenberg, or other party subordinates, Hitler's anti-Semitic harangues went on unabated, his only public anti-Jewish outbursts throughout a period of several months came at the beginning of the war, on the day Great Britain and France joined the conflict. On the afternoon of September 3 German radio broadcast four proclamations by Adolf Hitler: the first to the German people; the second and third to the armed forces on the Eastern and Western fronts; the last and most important one, to the National-Socialist Party. In the first proclamation the Nazi leader lashed out at those who had initiated this war: "that Jewish-plutocratic and democratic ruling class that wanted to turn all the nations

of the earth into its obedient slaves."[10] Whereas in the proclamation to the German people the attack against "Jewish
plutocracy" came only in the middle of the address, it opened
the proclamation to the party: "Our Jewish-democratic world
enemy has succeeded in pulling the English people into a state
of war with Germany." The real "world enemy" was clearly
identified once again: Party and state would have to act. "This
time," Hitler darkly warned, "those who hoped to sabotage
the common effort would be exterminated without any pity."[11]
Whether these dire threats were signals of steps to come or, at
this point, merely ritualized outbursts remains an open question.

Hitler's subsequent public restraint derived from obvious
political reasons (the hope of an arrangement with France and
Great Britain). Nothing was said about the Jews, either in the
annual address to the party "old fighters" on November 8, 1939,
or in the official announcement that followed the attempt on
Hitler's life on that same evening. In his 1940 New Year's message to the party, Hitler merely hinted that the Jews were not
forgotten: "Jewish-international capitalism, in alliance with reactionary forces, incited the democracies against Germany";
the same "Jewish-capitalist world enemy" had only one goal,
"to destroy the German people," but, Hitler announced, "the
Jewish capitalist world would not survive the twentieth century."[12] On January 30, in the annual speech commemorating
the "seizure of power," the same restraint was even more no-
ticeable; the Jews were not mentioned at all.

Notwithstanding Hitler's public restraint, Goebbels never
forgot the potential impact of Nazi anti-Jewish propaganda
beyond the Reich's borders, mainly among Germany's enemies. By endlessly repeating that the war was a "Jewish war,"
prepared and instigated by the Jews for their own profit and
their ultimate goal—world domination—Goebbels hoped to
weaken enemy resolve and foster a growing demand for an arrangement with Germany.

Immediately after the beginning of the war, Goebbels ordered the production of three major anti-Jewish films: *The Rothschilds*, *Jud Süss* (*Jew Süss*), and *The Eternal Jew*. Throughout the end of 1939 and the beginning of 1940, the minister devoted constant attention to the "Jew film," as he called *The Eternal Jew*. Synagogue scenes had been filmed at the Vilker synagogue in Lodz. The Germans assembled the congregation, ordered it to put on tallithim and tefillin and to stage a full-scale service. Shimon Huberband later recorded the details of the event for the underground historical archives kept in Warsaw (to which we will return). "A large number of high-ranking German officers came," Huberband noted, "and filmed the entire course of the service, immortalizing it on film!!" Then, the order was given to take out the Torah scroll and read from it: "The Torah-reader, a clever Jew, called out in Hebrew before beginning to read the scroll: 'Today is Tuesday.' This was meant as a statement for posterity that they were forced to read the Torah, since the Torah is usually not read on Tuesdays."

The Germans repeated the operation in the Jewish slaughterhouse: "The kosher meat slaughterers, dressed in *yarmulkes* [skullcaps] and *gartlekh* [sashes], were ordered to slaughter a number of cattle and recite the blessings, while squeezing their eyes shut and rocking with religious fervor. They were also required to examine the animals' lungs and remove the adhesions to the lungs."[13] Over the following days the Germans burned down one synagogue, then another, and announced that it was Polish revenge for the destruction by the Jews of the monument to the national hero and anti-Russian freedom fighter Tadeusz Kociuszko.

The SS *Einsatzgruppen* (SS "Operational Groups" set up by Heydrich, since mid-September 1939 chief of the SS Main Office for the Security of the Reich, or RSHA) were in charge of murdering Poles and of terrorizing the Jewish populations. Regarding the Jews, their wanton murder and destruction campaign was both a manifestation of generalized Nazi anti-Jewish hatred and a show of violence meant to incite the Jewish populations to flee from regions about to be incorporated in the Reich. More generally the *Einsatzgruppen* had probably received the instruction to drive as many Jews as possible beyond the San River to what was to become the Soviet-occupied area of Poland.

Men of SS General Udo von Woyrsch's mixed *Einsatzgruppe* of SD and Order Police excelled. In Dynow, near the San River, Order Police detachments belonging to the group burned a dozen Jews in the local synagogue, then shot some further sixty of them in the nearby forest. Such murder operations were repeated in several neighboring villages and towns. Overall the unit had murdered five to six hundred Jews by September 20. For the Wehrmacht, Woyrsch had transgressed all tolerable limits. Several army commanding officers demanded the withdrawal of the *Einsatzgruppe* and, atypically, Gestapo headquarters immediately complied. Woyrsch's case, however, was extreme; usually, the tension between the Wehrmacht and the SS did not lead to any measures against the SS units as such but rather to army complaints about the lack of discipline of Heydrich's men.

Massacring Jews may have been considered by the Wehrmacht as demanding disciplinary action, but torturing them was welcome enjoyment for both the soldiers and SS personnel. The choice victims were Orthodox Jews, given their distinctive looks and attire. They were shot at; they were compelled to smear feces on one another; they had to jump, crawl, sing, clean excrement with prayer shawls, and dance around bonfires of burning Torah scrolls. They were whipped, forced to eat pork, or had Jewish stars carved on their foreheads. The "beard game" was the most popular entertainment of all: Beards and sidelocks were shorn, plucked, torn, set afire, hacked off with or without parts of skin, cheeks, or jaws, to the amusement of a usually large audience of cheering soldiers.

Part of the invasion army itself was highly ideologized, even at that early stage of the war. In a "Leaflet for the Conduct of German Soldiers in the Occupied Territory of Poland," issued by the commander in chief of the army, Gen. Walther von Brauchitsch, on September 19, 1939, the soldiers were warned of the "inner enmity" of "all civilians that were not 'members of the German race.'" Furthermore the leaflet stated: "The behavior toward Jews needs no special mention for the soldiers of the National-Socialist Reich." It was therefore within the range of accepted thinking that a soldier noted in his diary, during these same days: "Here we recognize the necessity for a radical solution to the Jewish question. Here one sees houses occupied by beasts in human form. In their beards and kaftans, with their devilishly grotesque faces, they make a dreadful impression. Anyone who was not yet a radical opponent of the Jews must become one here."[14]

Looting, however, did not demand any ideological passion: "They knock at eleven in the morning," Sierakowiak noted on October 22. "A German army officer, two policemen and the superintendent came in. The officer asks how many persons are in the apartment, looks at the beds, asks about the bedbugs, and if we have a radio. He doesn't find anything worthy of taking and finally leaves disappointed. At the neighbors' (naturally they go only to Jews), he took away radios, mattresses, comforters, carpets, etc. They took away the Grabinski's only down quilt."[15]

All incentives were mixed, in fact: ideology, looting, and fun. . . . On October 13, 1939, the Polish physician and longtime director of the hospital in Szczebrzeszyn, near Zamość, Dr. Zygmunt Klukowski, recorded in his diary: "The Germans posted several new regulations. I am noting only a few: 'All men of Jewish religion between the ages of fifteen and sixty must report at 8 a.m. on the morning of October 14, at city hall with brooms, shovels, and buckets. They will

be cleaning city streets." On the next day he added: "The
Germans are treating the Jews very brutally. They cut their
beards; sometimes they pull the hair out." On the fifteenth
the Germans added more of the same, yet with a slightly different emphasis: "A German major, now town commandant,
told the new 'police' [an auxiliary Polish police unit] that all
brutalities against Jews have to be tolerated since it is in line
with German anti-Semitic policies and that this brutality has
been ordered from above. The Germans are always trying to
find new work for the Jews. They order the Jews to take at
least a half hour of exhaustive gymnastics before any work,
which can be fatal, particularly for older people. When the
Jews are marched to any assignment, they must loudly sing
Polish national songs."[16]

On September 21, 1939, Heydrich had issued the following guidelines to the commanders of the *Einsatzgruppen*:
(1) rounding up and concentration of Jews in large communities
in cities close to railway lines, "in view of the end goal";
(2) establishment of Jewish Councils in each Jewish community to serve as administrative links between the German authorities and the Jewish population; (3) cooperation with the
military command and the civil administration in all matters
relating to the Jewish population.[17]

The "end goal" in this context probably meant the deportation of the Jewish population of the Warthegau and later of the
western and central parts of former Poland to the easternmost
area of the General Government, the Lublin district. A few days
later Heydrich announced that the führer had authorized the
expulsion of Jews over the demarcation line [between German
occupied Poland and the Soviet occupation area]. Such an authorization meant that at this early stage the Germans had
no clear plans yet. Their anti-Jewish policies seemed to be in
line with the measures they had elaborated before the war regarding the Jews of the Reich—now applied with much greater

violence: identification, segregation, expropriation, concentration, emigration or expulsion.

By then, however, a new element had become part of the picture and considerably influenced the measures taken against Jews and Poles: the mass ingathering of ethnic Germans from Eastern and Southeastern Europe. Jews and Poles would be expelled and "ethnic Germans" would move in. On October 7, 1939, Himmler was appointed head of the new agency in charge of these population transfers: the Reich Commissariat for the Strengthening of Germandom (Reichskommissariat für die Festigung deutschen Volkstums, or RKFDV).

In recent years many historians have sought a link between these plans and the onset of the "Final Solution." Yet, as we shall see, these operations appear to have been distinct and to have stemmed from different motives and plans. Nonetheless, between 1939 and 1942, Himmler's population transfers led directly to the expulsions and deportations of hundreds of thousands of Poles and Jews, mainly but not exclusively from the Warthegau into the General Government.

In October 1939 the deportations of Jews from Vienna, Mährisch Ostrau, and Katowice to Nisko (a small town on the San, in the Lublin district) started. These deportations, agreed to by Hitler, had been demanded by local Gauleiter mainly to seize Jewish homes. Moreover, as far as Vienna was concerned, the city would thus recover its pristine Aryan nature. A few thousand Jews were deported, but within days the operation came to a halt, as the Wehrmacht needed the railway lines for transporting troops from Poland to the West.

Two other transfers were simultaneous and identical in their goals. The one, small in scale (by Nazi standards), was the deportation in February 1940 of some eighteen hundred Jews from the German towns of Stettin and Schneidemühl on the coast of the Baltic Sea to Lublin. The second operation was a formidable exercise in utter brutality: It aimed at the just-mentioned expulsion of hundreds of thousands of Jews and Poles from the annexed Warthegau into the General Government, over a period of several months. The abandoned homes and farms of the deportees were to be distributed to ethnic Germans from the Baltic countries, whose departure and ingathering into the Reich the Germans had negotiated with the USSR.

Nothing was ready for the Jews of Stettin and Schneidemühl in the snow-covered Lublin area, and they were either housed in temporary barracks or taken in by local Jewish communities. For the newly appointed SS and Police Leader (SSPF) of the Lublin District, Odilo Globocnik, there was no particular problem. On February 16, 1940, he declared that "the evacuated Jews should feed themselves and be supported by their countrymen, as these Jews had enough [food]. If this did not succeed, one should let them starve."[18]

The deportations from the Warthegau into the General Government soon became mired in total chaos, with overfilled trains blocked for days in freezing weather or maneuvering aimlessly to and fro. The ruthlessness of these deportations, mainly organized by Eichmann, now the RSHA specialist on the emigration and evacuation of Jews, in coordination with the newly established RKFDV, did not compensate for the complete lack of planning and of even minimal preparation of reception areas for the deportees. During the first weeks of the transfers, Governor-General Hans Frank seemed rather unconcerned about the sudden influx. But in early February 1940, after some two hundred thousand new arrivals into his domain had been counted, he traveled to Berlin and extracted an order to halt the transfers from Göring. Encouraged by this success, Frank took an initiative of his own: On April 12 he announced his intention to empty Kraków of its Jews. By the end of the year 43,000 Jewish inhabitants of the city had been expelled and those who remained were concentrated in the district of Podgorce, the ghetto. As for the Jews who had been ousted, they could not go very far. They settled mostly in the surroundings of Frank's capital, but at least the governor-general and the German civil and military administration in Kraków had chased most of the Jews out of their sight.

Although Frank was directly subordinate to Hitler himself, his own authority and that of his administration were constantly undermined by Himmler, in charge of all internal security matters also in the General Government. Moreover, as chief of the newly established RKFDV, Himmler took over the dumping of Poles and Jews into Frank's kingdom until the operation was temporarily stopped, as we saw. De facto, then, as 1940 began a dual administration was being put in place: Frank's civilian administration and Himmler's security and RKFDV administration. The tension between both rapidly grew, mainly at the district level and particularly in the Lublin district, where Himmler's appointee and protégé, the SS and police leader, the notorious Globocnik, established a quasi-independent administration, in direct defiance to the authority of District Governor Ernst Zörner.

Unexpectedly the first round in this ongoing power struggle was won by Frank. Not only did the governor-general succeed in halting the deportations into his domain but, in the Lublin district, he compelled Globocnik to disband his private police, the "Self-Defense," recruited among local ethnic Germans. This, however, was but round one; soon Globocnik would resume his terror activities on a far wider scale.

In the meantime, in accordance with Heydrich's guidelines, the Jews were increasingly concentrated in specific areas of cities and towns, although neither Heydrich nor Frank gave an overall order to establish closed ghettos. The initial marking and segregation of Jews began on December 1, when the Jews of the General Government above age ten were ordered to wear a white armband with a blue Star of David on their right arm. The armband was rapidly followed by a prohibition to change residence, the exclusion from a long list of professions, a ban on the use of public transportation, and barring from restaurants, parks, and the like. Expropriation and confiscation followed: On January 24, 1940, Jewish enterprises in the General Government were set under "trusteeship"; they could also be confiscated if "public interest" demanded it. On the same day Frank ordered the registration of all Jewish property: nonregistered property would be confiscated as "ownerless." Further expropriation measures followed and finally, on September 17, 1940, Göring would order the confiscation of all Jewish property and assets except for personal belongings and one thousand reichsmarks in cash.

Steps toward ghettoization were initiated locally and stemmed from different circumstances from place to place. It extended from October 1939 (Piotrkow Trybunalski) to March 1941 (Lublin and Kraków), to 1942, and even 1943 (Upper Silesia); in some cases no ghettos were established before the beginning of deportations to the extermination camps. The Lodz ghetto was established in April 1940 and the Warsaw ghetto in November 1940. Whereas in Warsaw the pretext for sealing the ghetto was mainly sanitary (the Germans' fear of epidemics), in Lodz it was linked to the resettlement of ethnic Germans from the Baltic countries in the homes vacated by the Jews.

From the outset the ghettos were considered temporary means of segregating the Jewish population before its expulsion. Once they acquired a measure of permanence, however, one of their functions became the ruthless and systematic exploitation of part of the imprisoned Jewish population for the benefit of the Reich (mainly for the needs of the Wehrmacht). Moreover, by squeezing the food supply and, in Lodz, by replacing regular money with a special ghetto currency as the only legal tender, the Germans put their hands on most of the cash and valuables that the Jews had taken along when driven into their miserable quarters.

The ghettos also fulfilled a useful psychological and "educational" function in the Nazi order of things: They rapidly became the showplace of Jewish misery and destitution, offering German viewers newsreel sequences that fed existing revulsion and hatred; a constant procession of German tourists (soldiers and some civilians) were presented with the same heady mix. "What you see," Fraulein Greiser, the Warthegau Gauleiter's daughter, wrote after touring the Lodz ghetto in mid-April 1940, "is mainly rabble, all of which is just hanging around. . . . Epidemics are spreading and the air smells disgustingly, as everything is poured into the drainpipes. There is no water either and the Jews have to buy it for 10 Pfennigs the bucket; they surely wash themselves even less than usually. . . . You know, one can really feel no pity for these people; I think that their feelings are completely different from ours and therefore they do not feel this humiliation and everything else." In the evening the young woman was back in the city and attended a big rally. "This contrast, in the afternoon the ghetto and in the evening the rally, which could not have been more German anywhere else, in one and the same city, that was absolutely unreal. . . . You know, I was again really happy and terribly proud of being a German."[19]

The most effective instrument of German control over the concentrated Jewish populations were the Jewish Councils (*Judenräte*), established in all Jewish communities. Of course, the councils were established by the Germans for their own purposes, but even during the early days of the war, communal activities were organized by the Jews themselves in order to cater to the basic needs of the population. In principle the twelve or twenty-four council members (according to the size of the community) were to be chosen from the traditional Jewish elites, the recognized community leadership. In fact, however, in many instances the council members did not belong to the foremost leadership of their communities but had mostly been previously active in public life.

Some of the councils' earliest German-ordered tasks acquired an ominous significance only when considered in hindsight; the potentially most fateful one was the census. The *Judenrat* itself needed the census to identify the pool of laborers at its disposal, for housing, welfare, food distribution, and the like; the immediate needs seemed more demanding and urgent than any long-term consequences. Nonetheless Kaplan, usually more farsighted than any other diarist and suspicious of German intentions on principle, sensed that the registration carried threatening possibilities: "Today, notices inform the Jewish population of Warsaw," he wrote on October 25, "that next Saturday [October 29] there will be a census of the Jewish inhabitants. The *Judenrat* under the leadership of Engineer Czerniaków is required to carry it out. Our hearts tell us evil—some catastrophe for the Jews of Warsaw lies in this census. Otherwise there would be no need for it."[20]

Bribery became an integral part of the relations between the Germans and the councils. In the words of historian Isaiah Trunk, "the Councils constantly had to satisfy all kinds of demands to remodel and equip German office premises, casinos and private apartments for various functionaries, as well as to provide expensive gifts. In dealing with a ghetto, each functionary considered himself entitled to be rewarded by its Council. On the other hand, the Councils themselves implemented an intricate system of bribes in an effort to try and 'soften the hearts' of the ghetto bosses or to win favors for the ghetto inmates from the 'good Germans.' This in turn enhanced the pauperization of the Jews."[21] The bribes may have briefly delayed some threats or saved some individuals; but, as the coming months would show, they never changed German policies. Additionally, bribing the Germans or their auxiliaries led to the spreading of corruption among the victims: a "new class" of Jewish profiteers and black marketeers was arising above the miserable majority of the population.

One of the immediate advantages that money could buy was exemption from forced labor. From mid-October 1939 on, the councils, mainly in Warsaw and Lodz, took it upon themselves to deliver the required numbers of laborers to the Germans in order to put an end to the brutal manhunt and the constant roundups that had been standard procedure. As could have been expected, the poorest part of the population bore the brunt of the new arrangement; the wealthier segments of the community either paid the councils or bribed the Germans.

While the German grip over the Jewish population of the Warthegau and the General Government was tightening, in the Soviet-occupied zone of Poland, the 1.2 million local Jews and the approximately 300,000 to 350,000 Jewish refugees from the western part of the country were getting acquainted with the heavy hand of Stalinism. There is little doubt that many local and refugee Jews in eastern Poland, threatened by the Germans and long-suffering victims of the Poles, welcomed the Soviet troops. Soon, however, many Jews became disenchanted with the new rulers: Economic hardship spread, Jewish religious, educational, and political institutions were disbanded, the Soviet secret police (NKVD) surveillance became all-intrusive and, in the spring of 1940, mass deportations, which had already targeted other so-called hostile groups, began to include segments of the Jewish population, such as the wealthier Jews, those who hesitated to accept Soviet citizenship, those who declared that after the war they wanted to return home. In view of these worsening conditions, thousands of Jews even attempted to return to the German occupied areas. Moshe Grossman's memoirs tell of a train filled with Jews going east that, at a border station, met a train moving west. When the Jews coming from Brisk [the Soviet zone] saw Jews going there, they shouted: "You are mad, where are you going?" Those coming from Warsaw answered with equal astonishment: "You are mad, where are you going?"[22] The story is obviously apocryphal, but it vividly illustrates the plight and the confusion of the Jews in both zones of Poland and, beyond it, the disarray spreading among the Jews of Europe.

In its great majority the Polish population under German occupation remained hostile toward the Jews and expressed fury at "Jewish behavior" in the Soviet-occupied part of the country. According to a comprehensive report written for the Polish government-in-exile in February 1940 by a young courier from Poland, Jan Karski, the Germans were striving to gain submission and collaboration from the Polish population by exploiting anti-Semitism. The concluding lines of the report were ominous: "The Jews have created here a situation in which the Poles regard them as devoted to the Bolsheviks and—one can safely say—wait for the moment when they will be able simply to take revenge upon the Jews. . . . The overwhelming majority (first among them of course the youth) literally look forward to an opportunity for 'repayment in blood.' "[23]

Already during the interwar period, the cultural separatism of the Jews—not different from that of other minorities living in the new Polish state—exacerbated the deep-rooted native anti-Semitism. This hostile attitude was nurtured by traditional Catholic anti-Judaism, by an increasingly fierce Polish economic drive to force the Jews out of their trades and professions, as well as by mythical stories of Jewish subversive activities against Polish national claims and rights.

In this fervently Catholic country, the role of the church was decisive. A study of the Catholic press between the wars opened with a resolutely unambiguous statement: "All Catholic journalists agreed . . . that there was indeed a 'Jewish question' and that the Jewish minority in Poland posed a threat to the identity of the Polish nation and the independence of the Polish state."[24] The general tenor of the articles published in the Catholic press was that all attempts to ease the conflict between Poles and Jews were unrealistic. There were even proposals to abandon the existing policy that acknowledged Jews as having the same rights as Poles and recognized them as equal citizens. The only diverging views dealt with the methods to be used in the anti-Jewish struggle. While part of the Catholic press (and hierarchy) advocated fighting "Jewish ideas," rather than the Jews as human beings, others went further and advocated "self-defense" even if it resulted in Jewish loss of life.[25]

The Polish government-in-exile was certainly aware of the anti-Jewish attitude of the devout Catholic Polish population; it was thus facing a quandary that was to grow with time. On the one hand, Prime Minister Władysław Sikorski's group knew that it could not denounce anti-Semitism in the home country without losing its influence on the population; on the other hand, abetting Polish hatred of the Jews meant incurring criticism in Paris, London, and particularly in the United States, where, the Polish government believed, the Jews were all-powerful. As for the future of Polish-Jewish relations it seems that Sikorski's men were giving up the hope, in 1940, that the Jews would help them in reclaiming the territories occupied by the Soviets. Some of them, moreover, hardly rejected the attitudes reported in the Karski memorandum.

In the meantime the social and economic situation of the approximately 250,000 Jews still living in Germany and annexed Austria was rapidly deteriorating. As we saw, already at the outbreak of the war, it was an impoverished, predominantly middle-aged or elderly community. Part of the male population had been drafted into compulsory labor and a growing number of families depended on welfare. Throughout the country the number of "Jew houses" was growing, as were the areas off-limits for Jews. The Jews of the Greater Reich were entirely segregated pariahs among some 80 million Germans and Austrians. Emigrating was their ever-present but rapidly dwindling hope.

On the first day of the war the Jews of Germany were forbidden to leave their homes after eight o'clock in the evening. "All police authorities in the Reich have taken this measure," a confidential instruction to the press explained, "because it has frequently happened that the Jews used the blackout to harass Aryan women."[26] On September 12 the Jews were ordered to shop only in special stores belonging to "reliable Aryans." Some of the store owners refused to cater to Jews, the SD reported from Cologne on September 29, until they were informed that they would not suffer any disadvantage from it. In that same city Jews could shop only from 8:00 to 9:30 a.m. "The mere presence of Jews in queues was felt as a provocation," the Bielefeld Gestapo explained on September 13: "One could not demand of any German to stand in front of a shop together with a Jew."[27] Five days later the Jews were ordered to build their own air-raid shelters. On Yom Kippur (September 23), the Jews had to hand in their radios. In November, after it occurred to the RSHA that Jews who had their radios confiscated could simply buy new ones, the names and addresses of all purchasers of new radios were registered. The radio issue was in and of itself the source of intense bureaucratic turmoil: How did the ruling apply to the non-Jewish spouses in a mixed marriage? What should be done about radios in a house still inhabited by both Jews and non-Jews? And what about the rights of Jewish wives whose Aryan husbands were fighting for the fatherland: Should they keep their radios or not? As for the distribution of the confiscated radios, elaborate hierarchies and priorities were established that had to take into account the rights of army units, party authorities, local grandees, and the like.

Jewish child nurses who still kept an office had to indicate on their doorplates that they were nurses for Jewish infants and children. From mid-December 1939 to mid-January 1940, Jews were deprived of the special food allocations for the holidays, receiving less meat and butter and no cocoa or rice. On January 3 they were forbidden to buy any meat or vegetables at all until February 4. A few weeks beforehand the food and agriculture ministers of all regions decreed that the Jews were not allowed to purchase any chocolate products or gingerbread.

Some anti-Jewish measures showed true creative "thinking." Thus the Reich Ministry of Education and Science announced on October 20, 1939, that, "in doctoral dissertations, Jewish authors may be quoted only when such quoting is unavoidable on scientific grounds; in such a case, however, the fact that the author is Jewish must be mentioned. In the bibliographies, Jewish and German authors are to be listed separately."[28] On February 17, 1940, a decree of the Ministry of the Interior authorized the training of Jewish female medical technicians or assistants, but only for Jewish institutions. However, they were not allowed to deal with [laboratory] cultures of live germs.

Full Jews were of course the prime targets of the regime's persecution policies. More complex was the situation of spouses and children in mixed marriages. Once the war started, the guidelines regarding mixed breeds of the first and second degrees were more confusing than ever: These mixed breeds were allowed to serve in the Wehrmacht and could even be decorated for bravery, but they were not allowed to fill positions of authority. As for the Jewish members of their families, they were not spared any of the usual indignities.

The Reich Association of the Jews in Germany remained in place as the war started. From the outset, however, its activities were entirely controlled by the Gestapo, particularly by Eichmann's Jewish Section. For all intents and purposes it was a Jewish Council on a national scale. It was the association which had to inform the Jewish communities of all Gestapo instructions, usually by way of the only authorized Jewish newspaper, the *Jüdisches Nachrichtenblatt*. The prime function of the association, until October 1941, was to foster and organize the emigration of Jews from Germany. But, as we saw, from the outset it was no less involved in welfare and education. After the beginning of the war state welfare allocations for needy Jews dropped sharply and most of the support had to be raised by the association. The pitiful "wages" paid to the tens of thousands of Jewish forced laborers could not alleviate the growing material distress. Furthermore, because Jewish students had been excluded from all German schools since November 1938, the association became solely in charge of the education of some 9,500 children and youngsters in the Old Reich.

On December 9, 1939, Klemperer recorded: "I was in the Jewish Community House, 3 Zeughausstrasse, beside the burned down and leveled synagogue, to pay my tax and Winter Aid. Considerable activity: the coupons for gingerbread and chocolate were being cut from the food ration cards. . . . The clothing cards had to be surrendered as well: Jews receive clothing only on special application to the Community. Those were the kind of small unpleasantnesses that no longer count. Then the Party official present wanted to talk to me: . . . You must leave your house by April 1; you can sell it, rent it out, leave it empty: that's your business, only you have to be out; you are entitled to a room. Since your wife is Aryan, you will be allocated two rooms if possible. The man was not at all uncivil, he also completely appreciated the difficulties we shall face, without anyone at all benefiting as a result—the sadistic machine simply rolls over us."[29]

While in Germany there was a continuity of Jewish leadership, in former Poland much of the prewar leadership was replaced, as we saw, when the Germans occupied the country and many Jewish community leaders fled. Both Chaim Rumkowski in Lodz and Adam Czerniaków in Warsaw were new to top leadership positions, and both were now appointed chairmen of the councils of their cities.

Mordechai Chaim Rumkowski's life to age sixty-two had been undistinguished: In business he apparently failed several times, in the Zionist politics of Lodz he did not leave much of an impact, and even his stewardship of several orphanages was criticized by some contemporaries. When the head of the prewar Lodz community, Leon Minzberg, fled, he was replaced by his deputy, and Rumkowski was elevated to the vice presidency of the community. It was Rumkowski, however, whom the Germans chose to lead the Jews of Lodz. The new "elder" appointed a council of thirty-one members. Within less than a month these council members were arrested by the Gestapo and shot. The hatred Rumkowski still inspired years after his death finds a telling expression in the insinuations of one of the earliest and most distinguished historians of the Holocaust, Philip Friedman, regarding this episode: "What was Rumkowski's part in the fate of the original council? Had he complained to the Germans about the intransigence of the council members? If so, did he know what was in store for them? These are grave questions, which we cannot answer on the basis of the evidence at our disposal."[30] A second council was set in place in February 1940.

Most contemporaries agree about Rumkowski's ambition, despotic behavior toward his fellow Jews, and his weird megalomania. These traits were vividly described by the diarist Emanuel Ringelblum (to whom we shall return), who recorded Rumkowski's visit to Warsaw on September 7, 1940: "Today there arrived from Lodz, Chaim, or, as he is called, 'King Chaim' Rumkowski, an old man of seventy, extraordinarily ambitious and pretty nutty. He recited the marvels of his ghetto. He has a Jewish kingdom there with 400 policemen, three jails. He has a foreign ministry and all other ministries too. When asked why, if things were so good there, the mortality is so high, he did not answer. He considers himself God anointed."[31]

In stark contrast to Rumkowski, Czerniaków's ordinariness was his most notable characteristic. Yet, his diary shows him to be anything but ordinary. His basic decency is striking in a time of unbridled ruthlessness. Not only did he devote every single day to his community, but he particularly cared for the humblest and the weakest among his four hundred thousand wards: the children, the beggars, the insane. An engineer by training, Czerniaków filled a variety of rather obscure positions and, over the years, also dabbled in city politics and in the Jewish politics of Warsaw. He was a member of the Warsaw City Council and of the Jewish Community City Council. As in Lodz, the chairman of the community fled at the outbreak of the war; Mayor Stefan Starzynski then nominated Czerniaków in his stead. On October 4, 1939, the fifty-nine-year-old Czerniaków was appointed head of the Warsaw Jewish Council.

Czerniaków could have left, but he stayed. In October 1939 he obviously could not foresee what would happen less than three years later, yet some of his witticisms have a premonitory tone: "Expulsions from Krakow," he writes on May 22, 1940. "The optimists, the pessimists and the sophists."[32] In Hebrew *soph* means "end." A witness tells that when the council convened for the first time, Czerniaków showed several members a drawer in his desk where he had put "a small bottle with 24 cyanide tablets, one for each of us, and he showed us where the key to the drawer could be found, should the need arise."[33]

CHAPTER 7

A New European Order

May 1940–December 1940

ON OCTOBER 22, 1940, the 6,500 Jews of the German provinces of Baden and the Saar-Palatinate were suddenly deported into nonoccupied France. According to a report from the prosecutor's office in Mannheim, on the morning of that day, eight local Jews committed suicide: Gustav Israel Lefo (age 74) and his wife, Sara Lefo (65), gas; Klara Sara Schorff (64) and her brother Otto Israel Strauss (54), gas; Olga Sara Strauss (61), sleeping pills; Jenny Sara Dreyfuss (47), sleeping pills; Nanette Sara Feitler (73), by hanging herself on the door of her bathroom; Alfred Israel Bodenheimer (69), sleeping pills.[1]

No major military operations had taken place from the end of the Polish campaign until early April 1940. The "winter war," which started with the Soviet attack against Finland in December 1939, ended in March 1940 after the Finns gave in to Soviet territorial demands in Karelia. This conflict in northern Europe had no direct impact on the major confrontation except possibly for strengthening Hitler's low opinion of the Red Army. During these same months of military inaction on the western front (the "phony war") optimism was rife in

London and in Paris, and consequently among Jewish officials who kept in touch with Western governments.

On April 9, in a sudden swoop, German troops occupied Denmark and landed in Norway. On May 10 the Wehrmacht attacked in the west. On the fifteenth the Dutch surrendered; on the eighteenth Belgium followed. On May 13 the Germans had crossed the Meuse River and, on May 20, they were in sight of the Channel coast, near Dunkirk. Some 340,000 British and French soldiers were evacuated back to England, thanks in part to Hitler's order to stop for three days before attacking and taking Dunkirk. At the time the decision appeared of "secondary importance," in German terms. In hindsight, it may have been one of the turning points of the war.

In early June the Wehrmacht moved south. On the tenth Benito Mussolini joined the war on Hitler's side. On the fourteenth German troops entered Paris. On the seventeenth French Prime Minister Paul Reynaud resigned and was replaced by his deputy, the elderly hero of World War I, Marshal Philippe Pétain. Without consulting his British ally, Pétain asked for an armistice. The German and Italian conditions were accepted, and on June 25, shortly after midnight, the armistice took effect. In the meantime the British government had been reshuffled. On May 10, the day of the German attack on the western front, Neville Chamberlain had been forced to resign; the new prime minister was Winston Churchill.

On July 19, in a triumphal address to the Reichstag, Hitler taunted England with a "peace offer." Three days later, in a radio broadcast, the foreign secretary, Lord Halifax (who a month beforehand had still been a supporter of a "peace of compromise"), rejected the German proposal and vowed that his country would continue to fight, whatever the cost. But did England have the military resources and did its population and its leadership have the resolve to pursue the war alone? None of this was obvious in the early summer of 1940. The appease-

ment camp remained vocal, and some highly visible personalities, the Duke of Windsor in particular, did not hide their
desire to come to terms with Hitler's Germany.

Stalin, who within days of the French collapse had occupied
the Baltic countries and wrung Bessarabia and northern Bukovina from Romania, snubbed Churchill's carefully worded
query about a possible rapprochement. The American scene
was contradictory. Roosevelt, an uncompromising "inter-
ventionist," had been nominated again as Democratic candi-
date at the Chicago convention on July 19. But in Congress
and among the American population, isolationism remained
strong; soon the America First Committee would give it a firm
political basis and a framework for militant propaganda. At
this stage even Roosevelt's reelection would be no guarantee
that the United States could move closer to war.

Throughout Europe, in occupied countries and among neu-
trals, a majority of the political elite and possibly a majority of
the populations did not doubt that Germany would soon prevail. Moreover many aspired to a "new order" and were open
to the "temptation of fascism."

The wide array of movements that came under the tag of
a new "Revolutionary Right" (as opposed to the traditional essentially conservative Right) did not spring only from a narrow
social background (the lower middle classes); inspired mainly
by fear of the mounting force of the organized Left on the one
hand and of the brutal and unaccountable ups and downs of
unrestrained capitalism on the other, the social background
of the New Right was wider and extended to parts of a disenchanted working class as well as to the upper middle classes
and to elements of the former aristocracy. It expressed violent
opposition to liberalism and to "the ideas of 1789," to social democracy and mainly to Marxism (later communism or bolshevism), as well as to conservative policies of compromise with
the democratic status quo; it searched for a "third way" that

would overcome the threats both of proletarian revolution and capitalist takeover. Such a "third way" had to be authoritarian in the eyes of the new revolutionaries; it carried a mystique of its own, usually an extreme brand of nationalism and a vague aspiration for an antimaterialist regeneration of society.

Whereas the antimaterialist, antibourgeois spirit surfaced both on the Right and among segments of the Left in pre–World War I Europe, and found strong support among Catholics and Protestants alike, its fusion with exacerbated nationalism, and the related cult of camaraderie, heroism, and death in the aftermath of the war, became standard fare of the New Right and of early fascism. Following the Russian Revolution of 1917, the fear of bolshevism added an apocalyptic dimension to the sense of looming catastrophe. It is in this context that the attraction of a "new order" (as the political expression of the "third way"), under the leadership of a political savior who could rescue a world adrift from the weak and corrupt paralysis of liberal democracy, grew in the minds of many.

The world economic crisis of the thirties merely brought the fears and the urges of earlier decades to a head: The Fascist regime in Italy, inaugurated by Mussolini's so-called march on Rome in October 1922, was outdistanced by the considerably more powerful and impressive Nazi phenomenon; the "new order" was becoming a formidable political and military reality. The defeat of France seemed to confirm the superiority of the new world over the old, of the new values over those that had so utterly failed.

The Danish government, kept in place by the Germans, issued a statement in July 1940 expressing its "admiration" for the "great German victories [that] have brought about a new era in Europe, which will result in a new order in a political and economic sense, under the leadership of Germany."[2] For several months the Belgian government, which had taken refuge in London, considered the possibility of rejoining King

Leopold III (who had stayed) and accepting German domination; in October 1940 it finally chose opposition and exile. By then Pétain's government had openly taken the path of collaboration with the Reich. As for the populations in most of Western Europe, they soon accommodated to the presence of an occupation army widely praised for its correct, even polite behavior.

Significant for the ready acceptance of a "new order" was the coalition between its carrier and most of the right-wing authoritarian regimes on the Continent. Common enemies, mainly communism, liberalism, and "materialism," superseded the social (and ideological) antagonisms existing between the traditional elites and the extremism inherent in Nazism or even Italian fascism. This alliance included, to various degrees, the main ingredients of modern anti-Jewish hostility; the "new order" was also becoming an intrinsically anti-Jewish new order.

Within this momentous ideological evolution, the influence of the churches and particularly that of the pope came to play a distinctive role. As mentioned, a few months before his death Pius XI requested the preparation of an encyclical against Nazi racism and anti-Semitism. He was presented with a draft of the encyclical *Humani Generis Unitas* as he lay dying. His successor must have known of the existence of the document and probably decided to shelve it.

Pius XII's attitude toward Germany and mainly toward the Jews has often been contrasted with that of his predecessor. The impression created was that Pius XII's policy was unusual, even aberrant. But in fact, Pius XI, as legate nuncio to Poland in the immediate aftermath of World War I, and during most of his pontificate, expressed unconcealed anti-Jewish attitudes, as had been the case among most of his predecessors in the modern era. The change that led to *Humani Generis Unitas* occurred during the last years of Pius XI's life and created a growing rift with the Curia, the Roman Jesuits of *Civiltà Cattolica*, the Vatican daily, *Osservatore Romano*, and possibly his secretary of state, Eugenio Pacelli, the future Pius XII. Thus it can safely be said that Pacelli himself, as secretary of state and later as pope, merely followed a well-established path.

The new pontiff, however, added a personal imprint and initiatives of his own to a well-honed tradition. Distant, autocratic, and imbued with the sense of his own intellectual and spiritual superiority, Pacelli was as fiercely conservative in politics as in church matters. Nonetheless he was considered an able diplomat during his tenure as nuncio in Munich (1916–20) and then in Berlin in the 1920s. His drive for centralization and for the control of the Vatican bureaucracy over the national churches led him to strive for a concordat with Germany, even at the cost of sacrificing the German Catholic Party in the process. The Concordat, as we have seen, was signed in July 1933 and ratified in September. The German signature was Adolf Hitler's.

Once Pacelli was elected pope, some of his first initiatives confirmed the persistence of an ultraconservative stance and showed an unmistakable desire to placate Germany. Thus in a radio broadcast in mid-April 1939, the pontiff congratulated the Spanish people on the return of peace and the achievement of victory (that of Franco). A few months later he rescinded his predecessor's excommunication of the French antirepublican, monarchist, furiously nationalist, and anti-Semitic Action Française. And on April 20, 1939, as a mark of special esteem, the pope congratulated Hitler on his fiftieth birthday in a message sent in German, a very unusual step.

The Nazi-Soviet pact, on the other hand, must have reinforced Pius XII's personal lack of confidence in the Nazi leader; it may explain why the pontiff maintained brief contacts with German opposition groups planning an anti-Hitler coup in the fall of 1939. From the outset, however, the pope was faced with a very different and no less pressing issue: What should his diplomatic and public reaction be in the face of ever more massive Nazi crimes?

Pius XII made it clear to his entourage that he would be personally in charge of the relations with Hitler's Germany. Intentionally, no doubt, the pro-Nazi and anti-Semitic Cesare Orsenigo was kept as nuncio in Berlin. Regarding the entire gamut of Nazi crimes, Pius's policy during the first phase of the war may be defined as an exercise in selective appeasement. The pope did not take a public stand about the murder of the mentally ill, but he made a plea for the "beloved Polish people" in his encyclical *Summi Pontificatus* of October 20, 1939. Concerning both euthanasia and the fate of the Catholics in Poland, the Vatican also appealed to Berlin via the nuncio (mainly about Poland) or in urgent pleas to the German bishops. In letters of December 1940 to both Cardinal Adolf Bertram of Breslau and Bishop Konrad Preysing of Berlin, Pius XII expressed his shock at the killing of the mentally ill. In both cases and otherwise, nothing was said about the persecution of the Jews.

Nazi domination over the newly conquered European territories was further facilitated by its rather pragmatic modes of control, which differed from country to country. Thus Denmark kept a semblance of freedom until the summer of 1943. Hitler had decided on this peculiar course to avoid unnecessary difficulties in a country strategically important (the passage to Norway and Sweden and the proximity of the English coast), "racially related," and mainly an essential supplier of agricultural products (more than 15 percent of Germany's needs by 1941). Norway and Holland—although also countries of "related racial stock"—were governed by Nazi Party appointees, Reichskommissare, who were both satraps and ideological envoys. Belgium and northern France remained under the authority of the Wehrmacht. The central and southern parts of France, on the other hand, were granted a measure of autonomy under Marshal Pétain's leadership; they became "Vichy France." Germany de facto annexed Luxembourg and kept the fate of the French provinces of Alsace and Lorraine in abeyance. A southeastern part of France was occupied by the Italian army, as a reward for Mussolini.

The Nazi terror system now controlled directly (or with the assistance of its satellites) around 250,000 to 280,000 Jews remaining in the Greater Reich, 90,000 in the Protectorate, 90,000 in Slovakia, 2.2 million in the German-occupied or -annexed parts of ex-Poland, 140,000 in Holland, 65,000 in Belgium, about 330,000 in both French zones, between 7,000 and 8,000 in Denmark, and 1,700 in Norway. Thus, at the beginning of the summer of 1940, a total population of almost 3,200,000 Jews was for all intents and purposes already caught in Hitler's clutches.

Germany's new victories triggered a wave of fear among the Jews of Europe. "On the Eiffel Tower, the swastika," the Romanian Jewish writer Mihail Sebastian noted in his diary two days after the fall of Paris. "At Versailles, German sentries. At the Arc de Triomphe, the 'unknown soldier' with a German 'guard of honor.' But the terrible things are not the trophies or the acts of provocation: they could even arouse and maintain a will to survive among the French population. What scares me more is the 'harmony' operation that is about to follow. There will be newspapers, declarations and political parties that present Hitler as a friend and sincere protector of France. When that time comes, all the panic and all the resentments will find release in one long pogrom. Where can Poldy [Sebastian's brother who lived in Paris] be? What will he do? What will become of him? And what of us here?"[3]

In 1940 the thirty-three-year-old Sebastian was already a

well-known novelist and playwright on the Romanian literary stage. He lived in Bucharest, in close touch with the local intellectual elite—some of whose members, such as E. M. Cioran and Mircea Eliade, were to achieve world fame in the postwar years—an elite massively drawn to fascism in Romanian garb and to the most vulgar and violent anti-Semitism. Yet Sebastian, strangely enough, tried to find excuses and rationalizations for the behavior and insulting outpourings of his former friends and, in fact, ongoing acquaintances. Whatever the peculiarity of Sebastian's forgiveness, his diary offers the faithful image of a society that was to support Nazi-like measures, including mass murder.

In Warsaw, Czerniaków noted the rapidly changing situation without adding comments. While Sierakowiak did not leave any notes for these months, Kaplan moved from wrath to despair and from despair to very-short-lived hope. Wrath at Mussolini's move, on June 11: "The second hooligan has dared, as well! Whether voluntarily or by compulsion it is difficult to say, but the fact remains that Benito Mussolini, the classic traitor, the Führer's minion, the monkey-leader of the Italian nation, has gone to war against England and France."[4]

Then came the dreadful news of Paris's fall and of the French demand for an armistice: "Even the most extreme pessimists," Kaplan noted on June 17, "among whom I include myself, never expected such terrible tidings." The unavoidable question followed: "Will England keep fighting?" Kaplan was doubtful at first, then again, three days later, filled with intense hope: "The war is not over yet! England is continuing to fight, and even France will henceforth carry on her battle from the soil of her empire, her colonies in all parts of the world." Thereupon Kaplan added an astute insight: "The Germans are, of course, the heroes of the war, but they require a short war; as they say in their language, a *Blitzkrieg*. They could not survive a long war. Time is their greatest enemy."[5]

As among Jews everywhere, Klemperer's mood switched from hope to despair and from despair to hope again with every bit of news, every rumor, even every chance remark. After England's rejection of Hitler's "peace offer," there was widespread belief that England was doomed among Germans—and among many Jews: "In the Jews' House," he noted on July 24, "I always play the role of the optimist. But I am not quite sure of my position at all." In the same entry Klemperer went on: "Peculiarity of the Jews' House that each one of us wants to fathom the mood of the people and is dependent on the last remark picked from the barber or butcher, etc. (I am too!). Yesterday a philosophical piano tuner was here doing his job: It will not last a long time, England is a world empire— even if there were to be a landing . . . immediately my heart felt lighter."[6]

Although throughout 1940 Hitler continued to maintain public restraint regarding the Jews, the Jewish issue was far from forgotten. As Himmler was busying himself with re-settlement plans, Hitler acquiesced in his henchman's memorandum of May 27, 1940, entitled "Some Thoughts on the Treatment of the Alien Populations in the East." The "ethnic mush" under German control would be deported to the General Government and the Jews would be shipped off to some colony "in Africa or elsewhere."[7] The island of Madagascar, which belonged to defeated France, seemed to be an obvious destination; such a deportation had for decades been a pet plan of anti-Semites of all hues (including French foreign minister Georges Bonnet).

For a short while, preparations moved into high gear, at least on paper. One of the main "planners" was the second-in-command to Martin Luther, chief of "Division Germany" of the Wilhelmstrasse, the fanatical anti-Semite Ernst Rade-macher. One sentence in his lengthy memorandum of July 3 should be kept in mind: "The Jews [in Madagascar] will remain in German hands as a pledge for the future good conduct of the members of their race in America."[8] The Madagascar fiction was abandoned over the next months, as the defeat of Great Britain was nowhere in sight.

At the same time Jewish emigration from the Reich and from occupied countries continued. As mentioned, Eichmann became the "chief of operations," in charge of both the deportations and the emigration of Jews (in Nazi eyes the two were identical at this stage). It is in line with the overall policy of expulsion that, particularly in the fall of 1939, Jews deported to the Lublin area were often driven by the SS over the Soviet demarcation line or were allowed to flee into Soviet-occupied territory. By mid-October 1939, however, this possibility tapered off, mainly due to a change in Soviet asylum policy. There also was a semiclandestine route out of Poland over the border into Hungary; it allowed for the flight of several thousand Jews but, as we shall see, not to lasting safety. During the first few months of the war Jews from Poland or Polish areas annexed to the Reich could also leave by applying for visas, as was the case in the Reich and the Protectorate.

The Germans soon established their priorities. In April 1940, as departures and border crossings became increasingly difficult, Heydrich issued a first set of guidelines: intensification of Jewish emigration from the Reich, except for men of military age; limitation and control of the emigration to Palestine; no emigration of Polish or ex-Polish Jews in concentration camps; no further deportation of Jews into the General Government. On October 25, 1940, Jewish emigration from the General Government was forbidden, mainly to keep the emigration possibilities from the Reich as open as possible.

In most cases, in that summer of 1940, immigration to the United States became a hopeless quest. It seems that the fear of enemy agents infiltrating the country as refugees had a significant influence on American decisions. No clash of policies existed between the bureaucratic level and the political level. Roosevelt's advisers believed in the "fifth column" threat as intensely as did the majority of the population swayed by a hysterical press campaign.

The stringent restrictions on entry to the United States had ripple effects on the policies of other states in the hemisphere. Jews intent on fleeing Germany after the beginning of the war often tried to obtain visas for Latin American countries, such as Chile, Brazil, Mexico, and Cuba. The end result was usually a matter of bribes and sheer luck. But in 1940 Chile and Brazil closed their doors, in part as a result of internal political pressures, also, however, because the United States had warned both governments that German agents could enter under the guise of Jewish refugees. The desperate candidates for emigration now helplessly watched the Western Hemisphere turn increasingly off-limits, except for a happy few.

Three routes remained available: illegal immigration to Palestine; semilegal transit via Spain and Portugal; or, as mentioned before, via Lithuania and the USSR to Japan and Shanghai, from where these Jews tried to reach overseas destinations, with the United States or some other countries of the Western Hemisphere still remaining the ultimate goal.

The unsavory but necessary cooperation between the leaders of the *Yishuv* and the Nazis (in the form of the Haavarah Agreement) took an unusual turn after Great Britain had closed the doors of Palestine to mass Jewish immigration for fear of pushing the Arab world toward the Axis: Heydrich and emissaries from the *Yishuv* joined forces to organize the illegal departure of Jews from Europe to Palestine. On the German side Eichmann was in charge of the practical aspects of the operation, including the negotiations with Jewish organizations: the Mossad L'Aliyah Beth (the agency for illegal immigration of the Jewish authorities in Palestine), the right-wing

Revisionist Zionists, or the American Jewish Joint Distribution Committee (JDC, or "Joint"), which financed a major part of the rescue effort.

For the Mossad and for the political leadership in Palestine, the outbreak of the war created an insoluble dilemma: Help Jews to flee Europe to Palestine in direct opposition to the British, while helping the British in their struggle against Germany and Italy. No clear priorities were set and, more often than not, the Mossad's operations were ill prepared almost to the point of recklessness. All in all, after the beginning of the war, less than thirteen thousand Jews managed to leave the Reich and the Protectorate for Palestine, and only part reached their destination. In March 1941 the Germans put an end to the common venture.

From the outset the British authorities were determined to foil any such illegal immigration attempts, in view of potential Arab reactions. That a number of high officials, particularly in the Colonial Office, were far from being philo-Semitic added an element of harshness to British policy. Measures aimed at deterring refugee ships from running the navy's blockade of the coast of Palestine became even more determined once Britain stood alone. In the fall of 1940 the Colonial Office decided that the illegal immigrants who succeeded in reaching Palestine would be deported to the island of Mauritius in the Indian Ocean and put in barrack camps surrounded by barbed wire. In response the Yishuv leadership hoped to arouse public opinion, mainly in the United States, by an act of defiance. In November 1940 explosives were affixed to the hull of the *Patria*, about to sail to Mauritius with its cargo of illegal immigrants, in order to disable it and prevent its departure. The ship sank and 267 refugees drowned; the remaining passengers were allowed to stay in Palestine, the only exception to the deportation policy.

For Jews another route to safety was over the Pyrenees. During the days just preceding and following the armistice this route was the easiest way to leave France. Approximately twenty-five to fifty refugees per day were allowed to cross the Spanish border if they carried valid passports and a visa to a country of final destination. Soon, however, the passage through Spain became conditional on French exit visas that could take months to obtain, due to a peculiar twist of French administrative sadism. Other restrictions followed: From November 1940, each Spanish transit visa needed permission from Madrid; the authorization from the American consulate in Marseille, for example, was not sufficient anymore. These Spanish regulations lasted throughout the war and did not discriminate between Jews and non-Jews. Ultimately the passage through Spain meant salvation for tens of thousands of Jews.

Portugal was even more restrictive. But while the Portuguese dictator Antonio del Oliveira Salazar ordered stringent anti-immigration measures, Portugal's consuls in several European countries delivered thousands of visas, notwithstanding Lisbon's explicit instructions. Some, like the consul general in Bordeaux, Aristides de Sousa Mendes, were to pay for their courage with their careers.

While Jews from the Reich and Western Europe were desperately trying to leave the Continent, as we saw, an unexpected and sudden deportation of 6,500 Jews from two German provinces, Baden and the Saar-Palatinate, was ordered by Hitler in October 1940. The operation, organized by the RSHA, ran smoothly and was hardly noticed by the population. Without any consultation with Vichy, the deportees were shipped to French camps in the nonoccupied zone (to which we shall return); there the cold weather, the lack of food, and the absence of the most elementary hygienic conditions took a growing toll. To the French authorities the Germans explained that these Jews would be sent to Madagascar in the near future.

It seems that Hitler had decided to take advantage of a clause in the armistice agreement with France that foresaw the expulsion of the Jews of Alsace-Lorraine into the unoccupied zone. The October 1940 expulsion was an "extension" of that clause, as Baden, the Palatinate, and the Saar, adjacent to the annexed French provinces, were meant to become part of the same *Gau*. The Jews of Alsace-Lorraine had already been expelled on July 16, 1940. Thus the new *Gau* Baden-Alsace would be entirely "free of Jews." On April 4, 1941, on Himmler's order, the property and assets belonging to the Jews deported from the two provinces were impounded.

Two days after the beginning of the deportations, Conrad Gröber, the Archbishop of Freiburg, wrote to the papal nuncio in Berlin, Cesare Orsenigo: "Your Excellency will have heard of the events of the last days concerning the Jews. What pained me most as Catholic bishop is that a great number of Catholic Jews were compelled to abandon home and work and to face an uncertain future far away, with only 50 pounds of movable property and 100 RM. In most cases, these are praiseworthy Catholics who appeal by way of my letter to the Holy Father to ask him . . . to change their lot or at least to improve it. . . . I urgently ask your Excellency to inform the Holy See of the fate of these Catholic Christians [*sic*]. I also ask your Excellency to use personally your diplomatic influence."[9] No answer is on record, either from the nuncio or from the pope.

While considering the deportation of all European Jews to Madagascar and ordering the expulsion of Jews from two German provinces to Vichy France, the supreme leader of the Greater German Reich did not miss any detail regarding the fate of the Jews living in his own backyard. On April 8, 1940, Hitler ordered that half-Jews—even men married to Jewish or half-Jewish spouses—be transferred from active service to Wehrmacht reserve units. Quarter-Jews could be maintained in active service and even promoted. Yet before the order could be implemented, the western campaign transformed the situation: Many Jewish soldiers received citations for courage. The Nazi leader had no choice and, in October 1940, had them turned into "full-blooded Germans," set on a par with their fellow German soldiers. The status of their Jewish relatives, however, would remain unchanged.

During the same weeks and months, most German state and party agencies were competing to make life ever harder for the Jews of the Reich. On July 7, 1940, the Reich minister of postal services and communications forbade Jews to keep telephones, "with the exception of 'consultants,' 'caretakers of the sick,' and persons belonging to privileged mixed marriages."[10] On October 4 the remaining rights of Jews as creditors in judicial proceedings were canceled. On October 7 Göring, as commander of the Luftwaffe, ordered that in air-raid shelters "the separation [of the Jews] from the other inhabitants be ensured either by setting aside a special area, or by a separation within the same area."[11] On November 13, 1940, Jewish shoemakers were allowed to work again in order to take some of the pressure off German shoemakers, but they could cater to Jewish clients only. As for German shoemakers who belonged to the party or affiliated organizations, they were not allowed to repair the shoes of Jews. Those who were not party members, "were to decide according to their conscience."[12] On the fifteenth of the same month, Himmler instructed all members of the German police to see *Jew Süss* during the winter. On December 12 the minister of the interior ordered that all mentally ill Jewish patients should henceforth be confined to one institution, Sayn-Bensdorf, in the Koblenz district, which belonged to the Reich Association of Jews in Germany. This was becoming technically possible as, since June, a great number of Jewish mental patients were being sent to their death.

On July 4, 1940, the police president of Berlin issued an order limiting the shopping time for Jews to one hour per day, from

4:00 to 5:00 p.m. "In regard to this police order," the decree indicated, "Jews are persons whose food cards are marked with a J or with the word ' "Jew.' "[13] In Dresden the shopping hours for Jews were not yet restricted at the beginning of the summer of 1940, but the J card was a constant problem. On July 6 Klemperer noted: "It is always horrible for me to show the J card. There are shops . . . that refuse to accept the cards. There are always people standing beside me who see the J. If possible I use Eva's 'Aryan' card. . . . We go for short walks after our evening meal and utilize every minute until exactly 9 p.m. [the summer curfew hour for Jews]. How anxious I was, in case we got home too late! . . . No one knows exactly what is allowed, one feels threatened everywhere. Every animal is more free and has more protection from the law."[14]

Under the hail of new regulations Jews in the Reich did not know exactly what was allowed and what was forbidden. Even the "Jewish Cultural Association" (Kulturbund) was often at a loss regarding what could be included in its programs. Thus, in mid-September 1939, after his first meeting with the overseer of the Kulturbund's activities, Erich Kochanowski from the Propaganda Ministry, the new artistic director of the association, Fritz Wisten, wrote in mock confusion about the contradictory and absurd instructions imparted to him. The performance of Ferenc Molnár's play *The Pastry Chef's Wife* was forbidden, as all plays with an "assimilatory" tendency ("assimilatory" meaning here encouragement for Jews to stay in Germany and assimilate to its society and culture). "I cannot see," Wisten wrote, "any assimilatory aims in 'The Pastry Chef's Wife.' "[15]

Although the ubiquitous propaganda minister was probably the source of the ever changing directives given to the Kulturbund, throughout the first half of 1940 Goebbels's attention seems to have been strongly focused, as it had been since October 1939, upon the production of his three anti-Semitic films. Hitler was regularly consulted and regularly demanded changes.

The premiere of *The Rothschilds* had taken place in July. Within two weeks, however, it became clear that the film had to be reworked and better focused. When it reappeared a year later it had finally received its full designation: *The Rothschilds: Stocks at Waterloo*. It was a story of Jewish world financial power and profiteering by the exploitation of misery and war.

The most effective of all Nazi anti-Jewish productions was *Jud Süss (Jew Süss)*. In the film Süss (in reality, Joseph Oppenheimer) befriended a Hapsburg military hero who became Duke of Württemberg in 1772; the duke appointed Süss his financial adviser. Some of the most basic Nazi anti-Semitic themes were the leitmotifs of the brilliantly directed and performed "historical" fabrication. Süss, played by Ferdinand Marian, opens the gates of Stuttgart to hordes of Jews, extorts money from the duke's subjects by the most devious means and seduces any number of beautiful German maidens. When the duke suddenly dies of a stroke, Süss is arrested, put on trial, sentenced to death, and hung in a cage. The Jews are expelled from Württemberg.

Jud Süss was launched at the Venice Film Festival in September 1940 to extraordinary acclaim; it received the "Golden Lion" award and garnered rave reviews. "We have no hesitation in saying that if this is propaganda, then we welcome propaganda," wrote then-young film critic Michelangelo Antonioni. "It is a powerful, incisive, extremely effective film. . . . There is not a single moment when the film slows, not one episode in disharmony with another: it is a film of complete unity and balance. . . . The episode in which Süss violates the young girl is done with astonishing skill."[16] The popular success of the film was overwhelming: By 1943, the number of German viewers had reached 20.3 million.

Ten days after the Reichsführer-SS had recognized the outstanding educational value of *Süss*, the third major screen production of the anti-Jewish campaign was completed: On November 29 *The Eternal Jew* opened throughout the Reich. The posters advertising the opening night in the capital carried the following warning: "As in the 6.30 p.m. presentation original images of Jewish animal slaughtering are shown, a shortened version presented at 4.00 p.m. is recommended to sensitive natures. Women are allowed only to the 4.00 p.m. presentation."[17]

In a particularly horrendous sequence of the film swarms of rats scurried through cellars and sewers, and, in rapid alternation, hordes of Jews moved from Palestine to the most remote corners of the world. The text was on a par: "Where rats turn up," the comment on that scene went, "they spread diseases and carry extermination into the land. They are cunning, cowardly and cruel; they mostly move in large packs, exactly as the Jews among the people."[18] Even worse was the ritual slaughter scene depicting the slow death throes of cattle and sheep, bathing in their own blood, heads partly severed, throats slit open while the laughing faces of the Jewish ritual slaughterers (filmed, let us remember, like the synagogue sequences, in the Jewish quarter of Lodz) were set in repeated contrast to the pitiful stares of the dying animals.

Notwithstanding dutifully positive press reviews, *The Eternal Jew* was a commercial failure. The SD reports from many regions of Germany and from Austria were unanimous: The horror scenes disgusted the viewers; the documentary was considered nerve racking; after having seen *Jud Süss* shortly beforehand, most people were saturated with "Jewish filth." Yet the commercial success of *Jud Süss* and the limited commercial appeal of *The Eternal Jew* should not be viewed as contrary results in terms of Goebbels's intentions. Images from both films were endlessly replicated in Nazi anti-Semitic posters or publications, all over the Reich and occupied Europe. The scurrying rats of *The Eternal Jew* or its hideously twisted Jewish faces may have ultimately settled in the "collective imagination" of European audiences at greater depth than the plot of *Jud Süss*. In both cases the goal was the same: to elicit fear, disgust, and hatred.

In the meantime the exclusion and segregation of the Jews in occupied Europe, east and west, became a top priority on the regime's agenda.

On May 1, 1940, the Germans hermetically sealed the shabbiest area of Lodz, the Baluty district; the 163,000 Jewish inhabitants of the city who had been ordered to move there were cut off from the outside world. The no-man's-land that surrounded the ghetto made any escape practically impossible. The city of Lodz as such, increasingly Germanized by a growing influx of Reich Germans and ethnic Germans—most of whom were enthusiastic Nazis—would certainly not have offered any hideout to a Jew. Thus, even more than in Warsaw, the Lodz ghetto would become a vast urban concentration and labor camp of sorts, without clandestine political or economic links to its surroundings, mostly deprived of information about the course of the war and the fate of Jews living and dying outside its own barbed-wire fence. As for the housing conditions in the ghetto, numbers are telling: apartments with drains, 613; with water pipes and drains, 382; with a toilet, 294; with toilet, drain, and bath, 49; lacking these amenities, 30,624.[19]

In the General Government, Frank had stopped the building of ghetto walls in the summer of 1940 in the belief that the Madagascar plan would materialize; by September he knew better. In a meeting with the heads of his administration, he announced his decision to enclose the ghetto in Warsaw. The ghetto was officially sealed off on November 16. The wall that surrounded it was built over a period of several months and paid for by the Jewish Council. The Poles who had lived in the area left; the Jews moved in. Some 380,000 Jews were now cut off from the world (their number, inflated by further arrivals from smaller towns or from the Warthegau, would peak at 445,000 in May 1941). The entire area comprised only 4.5 percent of the city; even this was later reduced.

By all counts the Warsaw ghetto was a death trap in the most concrete, physical sense. But cutting Warsaw off from the world also meant destroying the cultural and spiritual center of Polish Jewry and of Jewish life well beyond. Within the ghetto walls Emanuel Ringelblum, a professionally trained historian who, in the years before the war, helped set up the Warsaw branch of the Vilna Yiddish Scientific Institute (YIVO), began to document what was happening to the Jews of Poland. He was soon joined by others and a code name, Oneg Shabbat (Sabbath Rejoicing), was adopted, as the meetings usually took place on Saturday afternoons. Like so many other Jewish chroniclers of those days, the members of Oneg Shabbat, whether they sensed it or not, were assembling the materials for the history of their own end.

In France, Marshal Pétain's new regime introduced its first anti-Jewish measures, on its own initiative. Of the approximately 330,000 Jews of prewar France almost half were either foreigners or born of foreign parents. Among the foreigners 55,000 had arrived between 1933 and 1939. While anti-Semitism had been part of the French ideological landscape throughout the nineteenth century, first on the Left, then—increasingly so—on the conservative and the radical Right, it was the Dreyfus affair that turned it into a central issue of French politics in the 1890s and throughout the turn of the century. Yet World War I brought a significant decrease in anti-Jewish incitement and the immediate postwar years seemed to herald a new stage in the assimilation of native French Jewry into surrounding society.

The resurgence of a vociferous anti-Semitism from the early 1930s on was due to the presence of the deep-rooted anti-

Jewish tradition (even if dormant for a few years), to a series of financial-political scandals in which some Jews were conspicuously implicated (the Staviski affair, among others), to the rising "threat" of the Popular Front (a coalition of Left and Center Left parties) led by the Jewish socialist Léon Blum—and to Blum's brief government—to the influence of Nazi agitation and to the massive immigration of foreign Jews. A new sense of unease among the native Jews turned them against their non-French "brethren," whom they accused of endangering their own position. From then on, more forcefully than ever before, the native Jews—although they did set up an assistance organization for the refugees—insisted on establishing a clear dividing line between themselves and the newcomers.

On the morrow of the Hitler-Stalin pact, refugees in France, whether communists or not, Jews or not, came to be viewed with suspicion; the hysterical fear of a "fifth column" turned eager anti-Nazis into potential enemies. A law of November 18, 1939, ordered the internment of people "dangerous for the national defense." At the end of the same month some twenty thousand foreigners, among whom many Jewish German (or Austrian) male refugees were sent to camps or camplike facilities. Over the following weeks most of the internees were released, once their anti-Nazi credentials had been checked. Their freedom was cut short, however, by the German attack in the west. Once more, thousands of Jewish and other refugees from Hitler were assembled at Le Vernet, Les Milles, Gurs, Rivesaltes, Compiègne, and other camps at the very moment when the Germans shattered the French defenses. Some of the internees managed to escape the trap. Others never did: for them, the path to death began in the French camps, in the spring of 1940.

As France disintegrated, about one hundred thousand Jews joined the eight to ten million people fleeing southward. They had been preceded by some fifteen thousand Jews from Alsace-

Lorraine and around forty thousand Jews from Belgium, Holland, and Luxembourg. Overall the catastrophe was perceived in national terms; its specific Jewish aspect was, as yet, no more than a vague anxiety about the possibility of dire change.

On July 10 the French Republic scuttled itself. In the non-occupied zone of the country, the eighty-three-year-old Pétain became the leader of an authoritarian regime in which he was both "Chief of State" and head of government. Vichy, at the geographical center of the country, was chosen as the capital of the new state. The motto of the État Français, *Travail, Famille, Patrie* (work, family, fatherland), replaced that of the republic: *Liberté, Egalité, Fraternité.*

The hard-core French admirers of Nazism, the militant anti-Semites, stayed in Paris. Vichy was too conservative for them, too clerical, too hesitant in its subservience to Germany and its struggle against the Jews. This vociferous fringe did not recognize any limits. The writer Louis-Ferdinand Céline demanded an alliance with Germany, a racially kindred country in his view: "France," he proclaimed, "is Latin only by chance, through a fluke, through defeat . . . it is Celtic, three quarters Germanic. . . . Are we afraid of absorption? We shall never be more absorbed than we are right now. Are we to remain slaves of Jews, or shall we become Germanic once more?"[20] Céline's hatred of Jews was shared by a noisy phalanx of writers, journalists and public figures of all ilk; it was spewed day-in day-out, week after week, by an astonishingly high number of newspapers and periodicals with anti-Semitism as their core message. "To Finish with the Jews!" Lucien Rebatet titled an article in *Le Cri du peuple* on December 6, 1940.[21]

The strident collaborationism of the occupied zone was rarely heard in Vichy where, however, traditional anti-Semitism was rife from the very outset. Vichy's first anti-Jewish decree was issued on July 17. The new law limited civil service appointments to citizens born of a French father. On

July 22 a commission, chaired by Justice Minister Raphaël Ali-
bert, began checking all post-1927 naturalizations. On August
27 Vichy repealed the Marchandeau Law of April 21, 1939,
which forbade incitement on racial or religious grounds: The
floodgates of anti-Semitic propaganda reopened. On August
16 a National Association of Physicians was established whose
members had to be born of French fathers. On September 10
the same limitation was applied to the legal profession. And,
on October 3, 1940, Vichy, again on its own initiative, issued its
"Statute of the Jews."

In the opening paragraph of the statute, a Jew was defined
as any person descending from at least three grandparents of
the "Jewish race," or of two grandparents of the "Jewish race"
if the spouse too was Jewish (the German definition referred to
the grandparents' religion; the French, to their race). The following paragraphs listed all the public functions from which
Jews were barred. Paragraph 5 excluded Jews from all positions of ownership or responsibility in the press, theater, and
film. The next day, October 4, a law allowed the internment
of foreign Jews in special camps, if the administration of their
département so decided. A commission responsible for these
camps was established. Foreign Jews could also be assigned to
forced residence by the same regional administration. Vichy's
anti-Jewish legislation was generally well received by a majority of the population in the nonoccupied zone.

No Catholic prelate protested the "Statute of the Jews."
Some bishops even openly supported the anti-Jewish measures. In fact, on August 31, 1940, after being informed of
the forthcoming statute, the assembly of cardinals and archbishops meeting in Lyon discussed the "Jewish Question."
Émile Guerry, adjunct archbishop of Cambrai, summed up
the assembly's official stand: "In political terms, the problem
is caused by a community [the Jews] that has resisted all
assimilation. . . . The State has the right and the duty to

remain actively vigilant in order to make sure that the persistence of this unity [of the Jews] does not cause any harm to the common good of the nation."[22]

The most immediate reason for the French church's attitude stemmed from the unmitigated support granted by Pétain to the reinsertion of Catholicism into French public life, particularly in education. Whereas the republic had established the separation of church and state and thus banned the use of state funds for the support of religious schools, Vichy canceled the separation and all its practical sequels: In many ways Catholicism had become the official religion of the new regime.

In the occupied zone the Germans didn't remain idle either. On September 27, 1940, the "First Jewish Decree," defining as Jewish anybody with more than two grandparents of the Jewish religion or with two such grandparents and belonging to the Jewish faith or married to a Jewish spouse, was issued. The decree forbade Jews who had fled to the Vichy zone to return to the occupied zone; it instructed the French prefects to start a full registration of all Jews, as well as to identify Jewish businesses and register Jewish assets. On October 16 a "Second Jewish Decree" ordered the Jews to register their enterprises before October 31. From that day on Jewish stores carried a yellow sign reading "Jewish Business."

The registration of all Jews in the occupied zone started on October 3, the Jewish New Year. The vast majority of Jews, whether French or foreign, obeyed the orders without much hesitation. Some even turned the registration into a statement. The terminally ill philosopher, Henri Bergson, although exempted from the registration and for years far closer to Catholicism than to Judaism, dragged himself in slippers and dressing gown to the Passy police station in Paris to be inscribed as Jew; a Col. Pierre Brissac went in full military uniform. Pierre Masse, a former minister and senator of the Hérault Department wrote to Pétain on October 20: "I obey the laws of my country even if they are imposed by the invader." In his letter he asked the *maréchal* whether he should take away the officer stripes that several generations of his ancestors had earned in serving their country since the Napoleonic Wars.[23]

The two main personalities of the French Jewish community, the head of the Consistoire Central and the head of the Consistoire de Paris, Édouard and Robert de Rothschild, fled the country in June 1940. They left a Jewry in complete disarray in the feeble hands of the newly elected chief rabbi of France, Isaie Schwartz, and of the remaining members of the Consistoire, most of whom had sought refuge in the nonoccupied part of the country. Vague forebodings spread among native French Jews and, even more so, among the foreign Jews, whether they lived in the occupied or the nonoccupied zone. In fact nobody knew, in the summer of 1940, what to expect and what to fear.

Two very different chroniclers followed the events from "opposite" perspectives. The first, Raymond-Raoul Lambert, was a native French Jew belonging to an old Alsatian-Jewish family; the other, Jacques Biélinky, was born in Vitebsk and, after having been jailed in Russia for clandestine socialist activities, he arrived in France in 1909 as a political refugee. For the Germans, and for Vichy—both were first and foremost Jews. Lambert was French to the core: French schools, decorated front-line officer during World War I, briefly appointed to the Foreign Ministry; yet he remained consciously Jewish, even actively so: He organized the assistance to German Jews after 1933 and simultaneously was appointed editor in chief of *L'Univers Israélite*, the main periodical of the Jewish establishment, the Consistoire. When the war broke out, Lambert donned uniform once again, this time as a reserve officer.

Biélinky had been naturalized in 1927 and thus formally belonged to his adoptive France as much as Lambert. During the coming events, however, Biélinky's voice would be that of a

foreign Jew, of an *Ostjude*, to a point. He had worked as a journalist for various Jewish newspapers and although his formal
education had stopped with the heder [the traditional Jewish
religious elementary school] he acquired a solid knowledge of
painting, and it is as a reporter dealing with the Parisian artistic scene that he signed many of his articles. Between 1940
and 1943 Lambert's path would not be the same as Biélinky's;
their fate, however, would be identical in the end.

In two ways the situation of Dutch Jewry was different from
that of other Western countries at the onset of the German occupation. Whereas the Jews of Belgium were predominantly
foreign and one-half of the French community was not native,
in the Netherlands the twenty thousand foreign Jews represented only one-seventh of the Jewish population. Moreover,
even if some measure of traditionally religious anti-Semitism
lingered in the rural areas of Holland, in Amsterdam—where
half the Jews of the country were concentrated, and in larger
cities in general—anti-Jewish feelings did not lead to public in-
tolerance.

During the first months of the occupation, German domination seemed relatively mild. The Dutch were considered a kindred race who, ultimately, would be integrated into the greater
community of Nordic nations. The Dutch political scene was
not unfavorable either to the occupiers. Soon after the defeat a
major new party ("Union") received tentative acceptance from
the Germans and initiated a policy of moderate collaboration
not very different from the Vichy line.

It was in this "conciliatory" climate that the first anti-Jewish
measures were imposed by the Germans throughout the
summer of 1940. They did not seem ominous: Air-raid protection teams would no longer include Jews; Jews were forbidden
to work in Germany; Jews in the civil service could not be promoted, and no new appointments of Jews were allowed. But in
October the first standard German steps were taken: All civil

servants had to fill out forms about their racial origin, and an edict defining Jews, identical in essence to that of the Nuremberg laws, was proclaimed. It was from this stage on that the Dutch civil service as a whole displayed the compliance that would later have such fateful consequences. By mid-November all Jewish civil servants had been dismissed, and the Dutch Supreme Court voted to dismiss its own Jewish president. On October 21, 1940, the registration of Jewish businesses started. It was followed on January 10, 1941, by the compulsory registration of the Jews themselves; nearly everyone complied.

In Amsterdam the city council and municipal personnel at first went beyond the call of duty in obeying German demands: Although the Dutch law did not compel them to fill out the declarations of Aryan descent, all volunteered to do so in January 1941. Yet, when the Germans mentioned the possibility of establishing a ghetto in the city, the council expressed its opposition. In the meantime, however, a situation was developing, which, in principle, should have helped the German plans. Incited by the Germans, Dutch Nazis were initiating brawls in the Jewish neighborhoods of Amsterdam. On February 19, 1941, the owners of the "Koco" (Kohn and Cahn) ice-cream parlor in south Amsterdam mistook a German police unit for Dutch Nazis and sprayed them with ammonium gas. Three days later the Germans sealed off the Jewish quarter of the city and arrested 389 young Jewish men whom they deported to Buchenwald, then to Mauthausen: One survived.

Notwithstanding the widespread compliance with the new anti-Jewish measures, some members of the Dutch elites, mainly in academia and the churches, did protest. On November 26, 1940, Professor R. P. Cleveringa, the dean of the Law School at the University of Leiden, the oldest Dutch university, spoke in front of a packed hall in honor of his Jewish colleague, Professor E. M. Meijers, who, like all other Jewish professors, had been dismissed on German orders (as a civil servant). That afternoon the students in Leiden and Delft started a strike. Both universities were closed on German orders and some of the protesters, including Dean Cleveringa, were arrested.

As for the churches in Holland, a month before the manifestation in Leiden, the Dutch Protestant churches (Reformed churches), the Mennonites, and the Dutch Catholic Church addressed a jointly signed letter to Arthur Seyss-Inquart, Reichskommissar for the occupied Netherlands. After invoking Christian charity and the issue of converted Jews, the letter continued: "Finally, this issue [the statute of the Jews and the expulsion of Jews from public service] has also brought profound dismay because it applies to the people from which the Savior is born, . . . we turn to your Excellency, with the urgent request to take the necessary steps to cancel the aforementioned measures." The very last sentence may have been particularly galling for the Reichskommissar: "Besides, we wish to recall the solemn promise given by your Excellency to respect our national identity and not to impose on us a way of thinking that is foreign to us."[24] The text of the letter was read from the pulpits of all Reformed temples on the following Sunday. Simultaneously the first protest articles appeared in the Dutch clandestine press, calling upon the Dutch people to resist "this imported poison of hate against the Jews."[25] A few months later, one after the other, all the major clandestine publications in Holland joined in protest.

CHAPTER 8

A Tightening Noose

December 1940–June 1941

ON JUNE 15, 1941, in the afternoon, a week before the beginning of the assault against the Soviet Union, Goebbels was summoned to the Reich Chancellery. The Nazi leader's ruminations were first and foremost an exercise in self-reassurance: "The most powerful attack that history had ever seen," the minister recorded, " . . . what happened to Napoleon would not repeat itself . . . the Führer estimated that the entire campaign would take approximately 4 months; I think it will be much less." In Goebbels's view, the attack was a vital necessity both for global strategic reasons and no less so on ideological grounds: "It is not Czarism that will be brought back to Russia; an authentic socialism will replace Judeo-bolshevism. Every old Nazi will rejoice at the opportunity of witnessing these events. The pact with Russia was in fact a stain on our shield . . . what we have fought against throughout our life, we shall now exterminate. I say this to the Führer and he completely agrees with me." Suddenly Hitler added a comment as unexpected as it was untypical: "The Führer says," Goebbels recorded, "whether we are right or wrong, we must win. This is the only way. And, it is right, moral and necessary. And once we have won, who will ask us about the methods. In any case, we have so much to account for that we must win."[1]

Whether in the summer of 1940 Hitler had ever seriously considered the invasion of the British Isles (Operation Sea Lion) remains a moot question. Throughout those months the onslaught of the Luftwaffe against Britain's coastal defenses did not achieve the essential precondition for a landing: the control of the skies over southern England. The massive bombing of cities that followed, mainly the raids on London (the Blitz), did not break the population's morale, and in the fall the Battle of Britain was turning to the advantage of the Royal Air Force.

At the same time Hitler was considering his alternative strategy. After the defeat of France and the British rejection of his "peace proposal," the Nazi leader mentioned the global strategic impact of an attack against the Soviet Union on several occasions, particularly in the course of the military conference at the Berghof (Hitler's mountain retreat), on July 31, 1940. According to the notes of Gen. Franz Halder, cheif of the Army (OKH) General Staff, Hitler's argument ran as follows: "England's hope is Russia and America. If hope in Russia is eliminated, America also is eliminated because enormous increase in the importance of Japan in the Far East will result from the elimination of Russia."[2]

Yet, notwithstanding the order to start the military buildup for an attack in the east in the spring of 1941, Hitler still seemed to hesitate during the summer and fall of 1940. The Tripartite Pact, signed on September 27, 1940, between Germany, Italy, and Japan, was meant as a warning to the United States no less so than to the Soviet Union. But when, in mid-November 1940, the Soviet foreign minister, Vyacheslav Molotov, arrived in Berlin for negotiations, and when Hitler suggested a common front against Great Britain and the United States by turning the Tripartite Pact into a "Quadripartite" one, the Nazi leader may already have made up his mind. In any case Molotov steadily brought the discussions back to concrete issues: the full implementation of the 1939 agreement about the Soviet "sphere of interest," mainly in the Balkans (Bulgaria) and regarding Finland.

On December 18, 1940, the Nazi leader signed directive no. 21 and changed the previous code name of the attack on the Soviet Union from Fritz (presumably referring to the king of Prussia, Frederick the Great) to Barbarossa (the common appellation of the twelfth-century emperor Frederick I of the Hohenstaufen dynasty, who had embarked upon a crusade in the East against the infidels). The assault was to start on May 15, 1941.

There was another reason for acting rapidly. Roosevelt had been reelected for a third term in November. On December 14, in a press conference, the president used the garden hose metaphor: "If a neighbor's house is on fire, the man who owns a hose does not say: 'My garden hose costs fifteen dollars and you must pay me this sum before you can have it.' He simply lends his hose, helps to put out the fire and then takes the hose back. America," Roosevelt said, "would in the future lend some nations the equipment they needed for defending their lives and their freedom."[3] On December 17, on the eve of signing directive no. 21, Hitler told Gen. Alfred Jodl, deputy chief of staff of the OKW, that Germany should solve all continental problems in 1941, "because in 1942 the United States will be ready to intervene."[4]

Unexpected events modified the schedule set for the eastern campaign. On March 27, 1941, two days after Yugoslavia adhered to the Tripartite Pact, a military coup unseated the pro-German government in Belgrade. Hitler ordered immediate retaliation: Belgrade was bombed to rubble and the Wehrmacht rolled south. Yugoslavia and Greece were occupied, Bulgaria joined the Axis, and the British forces that had landed in

Greece were driven from the Continent and from the island of Crete. However, the attack against the Soviet Union had to be postponed by several weeks. The date now set was June 22, the longest day of the year.

The murder plans aimed against the Jews on Soviet territory appear at first as intended to accelerate the collapse of the Soviet system as a whole, in line with the Nazi identification of bolshevism, its elites and its structures with the omnipresence of Jews in power positions. Otherwise Hitler's public declarations during the first half of 1941 do not indicate that the anti-Jewish dimension of the campaign was a goal in itself.

In his annual Reichstag speech, on January 30, 1941, the Nazi leader returned to his dire prophecy of January 1939 regarding the ultimate fate of European Jewry, this time without explicitly mentioning extermination. Rather he prophesied that the war would "put an end to Jewry's role in Europe"[5]—a statement that could have meant complete segregation, deportation—or indeed total extermination. And, in meetings with foreign statesmen, in speeches made throughout the last months of 1940, and during the military buildup period preceding June 22, 1941, Hitler's allusions to the Jews were perfunctory and brief. Nonetheless, on March 3, 1941, he sent back a first draft of the campaign guidelines prepared by the Wehrmacht Supreme Command (OKW), adding, among other points, that "the Jewish Bolshevik intelligentsia, as the oppressor of the past, had to be liquidated."[6] The gist of the Nazi leader's notorious speech to his top commanders on March 30 was basically identical but the Jews were not mentioned as such: "The Bolshevik commissars and the Bolshevik intelligentsia have to be exterminated. . . . The struggle must be aimed at the poison of disintegration."

Hitler's antibolshevik creed quite naturally merged with a no less cardinal ideological theme inherited from pan-Germanism: the need for the *Volk* to control as vast an eastern

Lebensraum (vital space) as racially and strategically necessary, possibly all the way to the Urals. The conquered space would be open to Germanic colonization and would supply the Reich with all the raw materials and food it needed. As for native populations, they would be enslaved, partly decimated, or deported to Siberia. With the victory over the Soviet Union, huge eastern colonization projects could be launched.

On March 26, 1941, on Hitler's command, Heydrich and the quartermaster general of the armed forces, Gen. Eduard Wagner, drafted an agreement granting the SS full autonomy for maintaining security behind the front, in the newly occupied territories. On May 13 Keitel, the OKW chief, signed the order limiting the jurisdiction of military courts over means used by the troops in their fight against the enemy. The execution of suspects henceforth depended upon decisions taken by units in the field. On May 19 Keitel ordered officers and soldiers to take "ruthless action" against the carriers of the Judeo-bolshevik ideology. Finally, on June 6, the guidelines for the treatment of political commissars (the "commissar order") were issued by the OKW: The commissars were to be shot.

As preparations for the attack went ahead full force, a new "territorial plan" regarding the Jews was in the making: the deportation of the Jews of Europe to the conquered Soviet territories, probably to the Russian Far North, instead of Madagascar. Rosenberg, since the end of March "special adviser" for the occupied territories in the East, mentioned as much in a speech of March 28, in which he alluded to the deportation of the Jews of Europe "under police surveillance" to a territory outside Europe "that could not be mentioned for the time being."[7]

After the beginning of the campaign against the Soviet Union, Hitler repeatedly mentioned the new territorial plan.

Yet, beforehand, on June 2, 1941, during his meeting with Mussolini, the Nazi leader again mentioned Madagascar as a concrete option.[8] It appears almost certain that Hitler was waiting
for the completion of the eastern campaign before taking a
final decision. In the meantime the emigration of Jews from
the Reich was still allowed but, on May 20, 1941, Göring forbade any such emigration from Belgium and France "in view
of the undoubtedly forthcoming final solution of the Jewish
question."[9]

Throughout early 1941, mainly in the largest ghettos of the
Warthegau and the General Government, hundreds of thousands of Jews lived on the edge of starvation. Among German
officials two contrary approaches to the crisis were envisioned.
On the one hand, the new chief administrator of the Lodz
ghetto, Hans Biebow, favored a level of economic activity that
would grant at least minimum subsistence to its population;
on the other, Biebow's own deputy did not mind letting the
Jews starve to death. Arthur Greiser, the Warthegau's Gauleiter, opted for Biebow's policy; Biebow's deputy, Alexander
Palfinger, was transferred to Warsaw.

The path of reorganization was not clear, however, even
after the Gauleiter's decision to support a "productionist"
policy, in historian Christopher Browning's terms. Greiser
himself displayed an unusual talent for extortion: He levied
a 65 percent tax on all Jewish wages. Moreover local German
agencies and businesses withheld raw materials or food from
the ghetto (or delivered substandard products and pocketed
the difference). It was only in the late spring of 1941 that
Biebow was able to impose the regulations he had been demanding: "For working Jews, 'Polish rations' were to be a
minimum; nonworking Jews were to receive the long-prom-
ised 'prison fare.'"[10]

Rumkowski's mistakes sometimes added to the chronic

starvation. According to a ghetto survivor, the population was particularly incensed by the potatoes affair. "A lot of potatoes were brought into the ghetto," Israel U. told the American psychologist David Boder in a 1946 interview. "When Rumkowski was asked why he didn't distribute them, he answered: 'you have no business to meddle in my affairs. I will distribute the potatoes when I want.' Frosts came and the potatoes became rotten and they had to be thrown away. They were buried. And afterwards for three years people still searched for potatoes at this spot where they lay buried. Moreover, the people talked themselves into believing that they tasted better that way, because the water had evaporated from the potatoes."[11]

Over time, however, the chairman imposed a measure of equality among the inhabitants that did contrast with the situation in Warsaw. Even the elder's most adamant ideological opponents noted his initiatives with a derision tempered by acquiescence: "Rumkowski is leaving for Warsaw to bring doctors and is reorganizing the food-distribution system in the ghetto," Sierakowiak wrote on May 13. "The number of food cooperatives is increasing; separate vegetable units are being created, while the bread and other food units are being combined. Creation of new squares, lawns, and even cobblestone and construction works completes the 'Spring Program' in the ghetto, marching in 'glory on the road of ascent and highest achievement.' "[12]

Notwithstanding all "productivization" efforts, the food-supply situation never improved beyond chronic starvation for much of the population. We have some knowledge of everyday life from individual records but mainly from the detailed *Chronicle* in which, regularly, from January 1941 to July 1944, a group of "official" diarists (appointed by Rumkowski) wrote down what they considered of significance for "future historians." The chroniclers reported the events of everyday life and used documents assembled in the ghetto archives, a vast and ongoing collection of all available information pertinent to the ghetto, and to the life and work of the megalomaniac Rumkowski. Although they avoided comments on the material they thus kept for history, the chroniclers—by their very presentation of the evidence—told a story whose implications the reader could not miss.

In the first entry of the *Chronicle*, on January 12, 1941, the authors, among many more important items, noted a minor but telling incident: "Appearing at one of the precincts of the Order Service, an 8-year-old boy filed a report against his own parents, whom he charged with not giving him the bread ration due to him. The boy demanded that an investigation be conducted and that the guilty parties be punished."[13]

In Warsaw the lack of food became catastrophic in March 1941. Like his counterpart in the Warthegau, Frank had to take a decision; and he made the same choice as Greiser. A decree of April 19 reorganized the German administration of the ghetto: District Governor Ludwig Fischer appointed the young attorney Heinz Auerswald as "commissar for the Jewish district of Warsaw," directly under his own orders. Moreover a *"Transferstelle* for overseeing the ghetto's economic relations to the exterior" was set up as an independent institution under the management of the banker Max Bischoff. Needless to say the new authorities had but little control upon the demands and initiatives of the ever-present Security Police and SD.

It is in this administrative context that Bischoff launched his new economic policy, with some measure of success. The value of exports from the ghetto increased from four hundred thousand zlotys in June 1941 to 15 million in July 1942, when the deportations started. Most of this production came from Jewish firms and not from German firms in the ghetto employing Jews. The same computation indicates that the number of productively employed Jews in the ghetto rose from 34,000 in September 1941 to more than 95,000 in July 1942.

Notwithstanding this "economic upswing," as in Lodz, the minimum food level for the entire ghetto population was never ensured. The *Information Bulletin* of the Polish underground published a leading article on May 23, 1941, that seems to give a faithful description of the situation, as seen from the "outside." "Further crowding has resulted in conditions of ill-health, hunger and monstrous poverty that defy description. Groups of pale and emaciated people wander aimlessly through the overcrowded streets. Beggars sit and lie along the walls and the sight of people collapsing from starvation is common. The refuge for abandoned children takes in a dozen infants every day; every day a few more people die on the street. Contagious diseases are spreading, particularly tuberculosis. Meanwhile the Germans continue to plunder the wealthy Jews. Their treatment of the Jews is always exceptionally inhuman. They torment them and subject them constantly to their wild and bestial amusements."[14]

Outside help, massively provided by the "Joint," allowed for the internal organization of welfare on a significant scale. Thus the "Jewish Social Self-Help" (JSS) started coordinating the efforts of previously independent Jewish welfare agencies throughout Poland. The task of the JSS was overwhelming, although it tried to set priorities, beginning with the neediest: children and the elderly; in its first year of activity it helped some 160,000 people in Warsaw alone by distributing food and other basic necessities.

In Warsaw, none of this, however, would have sufficed without large-scale smuggling as an essential part of "self-help": "Smuggling is carried out through all the holes and cracks in the walls, through connecting tunnels in the cellars of buildings on the border, and through all the hidden places unfamiliar to the conqueror's foreign eyes," Kaplan noted in early 1941. "The conductors on the Aryan trolleys in particular make fortunes. . . . Aryan trolleys make no stops inside the ghetto, but that's not a handicap. The smuggled sack is thrown out at an appointed spot and caught by trustworthy hands. This is the way they smuggle in pork fat, in particular, which the religious leaders have permitted us to use in this time of destruction."[15] The smugglers, or rather the ringleaders, were the first to benefit from these operations. German and Polish guards pocketed substantial bribes—and so, on a lesser scale, did members of the Jewish ghetto police. On the face of it the German administration fought the smuggling, and the ghetto commissar took some measures to make the illegal traffic more difficult. Yet "for the most part, smuggling was tolerated, and the measures taken against it were meant only to restrict its magnitude."[16] As for the Jewish Council, it understood perfectly that, given the food-supply situation, smuggling could not and should not be stopped.

Notwithstanding smuggling, self-help, house committees, and packages that—until June 1941—arrived mostly from the Soviet Union or Soviet-occupied Poland, the majority went hungry. The number of deaths from starvation and disease between the closing of the ghetto in November 1940 and the beginning of the deportations in July 1942 may have been as high as one hundred thousand. A dramatic deterioration of the children's situation at the beginning of the summer of 1941 found an immediate expression in the diarists' entries. "A special class of beggars," Ringelblum recorded on July 11, 1941, "consists of those who beg after nine o'clock at night. . . . In the surrounding silence of night, the cries of hungry beggar children are terribly insistent and, however hard your heart, eventually you have to throw a piece of bread down to them— or else leave the house. Those beggars are completely unconcerned about curfews and you can hear their voices late at night at eleven or even at twelve. They are afraid of nothing and of no one. . . . It is a common thing for beggar children like these to die on the sidewalk at night. I was told about such a horrible scene . . . where a six-year-old beggar boy lay gasping all night, too weak to roll over to the piece of bread that had been thrown down to him from the balcony."[17]

Given the conditions prevailing in the Warsaw ghetto during the summer of 1941, death—that of children or of adults—was increasingly becoming a matter of indifference. Typhus was spreading and there was little the hospitals, "places of execution" according to the director of the Ghetto Health Department, could do: Either the patients died from the epidemics or from lack of food at the hospital.

Despite the overall misery, maintaining education for youngsters in the ghettos remained a constant and partly successful endeavor. Until 1941 Jewish schools were forbidden in the General Government. After Frank's agreement to the resumption of Jewish education, schooling became official and the councils took over, bit by bit, according to local German orders. In Lodz schools reopened in the spring of 1941; in Warsaw, only in November 1941. During the two years or so in which schooling had been prohibited in Warsaw, clandestine schools, run by teachers belonging to prewar educational institutions, spread throughout the ghetto, and clandestine libraries in the three languages of the ghetto attracted a vast readership.

Music filled a special role in the larger ghettos, mainly in Warsaw and Lodz. Orchestras were established, and a relatively rich and intense musical life developed. In Warsaw, the initiative of setting up a symphony orchestra came from a few musicians; but, was it their intention "to serve the noble art," in the words of the literary critic Marcel Reich-Ranicki, "or to provide joy and pleasure to others? Nothing of the sort—they wanted to earn some money in order to assuage their hunger."[18] An additional reminder of what counted most in ghetto life. Reich-Ranicki's comments regarding the avid attendance at the symphony concerts are equally telling: "It was not defiance that brought the hungry and the wretched into the concert halls, but a longing for solace and elevation. . . . They needed a counter-world."[19]

In Lodz, too, musical life was intense. During the first three weeks of March 1941, for example, the *Ghetto Chronicle* mentions concerts on the first, the fifth, the eighth, the eleventh, and the thirteenth: "On the 13th, which was Purim," the *Chronicle* recorded, "there was a violin performance by Miss Bronislawa Rotsztat, as well as a symphony concert conducted by Dawid Bajgelman in which Hazomir ["the nightingale," in Hebrew] chorus participated. On Saturday, March 15, that program was repeated in a performance for invited guests, the Chairman chief among them. This performance had a special ceremonial quality and lasted until ten o'clock in the evening. On March 17, the School Department organized a performance of music and vocals for schoolchildren. On the 18th, the 20th and the 22nd of March there were symphony concerts for factory workers and, finally, on the 22nd, there was a symphony concert dedicated to classical music and conducted by Theodor Ryder."[20]

Grassroots intellectual (ideological) activity was probably even more intense than public cultural manifestations. On May 8, 1941, Sierakowiak recorded his intention to meet on that same day with three other high school members of the [communist] "all youth unit of lecturers" to "discuss Lenin's famous work, *The State and Revolution,* and then . . . lecture on it to all other active youth units in the ghetto."[21] On May 10 "in the afternoon," Sierakowiak noted, "we had a meeting with girls, during which our most active members (Niutek, Jerzyk and I) had a difficult time explaining the concept of surplus value."[22]

Organized Jewish youth had been left to its own devices following the hasty departure of the envoys from Palestine and of much of the senior political or communal leadership at the beginning of the war. Whereas Bundist youth stayed in close contact with a senior leadership that remained in occupied Poland, the Zionist youth movements gradually lost touch with party headquarters in Palestine. The ideological fervor of this Zionist youth did not falter—it was possibly even heightened by the surrounding circumstances; the response from Palestine, however, soon dwindled to increasingly unrealistic and perfunctory advice and instructions, and often it lapsed into silence. Such indifference created a growing rift and soon turned into a desperate sense of independence among the local youth leaders, the oldest of whom were in their early twenties at most.

While the ongoing and intense debates that divided movements sharing, for example, the same Zionist-socialist outlook (like Hashomer Hatzair, Gordonia, or Dror) appear incomprehensible from hindsight, the considerable effort invested in these ideological-cultural activities and the publication of a large number of underground newspapers and periodicals—either in Polish, Yiddish, or Hebrew—became a form of resistance and, possibly, a psychologically necessary preparation for the armed resistance of later days.

The Council remained at the center of ghetto life. By mid-1941 the Warsaw *Judenrat*, for example, had become a tentacular bureaucracy employing some six thousand people in a whole array of departments; its achievements were real given the dearth of means, and yet, as mentioned, it encountered intense hostility among most of the Jewish population, a hostility that grew as time went by. "The Community Council is an abomination in the eyes of the Warsaw community," the acerbic Kaplan noted on April 23, 1941. "When the Council is so much as mentioned, everyone's blood begins to boil. If it were not for fear of the Authorities there would be bloodshed. . . . According to rumor, the President is a decent man. But the people around him are the dregs of humanity. . . . They are known as scoundrels and corrupt persons, who did not avoid ugly dealings even in the period before the war. . . . Everything is done in the name of the President. But in truth, everything is done without his knowledge and even without his consent, and perhaps also against his decisions and wishes."[23] Above and beyond the anger triggered by widespread corruption, popular resentment focused mainly on forced-labor conscription, taxation, and the brutality of the Jewish police.

While Jewish workers were increasingly employed by ghetto workshops, "labor battalions," set up by the councils, were daily marched to work. Furthermore in Upper Silesia tens of thousands of local Jews were toiling in special labor camps and Jewish slave laborers were ruthlessly driven by the SS in the eastern part of the General Government, mainly in Globocnik's Lublin district. There, the laborers were kept digging anti-tank trenches and constructing a defense line for no clear military purpose. The Supreme Command of the Army (OKH) had agreed to the enterprise, but its implementation was entirely left in the hands of Himmler's henchmen.

The conditions in the Lublin labor camps were the worst, but the situation in the Warsaw area was not much better. On May 10, 1941, after receiving a report from two council members who had just been allowed a short visit, Czerniaków noted: "The camp huts have spoiled straw to sleep on and the wind is blowing through the walls. The workers are shivering at night. There are no showers and restrooms. The workers' boots were ruined in wet sand and clay. There are no drugs or bandages. Treatment of the workers by the camp guards in many localities is bad." And yet, the ghetto poor kept volunteering in the hope of receiving some money and some food. In the same entry, Czerniaków added: "Wages are not paid. . . . Everything depends on nutrition." Barely a fraction of the promised food was handed out.[24]

Money would protect you from the labor camps. "If you

have not appeared before the [mustering] commission yet," Hersch Wasser of the Oneg Shabbat group, noted on April 28, 1941, "you can go to one of the doctors, pay down 150 zl. [zlotys] on the fee, and he will find some medical reason for requesting your release. . . . For an additional 200 zl., a work card is miraculously whisked into your home without toil or trouble. And if, God forbid, you have already undergone the medical examination and—o, woe!—been found capable, the procedure costs around 500 zl. for a certificate of being immune, inviolable."[25]

As for taxes, particularly in Warsaw they were blatantly unjust. The Council had opted for indirect taxation of the ghetto's most basic commodities and services, instead of direct taxation of the wealthy inhabitants; it meant that the poorest segments of the population (the immense majority) were carrying most of the tax burden. The wealthy inhabitants, the big smugglers, the profiteers of various ilk, practically avoided all direct levies on their assets.

Possibly the most common target of popular anger was the Jewish police, which in principle was under the orders of the Council and of the Germans. In Warsaw the ghetto police was some two thousand men strong and headed by a convert, a former colonel in the Polish police, Józef Szeryński. The policemen were mainly young men from the "better" class, from the "intelligentsia" at times. They had the necessary connections to get the coveted jobs, and, once in uniform, they did not hesitate to enforce the most unpopular orders issued by the councils (tax collection, escorting men to forced labor, guarding the inner fence of the ghetto, confiscations of property and the like) or by the Germans, often brutally. Although the policemen argued at the time—and after the war—that things would have been much worse if their jobs had been solely implemented by Germans or Poles, there is no doubt that "considerable segments of the ghetto police were morally and materially corrupt, that they enriched themselves on account of the oppressed and persecuted inmates when carrying out their assignments."[26]

For the Germans, Jewish policemen were as contemptible as any other Jews. "Yesterday," Mary Berg, a Jewish girl who lived in the ghetto with her American mother (and was allowed to emigrate in 1941), noted on January 4, 1941, "I myself saw a Nazi gendarme 'exercise' a Jewish policeman near the passage from the little to the big ghetto on Chlodna street. The young man finally lost his breath but the Nazi still forced him to fall and rise until he collapsed in a pool of blood."[27]

In his January 30, 1941, speech, Hitler concluded his prophecy of anti-Jewish retribution by expressing the hope that an increasing number of Europeans would follow the German anti-Semitic lead: "Already now," he declared, "our racial awareness penetrates one people after the other."[28] As he mentioned the growth of anti-Semitism, the Nazi leader probably had in mind the events that had occurred in Bucharest merely a few days before.

On January 21, 1941, the Romanian capital had been shaken by a brief and abortive attempt by the SS-supported Iron Guard to wrest power from its ally, the dictatorial head of state, Marshal Ion Antonescu. During their three-day rampage, Horia Sima's "legionaries" first and foremost vented their rage upon the Jews of the city. "The stunning thing about the Bucharest bloodbath," Sebastian recorded a few days after the events, "is the quite bestial ferocity of it. . . . It is now considered absolutely certain that the Jews butchered at Straulesti abbatoir were hanged by the neck on hooks normally used for beef carcasses. A sheet of paper was stuck to each corpse: 'Kosher Meat.' As for those killed in Jilava forest, they were first undressed (it would have been a pity for clothes to remain there), then shot and thrown on top of one another."[29] The guard was crushed and its leaders fled to Germany, but their anti-Jewish rage was deeply anchored in Romanian society.

It was widely believed that the 375,000 Jews living in Romania in early 1941 were guilty of the loss of Bessarabia and Bukovina to the Soviet Union in July 1940 and of northern Transylvania to Hungary. These territorial changes, needless to say, had been arranged by Germany in its secret agreement with the USSR and in its arbitration between Hungary and Romania in the summer of 1940. In any case, these latest accusations were but the tip of the iceberg of Romanian anti-Jewish hatred.

As in other Eastern European countries, the very foundation of Romanian attitudes toward the Jews was nurtured by virulent religious anti-Judaism, spewed, in this case, by the Romanian Orthodox Church. This brand of religious hostility had first flourished among the peasantry before spreading to the new urban middle classes, where it acquired its economic and mainly nationalist dimensions. "Romanianism" targeted ethnic and cultural minorities mainly in its struggle for domination of the borderland provinces, which were considered as rightfully belonging to Greater Romania: The Jews were deemed foreign and hostile both ethnically and culturally, and in the struggle for Romanianism they were accused of siding with the Hungarians or the Russians.

The anti-Semitic violence in Romania in early 1941 was but an indication of what was about to happen on local initiative in much of Eastern Europe and the Balkans with the beginning of the war against the Soviet Union. In various stages and diverse political and strategic circumstances, local hatred of Jews and German murder policies were soon to mix in a particularly lethal brew.

In the West the policies of collaboration developed according to different internal dynamics and, at a different pace; ultimately, however, the outcome was the same.

A Hitler-Pétain meeting took place in the little town of Montoire on October 24, 1940: "Collaboration" between Vichy France and the Reich was officially proclaimed. Yet, on December 13, Pierre Laval, the main proponent of this policy, was dismissed by the old *maréchal*. The turmoil was brief. German pressure and internal constraints set Vichy back on track: In early 1941 Adm. François Darlan replaced the moderate Pierre-Étienne Flandin at the head of the government and the collaboration with Germany tightened. Anti-Jewish measures spread.

In February 1941, out of the 47,000 foreigners imprisoned in French concentration camps, 40,000 were Jews. Aryanization progressed apace. Jewish businesses were increasingly put under the control of "French" supervisors who had full power to decide the businesses' fate. This, of course, encouraged scoundrels of all hues to buy all remaining wares from the Jewish owners (or the businesses themselves) at a fraction of the price. Simultaneously the largest French banks took steps of their own to interpret German ordinances as extensively as possible. In April 1941 the Jews were forbidden to fill any position—from selling lottery tickets to teaching—that would put them in contact with the public. Only a few "particularly deserving intellectuals" were exempted from this total professional segregation. As for the vast majority of the French population, it did not react. Anti-Jewish propaganda intensified, as did the number of acts of anti-Jewish violence. Individual expressions of sympathy were not rare, but they were volunteered in private, far from any public notice.

At the beginning of 1941 the Germans decided to set up a central office that would coordinate the anti-Jewish measures throughout both French zones. The function of that office would be to deal with all police matters regarding the arrest, surveillance, and registration of Jews; to exercise economic control; to organize propaganda activities; and to set up an anti-Jewish research institute. To avoid opposition to a German initiative the establishment of the new office would be left to the French authorities.

On March 29, 1941, the Vichy government indeed established the Central Office for Jewish Affairs (Commissariat Général aux Questions Juives, or CGQJ); its first chief was Xavier Vallat. Vallat belonged to the nationalist anti-Jewish tradition of the Action Française and did not share the racial anti-Semitism of the Nazis. Nonetheless, the CGQJ soon became the hub of a rapidly expanding anti-Jewish activity. Its main immediate achievement was the reworking of the Jewish Statute of October 3, 1940. The new Statut des Juifs was accepted by the government and became law on June 2, 1941. It aimed at filling the many gaps discovered in the October 1940 edict. In the case of French "mixed breeds," for example, with two Jewish grandparents who had converted to another religion, the cut-off date validating the conversion in terms of the decree was June 25, 1940, the official date of the armistice between Germany and France. Moreover conversion was considered valid only if the convert had chosen to join a confession recognized before the separation of church and state of December 1905. Only the CGQJ would be entitled to issue certificates of nonappurtenance to the Jewish race. Like the statute of October 1940, that of June 1941 did not establish any distinction between native and foreign Jews. On May 14, 1941, on German orders, French police arrested 3,733 Jewish immigrants. The next day, the collaborationist paper *Paris Midi* hailed the disappearance of "five thousand parasites from greater Paris." No other paper (apart from the Jewish press) deemed the event worth mentioning. [30]

There was a striking (possibly unperceived) relation between French attitudes toward the Jews and the behavior of representatives of native Jewry toward the foreign or recently naturalized Jews living in the country. The growing anti-Semitism of the thirties and its most violent outbursts following the defeat were, in their opinion, caused in large part by the influx of foreign Jews; the situation thus created could be mitigated by a strict distinction between native French Jews and the foreign Jews living in the country. The Vichy authorities had to be convinced of this basic tenet.

It was precisely this difference that Jacques Helbronner, the acting vice president of the Consistoire (after the Rothschilds had fled the country), attempted to convey to Pétain in a memorandum he sent him in November 1940. In this statement, entitled *Note sur la question juive*, Helbronner argued that the Jews were not a race and did not descend from the Jews who had lived in Palestine two thousand years beforehand. Rather, they were a community composed of many races and, as far as France was concerned, a community entirely integrated into its homeland. The problems began with the arrival of foreign Jews "who started to invade our soil." The open-door policies of the postwar government had been a mistake, resulting "in a normal anti-Semitism the victims of which were now the old French Israelite families."[31] Helbronner then suggested a series of measures that would free the native Jews from the limitations of the statute but not the foreign or recently naturalized Jews. His message went unanswered.

In Holland the population staged a small-scale rebellion in reaction to the German treatment of the hundreds of Jewish men arrested in the streets of Amsterdam on February 22, 1941. The communists called for a general strike: On February 25 Amsterdam was paralyzed, and soon the strike spread to nearby cities. The Germans reacted with extreme violence against the demonstrators, using both firearms and hand grenades: Seven people were killed, seventy-six wounded, scores arrested. The strike was quashed. The Dutch had learned that the Germans would not hesitate to pursue their anti-Jewish policies with utter ruthlessness; the Germans realized that converting the Dutch to National Socialism would not be an easy task.

Whether as a result of the Amsterdam events, or as the outcome of prior planning—Heydrich decided to establish a Central Office for Jewish Emigration in Amsterdam, on the model of the offices set up in Vienna in 1938, in Berlin and in Prague in 1939. The Zentralstelle was indeed established in April 1941, mainly, it seems, for economic extortion. In order to speed up the Aryanization of large enterprises, the Zentralstelle would allow for the departure of their Jewish owners, who would sell their businesses to German bidders. The German companies, as legal owners, could then claim rights to related foreign assets and avoid any lawsuits, particularly in the United States. The deals ensured unhindered emigration for the lucky few (around thirty families) within weeks from the time of the property transfer.

Later on the same racketeering would be applied to Jews in several countries in exchange for large sums in foreign currency. Eventually the German takeover of Jewish property would be much more systematic in Holland than in occupied France, in line with the Nazi master plan for a European economic "new order." The Dutch economy was destined for complete integration in the German system, whether the Dutch wished it or not. Once more, ideological creed and economic greed converged. In August 1941 the Jews of Holland were ordered to register all their assets with the formerly Jewish Lippman-Rosenthal bank; on September 15 real estate was included in the registration.

The February 1941 events led to the dismissal of the Amsterdam City Council and its replacement by an adequately subservient new group. The Amsterdam police force was put under the command of a new chief, Sybren Tulp. Tulp, as a member of the Dutch Nazi Party, had the appropriate ideological leanings, the more so that he was a great admirer of Adolf Hitler.

As Seyss-Inquart's delegate in Amsterdam, Dr. H. Böhmcker was considering the establishment of a ghetto in the Jewish quarter of Amsterdam, he demanded the creation of a unified representation of the Jews of the city. Abraham Asscher, a wealthy merchant involved in aiding Jewish refugees before the war, volunteered to preside over the new organization and asked for the appointment of his friend, David Cohen, as a copresident. Both Asscher and Cohen then chose the other members, mostly from their own social milieu, Amsterdam's small and wealthy Jewish high bourgeoisie. On February 12 the Council held its first meeting. On the next day, on Böhmcker's demand, Asscher spoke to an assembly of Jewish workers requesting the delivery of any weapons in their possession. As the historian Bob Moore pointed out, "In effect, the first steps towards Jewish collaboration with the Germans had begun with the self-appointed elite of the Jewish Council acting as a conduit for Nazi demands."[32]

Whatever the assessment of the Dutch Council's early behavior may be, the Germans did not ask for its approval when it came to dispatching the four hundred young Jewish men arrested after the Koco incident to their death. At first they were deported to Buchenwald, then to Mauthausen. They arrived in Mauthausen on June 17, 1941. A batch of fifty was immediately killed: "They were chased naked from the bathhouse to the electrified fence." The others were murdered in the main quarry of the camp, the "Vienna Ditch." According to the German witness Eugen Kogon, these Jews were not allowed to use the steps leading to the bottom of the quarry. "They had to slide down the loose stones at the side, and even here many died or were severely injured. The survivors then had to shoulder hods, and two prisoners were compelled to load each Jew with an excessively heavy rock. The Jews then had to run up the 186 steps. In some instances the rocks immediately rolled downhill, crushing the feet of those that came behind. Every Jew who lost his rock in that fashion was brutally beaten and the rock was hoisted to his shoulders again. Many of the Jews were driven to despair the very first day and committed suicide by jumping into the pit. On the third day the SS opened the so-called 'death-gate,' and with a fearful barrage of blows drove the Jews across the guard line, the guards on the watchtowers shooting them down in heaps with their machine guns. The next day the Jews no longer jumped into the pit individually. They joined hands and one man would pull nine or twelve of his comrades over the lip with him into a gruesome death. The barracks were 'cleared' of Jews, not in six but in barely three weeks. Everyone of the 348 prisoners perished by suicide, or by shooting, beating, and other forms of torture."[33] When asked by the local *Landrat* how the Dutch Jews had adapted to the hard work, Commandant Franz Ziereis answered: "Ah, hardly a one is still alive."[34]

As the news of the deaths of this first group of Amsterdam Jews was trickling back to Holland, an attack on the Luftwaffe telephone exchange at Schiphol Airport on June 3, 1941, seriously wounded one of the soldiers. In retaliation the Germans tricked council members Cohen and Gertrud van Tijn into giving them the addresses of two hundred young German Jewish refugees. These were arrested together with other young Amsterdam Jews, sent to Mauthausen, and murdered.

Etty (Esther) Hillesum was still a young student in Slavic languages at Amsterdam University during those spring months of 1941. For years Etty's father had been the headmaster of a municipal gymnasium in Deventer; her mother, it seems, introduced a tempestuous Russian Jewish personality into the staid Dutch bourgeois environment. Etty's two brothers were unusually gifted: The older, Mischa, as a brilliant concert pianist from age six, and the younger, Jaap, as a budding biochemist who discovered a new vitamin at age seventeen. As for Etty, she was a born writer and a free spirit. At the Amsterdam house she rented with several other Jewish friends, she launched into a complicated love life, branching out into several simultaneous directions, and started on an idiosyncratic spiritual path tinged with Christianity and some esoteric and mystical components. And, she began keeping her diary.

"Sometimes when I read the papers or hear reports of what is happening all around," Etty noted on March 15, 1941, "I am suddenly beside myself with anger, cursing and swearing at the Germans. And I know that I do it deliberately in order to hurt Käthe [the German cook who lived in the house], to work off my anger as best I can. . . . And all this when I know perfectly well that she finds the new order as dreadful as I do. . . . But deep down she is of course one of her people, and while I understand, I sometimes cannot bear it. . . . And now and then I say nastily, 'They are all scum,' and at the same time I feel terribly ashamed and deeply unhappy but cannot stop even though I know that it's all wrong. . . ." The peace of mind that Etty was arduously trying to acquire in the midst of the growing turmoil was badly shaken by the new arrests: "More arrests, more terror, concentration camps, the arbitrary dragging off of fathers, sisters, brothers," she noted on June 14, "Everything seems so menacing and ominous, and always that feeling of total impotence."[35]

The setting up of the Jewish Council, the Aryanization drive, the two waves of arrests were but one aspect of the German terror campaign; the other aimed at cutting off the Jews from the surrounding Dutch population, at increasingly isolating them, even if publicly marking them was still a year away. At the end of May 1941, as the hot-weather season was starting, the Germans not only barred all Jews from parks, spas, and hotels, but also from public beaches and swimming pools. Shortly afterward Jewish elementary and high school students were ordered to fill out special registration forms.

Soon, they were excluded from Dutch schools and only allowed to attend Jewish schools.

Anne Frank, her sister, Margot, her father, Otto, and her mother, Edith, had emigrated from Frankfurt to Amsterdam during the second half of 1933. The father received the franchise for the jelling agent pectin from the Pomosin-Werke in Frankfurt. Over time Frank's modest dealership reached a measure of stability, thanks to a small group of devoted Dutch employees. Commenting on the prohibition to use swimming pools, twelve-year-old Anne Frank wrote to her grandmother living in Basel: "We're not likely to get sunburned because we can't go to the swimming pool . . . too bad, but there is nothing to be done."[36]

The official positions of the national Catholic Churches throughout the Continent (and those of the Vatican) were not essentially different from one another regarding the increasingly harsh anti-Jewish measures. In France, as we saw, the assembly of cardinals and bishops welcomed the limitations imposed on the country's Jews, and no members of the Catholic hierarchy expressed any protest regarding the statutes of October 1940 and June 1941. In neighboring Belgium, Joseph-Ernest Cardinal van Roey, archbishop of Mechelen, remained equally silent about the anti-Jewish edicts of 1940 and 1941; in so doing the cardinal was in step with the upper echelons of his church and neither able nor willing to oppose the militant Catholic-nationalist anti-Semitism of the Flemish radical Right, mainly active in Antwerpen.

In East-Central Europe pride of place has to be granted to the Polish Catholic Church. A report originating with the Polish Church itself, covering the period between June 1 and July 15, 1941, and transmitted to the government-in-exile in London, is telling: "The need to solve the Jewish Question is urgent," the report stated. "Nowhere else in the world has that question reached such a climax, because no fewer than four million [sic] of these highly noxious and by all standards dangerous elements live in Poland, or to be more precise, off Poland."

Two documents from the first half of 1941 may add some insight regarding the pope's own attitude at that time, and the views shared by some of the Vatican's most authoritative personalities about the anti-Jewish measures. "Your Holiness is certainly informed about the situation of the Jews in Germany and in the neighboring countries," Bishop Preysing of Berlin wrote to Pius XII on January 17, 1941. "I would like to mention that I have been asked by Catholics as well as by Protestants whether the Holy See couldn't do something in this matter, issue an appeal in favor of these unfortunate people?"[37] On March 19 the pope answered several of Preysing's letters and particularly praised the Berlin bishop for his denunciation of euthanasia in a March 6 sermon. Not a word, however, alluded to Preysing's unmistakable plea for a papal reaction to the persecution of the Jews.

The second document was no less indicative. In response to an inquiry regarding the Vatican's attitude toward the anti-Jewish legislation, demanded by Pétain in August 1941, Léon Bérard, Vichy's ambassador to the Holy See, provided an exhaustive answer on September 2. First the French diplomat informed the *maréchal* that although there existed a fundamental conflict between racial theories and Church doctrine, it did not follow that the Church necessarily repudiated every measure taken by particular countries against the Jews. The Church recognized, Bérard wrote, that religion was not the only special characteristic of Jews and that there were also certain ethnic—not racial—factors that set them apart. Historically the Church's practice and feeling over the centuries had been that Jews should not have authority over Christians. It was legitimate, therefore, to exclude them from certain public offices and to restrict their access to universities and the professions. He recalled also that ecclesiastical law had required the Jews to wear a distinctive garb.

One of the major problems, the ambassador continued, was that of marriages. The new racial legislation in Italy and elsewhere prohibited marriages between Christians and Jews. The Church felt that it had the authority to perform such marriages, if the Jewish partner had been baptized or if an ecclesiastical dispensation had been obtained. In France, Bérard believed, there would not be similar problems because the circumstances were different (marriages between Jews and non-Jews had not been prohibited on racial grounds). For Pétain, Bérard's report must have been reassuring.

Given the absence of any significant assistance from the major Christian Churches to nonconverted Jews, the role of private institutions and of (sometimes unlikely) individuals grew in importance. The role of Jewish organizations was preeminent, particularly that of the "Joint," the Organization for Rehabilitation and Training (ORT), and the Oeuvre de Secours aux Enfants (OSE), as well as organizations belonging more directly to Jewish political parties (Zionists, Orthodox, Bundists, Communists) or to various Jewish immigrant associations in Western Europe. Non-Jewish charitable organizations also extended generous help: the American Friends Service Committee, the YMCA, the French Protestant student group CIMADE, and others.

The initiatives of individuals carried a particular moral significance. Even during this early period, and even outside the Reich, the risks incurred were often considerable, albeit mainly in professional and social terms. The qualified stand taken by the head of the French Protestant community, Pastor Marc Boegner, against Vichy's anti-Jewish policies could, for example, have endangered his position within his own flock; the smuggling of Jews across the Swiss border on the eve of the war put an end to Paul Grüninger's career in St. Gallen's border police; several Swiss consular officers, mainly in Italy, were reprimanded for disregarding the rules about Jewish immigration. As already mentioned, after the defeat of France, the Portuguese consul general in Bordeaux, Aristides de Sousa Mendes, started issuing entry visas to Jews, notwithstanding contrary instructions from Lisbon; he was recalled and dismissed from the foreign service. Like Grüninger, he was rehabilitated only several decades after the end of the war. The American Varian Fry, sent on a brief fact-finding mission by the New York based Emergency Rescue Committee (set up on June 25, 1940, to identify refugees from southern France deemed valuable to the United States) took it upon himself to smuggle hundreds of endangered and "valuable" refugees—Jews and non-Jews—out of Vichy France by, among other means, forging exit and transit visas. In August 1941, Fry was briefly arrested by the French and recalled.

One of the most unlikely cases in many ways was that of Chiune Sugihara, the Japanese consul in the Lithuanian capital, Kovno (Kaunas). Sugihara had been transferred from Helsinki to Kovno in October 1939. When Lithuania was annexed by the Soviet Union, the Japanese consulate had to close down, and Sugihara was posted to Berlin, then Prague, later to Königsberg. From the outset his real mission had been to observe troop movements and related military developments. But, in order to keep the appearances of his official cover, he fulfilled all the regular functions of a genuine consul; mainly he issued visas. On August 10, 1940, against instructions of the Foreign Ministry in Tokyo, Sugihara started issuing Japanese transit visas to all the Jews who could reach his consulate. Almost none of them had an entrance permit to a country of final destination; many didn't even have valid passports of any sort.

Within days admonishments from Tokyo reached the wayward consul. Sugihara remained undeterred: He continued signing visas even from the window of the already moving train, as he and his family were leaving for Berlin. He issued more visas in Prague, and possibly in Königsberg. Sugihara may have issued up to ten thousand visas, and possibly half the number of Jews who received them managed to survive. "I did not pay any attention [to consequences]," he wrote after the war, "and just acted according to my sense of human justice, out of love for mankind."[38]

CHAPTER 9

The Eastern Onslaught

June 1941–September 1941

O N SEPTEMBER 29, 1941, the Germans shot 33,700 Kiev Jews in the Babi Yar ravine near the city. As the rumors about the massacre spread, some Ukrainians initially expressed doubts. "I only know one thing," Iryna Khoroshunova wrote in her diary on that same day. "There is something terrible, horrible going on, something inconceivable, which cannot be understood, grasped or explained." A few days later her uncertainty had disappeared: "A Russian girl accompanied her girlfriend to the cemetery, but crawled through the fence from the other side. She saw how naked people were taken toward Babi Yar and heard shots from a machine gun. There are more and more such rumors and accounts. They are too monstrous to believe. But we are forced to believe them, for the shooting of the Jews is a fact. A fact which is starting to drive us insane. It is impossible to live with this knowledge. The women around us are crying. And we? We also cried on September 29, when we thought they were taken to a concentration camp. But now? Can we really cry? I am writing, but my hair is standing on end."[1]

After the end of the Babi Yar massacre, a few elderly Jews returned to Kiev and sat by the Old Synagogue. Nobody dared to approach or leave food or water for them, as this could mean immediate execution. One after the other, the Jews died until only two remained. A passerby went to the German sentry standing at the corner of the street and suggested shooting the two old Jews instead of letting them starve to death. "The guard thought for a moment and did it."[2]

Of necessity the Lodz chroniclers had to keep to the barest facts about the new war in the East: "In connection with the war against the Soviets, in the last ten days of June there has been a sudden increase in the price of packaged goods, which the ghetto had received mostly from the USSR," they recorded in their entry of June 20–30, 1941.[3] The German attack in the East elicited no further comment. The restraint imposed on the official ghetto recorders was not shared by the individual diarists. Young Sierakowiak was elated: "Incredible, wonderful news!" he wrote on the twenty-second, though he was not yet entirely sure that the "free, beloved, great Soviets" were not being attacked by a German-British coalition.[4] On the twenty-third he triumphantly confirmed: "It is all true! . . . The entire ghetto is buzzing like one big beehive. Everybody feels that a chance for liberation is finally possible."[5]

Not all Jewish diarists were in tune with Sierakowiak's high spirits. In Romania—which had joined the antibolshevik crusade—fear spread: "In the evening, we gather early at the house," Sebastian noted on June 22. "With the shutters drawn and the telephone out of service, we have a growing sense of unease and anguish. What will happen to us?"[6] In Vilna, Hermann Kruk did not share Sierakowiak's enthusiasm either. Kruk had fled from Warsaw to Lithuania a few days after the beginning of the war. In the Polish capital he had been active in Yiddish cultural circles and was in charge of the cultural activities of the Bund's youth movement, *Zukunft*, and of the central Yiddish library. On June 22, 1941, he thought of fleeing again but did not succeed. Fatalistically he resigned himself to staying and recording the oncoming events: "I make a firm decision," he noted on June 23, "I leave myself to the mercy of God; I am staying. And, right away, I make another decision: if I am staying anyway and if I am going to be a victim of fascism, I shall take pen in hand and write a chronicle of a city. Clearly, Vilna may also be captured. The Germans will turn the city fascist. Jews will go into the ghetto—I shall record it all. My chronicle must see, must hear, and must become the mirror and the conscience of the great catastrophe and of the hard times."[7]

In the Warsaw ghetto, like in Lodz, the immediate, everyday consequences of the new war seemed to be the main concern. "A newspaper special on the war with the Soviets," Czerniaków noted on June 22. "It will be necessary to work all day, and perhaps they will not let one sleep at night."[8] For days on end the Warsaw Chairman hardly mentioned the war in Russia; he had other, more urgent worries. "In the streets the workers are being impressed for labor outside the ghetto, since there are few volunteers for a job which pays only 2.80 zlotys and provides no food," he noted on July 8. "I went to [Ferdinand von] Kamlah to obtain food for them. So far, no results. Considering their dire predicament, the Jewish masses are quiet and composed."[9]

Among the Germans, as far as Klemperer could observe, the news of the campaign in the East was well received: "Cheerful faces everywhere," he noted on June 22. "The Russian war is a source of new pride for people, their grumbling of yesterday is forgotten."[10]

Indeed, during the first days and weeks of the campaign, the German onslaught seemed irresistible. Despite repeated warnings from the most diverse sources, Stalin and the Red Army had been caught by surprise. Optimism pervaded the high-level meeting convened at Hitler's headquarters on July

16 and attended by Göring, Bormann, Lammers, Keitel, and Rosenberg. In a memorable formula, the "greatest military leader of all times," according to Keitel, set the guidelines for German policy in the occupied Soviet Union: "We have to divide this enormous cake in the right way in order, first, to rule it, second, to administer it, third, to exploit it." In this context the Nazi chief considered Stalin's July 3 appeal to Red Army soldiers to start partisan warfare behind the German lines as one more favorable development: "This partisan warfare gives us an advantage by enabling us to destroy everything in our path . . . in this vast area, peace must be imposed as quickly as possible, and to achieve this it is necessary to execute even anyone who doesn't give us a straight look."[11]

It was at the same meeting that Rosenberg was officially appointed Reich minister for the occupied eastern territories; yet Himmler's responsibility for the internal security of the territories was reaffirmed. According to the formal arrangement, Rosenberg's appointees would have jurisdiction over Himmler's delegates in their areas, but de facto the higher SS and police leaders (HSSPF) got their operational orders from the Reichsführer. The arrangement, which was meant to safeguard both Himmler's and Rosenberg's authority, was of course a recipe for constant infighting. But although the tension between both systems of domination has often been highlighted, the "results" prove that cooperation in implementing the tasks on hand, particularly in regard to mass murder, usually overcame competition; together with the Wehrmacht, they were intent, beyond anything else, to impose German domination, exploitation, and terror in the newly conquered territories.

But as weeks went by, neither the Red Army nor Stalin's regime collapsed; the progress of the Wehrmacht slowed, and German casualties steadily mounted. In mid-August, Hitler—against his generals' advice to concentrate all available forces for an attack on Moscow—decided that Army Group Center would first conquer the Ukraine before turning northward for the final assault on the Soviet capital. Kiev surrendered on September 19 and more than six hundred thousand Russian soldiers—and their equipment—fell into German hands. Hitler was again in an ebullient mood; yet, time was running dangerously short for the attack on the center of Soviet power.

The international situation too was becoming more ominous for Germany. On March 11, 1941, Roosevelt signed the Lend-Lease Bill. Within days British ships were carrying "lent" American weapons and supplies across the Atlantic. In the early summer similar American assistance to the Soviet Union started. The major problem for Washington was not whether to supply the Communist victim of German aggression but to get the American supplies to their destination in the face of increasingly successful German submarine operations. In April, invoking the Monroe Doctrine and the need to defend the Western Hemisphere, Roosevelt sent American troops to Greenland; two months later U.S. forces established bases in Iceland. Then, in mid-August, Roosevelt and Churchill met off the coast of Newfoundland, and, at the end of the talks, proclaimed the rather hazy principles of what became known as the Atlantic Charter. In Berlin, as elsewhere, the meeting was interpreted as signaling a de facto alliance between the United States and Great Britain. Secretly Roosevelt had indeed promised Churchill that the U.S. Navy would escort British convoys at least half way across the Atlantic. By September major incidents between American naval units and German submarines had become unavoidable.

By midsummer 1941 the German population showed some signs of unease. The war in the East was not progressing as rapidly as expected, casualties were growing, and regular food supply became a source of mounting concern. It is in these circumstances that a major incident rattled the Nazi leadership. On Sunday, August 3, Bishop Clemens von Galen defied Hitler's regime. In a sermon at the Münster cathedral, the prelate forcefully attacked the authorities for the systematic murder of the mentally ill and the handicapped. The sermon came four weeks after the German episcopate had issued a pastoral letter, read from every pulpit in the country, denouncing the taking of "innocent lives." Protestant voices also rose.

The Nazi leader decided not to retaliate against Galen at this crucial stage of the war. Accounts with the church would be settled later, he declared. Officially operation T4 was discontinued but, in fact, the selective murder of "lives unworthy of living" continued nonetheless in less visible ways. Henceforth the victims were mainly chosen from prisoners of concentration camps: Poles, Jews, "criminals against the race," "asocials," cripples. Under the code name 14f13, Himmler had already launched these killings in April 1941 in Sachsenhausen; after mid-August 1941 it became the modified euthanasia operation. Moreover, in the mental institutions "wild euthanasia" took the lives of thousands of resident inmates. Yet, notwithstanding the circuitous pursuit of the killings, it was the first and only time in the history of the Third Reich that prominent representatives of the Christian churches in Germany voiced a public condemnation of the crimes committed by the regime.

On June 22, on the very first day of the war, Reich Press Chief Otto Dietrich, in his "theme of the day" for the German press, insisted on the Jewish dimension of the bolshevik enemy: "It has to be pointed out that the Jews pulling the strings behind the Soviet scene have remained the same, and so did their methods and their system . . . Plutocracy and Bolshevism have an identical starting point: the Jewish striving for world domination."[12] The tone was set. It would be sustained in innumerable variations, to the very end. Goebbels's first personal contribution came on July 20, in a massive anti-Jewish attack published in *Das Reich* under the title: "Mimicry." Under the minister's pen, the Jews became quintessential mimics: "It is difficult to detect their sly and slippery ways. . . . Moscow's Jews invent lies and atrocities, the London Jews cite them and blend them into stories suitable for the innocent bourgeois."[13] The argument was clear: The Jews camouflaged their presence and moved to the background in order to maneuver behind the scenes. The conclusion of Goebbels's tirade was foreseeable: The nations that had been deceived would see the light. From then on and throughout the summer the minister repeatedly returned to the same theme on every available occasion.

In those same days Goebbels discovered a "sensational" document. Theodore Kaufman, a Jewish native of New Jersey, had a small advertising business in Newark, selling mainly theater tickets. In early 1941 he set up the Argyle Press solely in order to publish a pamphlet he had authored: "Germany Must Perish." He demanded the sterilization of all German men and the division of the country into five parts, to be annexed by the Reich's neighbors. After printing his pamphlet Kaufman personally wrapped the copies and sent them to the press. The pamphlet found no echo, except for a notice in the March 24, 1941, issue of *Time* magazine under the sarcastic title "A Modest Proposal," which also included a few details about the author and his one-man enterprise. Thereafter Kaufman faded back into obscurity in the United States but not in Germany.

On July 24, 1941, the *Völkischer Beobachter* ran a front-page story under the bloodcurdling title: "Roosevelt demands the sterilization of the German People" and the shocking subtitle: "A Monstrous Jewish Extermination Plan. Roosevelt's Guidelines." Kaufman was turned into a close friend of Roosevelt's main speechwriter—the Jew Samuel Rosenman, and was himself a leading personality of American Jewry. According to the story the president was the real initiator of Kaufman's ideas; he had even personally dictated parts of the shameful work.

The German press and radio carried the Kaufman story in

endless variations and presented it as the hidden agenda of the mid-August Churchill-Roosevelt meeting. In September the Propaganda Ministry published a pamphlet including translated and annotated excerpts from Kaufman's text; it was launched in millions of copies, precisely when the Jews of the Reich were compelled to wear the star. And, while the Kaufman story was being relentlessly spread, reports about bolshevik atrocities were regularly carried by all of Goebbels's channels; of course they were attributed to Jewish executioners.

In a July 2 message to the higher SS and police leaders in the newly occupied eastern territories, Heydrich summed up the instructions previously given to the *Einsatzgruppen*: All Jewish party and state officials were to be executed and local pogroms were to be encouraged. Then, on July 17, Heydrich ordered the execution of all Jewish prisoners of war. During the first weeks, mostly Jewish men were killed, then all Jews without distinction were murdered by SS *Einsatzgruppen* and other special SS units, by Order Police battalions, assisted at the outset by the local populations, then by local auxiliaries, and often by regular Wehrmacht troops. By the end of 1941 about six hundred thousand Jews had been murdered in the newly conquered eastern regions.

Contrarily to what had long been assumed, Himmler did not give the order for the general extermination of all Jews on Soviet territory during his August 15 visit to Minsk, when, upon his request, he attended a mass execution of Jews on the outskirts of the city. The move from selective to mass murder had started earlier, probably as a result of Hitler's remarks during the July 16 conference regarding the "possibilities" offered by "antipartisan" operations. All Jews may not have been partisans in German eyes, but why not assume that they would offer assistance to partisans if they could?

That some of the killings were directly linked to the planned reduction of food supply to Soviet POWs, Jews, and wider Slav populations in order to feed the *Ostheer* (Eastern Front Army) is probable. But while this "murder for food supply" strategy was applied systematically regarding the POWs, it was not a decisive factor in the murder of Jews during the summer of 1941. Otherwise the killing of Jews would not have been selective from the outset, and some trace of such plans would have surfaced in Heydrich's directives or in the reports of the *Einsatzgruppen* and the police battalions. In the meantime, the Wehrmacht propaganda units were hard at work to promote anti-Jewish rage in the ranks of the Red Army and among the Soviet populations. In early July 1941 the first major drops of millions of German leaflets over Soviet territory started. The "Jewish criminals," their murderous deeds, their treacherous plots, were the mainstays in an endless litany of hatred. And, more virulently than during the Polish campaign, soldiers' letters demonstrate the impact of the anti-Jewish slogans among members of the *Ostheer*.

On July 3 Corporal F marched through an eastern Galician town. After describing the discovery of the massacres that had taken place in local jails before the Soviets departed, he commented: "Here, one witnesses Jewish and Bolshevik cruelty of a kind that I hardly thought possible. . . . This kind of thing calls for vengeance and it is being meted out."[14] In the same area Corporal WH described the houses in the Jewish quarter as "robber dens" and the Jews he encountered as the most sinister beings. His comrade Helmut expressed their feelings: "How was it possible that this race claimed for itself the right to rule all other nations."[15]

Before retreating from eastern Galicia, the NKVD, unable to deport the jailed Ukrainian nationalists, decided to murder them on the spot. The victims, in the thousands, were found inside the jails and mainly in hastily dug mass graves when the Germans, accompanied by Ukrainian units, marched into the main towns of the area. As a matter of course the Ukrainians accused the local Jews of having sided with the Soviet occupation regime in general, and particularly of having helped the NKVD in its murderous onslaught against the Ukrainian elite.

Such accusations were rooted in a long tradition of Ukrainian hatred of Jews, originating in Christian anti-Jewish hostility. It was later reinforced by the frequent employment of Jews as estate stewards for Polish nobility, and thus their being perceived as the representatives of Polish domination over the Ukrainian peasantry. Drawing on such hostility, modern Ukrainian nationalists accused Jews of siding with the Poles on the morrow of World War I in fought-over areas such as eastern Galicia (while the Poles accused the Jews of siding with the Ukrainians) and, throughout the interwar period, as being part and parcel either of bolshevik oppression or of Polish measures against the Ukrainian minority.

Within the Ukrainian nationalist movement itself, the extremists, led by Stepan Bandera and supported by the Germans, gained the upper hand. Bandera's men led the OUN–B (Organization of Ukrainian Nationalists–Bandera) auxiliary units that marched into eastern Galicia in June 1941 together with the Wehrmacht. In Lwów the Ukrainians herded local Jews and forced them to dig up the corpses of the NKVD's victims from their mass graves or retrieve them from the jails. Then the Jews had to align the bodies of those recently murdered and also of already badly decomposed corpses along open graves, before being themselves shot into the pits—or being killed in the jails and the fortress, or on the streets and squares of the main eastern Galician towns.

On July 6 Private Franzl recorded the events at Tarnopol for the enjoyment of his parents in Vienna. The discovery of the mutilated corpses of *Volksdeutsche* and Ukrainians led to vengeance against the local Jews: They were forced to carry the corpses from the cellars and line them up by newly dug graves;

afterward the Jews were beaten to death with truncheons and spades. "Up to now," Franzl went on, "we have sent approximately 1,000 Jews to the other world, but this is by far too little for what they have done." After asking his parents to spread the news, Franzl ended his letter with a promise: "If there are doubts, we will bring photos. Then, no more doubts."[16]

In smaller towns of eastern Galicia most of the murderous anti-Jewish outbreaks during these early days of occupation took place without apparent German intervention. Decades later witnesses from Brzezany, a town to the south of Zloczow, described the sequence of events: As the Germans entered the town "the Ukrainians were ecstatic. Throngs of Ukrainian peasants, mostly young people, carrying yellow-and-blue flags adorned with the Ukrainian trident, filled the . . . streets. They came from the villages, dressed in Ukrainian national costumes, singing their Ukrainian songs . . ." What followed was to be expected: "Most of the Jews who perished in Brzezany on that day were murdered with broomsticks with nails attached to them. . . . There were two rows of Ukrainian bandits, holding big sticks. They forced those people, the Jews, in between the two rows and murdered them in cold blood with those sticks."[17]

On August 1, 1941, eastern Galicia was annexed to the General Government and became part of the district of Galicia, with Lwów as its main administrative center. For several months Hans Frank forbade the setting up of ghettos in order to keep the option of transferring these additional Jewish populations "to the East," eventually to the Pripet swamps area. In Lwów, for example, ghettoization started only in October 1941. Frank's desire to get rid of his newly acquired Jews was so intense that little was done to hinder thousands of them from fleeing to Romania and Hungary. Otherwise tens of thousands of Jewish men from Galicia were soon herded into labor camps, mainly along the new strategic road that would link Lwów to the southern Ukraine and eventually to the Black Sea. This notorious *Durchgangstrasse IV* (transit road IV) would be useful both to the Wehrmacht and to Himmler's colonization plans. It is this project that, in the later summer of 1941, inaugurated de facto the systematic annihilation of Jews by way of slave labor.

In Lithuania the first victims of the Germans were the 201 mostly Jewish men of the small border town Gargždai (Garsden), executed on June 24. The Jewish women and children (approximately three hundred), spared at the outset, were locked up in barns and shot in mid-September. A few days later, the killings started in the main cities, Vilna and Kovno, and went on in several waves during the summer and the fall; at the same time the Jewish population in small towns and villages was entirely exterminated.

Vilna, a city inhabited on the eve of the German occupation by some sixty thousand Jews, was for centuries one of the most important centers of Jewish life in Eastern Europe. In the eighteenth century Rabbi Elijah ben Solomon, the "Vilna Gaon," carried religious scholarship to rarely equaled heights, albeit in a tradition of strict intellectual orthodoxy that fiercely opposed Hasidism, the emotional and popular Jewish revivalism born at the same time in the Ukrainian borderlands. It was also in Vilna that the Jewish workers' party, Bund, was created at the end of the nineteenth century. Though a fervent protagonist of the international proletarian struggle, the Bund was decidedly antibolshevist; it advocated Jewish cultural (Yiddish) and political (socialist) autonomy in Eastern Europe and thus opposed the Zionist brand of Jewish nationalism. It was possibly the most original and numerically important Jewish political movement of the interwar period—and the most unrealistic.

In the wake of World War I the Baltic countries became independent, but Lithuania lost Vilna to Poland. At that stage the hatred of Lithuanian nationalists and of their fascist fringe, the "Iron Wolf" movement, was essentially directed against the Poles, much less so against the Jews. Stepwise, however, from 1926 on, Lithuania moved to the right. Yet the Lithuanian government, under Antanas Smetona, did not initiate any anti-Semitic laws or measures.

During these same years the Jewish minority in Polish-controlled Vilna energetically developed its cultural and internal political life. Apart from a vast school system in Yiddish, Hebrew, and Polish, the Vilna community boasted a Yiddish theater, a wealth of newspapers and periodicals, clubs, libraries, and other cultural and social institutions. The city became home to major Yiddish writers and artists, as well as to the YIVO research center in the Jewish humanities and social sciences, founded in 1925—a Jewish university in the making.

The political scene changed radically with the Soviet annexation of Lithuania and the other Baltic countries in July 1940. Any kind of balanced assessment of Jewish involvement in the new political system is rendered quasi impossible by contrary aspects in various domains: Jewish religious institutions and political parties soon became targets of the NKVD; at the same time Jews were highly represented in officer schools, midrank police appointments, higher education, and various administrative positions. Thus it was not too difficult for extremist Lithuanian right-wing émigrés who had fled to Berlin, and who, together with the Germans, were fostering anti-Soviet operations in the home country, to identify the Jews with the bolsheviks. Elimination of the Jews from Lithuania became a goal of the underground Lithuanian Activists' Front (LAF). When, a week before the German invasion, the NKVD deported some 35,000 Lithuanians to the Soviet interior, the Jews were widely accused of being both agents and informers.

The Wehrmacht occupied Vilna in the early morning hours of June 24, 1941. The systematic killings in the city began on July 4. Lithuanian gangs had started rounding up hundreds of male Jews whom they either slaughtered on the spot or in the woods of Ponar, close to the city. Women and children were included from August onward; the German aim seems to have been the extermination of the Jews unable to work, while workers and their families were left alive. A first *Judenrat* was established in Vilna in July; most of its members were among the Jews murdered in early September. A second Jewish Council was appointed under the chairmanship of Anatol Fried. On September 6, 1941, the remaining Jews were ordered to move into the ghetto. This concentration, along with the help of the Germans' willing auxiliaries—the Lithuanians—facilitated the killing operations, which lasted throughout December and claimed the lives of some 33,000 Jewish inhabitants of Vilna.

Itzhok Rudashevski, a Vilna schoolboy not yet fourteen, described in his diary the roundup of Yom Kippur: "Today the ghetto is full of storm troopers. They thought Jews would not go to work today, so they came to the ghetto to take them. At night things suddenly became turbulent. The people get up. The gate opens. An uproar develops. Lithuanians have arrived. I look at the courtyard and see them leading away people with bundles. I hear boots pounding on the stairs. Soon, however, things calmed down. The Lithuanians were given money and they left. In this way the defenseless Jews attempted to rescue themselves. In the morning the terrible news spread. Several thousand people were uprooted from the ghetto at night. These people never came back again."[18] Rudashevski's last sentence indicates clearly that this entry must have been written some time after the events; it also shows that during the roundups neither he nor the Jews being taken away had any idea what was going on and where they were headed.

In Kovno, Lithuanian murder squads ran wild during the early days of the occupation. Some reports describe the enthusiastic attendance of the Lithuanian population (many women with children settling in "front rows" for the day) and of throngs of German soldiers, all of them egging on the killers with shouts and applause. Over the following days groups of Jews were shoved off to the forts surrounding the city and shot. After the first wave of killings the remaining thirty thousand Jews were expelled into the old Jewish suburb of Slobodka, across the river, where on July 10, 1941, a ghetto was officially established; its chairman was the highly respected physician Dr. Elchanan Elkes.

The extermination frenzy that engulfed the immense majority of the Jews of Lithuania raged throughout the other two Baltic countries. By the end of 1941 almost all of the two thousand Jews of Estonia had been killed. A year later the approximately 66,000 Jews of Latvia had been almost entirely exterminated as well (some 12,000 Jews remained on Latvian territory, 8,000 of whom were deportees from the Reich).

The massacres spread throughout the eastern occupied territories. Even the Reich's downtrodden victims, the Poles, took a hand in the mass killing of Jews. The best-known massacres occurred in the Białystok district, in Radzilow and in Jedwabne, on July 10. After the Wehrmacht occupied the area, the inhabitants of these small towns exterminated most of their Jewish neighbors by beating them, shooting them, and burning scores of them alive in local barns.

At times, however, local populations refused to participate in the anti-Jewish violence. In Brest-Litovsk, for example, both the White Russians and the Poles expressed quite openly their pity for the Jewish victims and their disgust for the "barbaric" methods of the Germans, the "hangmen of the Jews." The same reluctance to initiate pogroms was noticed in the Ukraine, in the Zhytomyr region, among others. Similar attitudes were indirectly confirmed in Wehrmacht reports dealing with the impact of anti-Semitic propaganda operations on the Russian population.

While the Germans and their local auxiliaries actively pursued their killing campaign in the north, center, and south of the eastern front, the Romanian army and gendarmerie were outperforming the *Einsatzgruppen*. In fact, over a one-year period, the Romanians were to massacre some 270,000 Jews. And while they could not compete with the Germans in the total number of victims, like the Latvians, the Lithuanians, the Ukrainians, and the Croats, they were ingenious tormentors and murderers.

The earliest large-scale massacre of Romanian Jews took place in Iasi, the capital of Moldavia. On June 26, 1941, in "retaliation" for two Soviet air raids, the killings started, organized by army intelligence officers and local police authorities. After thousands had been massacred in the city, several thousand more were packed into the hermetically closed cars of two freight trains and sent on an aimless journey lasting several days. In the first train 1,400 Jews suffocated or died of thirst; 1,194 bodies were recovered from the second one. The exact number of the victims of the Iasi pogrom remains in dispute, but it may have exceeded ten thousand.

The decimation of the Jews of Bessarabia and Bukovina first began as a local initiative then on orders from Bucharest. On July 8 Ion Antonescu harangued his ministers: "I beg you, be implacable. Saccharine and vaporous humanitarianism have no place here. . . . If need be, shoot with machine guns, and I say that there is no law."[19] The massacre of Jews became an everyday occurrence; tens of thousands were herded into ghettos until, in the autumn, they were driven over the river Dniester into "Transnistria," the area of southern Ukraine that was Romanian-occupied and was to remain under Romanian control.

After the German victory in the Balkans, Yugoslavia had been divided: The Germans occupied Serbia and the Italians, large stretches of the Dalmatian coast; the Hungarians were given the Backa and Baranya regions, and the Bulgarians re-

ceived Macedonia. An independent Croatian state was established under the leadership of Ante Pavelić and his Ustasha
movement. While the Dalmatian coast of Croatia remained
partly under Italian control, some German troops also stayed
on Croatian territory.

In Serbia, the Germans set up a collaborationist government under Prime Minister Milan Nedić, a fervent anticommunist. Nedić hardly mattered, and soon after the German
attack against the Soviet Union, armed resistance started
mainly in the countryside. Throughout the summer relatively
small and untrained Wehrmacht forces fought a losing battle
against the spreading insurrection of Tito's (Josip Broz) communist and Draža Mihajlović's Serbian nationalist guerrillas.
Notwithstanding the widespread shooting of hostages (Serbs
and mainly Jews) by the Germans, the destruction of villages,
and the killing of their inhabitants, the rebellion spread. In September, Hitler appointed the Austrian general Franz Boehme,
a notorious Serb hater, as commanding general of the forces
stationed in Serbia and gave him a free hand to use "severe
methods" to regain control of the situation. Boehme complied
enthusiastically.

In Croatia no sooner did Pavelić establish his new regime—
a mixture of fascism and devout Catholicism—that, as the
German envoy to Zagreb, Edmund von Glaise Horstenau,
reported "the Ustasha went raging mad."[20] The new leader
launched a genocidal crusade against the 2,200,000 Christian-
Orthodox Serbs (out of a total population of 6,700,000) living
on Croatian territory, and against the country's 45,000 Jews,
particularly in ethnically mixed Bosnia. The Catholic Ustasha
did not mind the continuous presence of Muslims or Protestants, but Serbs and Jews had to convert, to leave, or to die.
According to the historian Jonathan Steinberg, "Serbian and
Jewish men, women and children were literally hacked to
death. Whole villages were razed to the ground and the people

driven to barns to which the Ustasha set fire. There is in the Italian Foreign Ministry archive a collection of photographs of the butcher knives, hooks and axes used to chop up Serbian victims. There are photographs of Serb women with breasts hacked off by pocket knives, men with eyes gouged out, emasculated and mutilated."[21]

While Archbishop Alojzije Stepinac, the head of the Catholic Church in Croatia, hesitated for months to publicly denounce the savage murder campaign, some local bishops rejoiced at the extermination of the schismatics and the Jews, or at their forced conversion. In the words of the Catholic bishop of Mostar, "There was never such a good occasion as now for us to help Croatia to save the countless souls."[22] And while bishops blessed the unique occasion to save souls, some Franciscan monks took a leading role in the most vicious murder operations and in the decimation of Serbs and Jews in the uniquely Croat Jasenovac extermination camp.

There was much in common in the mixture of Christian beliefs, fascist policies, and savage murderousness between the Croat Ustasha and the Romanian Iron Guard, or even Antonescu's regime; the same extremist ingredients characterized the Ukrainian nationalists, mainly Bandera's faction in the OUN, and the sundry groups of Lithuanian and Latvian "partisans." For all of these radical killer groups, local Jews were a prime target, as we saw. Similar ideological components also characterized the Slovak People's Party. From the outset the People's Party was divided between traditional conservatives and a militant quasi-fascist wing led by Vojtech Tuka, a fierce nationalist and no less fierce anti-Semite. In March 1939 Dr. Jozef Tiso, a conservative priest, became the chief of the party and the president of independent Slovakia, while Tuka drifted ever closer to National Socialism and was soon appointed prime minister of the new state. Of course the new Slovak regime did not forfeit the confidence of its Berlin masters—nor could it; its anti-Semitism was inherent to a religious tradition and to direct German influence.

The great majority of a largely rural Slovak population of approximately 2,600,000 inhabitants was devoutly Catholic; the Evangelical community counted around 15 percent of the population, and at the end of 1940, the Jews represented some 80,000 people, that is, around 3.3 percent of the population.

When Tiso, Tuka, and Interior Minister Sano Mach were received by Hitler on July 28, 1940, the Nazi leader demanded that his Slovak partners align their anti-Jewish legislation on the German one. Soon thereafter a Central Office for the Economy (UHU) was established to oversee the Aryanization of Jewish property and expel the Jews from any significant functions in business life; a Jewish Council (UŽ) was set up, and in September 1941, the "Jewish Codex," a whole array of anti-Jewish laws, was promulgated. The new decrees included the wearing of the Jewish star and compulsory labor. The stage was set for further steps that would lead Catholic Slovakia to be the first country—after the Reich—to start the deportation of its Jews.

Hungary remained relatively calm; in 1941, some 825,000 Jews lived within its borders, by then vastly expanded by recent annexations. In the larger cities and mainly in Budapest, most Jews were a highly assimilated community that had thrived in a quasi symbiosis with the country's social elite until the end of World War I. In 1918 the political situation radically changed. A defeated and dismembered Hungary was engulfed by revolution. Although Béla Kun's Communist dictatorship lasted only 133 days, his own Jewish origins and the massive presence of Jews in his government triggered a violent anti-Semitic reaction which left thousands of Jewish victims in its wake. Moreover, the presence of a substantial minority of non-assimilated, mainly Polish Jews added to a growing anti-Jewish hostility; it was fueled over the following years by nationalist revisionism, militant anticommunism, and, increasingly so, by the ever stronger pull of Nazism.

Yet, through the interwar period, the regent, Admiral Miklos Horthy, succeeded in keeping conservative governments in power and in staving off small fascist and rabidly anti-Semitic movements. One of the methods chosen by Horthy and the traditional conservatives to stem the extremist tide was to enact anti-Jewish discriminatory laws. An early law of 1920 introducing an anti-Jewish quota in the universities—the first anti-Semitic law in postwar Europe—was adopted but not applied very stringently. The laws of 1938 and 1939, however, concretely limited Jewish participation in the political and economic life of the country, at least as far as the Jewish middle class was concerned (the Jewish banking and industrial elite generally remained untouched). The "third law," that of August 1941—was a replica of the Nuremberg racial legislation. In most of these policies Horthy was backed by the Hungarian Catholic Church and by the Protestant churches. The Hungarian episcopate readily accepted the anti-Jewish decrees of 1938 and 1939, but, as could be expected, balked at the law of August 1941 because of its openly racial dimension, a threat to Jewish converts.

Thousands of foreign Jews who lived in Hungary had to pay for the regent's appeasement tactics. In the course of August 1941, 18,000 of these foreign Jews (almost all Polish) were rounded up by the Hungarian police and turned over to the SS in the western Ukraine. On August 27–28, the expellees and a few thousand local Jews (around 23,600 in all) were exterminated. When the news of the massacre seeped back to Hungary, the minister of the interior ordered an end to the deportation. In the meantime, however, first thousands, then tens of thousands of Jewish men were being drafted for forced-labor service in the occupied Ukraine. By the end of 1941 some fifty thousand Jews had been conscripted; some forty thousand belonging to this first lot would not return. It became apparent however that Horthy was not ready to overstep a certain limit in his anti-Jewish measures, despite repeated German prodding. A stabilization of sorts would last from March 1942, when the relatively liberal Miklós Kállay replaced the pro-German László Bárdossy as the head of government, until the German occupation of the country in March 1944.

The rapid expansion of the murder operations in the newly occupied eastern territories from Jewish men only to that of entire Jewish communities demanded the most efficient mass murder methods. The execution of women and children seemed to Himmler to be too stressful for his commando members; toxic gas was more promising. In the euthanasia program the gassing of mental patients had been used alongside other killing methods. Carbon monoxide was released from bottles into stationary gas chambers or into vans. In September 1941 a technical modification in the euthanasia gas vans, developed at the Criminal Technical Institute of the RSHA, opened new possibilities. The redesigned vans would become mobile suffocating machines for batches of around forty people per van: A metal pipe connected to the exhaust gas hose would be inserted into a sealed van. Running the engine sufficed to asphyxiate its human cargo.

In his postwar testimony commando member Lauer described the process: "Two vans were in service [in Poltava]. . . . They drove into the prison yard and the Jews—men, women and children—had to get straight into the vans from their cells. . . . The exhaust fumes were piped into the interior of the vans. I can still hear the hammering and the screaming of the Jews—"Dear Germans, let us out!" . . . As soon as the doors were shut, the driver started the engine. He drove to a spot outside Poltava. I was there when the van arrived. As the doors were opened, dense smoke emerged, followed by a tangle of crumpled bodies. It was a frightful sight."[23] Within a few months some thirty gas vans were to become operational in the Baltic countries, in Belorussia, in the Ukraine, in the Warthegau, and in Serbia.

It was but a short step from the gas van to the stationary gas chamber, which functioned according to the same technical principles: the use of carbon monoxide produced by attached engines. As we shall see, while several gas vans were used at the Chelmno extermination site in the Warthegau from early December 1941 on, the construction of gas chambers—activated by the exhaust gas from attached engines—began in November on the site of the future Belzec extermination camp. Somewhat earlier, in September of 1941, a different set of murder experiments by gas had started at Auschwitz.

Auschwitz had undergone several stages of development since opening its gates in June 1940 as a concentration camp for Polish political prisoners. Situated near the Upper Silesian town of the same name (half of whose 14,000 inhabitants were Jewish), it was conveniently located between the rivers Vistula and Sola and close to a railway junction of some importance. On April 27, 1940, Himmler had decided about the setting up of the camp, and on May 4 Rudolf Höss, formerly part of the Dachau staff, was put in charge. On June 14, as the Wehrmacht marched into Paris, the first transport of 728 Polish political prisoners from Tarnow in Galicia arrived at the new camp.

In March 1941, Himmler visited the Upper Silesian camp in the company of representatives of the chemical industry giant, I.G. Farben. This visit had been preceded by arduous negotiations between I.G. Farben, officials of Göring's Four-Year Plan administration, and the SS. The continuation of the war with England and the planned attack against the Soviet Union had convinced Hitler and Göring that the production of synthetic rubber and gasoline should be given the highest priority.

I.G. Farben, the German pioneer in this domain, was ordered to expand its production capability considerably. A new plant had to be built as rapidly as possible: Auschwitz was one of the potential sites. In March and April of 1941, Himmler finalized the deal, promising the supply of cheap slave labor and the construction of adequate housing for the German personnel. Höss was ordered to expand the capacity of the camp from 11,000 to 30,000 inmates. The Jews from the town of Auschwitz were expelled and their homes taken over, while Poles were rounded up for construction work both at the camp and at I.G. Farben's future Buna plant site at Dwory.

As these vast expansion plans were set in motion, by sheer coincidence, an Auschwitz disinfection team "discovered" that the powerful pesticide Zylon B—used for the decontamination of ship hulls and military barracks and thus also regularly utilized in Auschwitz—could kill animals and therefore human beings. Testing on a small group of Soviet prisoners of war successfully took place in early September 1941 in the cellar of block 11 in the main camp.

While technical improvements in the murder methods were rapidly progressing, at the top of the Nazi hierarchy hesitation about several possible "solutions" of the Jewish question persisted throughout the summer of 1941. On occupied Soviet territory, as we saw, the extermination was first aimed at Jews as carriers of the Soviet system, then at Jews as potential partisans, and finally as hostile elements living in territories ultimately destined for German colonization: the three categories merged of course into one but did not apply, at least during the summer and the fall of 1941, to the entire European continent. In terms of mass murder the first phase of what was to become the "Final Solution of the Jewish Question in Europe" had started on Soviet territory, but it was probably not yet seen as part of an overall extermination plan of all European Jews.

How then should we interpret the letter addressed by Göring to Heydrich on July 31, 1941?

"In completion of the task which was entrusted to you in the edict dated January 24, 1939, of solving the Jewish question by means of emigration or evacuation in the most convenient way possible . . . ," Göring wrote, "I herewith charge you with making all the necessary preparations . . . for an overall solution of the Jewish question in the German sphere of influence in Europe." The letter went on: "Insofar as the competencies of other central organizations are affected, they are to cooperate with you. I further charge you with submitting to me promptly an overall plan of the preliminary organizational, practical and financial measures for the execution of the intended final solution of the Jewish question."

Göring's letter had been drafted by Heydrich and submitted to the Reichsmarschall for his signature; this much we know from Eichmann's deposition at his 1961 trial in Jerusalem. Manifestly the document was meant to ensure Himmler's and thus Heydrich's authority on all matters pertaining to the fate of the Jews, either in regard to all ongoing operations on Russian territory or in regard to the expected deportations after victory in the East. In other terms the letter was meant to inform all concerned that, in practical terms, the solution of the Jewish question was Himmler's domain (subject of course to Hitler's instructions).

Göring's letter was also appropriately vague concerning any particular time frame, as it seems that Hitler still held to the view that the general evacuation of the European Jews to northern Russia would take place only after the end of the campaign. This was confirmed by Eichmann in early August 1941, at a conference of high officials of the Propaganda Ministry convened to prepare Goebbels's forthcoming visit to his leader. "The Führer," Eichmann declared, "had rejected Obergruppenführer Heydrich's official request regarding evacuations [of Jews] during the war." Consequently Heydrich drew up a proposal for a partial evacuation of Jews from the main Eastern cities. The same idea was submitted to Hitler when Goebbels met him at the Rastenburg headquarters on August 18 and was once more rejected.

During that conversation the Nazi leader again mentioned his "prophecy" regarding the price the Jews would pay for unleashing the war. "The Führer is convinced," Goebbels recorded, "that the prophecy he made in the Reichstag, namely that if Jewry succeeded once again in unleashing a world war, it would end with the extermination of the Jews, is being fulfilled. It [the prophecy] is being confirmed during these last weeks and months with what appears to be an almost uncanny certainty. In the East, the Jews are paying the bill; in Germany, they have already paid it in part and will have to pay more in the future. Their last refuge is North America; and there, either in the long or the short run, they will have to pay as well." Hitler's declarations to Goebbels were indeed highly threatening; still, it is notable that these threats remained vague. The Jews of Germany "will have to pay more in the future" could mean that after victory was achieved in the East, the Jews of Germany would be deported to northern Russia and there "under a hard climate, they would be worked over." Mass death was implicit in Hitler's words; however, it is unlikely that at this stage the Nazi leader's declaration meant organized, generalized, and immediate extermination.

In the meantime, on September 1, 1941, with Hitler's authorization, a decree ordered that all Jews of the Greater Reich and the Protectorate aged six and above should wear a yellow six-pointed star with the word *Jude* inscribed on it in (twisted) black letters. The star had to be sewn onto clothing, on the left side of the breast, at the height of the heart, so as to be fully visible when a Jew was in a public place. From the same date it was forbidden to Jews to leave their area or residence without

police authorization, as well as to carry medals, honorary dec-
orations, and any other kind of badge.

"Today, the Jew's star," Klemperer wrote on September 19:
"Frau Voss has already sewn it on, intends to turn her coat
back over it. Allowed? I reproach myself with cowardice. Yesterday Eva wore out her feet on the pavements and must now
go shopping in town and cook afterwards. Why? Because I
am ashamed. Of what? From Monday I intend to go shopping
again"[24] (Klemperer's wife, Eva, not being Jewish, did not have
to wear the star). How did the German population react?

According to a September 26 SD report from Westphalia,
the new measure was often greeted with satisfaction by the
German population; criticism was rather directed at the existence of exceptions. Why were the Jewish spouses of Aryans
exempted from the tag? As the saying went, there were now
"Aryan Jews" and "non-Aryan Jews." An SD report from the
previous day mentioned the general opinion that the Jews
should also carry the star on the back of their clothes for better
visibility: It would compel those still remaining in Germany to
"disappear."

And yet, many witnesses also recorded different reactions.
On September 20, Klemperer described what happened to
Frau Kronheim: "The latter took the tram yesterday—front
platform. The driver: Why was she not sitting in the car? Frau
Kronheim is small, slight, stooped, her hair completely white.
As a Jewess she was forbidden to do so. The driver struck the
panel with his fist: 'What a mean thing!' Poor comfort." The
most extraordinary expression of sympathy was recorded on
November 25: "Frau Reichenbach . . . told us a gentleman had
greeted her in a shop doorway. Had he not mistaken her for
someone else?—'No, I do not know you, but you will now be
greeted frequently. We are a group who greet the Jew's star.' "[25]
It seems indeed that such expressions of sympathy were not
infrequent. In the historian David Bankier's nuanced assess-

ment, it was the visibility of the persecution that caused so many Germans to react as they did, at least for a while: "As long as anonymous Jews were persecuted, the population could remain emotionally distant from the moral consequences of the affliction they had helped to cause, easily coming to terms with persecution since shame and guilt were not involved. Labeling the victim, however, made him an accusing public witness who testified to the cost of conformity and adjustment in a murderous system. . . . These disturbing feelings obviously did not last long. As had happened with other measures, the penalties exacted from those who sympathized with Jews plus mounting insensibility to what became a common sight, produced increasing apathy and insensitivity."[26]

Whether as an afterthought in the wake of the star decree or as an early sign of decisions to come, on September 11, 1941, the Gestapo disbanded the Kulturbund. Most of its cultural activities had already been forbidden beforehand. Thus in July the association's musicians met for the last time to celebrate Verdi; then their instruments were confiscated and handed out to SA and SS units, the pianos were sent to Nazi welfare organizations and Wehrmacht sanatoriums and their records were recycled by the German record industry. In Germany the last remains of authorized Jewish cultural activity had been snuffed out.

After the proclamation of the new statute of June 1941, the Vichy government forged ahead: On July 22 Aryanization was introduced in the nonoccupied zone according to the same criteria and methods used in the north. Businesses were liquidated or put under "French" control, assets were seized and the proceeds were deposited in a special government bank.

For Darlan and Vallat this did not suffice. On the day the June statute was published, the registration of all Jews (according to the new definition) in the Vichy zone was mandated. More ominous was Darlan's order of December 1941 to register all Jews who had entered France after January 1, 1936; this identification was to become an essential element of the Franco-German agreements concerning the roundups and deportations that were to come. On August 20, 1941, on German instructions, the Paris police arrested a further 4,230 Jews; they were sent to Drancy, the newly established assembly and concentration camp near the French capital. This second roundup was probably undertaken in reprisal for the anti-German demonstrations organized in the city on August 13 by communist youth organizations; the police had supposedly noticed a substantial number of Jews among the demonstrators. This time some French Jews, particularly communists, were also arrested.

In the autumn, attacks against German military personnel drew reprisals, mainly, at first, against communists (Jewish or not). Even the execution of fifty hostages after the killing of the Feldkommandant of Nantes, Lt. Col. Karl Holtz, on October 20, 1941, did not specifically target Jews. For Heydrich, the anti-Jewish reprisals were too mild, and it is against this background that French pro-Nazi militants perpetrated bomb attacks on three Paris synagogues on October 3. On November 28, 1941, another attack against German soldiers took place. This time, on December 12, 743 Jewish men, mainly French and mostly belonging to the middle classes, were seized by the German police and sent to Compiègne, a camp under direct German command. In March 1942 this group and additional Jewish prisoners were deported to Auschwitz. Thus, in France it was the army high command that put into effect increasingly drastic anti-Jewish measures. While the execution of French hostages caused qualms, the deportation of Jews to their death was taken in stride and implemented by the largely non-Nazi military elite.

Simultaneously with the multiplication of anti-Jewish measures, with the arrests and the early deportations, Eichmann's envoy in Paris, the SD officer in charge of Jewish affairs, Theodor Dannecker, exercised growing pressure on the Jewish organizations to transform the "coordination committee" into a full-fledged Jewish Council. The Germans expected Vichy to take the initiative of imposing the new institution. In the fall of 1941 it became obvious to the Jewish leaders, natives and foreigners alike, that they would have to accept the Diktat. Yet the common fate imposed upon all did not heal the rift between the two communities. Against this background of internecine squabbles, a group of French Jewish personalities—among whom Lambert came to play an increasingly important role—decided to go along with Vichy's decisions and to participate in repeated consultations with Vallat, against the will of the Consistoire. On November 29, 1941, Vallat signed the decree establishing the Union Générale des Israélites de France. On January 9, 1942, the executive boards of the UGIF-North (occupied zone) and UGIF-South (Vichy zone) were officially appointed. De facto, Lambert became the dominant personality of UGIF-South.

It has been argued that anti-Jewish measures were less readily applied in the countries of Western Europe under direct German military authority than in those under civilian Nazi rule. While this was not the case in occupied France, it seems that in Belgium the commander in chief of the Wehrmacht, Gen. Alexander von Falkenhausen, was indeed reticent in regard to measures that could create unrest in the population. Yet, the usual anti-Jewish measures enacted in Holland and in France were imposed in Belgium at approximately the same time. Thus in October 1940 the military administration imposed a "Statut des juifs," similar to the French and Dutch ones, upon the 65,000 to 75,000 Jews living in Belgium at the time. Registration was ordered, identity cards marked, Jewish businesses listed, Jewish officials dismissed, Jews expelled from the legal professions and from journalism, like elsewhere in the West. In the spring of 1941, the registration of all Jewish property followed, as well as further segregation measures like those implemented in neighboring Holland, and approximately at the same time. In the fall of that same year a Jewish Council, the Association des Juifs en Belgique (AJB) was imposed; a few days later the UGIF was established in France.

There were some differences, however, between the situation of the Jews of Belgium and those of Holland and France. Whereas two-thirds of the Jews of Holland and half of the Jews of France were native or naturalized citizens in 1940, only 6 percent of the Jews of Belgium were Belgian citizens. Whereas in the three Western countries, small pro-Nazi movements had damaged Jewish property and attacked individual Jews once German presence eased the way, only in Belgium did large-scale pogromlike riots take place on April 14 and 17, 1941. In Antwerp several hundred militants of the nationalist Flemish political party (VNV) set fire to synagogues and to the chief rabbi's house on Easter Monday after attending the screening of *Jud Süss*. And, as 1941 was coming to an end, neither the Belgian church dignitaries nor the resistance movements took a strong stand against the German anti-Jewish measures or against the violence of the Belgian extreme Right. A liberal underground publication did protest against the Antwerp riots, concluding: "Dear readers—Do not think that we Belgians are pro-Jewish. No, far from it. Yet, even a Jew is a human being."[27]

CHAPTER 10

The "Final Solution"

September 1941–December 1941

ON NOVEMBER 12, 1941, Himmler ordered Friedrich Jeckeln, the HSSPF Ostland,[1] to murder the approximately thirty thousand Jews of the Riga ghetto. On the eve of the operation, on November 29, the able-bodied Jews were separated from the bulk of the ghetto population. In the early morning hours the trek from the ghetto to the nearby Rumbula forest began. Some seventeen hundred guards were ready, including around a thousand Latvian auxiliaries. In the meantime several hundred Soviet prisoners had dug six huge pits in the sandy terrain of Rumbula. As group after group of the ghetto inhabitants reached the forest, a tightening gauntlet of guards drove them toward the pits. Shortly before approaching the execution site, the Jews were forced to dispose of their suitcases and bags, take off their coats, and, finally, remove their clothes. Then the naked victims descended into the pit over an earthen ramp, lay facedown on the ground or on the bodies of the dying and the dead and were shot at the back of the head with a single bullet from a distance of about two meters. Jeckeln stood on the edge of the pits surrounded by a throng of SD, police and civilian guests. Twelve marksmen working in shifts shot the Jews throughout the entire day. The killing stopped sometime between 5 and 7 p.m.; by then, about fifteen thousand Jews had been murdered. A week later, on December 7 and 8, the Germans murdered the remaining half of the ghetto population.

The historian Simon Dubnow, who lay ill, had been overlooked during the first massacre. The second time he was caught in the dragnet. The sick and feeble ghetto inhabitants were brought to the execution area in buses; as Dubnow could not board the bus fast enough, one of the Latvian guards shot him in the back of the head. The next day, he was buried in a mass grave in the ghetto. According to rumor, on his way to the bus Dubnow repeated: "People, do not forget; speak of this, people; record it all."[2]

On the day of the first massacre of the Riga Jews, in the early morning hours, a transport of one thousand Jews from Berlin had arrived at the city's railway station. The Berlin Jews were transported straight from the station to the forest and killed on the spot. The deportees transported from the Reich to Riga were but one group among others who, since October 15, following an unexpected decision taken by Hitler, were being sent off from cities in Germany and the Protectorate to ghettos in former Poland or the Ostland. Merely a month earlier Hitler had told Goebbels that the deportation of the Jews of Germany would take place after the victory in Russia and would be directed to the Russian Far North. What could have triggered the Nazi leader's sudden initiative?

Hitler's decision has been attributed to information about Stalin's order to deport the entire population of Volga Germans to Siberia. Yet Hitler could hardly have believed that deporting the Jews of Germany to avenge the Volga Germans would impress somebody of Stalin's ilk. The Volga Germans could have been a convenient pretext for a decision taken earlier for an entirely different reason: Roosevelt's steady efforts to involve the United States in the war. This assessment tallied perfectly with Hitler's belief that the Jews were the threatening force behind Roosevelt. How else could one explain the readiness of the leader of world capitalism to rush aid and assistance to the threatened fortress of Bolshevism? And, as speeches and threats did not seem to deflect the American president from his course, the Nazi leader may have thought that direct and highly menacing steps against the Jews of Germany would have some effect on Roosevelt's Jewish "entourage." The German Jews became, concretely and visibly, hostages on the brink of a dire fate if the United States moved further toward war.

The need to put pressure on Roosevelt may have seemed increasingly urgent to Hitler during the first days of September 1941. On September 4 a German submarine dangerously trailed by the U.S. destroyer *Greer*—and attacked by British aircraft guided by the *Greer*—attempted to torpedo the American vessel. Both the *Greer* and the U-652 escaped unharmed, but a week later, on September 11, Roosevelt gave a distorted account of the incident; two days later American naval forces received the order to "shoot on sight" at all Axis ships encountered within the American "neutrality zone" [unilaterally defined by the United States and extending to mid-Atlantic].[3] One may assume that, in Hitler's mind, the counterthreat could work both ways: Either the fate menacing the Jews of Germany would eventually stop Roosevelt in his tracks or, if Roosevelt and the Jews were bent on war with the Reich, the most dangerous internal enemy would already have been expelled from German territory.

According to Himmler's initial orders the main deportation site was to be the Lodz ghetto, but as Lodz could not take in more than twenty thousand Jews, the ghettos of the Ostland were added. On October 15 the first transport left Vienna for Lodz; it was followed by transports from Prague and Luxembourg on the sixteenth and from Berlin on the eighteenth. By November 5 twenty transports carrying 19,593 Jews completed the first phase. Then, on November 8, the second phase started and lasted until mid-January 1942. This time, twenty-two transports with some 22,000 Jews in all were headed to Riga, Kovno, and Minsk. Of the transports destined for Riga, five were rerouted to Kovno; none of these 5,000 deportees ever set foot in the ghetto: Upon their arrival they were immediately transferred to Fort IX and shot in two batches on November 25 and 29. A month beforehand, on October 28, approximately 10,000 inhabitants of the Kovno ghetto had been murdered. In Minsk, 13,000 local Jews were exterminated on November 7 and a further group of 7,000, on November 20. Clearly the mass slaughters of October and November 1941 were intended to make space for the new arrivals from the Reich. And, as we saw, at times some of the new arrivals were killed upon reaching their destination.

Soon the Reichsführer was receiving a growing number of complaints about the inclusion of *Mischlinge* and decorated war veterans in the transports. And, as information about the Kovno massacres spread, Himmler precipitously ordered on Sunday, November 30, that no liquidation of the Jews deported from Berlin to Riga should take place. The order reached Riga too late and the irate SS chief threatened Jeckeln with punishment for acting on his own. During the following months mass executions of Jews deported from Germany stopped. It was but a brief respite.

Typhoon, the Wehrmacht's offensive against Moscow, was launched on October 2; it was Germany's last chance to win the war in the East before the onset of winter. For a few days victory again seemed within reach. As in July, Hitler's euphoric state of mind was shared by the OKW and also by Fedor von Bock, the commander of Army Group Center, the main force advancing on the Soviet capital. On October 4, when the Nazi chief returned to Berlin for a major speech at the Sportpalast,

Goebbels noted: "The *Führer* is convinced that if the weather remains half way favorable, the Soviet army will be essentially demolished in 14 days."[4]

All over Europe, Jews were following the military news like an anxious choir, in despair at first, with hope somewhat later, then with exaltation at the end of the year. "Hitler is reported to have given a speech in which he said that he has begun a gigantic offensive in the east," Sierakowiak noted on October 3. "I wonder how it will develop. It looks like this one will be as victorious as all the previous ones."[5] And on October 10: "The Germans have supposedly broken the Russian front with their 3 million-man army and are marching on Moscow. Hitler has personally taken command on the front. . . . The Germans are really invincible. We'll rot in this ghetto for sure."[6] A few days later Kaplan became the voice of despair: "The Nazis continue to advance on the Eastern front," he recorded on October 18, "and have reached the gates of Moscow. The city is still fighting desperately but its fate has been decided; it will surely be captured by the Nazis. And when Moscow falls, all the capitals of Europe will be under the Nazi rule. A Nazi victory means complete annihilation, morally and materially, for all the Jews of Europe."[7] Among Jews farther west, opinions may have been more starkly divided: "The events in Russia divide the Jews into two groups," Biélinky noted on October 14. "There are those who consider Russia as already defeated and who hope for some generous gesture on the part of the victor. The others keep a robust faith in Russian resistance."[8]

Strangely enough the misperception of the military situation on the German side went on until early November. Halder, the cool planner, envisioned an advance of two hundred kilometers eastward of Moscow, the conquest of Stalingrad, and the capture of the Maykop oil fields, no less. It was actually Hitler who brought his generals' fantasies down to earth and to the more modest goal of taking Moscow. On November 1 the Nazi leader ordered the resumption of the offensive against the Soviet capital. By then, however, stiffening Soviet resistance, lack of winter equipment, subzero temperatures, and sheer exhaustion of the troops brought the Wehrmacht to a halt. By the end of November, the Red Army had recaptured Rostov-on-Don, which the Germans had occupied a few days earlier; it was the first major Soviet military success since the beginning of the campaign. On December 1 the German offensive was definitively halted. On December 5 fresh Soviet divisions transferred from the Far East counterattacked in front of Moscow: The German retreat started.

While the Wehrmacht faced a perilous situation on the Eastern front, the United States further inched toward war. On October 17 a German submarine attacked the U.S. destroyer *Kearney*, killing eleven sailors; an American merchant ship, the *Lehigh*, was torpedoed off the African coast a few days later; and on October 31, the destroyer *Reuben James* was sunk and more than one hundred American sailors perished. In the midst of this undeclared naval war (apparently the German submarines did not identify the nationality of the vessels in time), the American president announced that he was in possession of documents showing Hitler's intention to abolish all religions, and of maps indicating German plans to divide Latin America into five Nazi-controlled states. Roosevelt's allegations were false, but his intentions were clear enough. Congress—and public opinion—did not remain indifferent: On November 13 the Neutrality Act, which considerably hampered the delivery of American aid to Britain and the Soviet Union, was repealed.

Besides the pressure Hitler may have hoped to put upon "the Jewish clique" around Roosevelt by deporting the Jews of Germany, the best chance of avoiding American entry into the war rested upon the success of the isolationist campaign. The antiwar agitation was led, at this stage, by the America

First Committee and its star speaker, Charles A. Lindbergh, the world-famous pilot and tragic father of a kidnapped and murdered son.

On September 11, following Roosevelt's "active defense" speech, Lindbergh delivered his most aggressive address yet, titled "Who are the War Agitators?" before some eight thousand Iowans packed into the Des Moines Coliseum. Lindbergh indicted the administration, the British, and the Jews. Regarding the Jews, he began by expressing compassion for their plight and their reasons to wish the overthrowing of the regime in Germany. "But no person of honesty and vision," he added, "can look on their pro-war policy here today without seeing the dangers involved in such a policy, both for us and for them."[9] Lindbergh's second point in no way mitigated the impact of the first: "Their greatest danger to this country lies in their large ownership and influence in our motion pictures, our press, our radio and our Government." The final part regarding the Jews was, implicitly, the most provocative of all: "I am not attacking either the Jewish or British people," he declared. "Both races, I admire. But I am saying that the leaders of both the British and Jewish races, . . . for reasons which are not American, wish to involve us in the war. . . . We cannot allow the natural passions and prejudices of other peoples to lead our country to destruction."[10]

The widespread outrage provoked by Lindbergh's speech not only put a de facto end to his political activity, but also demonstrated that, notwithstanding strong anti-Semitic passions among segments of American society, the great majority would not admit any exclusionary talk, even if presented in "reasonable terms." Goebbels missed neither the speech nor the reactions. "One cannot but admire Lindbergh," he recorded on September 14. "Solely relying on himself he has dared to face this association of business manipulators, Jews, plutocrats and capitalists."[11]

On December 7 the Japanese attacked Pearl Harbor. On December 11, preempting the inevitable, the Nazi leader declared war on the United States.

Hitler's prolonged low-key rhetorical stance regarding the Jews came to an abrupt end in the fall of 1941: The restraint of the previous months gave way to an explosion of the vilest anti-Jewish invectives and threats. This sharp turnabout closely followed the decision to deport the Jews of Germany; it was inaugurated by what must have been the most bizarre "order of the day" in modern times. On the eve of Typhoon, on October 2, in addressing the millions of soldiers poised for what was to be "the last of the great decisive battles of the year," Hitler left no doubt about the true identity of the "horrendous, beast-like" foe that had been about to "annihilate not only Germany, but the whole of Europe." Those who upheld the system in which bolshevism was but the other face of the vilest capitalism were in both cases the same: "Jews and only Jews!"[12] The next day, in his Sportpalast speech to mark the opening of the "winter relief" campaign, Hitler designated the Jews as "the world enemy."[13] From then on his anti-Jewish diatribes became torrential. Day after day, sheer naked anti-Semitic rage had become the German leader's obsessional theme in private talks and public declarations.

On December 12, one day after Hitler announced to the Reichstag that Germany was declaring war on the United States, the Nazi leader addressed the Reichsleiter and Gauleiter in a secret speech summed up by Goebbels: "In regard to the Jewish question, the *Führer* is determined to wipe the slate clean. He prophesied to the Jews that if they once more brought about a world war, they would be annihilated. These were not mere words. The world war is here, the extermination of the Jews must be its necessary consequence."[14]

Then, according to an entry in Himmler's appointment

calendar dated December 18, the Nazi leader gave him the instruction: "Jewish question: exterminate as partisans."[15] The identification of the Jews as "partisans" obviously did not refer to the Jews on Soviet territory, who were already being exterminated for six months. It referred to the deadly internal enemy, the enemy fighting within the borders of one's own territory, who, by plotting and treachery could, as in 1917–18, stab the Reich in the back, now that a new world war on all fronts rekindled all the dangers of the previous one. One may, moreover, associate "partisans" with the most general connotation used by Hitler in his declaration at the conference of July 16, 1941: All potential enemies within Germany's reach; it was understood, as we saw, to include any civilians and entire communities at will. Thus, the order was clear: Extermination without any limitation, here applied to the Jews.

Even before the departure of the first transport from the Reich, Heydrich convened a meeting in Prague on October 10, attended by the highest local SS commanders and by Eichmann. Fifty thousand deportees, the RSHA chief told his acolytes, would be sent to the *Ostland*. Regarding the Jews of the Protectorate, Heydrich planned the establishment of two transit camps, one in Moravia and one in Bohemia, from which the Jews would leave eastward. On October 13 the Reichsführer met Globocnik and Friedrich Wilhelm Krüger (HSSPF in the General Government). It was probably at this meeting that the SS chief ordered Globocnik to start building the Belzec extermination camp. We do not know with any certainty whether the camp was "only" being set up to exterminate Jews of the Lublin district in order to make space for Jewish deportees from the Reich or whether the killing of all Jews of the district was also linked to colonization plans in the area, as a first step of the constantly reworked "General Plan East"—part of Hitler's Lebensraum plan to cleanse the territories occupied by Germany in Eastern Europe. It may have been intended for both objectives.

We do know that it was essentially in order to deal with the influx of deportees from the Reich to Lodz that preparations for mass murder were initiated in the Warthegau. The extermination sites planned for the *Ostland* were most probably also part of the same immediate murder projects regarding the local ghetto populations. With Himmler's agreement a few euthanasia experts had already been sent to Lublin in early September. If Hitler's order about the deportation from the Reich had been conveyed to the Reichsführer at the beginning of September, the arrival of euthanasia experts at that time meant that the elimination of part of the ghetto populations was considered from the outset as the best solution to the overcrowding issue. Additional indications pointing to the initially "local" function of Belzec and Chelmno include the technically "limited capacity" of the Belzec gassing installations and the letter sent by Greiser to Himmler in May 1942, indicating that Chelmno was meant to exterminate part of the Jewish population of the Warthegau, including Lodz. On November 1 the construction of Belzec started. The killing installation in Chelmno was much simpler: Three gas vans were delivered by the RSHA sometime in November, and by early December everything was ready for the first batch of victims.

A few days after his meeting with Krüger and Globocnik, Himmler ordered the cessation of all Jewish emigration from the Reich "in view of the forthcoming 'Final Solution' of the Jewish Question." Furthermore, on the eve of Himmler's order, a step, puzzling at first glance, had been taken by Heydrich. The chief of the RSHA rejected an offer from the Spanish government to evacuate to Morocco two thousand Jews of Spanish nationality arrested over the previous months in Paris. Heydrich argued that the Spaniards would be unwilling and unable to guard the Jews in Morocco and that, moreover, "these Jews would also be too much out of the direct reach of measures for a basic solution to the Jewish question to be enacted after the war."[16] Heydrich demanded that this explanation be conveyed to the Spaniards.

While Heydrich was dealing with the Spaniards, on October 25 one of Rosenberg's acolytes in the ministry for the occupied eastern territories, Eberhard Wetzel, ventured to issue instructions of his own: There were no objections in his view that those Jews from the Ostland ghettos who were unable to work and Reich Jews of the same category should be "removed by Brack's device" [gas vans].[17] This would have been a first direct allusion to a general extermination plan, except for the fact that neither Wetzel nor Rosenberg had any say in the matter. Moreover it should be kept in mind that Rosenberg may have been informed of a general extermination plan in mid-November at the earliest (if such a plan existed at the time) and otherwise only in December. A number of other documents, mostly of less intrinsic significance, have been adduced to argue that Hitler's final decision to exterminate the Jews of Europe was taken sometime in late September or early October 1941; others, obversely, have been introduced to demonstrate that the decision was taken after the American entry into the war.

Either way the Nazi leader's decision was taken sometime during the last three months of 1941. His rhetoric, the new deportations, the expansion of the killings all pointed to the same direction: Faced with the reality of a new world war, the Nazi leader was determined to eliminate the one internal enemy he deemed responsible for Germany's defeat in 1914–18—the Jews.

In the Reich, information about massacres perpetrated in the East was first and foremost spread by soldiers, who often wrote home quite openly about what they witnessed and quite approvingly so as well. "In Kiew," Cpl. LB wrote on September 28, "mines explode one after the other. For eight days now the city is on fire and all of it is the Jews' doing. Therefore all Jews aged

14 to 60 have been shot and the Jewish women will also be shot, otherwise there will be no end to it."[18] On November 2 Pvt. XM described a former synagogue, built in 1664, that was in use up to the war. Now only the walls remained. "It won't ever be used in the previous function," XM added. "I believe that in this country [the Soviet Union] the Jews will soon not be in need of any prayer house. I already described to you why it is so. For these dreadful creatures it remains after all the only right redemption."[19]

The information about the gigantic exterminations of Jews in the East was of course not conveyed by soldiers' letters only. As early as July 1941 Swiss diplomatic and consular representatives in the Reich and in satellite countries were filing detailed reports about the mass atrocities; their information all stemmed from German or related sources. Senior and even midlevel officials in various German ministries had access to the communications of the *Einsatzgruppen* and to their computations of the staggering number of Jews whom they had murdered. Such information was mentioned in internal Foreign Ministry correspondence in October 1941 and not even ranked "top secret."

In a letter addressed to his wife, Freya, Helmuth von Moltke, an active member of the opposition to Hitler, displayed a clear understanding of what was going on: "The news from the East is terrible again. Our losses are obviously very, very heavy. But that could be borne if we were not burdened with a hecatomb of corpses. Again and again one hears reports that in transports of prisoners or Jews only 20% arrive. . . . What will happen when the nation as a whole realizes that this war is lost, and lost differently from the last one? With a blood guilt that cannot be atoned for in our lifetime and can never be forgotten. . . ."[20] These lines were written at the end of August 1941. Later that year, in October and November, Moltke commented on the deportations: "Since Saturday," he wrote to Freya on October 21, "the Berlin Jews are being rounded up. . . . Then they are sent off, with what they can carry to Lodz and Smolensk. We are to be spared the sight of them being simply left to perish in hunger and cold, and that is why it is done in Lodz and Smolensk."[21] And, on November 13: "I find it hard to remember these two days. Russian prisoners, evacuated Jews, evacuated Jews, Russian prisoners. . . . This was the world of these two days. Yesterday, I said goodbye to a once famous Jewish lawyer who has the Iron Cross First and Second Class, the Order of the House of Hohenzollern, the Golden Badge for the Wounded, and who will kill himself with his wife today because he is to be picked up tonight."[22]

Regarding the killings in occupied Soviet territories, Ulrich von Hassell commented on October 4 about "the continuation of the most disgusting atrocities mainly against the Jews who are executed row after row without the least shame. . . . A headquarters commanding medical officer . . . reported that he tested Russian dum-dum bullets in the execution of Jews and achieved such and such results; he was ready to go on and write a report that could be used in [anti-Soviet] propaganda about this ammunition!"[23]

German populations were also quite well informed about the goings-on in the concentration camps, even the deadliest ones. Thus people living in the vicinity of Mauthausen, for example, could watch what was happening in the camp. On September 27, 1941, Eleanore Gusenbauer sent a letter of complaint to the Mauthausen police station: "In the Concentration Camp Mauthausen at the work site in Vienna Ditch inmates are being shot repeatedly; those badly struck live for yet some time, and so remain lying next to the dead for hours or even half a day long. My property lies upon an elevation next to the Vienna Ditch, and one is often an unwilling witness to such outrages. I am anyway sickly and such a sight makes a demand on my nerves that in the long run I cannot bear. I request that it be arranged that such inhuman deeds be discontinued, or else done where one does not see [them]."[24]

As for the fate of Jewish deportees from the Reich, some information seeped back from the very outset. The killers themselves were not shy about describing their deeds, even regarding mass executions in the supposedly secret operation 14f13. During the last months of 1941 Dr. Friedrich Mennecke, one of the SS physicians directly involved in the operation, left a few notorious letters to his wife—and to posterity. On November 26, for example, he reported to his "dearest Mommy" from Buchenwald: The first "portion" of victims was Aryan. "A second portion of some 1200 Jews followed, who need not be 'examined,' but for whom it suffices to take the incarceration reasons (often considerable!) from the file and transfer them to the form. Thus it is a purely theoretical task."[25] A few days later the Jews were transported to Bernburg and gassed.

Throughout the weeks and months of the fall of 1941, as the deportations from the Reich started and the signal for the extermination of all the Jews of Europe was given, "ordinary" persecution of Jews in the Reich did not abate. Moreover legislation dealing with the practical sequels of the deportations was finalized, mainly to allow a smooth takeover of all assets and property left behind. Three issues were at the top of the agenda: the judicial status of Poles and Jews; the legal situation of Jewish laborers, and finally, the status of Jews who were still German nationals but were no longer living in the Reich.

By mid-October 1941 the first law was ready: almost any offense committed by a Pole or a Jew was punishable by death. The new "Labor Law" for Jews was published on November 4: A Jewish laborer had no rights whatsoever and could be dismissed from one day to the next. Apart from a minimal daily salary, a Jew could not claim any social benefit or compensation. Nonetheless Jewish laborers had to give up nearly half of their meager salary in income tax and social benefits payments.

The "Eleventh Ordinance to the Reich's Citizenship Law,"[26] promulgated on November 25, 1941, stated that German Jews residing outside the Reich would lose their citizenship, and all their assets would become the property of the state ("outside the Reich" designated of course some of the major deportation areas).

The German churches could no longer disregard the new anti-Jewish measure, as some of the victims were converted Jews. On September 17, two days before the enforcement of the star decree, Theodor Cardinal Innitzer of Vienna sent out a pastoral letter commending respect and love toward the Catholic Jews; the next day his message was withdrawn and replaced by a short text from which any mention of love and respect had disappeared; it merely allowed non-Aryan Christians to continue and participate in church life as previously. Also on September 17, Breslau's Cardinal Bertram set the guidelines for the church in the Reich. He reminded the bishops of the equal standing of all Catholics, Aryans or non-Aryans, and demanded that discriminatory measures in church services be avoided "as long as possible." But, if asked by (non-Aryan) Catholics, priests should recommend "attendance of early morning services."[27] If disturbances were to occur, then—and only then—a statement reminding the faithful that the church did not recognize any differences among its members, whatever their background, should be read, but separate church attendance should also be considered. A month later, however, Bertram wrote to Munich's Cardinal Faulhaber that the church had more urgent issues to deal with than the problem of the converted Jews. As for the Jews as such, they were not even mentioned.

Bernhard Lichtenberg, prior of Sankt Hedwig Cathedral in Berlin, was a lone exception. From November 1938 on, during every evening service he prayed aloud for the Jews. On August 29, 1941, two women parishioners denounced him to the Gestapo.

He was arrested on October 23, interrogated, and sentenced to prison. He died on his way to Dachau, on November 3, 1943.

Among Protestants stark differences appeared between the Confessing communities and the "German Christians." Some members of the Confessing Church demonstrated outright courage. Thus, in September 1941, Katerine Staritz, a church official in Breslau published a circular letter in support of the star bearers, calling on her congregation to show an especially welcoming attitude toward them. The SD reported on the circular; the *Schwarze Korps* commented on it, and the officials of the church dismissed Staritz from her position as "city curate." A few months later she was shipped to Ravensbrück for a year. Upon her return she was not allowed to perform any significant duties in the church and had to report twice a week to the Gestapo.

As could be expected, the German Christians reacted with glee to the new measure. A few weeks before, they had published a manifesto praising the antibolshevik campaign in the East: "We are opposed," they declared in their message, "to a form of Christianity which allies itself with Bolshevism, which regards the Jews as the Chosen People, and which denies that our Volk and our Race are God-given." For them the introduction of the star allowed barring "Jewish Christians from attending services, entering church buildings or being buried in Christian cemeteries."[28]

In late 1941, as details about the fate of the Jews in the East were seeping back into the Reich, British high officials were also becoming aware of the mass murders on Soviet territory from decoded German messages. However, any such information remained strictly secret to protect the most precious trump card of the war: British possession of a German "Enigma" encoding machine that gave access to a large proportion of enemy radio communications.

In the meantime the leadership of American Jewry and that of the Jewish community in Palestine seemed rather unconcerned about the European situation, both because of inadequate information and more pressing and immediate challenges. For American Jews their veneration of Roosevelt and their fear of anti-Semitism added to the reticence regarding any interventions that may have displeased "the Chief" and the higher levels of the administration.

More perplexing in many ways was the attitude of the Jewish leadership in Palestine. In February 1941 David Ben-Gurion, leader of Mapai, the strongest political party in the *Yishuv*, and of its highest executive body, the Jewish Agency, returned to Palestine after a lengthy stay in Great Britain and the United States. His comments at a meeting with his Mapai colleagues offer an indication of what had been and would be his approach to the events in Europe: "No one can estimate the enormity of the destruction of the Jewish people. . . . What we must do now . . . above all and before anything, for ourselves and for the Diaspora, that same small Diaspora still left to us, is [create] Zionist commitment."[29] In other words, for Ben-Gurion there was but one way of helping European Jewry: achieving the goals of Zionism. And simultaneously such help would eventually allow a Jewish state in Palestine to survive. Notwithstanding Ben-Gurion's exhortations, no concrete assistance or rescue plans emerged from the *Yishuv* throughout most of 1941. The Jewish Agency hardly paid attention to the situation in Europe, and the common opinion was that nothing much could be done to alleviate whatever suffering there was.

Throughout the Reich and the Protectorate the local Jewish community offices were informed well in advance of the date of deportations from their area. The local Gestapo station received the lists of names from the district office of the Reichs-vereinigung and decided whom to include in the upcoming transport. Those designated for departure were given a serial number and informed by the Reichsvereinigung or by the Gestapo about the procedures regarding assets, homes, outstanding bills, the amount of cash allowed, the authorized weight of the luggage, the amount of food for the journey, as well as the date by which they had to be ready. From then on they were forbidden to leave their homes without permission from the authorities. On the departure day these Jews were assembled by the Schutzpolizei (ordinary police) and marched or driven in trucks to a waiting area where they would be kept, sometimes for several days, before being marched again or driven to the railway station, often in broad daylight and in full view of the population.

Some Jews avoided deportation. "Nineteen Jews who should have gone with the first transport from Vienna to Lodz on October 15 took their own lives, either by jumping from windows or by gassing themselves, by hanging, with sleeping tablets, by drowning, or by means unknown. Within the space of three weeks, the Gestapo reported 84 suicides and 87 suicide attempts in Vienna." According to statistics of the Berlin police, 243 Jews took their lives during the last three months of 1941 (from the beginning of the deportations to the end of the year). The quota was filled with other Jews, of course.

On September 23 Rumkowski had been informed by the Germans of the coming deportations into the ghetto. Statistics assembled by the elder regarding overcrowding obviously had no effect whatsoever. For the 143,000 inhabitants of the ghetto in the fall of 1941, first the arrivals of Jews from Włocławek and other surrounding small towns, then of the twenty thousand Jews from the Reich and the Protectorate and of five thousand Gypsies, meant a sudden 20 percent increase in the population. Seen from the perspective of the new arrivals it meant sleeping in evacuated school buildings and halls of all types, often on the floor and without heating or running water; for most, toilets were located a few buildings away. For the ghetto inhabitants it meant greater overcrowding, less food and other unpleasant consequences, as we shall see. Tension between the newcomers and the ghetto population became unavoidable.

Sierakowiak kept his own recordings of the events. "October 16: The first transport of deportees from Vienna arrived. . . . There are thousands of them, pastors and doctors among them, and some have sons on the front. They have brought a carload of bread with them and excellent luggage, and are dressed splendidly. Every day the same number is supposed to arrive, up to 20,000. They will probably overwhelm us completely."[30] The next day Sierakowiak witnessed the arrival of a transport from Prague; again he noticed the cartloads of bread, the luggage, the clothes: "I have heard," he added, "that they have been inquiring whether it's possible to get a two-room apartment with running water. Interesting types."[31] On October 19, however, the first practical consequences of the influx of the new deportees were recorded: "More Luxembourg Jews arrived today. They are beginning to crowd the ghetto. They have only one patch on the left breast with the inscription *Jude*. They are dressed splendidly (you can tell they haven't lived in Poland). They are buying up all they can in the ghetto, and all the prices have doubled. . . . Although they have been here only a few days, they already complain about hunger. So what can we say, we who haven't had our stomach full for more than a year? You can apparently get used to everything."[32]

The economic disruption soon worsened: "From the moment they arrived," the *Chronicle* reported in November 1941, "the newcomers began selling their personal property and, with the cash they received, began to buy up literally everything available on the private food market. In time, this caused a shortage in the food supply and prices rose horrendously with indescribable speed. On the other hand, the availability of all sorts of items which had been lacking in the ghetto for quite a while has caused trade to become brisk, and a few of the ghetto's stores have shelves filled with goods that have not been seen in the ghetto for a long time. Because of the newcomers . . . who are popularly known as *Yekes*, stores never really closed their doors in the month of November. They sold their clothing, shoes, linen, cosmetics, traveling accessories, and so forth. For a short while this caused a decline in prices for the most varied items; however, to match the price increase on the food market, the newcomers began to raise the prices of the items they were selling. From the point of view of the ghetto's previous inhabitants, this relatively large increase in private commerce has caused undesired disturbances and difficulties and, what is worse, the newcomers have, in a short span of time, caused a devaluation of the [ghetto] currency. That phenomenon is particularly painful for the mass of working people, the most important segment of ghetto society, who only possess the money they draw from the coffers of the Eldest of the Jews."[33]

As transports of deportees were arriving in Lodz from the Reich and Protectorate, the Germans started murdering part of the ghetto's inhabitants. On December 6 the Chelmno gas vans had become operational and on that same day, Rumkowski was ordered to have twenty thousand of "his" Jews [the local Jews] ready for "labor deployment outside the ghetto." The number was finally reduced to ten thousand. Shortly afterward the *Chronicle* recorded a sudden interruption of all mail services between the ghetto and the outside world. On the face of it the chroniclers could not make any sense of the order: "There have been various stories concerning the suspension of mail service, and a question of fundamental interest has been whether this was a purely local event or whether there have been nation-wide restrictions. There are, in addition, conjectures about the reasons behind this latest restriction."[34] Obviously the chroniclers could not write that these conjectures pointed to the forthcoming deportations. As rumors continued to spread, Rumkowski decided to address the issue in a speech at the House of Culture on January 3, 1942: "The stories circu-lating today are one hundred percent false. . . . The authorities are full of admiration for the work which has been performed in the ghetto. . . . Their approval of my motion to reduce the number of deportees from 20,000 to 10,000 is a sign of that con-fidence. . . . Nothing bad will happen to people of good will."[35]

The deportations continued in February and March: By April 2 a further 34,073 ghetto Jews had been deported and murdered. "Nobody was safe anymore from being deported," noted Oskar Rosenfeld, a writer and a journalist who was de-ported from Prague to Lodz in early November 1941; "at least eight hundred people had to be delivered every day. Some thought they would be able to save themselves: chronically ill old people and those with frozen limbs, not even that helped. The surgeons in the hospital were very busy. They amputated hands and feet of the poor 'patients' and discharged them as cripples. The cripples too were taken away. On March 7, nine people froze to death at the railway station where they had to wait nine hours for the departure of the train."[36]

The killing capacity of Chelmno was approximately a thou-sand people a day. The first victims were the Jews from villages and small towns in the Lodz area. Then, before the deporta-tion of the Jews from the Lodz ghetto started, came the turn of the Gypsies herded in a special area of the ghetto (the Gypsy camp). Approximately 4,400 Gypsies were killed in Chelmno, but there were few witnesses.

As mentioned, the vast majority of the Lodz ghetto inhab-itants remained unaware of Chelmno although over time in-formation reached them in diverse ways. Strangely enough, some information was even sent by mail. Thus, some five weeks after the beginning of the exterminations, a letter based on an eyewitness account was sent by the rabbi of Grabow to his brother-in-law in Lodz: "Until now I have not replied to your letters because I did not know exactly about all the things people have been talking about. Unfortunately, for our great tragedy, now we know it all. I have been visited by an eye witness who survived only by accident, he managed to escape from hell. . . . I found out about everything from him. The place where all perish is called Chelmno. . . . People are killed in two different ways: By firing squad or by poison gas. This is what happened to the cities Dabie, Isbicza, Kujawska, Klodawa and others. Lately thousands of Gypsies have been brought there from the so-called Gypsy camps of Lodz and, for the past several days, Jews have been brought there from Lodz and the same is done to them. Do not think that I am mad. Alas, this is the tragic cruel truth. O Creator of the world, help us! Jakob Schulman."[37] The eyewitness was probably the man called the "grave-digger from Chelmno," Yakov Groyanowski from Izbicza, a member of the Jewish commando that dug the pits into which the corpses were thrown in the forest. The gravedigger's story reached Ringelblum in Warsaw. He told of people undressing in the castle for showering and disinfection, then being pushed into the vans and suffocated by the exhaust gas pumped in during the ride to the forest, some sixteen kilometers away. "Many of the people they [the grave-diggers] dealt with had suffocated to death in the truck. But there were a few exceptions, including babies who were still alive; this was because mothers held the children in blankets and covered them with their hands so the gas would not get to them. In these cases, the Germans would split the heads of the babies on trees, killing them on the spot."[38] Groyanowski managed to flee, and hid in small communities until he reached Warsaw in early January 1942.

In the *Ostland*, as we saw, mass killings had followed one another throughout October and November 1941, to make space for the deportees from the Reich. In Kovno in early October some sporadic "actions" targeted the hospital and the orphanage which the Germans burned with their inmates. Then, on October 25, the council was informed by SS Master Sgt. Helmut Rauca, the man in charge of the Jewish desk at the Kovno Gestapo, that all the inhabitants—that is, all 27,000 of them—had to assemble on October 28 at 6 a.m., at Demokratu Square, to allow a reallocation of food rations to those who did labor for the Germans as one category, and to the nonworkers as another; the nonworkers would be transferred to the "small ghetto." The council was ordered to announce the general roll call to the inhabitants.

On the morning of the twenty-eighth the whole population assembled at the square; each and every adult Jew who did not possess a working permit carried some document, a school certificate, a commendation from the Lithuanian army, and the like: Maybe it could help. At the square Rauca was in charge of the selection: The "good" side was the left. Those sent to the right were counted and pushed to an assembly point in the small ghetto. From time to time Rauca was informed of the number of Jews who had been moved to the right. After nightfall the quota of ten thousand people had been reached: The selection was over; seventeen thousand Jews were returning home. Throughout the entire day Elkes had been at the square; in some rare cases he could appeal to Rauca and achieve a change of decision. When he reached home that evening, a crowd besieged him and each Jew implored him to save somebody. On the next day, as the first column of Jews started the trek from the small ghetto to Fort IX, Elkes with a list of names in hand tried once more to intervene. Rauca granted him one hundred people. But, when Elkes tried to remove these one hundred from the columns, he was hit by the Lithuanian guards and collapsed. Days went by before Elkes's wounds healed and he could stand on his feet again. In the meantime, from the dawn of the twenty-ninth to noon, the ten thousand Jews from the small ghetto marched to Fort IX where, batch after batch, they were shot. Days beforehand pits had been dug behind the fort: they were not for the Lithuanian Jews, however, but, as we saw, for the Jews from the Reich and the Protectorate who arrived in November and disappeared without ever reaching the ghetto.

In a longer than usual description of several weeks in the life of the Vilna ghetto, probably written sometime in December 1941, Rudashevski noted: "I feel we are like sheep. We are being slaughtered in the thousands and we are helpless. The enemy is strong, crafty, he is exterminating us according to a plan and we are discouraged."[39] For the fourteen-year-old diarist there was little that the ghetto inhabitants could do other than hope for quick liberation from the outside.

Other Vilna Jews also drew conclusions from the events, yet without any such hopefulness. In the eyes of some members of the Zionist youth movements, the systematic manner in which the Germans carried out the killings indicated the existence an extermination project that would ultimately extend to all the Jews of the continent. One of the first to grasp the significance of the Vilna massacres was the twenty-three-year-old poet and member of Hashomer Hatzair, Abba Kovner, who was hiding in a monastery close to the city. He found the words and the arguments that convinced an increasing number of his fellow youth movement members. And, if his interpretation was correct, if sooner or later death was unavoidable, only one conclusion remained possible: The Jews had to "die with dignity"; the only path was armed resistance.

Kovner was asked to write a proclamation that would be read at a gathering of members from all youth movements in the ghetto. The meeting, which took place under the guise of a New Year celebration on December 31, 1941, brought together some 150 young men and women at the "Pioneers Public

Kitchen," on Straszun Street. There, Kovner read the manifesto that was to become the first call for a Jewish armed resistance. "Jewish Youth," Kovner proclaimed, "do not believe those that are trying to deceive you. . . . Of those taken through the gates of the ghetto not a single one has returned. . . . Hitler plans to destroy all the Jews of Europe, and the Jews of Lithuania have been chosen as the first in line. We will not be led like sheep to the slaughter. True we are weak and helpless, but the only response to the murderer is revolt! Brothers! It is better to die fighting like free men than to live at the mercy of the murderers. Arise! Arise with your last breath!"[40]

Within a short time, Kovner's appeal led to the creation of the first Jewish resistance organization in occupied Europe, the FPO, the United Partisans Organization. It brought together young Jews from the most diverse political frameworks, from the communists to the right-wing Zionists of Betar. Yet, precisely in Vilna, the situation seemed to change again: A relative stability that was to last for more than two years settled upon the remaining 24,000 Jews of the ghetto—most of whom worked for the Germans—and upon the members of their immediate families.

When the Vilna massacres of the summer and fall of 1941 became known in Warsaw, they were generally interpreted as German retribution for the support given by the Jews of Lithuania to the Soviet occupation. It was only among a minority within the youth movements that a different assessment was taking shape. Yitzhak "Antek" Zuckerman, leader of Dror Hechalutz Zionist Youth Movement in the ghetto, explained the change of perception that was emerging in his group: "My comrades and the members of Hashomer Hatzair had already heard the story of Vilna [the massacres of Jews in Ponar]. We took the information to the Movement leadership, to the political activists in Warsaw. The responses were different. The youth absorbed not only the information but also accepted the

284 NAZI GERMANY AND THE JEWS, 1933–1945

interpretation that this was the beginning of the end. A total death sentence for the Jews. We didn't accept the interpretation that this was all because of Communism. . . . Because if it had been German revenge against Jewish Communists, it would have been done right after the occupation. But these were planned and organized acts, not immediately after the occupation, but premeditated actions."⁴¹

As the fateful year 1941 reached its last day and the course of the war seemed to be turning, the mood of a vast majority of European Jews starkly differed from that of the tiny minority of would-be resisters. In Bucharest, Sebastian had overcome his worst fears: "The Russians have landed in eastern Crimea," he noted on December 31. " . . . I carry inside myself the 364 terrible days of the dreadful year we are closing tonight. But we are alive. We can still wait for something. There is still time; we still have some time left."⁴² Klemperer, for once, was even more ebullient than Sebastian. At a small New Year's Eve gathering at his downstairs neighbors', he made a speech: "It was our most dreadful year, dreadful because of our own real experience, more dreadful because of the constant state of threat, most dreadful of all because of what we saw others suffering (deportations, murder), but at the end it brought optimism. My adhortatio was: Head held high for the difficult last five minutes!"⁴³

PART III

SHOAH

January 1942–May 1945

The struggle to save myself is hopeless. . . . But that's not important. Because I am able to bring my account to its end and trust that it will see the light of day when the time is right. . . . And people will know what happened. . . . And they will ask, is this the truth? I reply in advance: No, this is not the truth, this is only a small part, a tiny fraction of the truth. . . . Even the mightiest pen could not depict the whole, real, essential truth.

—STEFAN ERNST, "THE WARSAW GHETTO,"
WRITTEN IN HIDING IN 1943 ON THE
"ARYAN SIDE OF WARSAW"

CHAPTER 11

Total Extermination

January 1942–June 1942

O N DECEMBER 15, 1941, the SS *Struma*, with 769 Jewish refugees from Romania on board, was towed into Istanbul Harbor and put under quarantine. The ship, a rickety schooner originally built in the 1830s, patched up over the decades, and equipped with a small engine, had left Constanța a week beforehand and somehow made it to Turkish waters. Five days later the British ambassador in Ankara, Sir Hughe Knatchbull-Hugessen, gave a wrong impression of British policy to a Turkish Foreign Ministry official: "His Majesty's Government did not want these people in Palestine," the ambassador declared, ". . . but from the humanitarian point of view, I did not like his [the Turkish official's] proposal to send the ship back into the Black Sea. If the Turkish government must interfere with the ship on the ground that they could not keep the distressed Jews in Turkey, let her rather go towards the Dardanelles [on the way into the Mediterranean Sea]. It might be that if they reached Palestine, they may, despite their illegality, receive humane treatment."[1]

The ambassador's message provoked outrage in official circles in London. The sharpest rebuff came from the colonial secretary, Lord Moyne, in a letter sent on December 24 to the parliamentary undersecretary at the Foreign Office, Richard Law: "The landing [in Palestine] of seven hundred more immigrants will not only be a formidable addition to the difficulties of the High Commissioner . . . but it will also have a deplorable effect throughout the Balkans in encouraging further Jews to embark on a traffic which has now been condoned by His Majesty's Ambassador. . . . I find it difficult to write with moderation about this occurrence which is in flat contradiction of established Government policy, and I should be very glad if you could perhaps even now do something to retrieve the position, and to urge that [the] Turkish authorities should be asked to send the ship back to the Black Sea, as they originally proposed."[2]

As weeks went by the British decided to grant the seventy children on board visas to Palestine. The Turks, however, remained adamant: None of the refugees would be allowed to disembark. On February 23 they towed the boat back into the Black Sea. Soon thereafter a torpedo, almost certainly fired by mistake from a Soviet submarine, hit the ship: The *Struma* sank with all its passengers, except for one survivor.

"Yesterday evening," Sebastian noted on February 26, "a Rador dispatch reported that the Struma had sunk with all on board in the Black Sea. This morning brought a correction in the sense that most of the passengers—perhaps all of them—have been saved and are now ashore. But before I heard what had really happened, I went through several hours of depression. It seemed that the whole of our fate was in this shipwreck."[3]

On December 19, 1941, Hitler dismissed Brauchitsch and personally took over the command of the army. During the following weeks the Nazi leader stabilized the eastern front. But despite the hard-earned respite and despite his own rhetorical posturing, Hitler probably knew that 1942 would be the year of "last chance." Only a breakthrough in the East would turn the tide in favor of Germany.

On May 8, 1942, the first stage of the German offensive started in the southern sector of the Russian front. After withstanding a Soviet counteroffensive near Kharkov, the German forces rolled on. Once again the Wehrmacht reached the Donetz. Further south the Germans recaptured the Crimea and, by mid-June, Sevastopol was surrounded. On June 28 the full-scale German onslaught (Operation Blue) began. Voronezh was taken, and while the bulk of the German forces moved southward toward the oil fields and the Caucasus foothills, Gen. Friedrich Paulus's Sixth Army advanced along the Don in the direction of Stalingrad. In North Africa, Bir Hakeim and Tobruk fell into Gen. Erwin Rommel's hands, and the Afrika Korps, under his command, crossed the Egyptian border: Alexandria was threatened. On all fronts—and in the Atlantic—the Germans heaped success upon success; so did their Japanese allies in the Pacific and in Southeast Asia.

In the meantime the Nazi leader's anti-Jewish exhortations continued relentlessly, broadly hinting at the extermination that was unfolding and endlessly repeating the arguments that, in his eyes, justified it. On January 30, in the ritual yearly address to the Reichstag, this time delivered at the Berlin Sportpalast, Hitler reiterated his deadly threats in full force: "For the first time, the ancient Jewish rule will now be applied: 'Eye for eye, tooth for tooth!'" Thereupon messianic ardor took hold of the Nazi leader: "World Jewry should know that the more the war spreads, the more anti-Semitism will also spread. It will grow in every prisoner-of-war camp, in every family that will understand the reasons for which it has, ultimately, to make its sacrifices. And the hour will strike when the most evil world enemy of all times will have ended his role at least for a thousand years."[4] The millennial vision of a final redemption capped the litany of hatred.

In Warsaw, Kaplan understood the main thrust of Hitler's speech: "The day before yesterday," he noted on February 2, "we read the speech the *Führer* delivered celebrating January 30, 1933, when he boasted that his prophecy was beginning to come true. . . . For us the speech serves as proof that what we thought were rumors are in effect reports of actual occurrences. The *Judenrat* and the Joint have documents which confirm the new direction of Nazi policy toward the Jews in the conquered territories: death by extermination for entire Jewish communities."[5]

Again and again during the first months of 1942, the Nazi leader repeated his announcement about the forthcoming extermination of the Jews. The crescendo of anti-Jewish abuse and threats that Hitler unceasingly spewed were immediately echoed in the German press: "A proper understanding of Jews and Judaism cannot but demand their total annihilation," *Volk und Rasse* proclaimed in May 1942.[6] In *Der Angriff* of that same month, the labor minister Robert Ley's threats competed with his master's prophecies: "The war will end," the minister announced to the three hundred thousand readers of the weekly magazine, "with the extermination of the Jewish race."[7] The upsurge in anti-Jewish hatred probably explains why the *Völkischer Beobachter* of April 30, 1942, could, without qualms, carry a detailed article (thinly veiled as rumor) about SD operations in the East: "The rumor has spread among the population that it is the task of the Security Police to exterminate the Jews in the occupied territories. The Jews were assembled in the thousands and shot; beforehand they had to dig their own graves. At times the execution of the Jews reached such proportions that even members of the *Einsatzkommandos* suffered nervous breakdowns."[8]

Initially scheduled for December 9, 1941, the high-level meeting convened by Heydrich in Berlin at the guesthouse of the Security

Police on Wannseestrasse, opened on the morning of January 20, 1942. Fourteen people assembled: several state secretaries or other high-ranking officials and a few SS officers, including Adolf Eichmann, who had sent the invitations (in Heydrich's name) and who drew up the minutes of the meeting. Heydrich opened the meeting by reminding the participants of the task Göring had delegated to him in July 1941 and of the ultimate authority of the Reichsführer-SS in this matter. The RSHA chief then presented a brief historical survey of the measures already taken to segregate the Jews of the Reich and force them to emigrate. After further emigration had been forbidden in October 1941, Heydrich went on, another solution had been authorized by the führer: the evacuation of the Jews of Europe to the East. Some 11 million persons would be included, and Heydrich listed this Jewish population, country by country, including all Jews living in enemy and neutral countries of Europe (Great Britain, the Soviet Union, Spain, Portugal, Switzerland, and Sweden). A small part of the evacuated Jews would be assigned to heavy forced labor, which naturally would greatly reduce their numbers; the remnant, "the strongest elements of the race and the nucleus of its revival," would have to be "treated accordingly." To implement the operation Europe would be "combed from West to East," whereby the Reich would be given priority "because of the housing problem and other socio-political considerations." Jews over sixty-five years old, war invalids, or Jews decorated with the Iron Cross would be evacuated to the newly established "old people's ghetto," Theresienstadt. The beginning of major evacuations would greatly depend upon the evolution of the military situation.

The statement regarding the "military situation" was strange and has to be understood in relation to the formula "evacuation to the East" used from then on to mean extermination. To maintain the linguistic fiction, a general comment about the war was necessary given the impossibility of deportations "to the East" in January 1942. The country-by-country listing of the Jews who would be targeted in the "Final Solution" meant to convey that every Jew in Europe would eventually be caught. None would escape or be allowed to survive. Moreover, all Jews, everywhere, even in countries or areas still outside Germany's reach, would be subjected to Himmler's and Heydrich's authority.

Heydrich then moved to the issue of mixed breeds and mixed marriages. During the discussion that followed, State Secretary Stuckart of the Ministry of the Interior warned of the considerable amount of bureaucratic work that the *Mischlinge* and mixed-marriage issues would create and strongly recommended the generalized sterilization of mixed breeds of the first degree as policy. Moreover Stuckart favored annulling mixed marriages by law. State Secretary Erich Neumann of the Four-Year Plan did not wish Jews working in essential war industries to be included in the evacuations; Heydrich answered that currently this was not the case. (In fact further discussions about the fate of mixed breeds and mixed marriages, on March 6 and on October 27, at the RSHA headquarters, did not lead to any definitive agreement.)

State Secretary Josef Bühler pleaded for starting the evacuations in the General Government, where transport was a minor issue, the Jews were not part of the workforce, and where, moreover, they were a source of epidemics and of economic instability as black marketers. Bühler's request demonstrates that he perfectly understood what Heydrich had omitted to spell out: The nonworking Jews were to be exterminated in the first phase of the overall plan. The conference ended with Heydrich's renewed appeal to all the participants to extend the necessary help for implementing the solution.[9]

Aside from the evolution of the war and of its overall impact, the major factors influencing the course of the "Final Solution," from early 1942 on, were the need for Jewish slave labor in an increasingly overextended war economy on the one hand, and the "security risk," which the same Jews represented in Nazi eyes, on the other.

In Lodz, Sierakowiak had been assigned to a saddler's workshop. "The ghetto population," he recorded on March 22, 1942, "has been divided into three categories: 'A,' 'B,' and 'C.' "A": workshop workers and clerks; 'B': clerks and ordinary laborers; 'C': the rest of the population."[10] Wave after wave, the "rest of the population" was shipped to Chelmno. In the General Government, a "substitution" policy developed, at least for a short while: Jewish labor gradually replaced Polish workers sent to the Reich. It became standard procedure to stop deportation trains from the Reich and Slovakia in Lublin in order to select the able-bodied Jews for work in the General Government; the others were sent on to their death in Belzec. Hans Frank himself seemed more than ready to move from the ideological stance to the pragmatic one: "If I want to win the war, I must be an ice-cold technician. The question what will be done from an ideological-ethnic point of view I must postpone to a time after the war."[11]

Two unrelated events which followed each other during the second half of May 1942 may have led to a slow-down in the use of Jewish slave labor on the one hand and the general acceleration of the "Final Solution" on the other. On May 18 an incendiary device exploded on the site of the anti-Soviet exhibition, The Soviet Paradise, in Berlin's Lustgarten. Within days the Gestapo caught most members of the small procommunist "Herbert Baum group," which had organized the attack. As Goebbels wrote on May 24, "characteristically five are Jews, three half-Jews and four Aryans."[12] The propaganda minister then recorded Hitler's reaction: "He is extraordinarily outraged and orders me to see to it as soon as possible that the Jews of Berlin be evacuated. . . . Moreover the *Führer* allows me to arrest 500 Jewish hostages and to react with executions to any new attempts."[13] On May 29 the Nazi leader ordered Speer to replace the Jews employed in the armament industries with foreign workers "as soon as possible."[14] In Hitler's mind the elimination of the Jews ensured that no repeat performance of the revolutionary activities of 1917/1918 would occur; the Baum attempt was a warning: The extermination of the Jews had to be completed as rapidly as possible.

A second event may also have accelerated the extermination process, albeit indirectly. On May 27 Heydrich, who had recently become the de facto Reichsprotektor, was fatally wounded by Czech commandos parachuted by the British into the Protectorate; he died on June 4. On the day of the state funeral Hitler ordered the murder of most of the population of Lidice (a small town near Prague where, the Germans thought, Heydrich's assailants had hidden). All men aged fifteen to ninety were shot; all women sent to concentration camps, where most of them perished; some children were "Germanized" and brought up in German families under new identities; the great majority of the children who did not show Germanic traits were sent to Chelmno and gassed. As for the town, it was leveled.

Himmler met Hitler on June 3, 4, and 5. Whether it was during these meetings that the Nazi leader and his henchman decided to accelerate the extermination process and set a deadline for the completion of the "Final Solution" is not known but seems plausible in light of the Baum attempt and Heydrich's death. More than ever the Jews were an internal threat. On June 9, in the course of a lengthy memorial address for the RSHA chief, Himmler declared, as if incidentally: "We will certainly complete the migration of the Jews within a year; after that, none of them will wander anymore. It is time now to wipe the slate clean."[15] Then, on July 19, on the morrow of a two-day visit to Auschwitz, the Reichsführer sent the following order to Krüger: "The resettlement of the entire Jewish population of the General Government should be implemented and completed by December 31, 1942. On December 31, 1942, no persons of Jewish origin are allowed to stay in the General Government, except if they are in assembly camps in Warsaw, Krakow, Czestochowa, Radom and Lublin. All projects that employ Jewish labor have to be completed by that date or transferred to the assembly camps."[16]

The majority of the Jews of Europe were exterminated after being held for different periods of time in camps or assembly areas in the West or in ghettos in the East. Most of these concentration or assembly areas were established before general extermination was decided upon, but some, such as Theresienstadt, were set up as part ghettos, part holding pens at the very outset of the "Final Solution."

Theresienstadt (Terezín in Czech) was a small fortified town in northern Bohemia that, at the end of 1941, housed some seven thousand German soldiers and Czech civilians; an annex (the small fortress) was already the central Gestapo prison in the Protectorate. At the end of 1941 Jewish labor details started preparing Theresienstadt for its new function as a fake Jewish "model camp" and, in early January 1942, the first transports arrived with around ten thousand Jews.

A "Jewish elder" and a council of thirteen members were appointed. The first "elder" was the widely respected Jakob Edelstein, an active socialist Zionist. Although quite unremarkable in appearance and in his professional life as a salesman, Edelstein soon proved to be an able public speaker, much in demand at Zionist meetings. Shortly after the Nazi accession to power in Germany, Edelstein was called to head the "Palestine office" in Prague, to assist the growing flow of refugees ready to immigrate to Palestine. His common sense—and his courage—made him, de facto, the central personality of Czech

Jewry in its contacts with the Germans. When, in the fall of that same year, Heydrich decided to deport the Jews of the Protectorate to an assembly camp on Bohemian territory, Edelstein was naturally chosen to head the "model ghetto."

At the outset the camp leadership was criticized for its Zionist slant; soon however, the increasing harshness of everyday life dampened ideological confrontations. and the Zionist commitment of the majority of the leadership remained unchanged. Thus, a twenty-three-year-old teacher in a Jewish school in Prague, Egon "Gonda" Redlich, became head of the Youth Welfare Department. Gonda and his associates created a quasi-autonomous domain of the young for the young (that over time comprised on average three to four thousand youngsters); there, in particular, a strongly Zionist-inspired youth culture developed.

Nothing, however, could protect either the young or the old from deportation to killing sites. "I heard a terrible piece of news," Redlich noted in his diary on January 6, 1942. "A transport will go from Terezin to Riga. We argued for a long while if the time had not yet come to say 'enough.'" His next day entry carried on in the same vein: "Our mood is very bad. We prepared for the transport. We worked practically all night." And, on January 7: "We were not able to work because we were locked in the barracks. I asked the authorities to remove children from the transport and was told that the children will not be traveling."[17]

As the summer of 1942 began, tens of transports of elderly Jews from the Reich and the Protectorate were sent on their way to the Czech "ghetto." "In June," Redlich recorded: "twenty-four transports arrived and four left. Of those entering, fifteen thousand came from Germany proper, most of them very old." On June 30: "I helped Viennese Jews yesterday. They are old, lice-ridden, and they have a few insane people among them."[18] Among its "insane" passengers, the transport from Vienna included Trude Herzl-Neumann, the youngest daughter of the founder of political Zionism, Theodor Herzl.

The number of incoming transports kept growing throughout July. "People arrive by the thousands," Redlich wrote on August 1, "the aged that do not have the strength to get the food. Fifty die daily."[19] Indeed, the mortality rate in the "old people's ghetto" shot up, and in September 1942 alone, some 3,900 people from a total population of 58,000 died. Approximately at the same time transports of the elderly inmates from Theresienstadt to Treblinka started. By then, as we shall see, the waves of deportations from Warsaw were subsiding and the gas chambers of the latest of the "Aktion Reinhard" camps (which, along with Belzec and Sobibor, were named in Heydrich's memory) could take in the 18,000 new arrivals from the Protectorate ghetto.

It is in one of the September transports from Vienna that teenage Ruth Kluger and her mother arrived in Theresienstadt. Ruth was sent to one of the youth barracks that stood under Redlich's supervision. There, as she writes, she became a Jew: The lectures, the all-pervading Zionist atmosphere, the sense of belonging to a community of *haverim* and *haveroth* [male and female comrades, in Hebrew], where one didn't say *Gute Nacht* but *Laila tov* ("good night" in Hebrew), gave the young girl a new feeling of belonging. And yet, even in Theresienstadt, even among the young, one part of the inmates kept feeling superior to the other and showed it: "The Czechs in L410 [the children's barracks] looked down on us because we spoke the enemy's language. Besides, they really were the elite because they were in their own country. . . . So even here we were disdained for something that wasn't in our power to change: our mother tongue."[20]

Throughout its existence Theresienstadt offered a dual face: On the one hand transports were departing to Auschwitz and Treblinka, on the other the Germans set up a "Potemkin village" meant to fool the world. "Will money be introduced?" Redlich asked in an entry on November 7, 1942. "Of course it could be. The thing could be an interesting experiment in national economics. Anyway, a coffee house has been opened (they say there will even be music there, a bank, a reading room)." Two days later: "They are making a film. Jewish actors, satisfied, happy faces in the film, only in the film . . ."[21] This was to be the first of two Nazi films about Theresienstadt.

In the meantime the killings in Chelmno ran smoothly on; the building of Belzec, which had started on November 1, 1941, progressed apace and on March 17, 1942, the camp opened its gates. At first, some 30,000 out of the 37,000 Jews of the Lublin ghetto were exterminated. Simultaneously another 13,500 Jews arrived from various areas of the district and from the Lwów area; in early June, deportees from Kraków followed. Within four weeks some 75,000 Jews had been murdered in this first of the three "Aktion Reinhard" camps; by the end of 1942 about 434,000 Jews would be exterminated in Belzec alone. Two survived the war.

Sometime in late March or in April, 1942, the former Austrian police officer and euthanasia expert Franz Stangl traveled to Belzec to meet its commandant, SS-Hauptsturmführer Christian Wirth. Forty years later, in his Düsseldorf prison, Stangl described his arrival in Belzec: "I went there by car. As one arrived, one first reached Belzec railway station, on the left side of the road. It was a one-story building. The smell . . ." he said. "Oh God, the smell. It was everywhere. Wirth wasn't in his office. I remember, they took me to him. . . . He was standing on a hill, next to the pits . . . the pits . . . full . . . they were full . . . not hundreds, thousands, thousands of corpses. . . . Oh God. That's where Wirth told me—he said that was what Sobibor was for. And that he was putting me officially in charge."[22]

Some two months later Sobibor—whose construction

started at the end of March 1942—was in operation and Stangl, its attentive commandant, usually toured the camp in white riding attire. About ninety to one hundred thousand Jews were murdered in Sobibor during the first three months of operation; they came from the Lublin district, from Austria, the Protectorate, and the *Altreich*. And, while the exterminations were launched in Sobibor, the construction of Treblinka began.

Extermination in the "Aktion Reinhard" camps followed standard procedures. Ukrainian auxiliaries, usually armed with whips, chased the Jews out of the trains. As in Chelmno, the next step was "disinfection"; the victims had to undress and leave all their belongings in the assembly room. Then, the throng of naked and terrified people was pushed through a narrow hallway or passage into one of the gas chambers. The doors were hermetically sealed; the gassing started. At the beginning bottles of carbon monoxide were still used in Belzec; later, they were replaced by various engines. Death was slow to come in these early gas chambers (ten minutes or more): Sometimes the agony of the victims could be watched through peepholes. When all was finished the emptying of the gas chambers was left, again as in Chelmno, to Jewish "special commandos" (*Sonderkommandos*) who would themselves be liquidated later on.

By April 1942 gassings had reached their full scale in Chelmno, Belzec, and Sobibor; they were just starting in Auschwitz and would soon begin in Treblinka. Simultaneously within a few weeks huge extermination operations by shooting or in gas vans would engulf further hundreds of thousands of Jews in Belorussia and in the Ukraine (the second sweep); "standard" on-the-spot killings remained common throughout the winter in the occupied areas of the USSR, in Galicia, in the Lublin district, and several areas of eastern Poland.

At the same time, slave-labor camps were operating through-

out the East and in Upper Silesia; some camps in this last category were a mix of transit areas, slave labor, and killing centers: Majdanek near Lublin or Janowska Road, at the outskirts
of Lwów, for example. And, next to this jumble of slave-labor
and extermination operations, tens of thousands of Jews toiled
in ordinary factories and workshops; in work camps, ghettos,
or towns; and hundreds of thousands were still alive in former
Poland, in the Baltic countries, and farther eastward. While
the Jewish population in the Reich was rapidly declining as deportations had resumed in full force, in the West most Jews
were leading their restricted lives without a sense of immediate danger.

In the occupied territories of the Soviet Union, given the
immense territories they had under their control and the variety of languages or dialects of the local populations, the
Germans relied from the outset on the help of local militias,
which, over the months, became regular auxiliary forces, the
Schutzmannschaften. The "Order Police" units and the gendarmerie were German; the *Schutzmannschaften* soon widely out-
numbered them and participated in all activities, including the
killings of Jews in some major operations, such as the extermination of part of the Jewish population of Minsk in the late
fall of 1941. There the Lithuanian *Schutzmannschaften* distinguished themselves.

The two Reichskommissare, Hinrich Lohse in the *Ostland*
and Erich Koch in the Ukraine, enthusiastically supported the
mass-murder operations. Koch in particular requested that in
the Ukraine all Jews be annihilated in order to reduce the local
food consumption and fill the growing food demands from the
Reich. As a result the district commissars, at their meeting in
August 1942, agreed with the head of the Security Police, Karl
Pütz, that all the Jews of the *Reichskommissariat* Ukraine, with
the exception of five hundred specialized craftsmen, would be
exterminated. In the Baltic countries—in Lohse's domain—

particularly in Lithuania, by February 1, 1942, the *Einsatz-gruppen* had executed 136,421 Jews, 1,064 communists, 56 partisans, 653 mentally ill, 78 others. Total: 138,272 (of whom 55,556 were women and 34,464 were children). In late July 1942 approximately half of the remaining Minsk ghetto population of 19,000 Jews were massacred.

Calls for Jewish armed resistance, such as Kovner's manifesto in Vilna, arose from the ranks of politically motivated Jewish youth movements, and the first Jews to fight the Germans as partisans, in the East or in the West, usually belonged to non-Jewish underground political-military organizations. In western Belorussia, however, a uniquely Jewish unit, without any political allegiance except for its aim of saving Jews, sprang up in early 1942: the Bielski brothers' group. The Bielskis were villagers who had lived for decades in Stankiewicze. Like their peasant neighbors they were poor, notwithstanding the mill and the land they owned. The only Jews in their village, they fully belonged to it in most ways. They knew the people and the environment, particularly the nearby forests. The younger generation included four brothers: Tuvia, Asael, Zus, and Arczik.

In December 1941 the Germans murdered four thousand inhabitants of the Nowogrodek ghetto, among them the Bielski parents, Tuvia's first wife, and Zus's wife. In two successive groups, the first led by Asael, the second by Tuvia, the brothers moved to the forests, in March, then in May 1942. Soon all deferred to Tuvia's leadership: An even larger number of family members and other Jews fleeing the surrounding ghettos joined the "Otriad" (a partisan detachment); weapons were acquired and food was secured. By the end of the German occupation the Bielski brothers had assembled some fifteen hundred Jews in their forest camp, notwithstanding almost insuperable odds.

While the Bielski group was one of its kind, other Jewish resistance movements, organized within the ghettos of the occupied Soviet Union, did often receive support from the council
leadership. In Minsk, for example, the head of the *Judenrat,* the
noncommunist Ilya Moshkin, was in regular contact with the
commander of the communist underground in the ghetto and
the city, Hersh Smolar. Such regular cooperation—for which
Moshkin ultimately paid with his life—was entirely atypical
farther west, in the Baltic countries and in former Poland, for
fear of German reprisals against the ghetto population. The
only partly comparable situation to that in Minsk was, for
a time at least, that of the Białystok ghetto, where Ephraim
Barash's *Judenrat* kept in touch for more than a year with Mordechai Tenenbaum's underground organization, a case to
which we shall return.

In the meantime the total exclusion of Jews from German society continued to be "perfected." In early 1942 Goebbels had
prohibited the sale of any press items (newspapers, journals,
periodicals) to Jews. Some two weeks earlier the use of public
phones had also been forbidden. Private phones and radios had
already been confiscated long before; the new instructions
would close another gap. Furthermore the growing scarcity
of paper seemed to add greater urgency to curtailing the distribution of newsprint. Unexpected opposition arose, however,
from the RSHA. In a February 4 letter to Goebbels, Heydrich
argued that it would be impossible to inform the Jews of all
the measures they had to heed only by way of the Jewish News
Bulletin. Moreover professional periodicals were essential for
Jewish "caretakers of the sick" or for "consultants." "As I have to
keep the Jews firmly in hand," Heydrich added, "I must ask to
ease these instructions, the more so because they were issued
without the essential consultation with my office."[23] By March,
Goebbels's regulations had been partly abandoned.

The prohibition of Jewish emigration led to the closing, on February 14, 1942, of the Reichsvereinigung offices, which advised and helped the emigrants. As for the public identification of Jews, the individual star did not suffice; on March 13 the RSHA ordered the fixing of a white paper star to the entrance door of every apartment inhabited by Jews or to the entrance of any Jewish institution. The display of signs and badges, favored by the RSHA, was in turn questioned by the propaganda minister. Thus on March 11 Goebbels rejected an SD proposal that Jews allowed to use public transportation should display a special badge. The minister, who wanted to avoid further public discussion of the star issue, suggested that these Jews be given a special permit to be presented to the ticket taker or, on demand, to army officers and party officials. On March 24 Heydrich forbade Jews the use of public transportation, except for holders of the special police permit.

Random Gestapo raids on Jews' houses were particularly feared. At the Klemperers' the first of these "house visits" took place on May 23, 1942, a Sunday afternoon, while Victor was not at home: the house was left upside down, its inhabitants had been slapped, beaten, and spat on, but, as Klemperer noted, "we got away not too badly this time."[24] On May 15 Jews were forbidden to keep pets. "Jews with the star," he recorded, "and anyone who lives with them, are with immediate effect forbidden to keep pets (dogs, cats, birds); it is also forbidden to give the animals away to be looked after. This is the death sentence for [their cat] Muschel, whom we have had for more than eleven years and to whom Eva is very attached. Tomorrow he is to be taken to the vet."[25]

In mid-June, Jews had to give up all electrical appliances, including any electric cooking and household appliances, as well as cameras, binoculars, and bicycles. On June 20 the Reichsvereinigung was informed that by the end of the month all Jewish schools would be closed: No further schooling was available for Jews in Germany. A few days later, an order forbade the use of freight cars for the transportation of the corpses of Jews. On September 2, upon a decree from the Ministry of Agriculture and Food Supply, Jews would no longer receive meat, milk, white bread, or tobacco wares, or any scarce commodities; pregnant women and sick people were not excepted.

At the same time the rhythm of deportations from the Reich accelerated. "Before a deportee goes," Klemperer recorded on January 21, 1942, "the Gestapo seals up everything he leaves behind. Everything is forfeit. Yesterday evening, Paul Kreidl [Klemperer's about-to-be-deported neighbor] brought me a pair of shoes that fit me exactly and are most welcome given the terrible condition of my own. Also a little tobacco which Eva mixes with blackberry tea and rolls in cigarettes. . . . The transport now includes 240 persons; there are said to be people among them who are so old, weak and sick that it is unlikely that everyone will still be alive on arrival."[26]

The information available about the trains' destinations was scant, often disbelieved, mixed with fantastic rumors, and yet sometimes astonishingly close to reality. "In the last few days," Klemperer noted on March 16, "I heard Auschwitz (or something like it), near Königshütte in Upper Silesia, mentioned as the most dreadful concentration camp. Work in a mine, death within a few days. Kornblum, the father of Frau Seligsohn, died there, likewise—not known to me—Stern and Müller."[27] In March 1942 Auschwitz was just becoming a major extermination center. Yet, through channels hard to trace, rumors seeped back to the Reich.

While the deportations from the Reich were engulfing all segments of the Jewish population, a few small groups of Germans, mainly in Berlin, offered their help; they hid Jews on the run, they produced forged identity papers, fake draft deferrals, food ration cards, and the like. And, beyond the immediate practical help, they offered humaneness and some hope. Of course there was only so much that two or three dozen anti-Nazis determined to help Jews could do, mainly in 1942 or 1943. In her diary Ruth Andreas-Friedrich, a journalist, bestselling writer and the driving force behind the "Uncle Emil" group, admits to many a tragic failure in this first half of 1942. Margot Rosenthal, one of the Jewish women whom the group was hiding, was denounced by her concierge as she briefly slipped back into her apartment. On April 30 Ruth and her friends received a piece of tissue paper: Margot and 450 other Jews were about to be sent away: " . . . knapsack, blanket roll, and as much baggage as one can carry. I can't carry anything, and so shall simply leave everything by the roadside. This is farewell to life. I weep and weep. God be with you forever, and think of me!" One after another most of Ruth's Jewish friends were caught: "Heinrich Muehsam, Mother Lehmann, Peter Tarnowsky, Dr. Jakob, his little Evelyn, his wife and the Bernsteins, his father-and mother-in-law."[28] Some other hiding strategies would have to be devised, for the few and by the few.

The first transport of Jewish deportees left Slovakia for Auschwitz on March 26, 1942. It carried 999 young women. Tiso's country thereby acquired the doubtful distinction of immediately following the Reich and the Protectorate in delivering its Jews to the camps. The deportation was the result not of German pressure but of a Slovak request. The Slovak initiative had its own rationality. Once the Aryanization measures had despoiled most Jews of their property, getting rid of this impoverished population followed strict economic logic. In early 1942 the Germans had demanded twenty thousand Slovak workers for their armament factories; Tuka's government offered twenty thousand able-bodied Jews. After some hesitation Eichmann accepted; he could use young Jewish workers to accelerate the building of Birkenau after Soviet laborers had almost all died; he could even take in their families. The Slovaks would pay five hundred reichsmarks per deported Jew (to cover the German expenses), and in exchange the Reich allowed them to keep the deportees' property. Moreover they received the assurance that the deported Jews would not return. This was the "Slovak model" that Eichmann hoped to apply elsewhere over time.

By the end of June 1942, some 52,000 Slovak Jews had been deported, mainly to Auschwitz and to their death. Then, however, the deportations slowed to a standstill. The intervention of the Vatican, followed by the bribing of Slovak officials upon the initiative of a group of local Jews, did eventually play a role. The bribing operation was initiated by the "Working Group," led by the ultra-Orthodox rabbi Michael Dov Ber Weissmandel, a female Zionist activist, Gisi Fleischmann, and other personalities representing the main segments of Slovak Jewry. The "Working Group" also made substantial payments to Eichmann's representative in Bratislava, Dieter Wisliceny. That bribing the Slovaks contributed to a halt in the deportations for two years is most likely; whether the sums transferred to the SS had any influence remains an open question. Completing the deportations from Slovakia was not a German priority, as we shall see; this may have allowed the SS to trick the "Working Group" into paying much-needed foreign currency in the belief that they were helping postpone the dispatch of the remaining Slovak Jews, and possibly of other European Jews, to their death.

The major operational decision regarding the deportations from France, Holland, and Belgium was taken just after Heydrich's death, at a meeting convened by Eichmann at the RSHA on June 11. The immediate goal was to deport 15,000 Jews from Holland, 10,000 from Belgium, and a total of 100,000 from both French zones. Eichmann suggested that in France, a law similar to the Eleventh Ordinance be passed, whereby

French citizenship of any Jew having left the French territory would be abolished and all Jewish property would be transferred to the French State. In the same way as in Slovakia, the Reich would be paid approximately seven hundred reichsmarks per deported Jew. During the second half of June, however, it became obvious to the Germans that they would not be able to arrest and transport more than 40,000 Jews from France during a first six-month phase; to make up for the loss the number of deportees from Holland, where direct German domination simplified matters, was raised from 15,000 to 40,000.

The Germans could rely upon the subservience of the Dutch police and of the civil service; the grip on the country's Jews progressively tightened. On October 31, 1941, the Germans appointed the Amsterdam Jewish Council as the sole council for the whole country. Soon thereafter, the deportation of Jewish workers to special labor camps started. On January 7, 1942, the council called on the first contingent of workers: unemployed men on public welfare. Over the following weeks the German demands for laborers steadily increased, and the array of those being called up grew. Although the Council operated in coordination with the Amsterdam and the Hague Labor Offices, the admonishments to report originated from the Jewish leaders.

The labor camps, using Jewish and non-Jewish forced labor, were mainly staffed by Dutch Nazis who often outdid the Germans in sheer sadism. Westerbork (from July 1942 on, the main transit camp to Auschwitz, Sobibor, Bergen-Belsen, and Theresienstadt) had been a camp for a few hundred German Jewish refugees since the beginning of the war; by 1942 they had become "old-timers" and de facto ruled the camp, under the supervision of a German Kommandant. In early 1942 transports of foreign Jews were increasingly sent to Westerbork, while Dutch Jews from the provinces were being concentrated in Amsterdam. Dutch police supervised the transfer operations and the access to the vacated Jewish homes. The Germans dutifully registered furniture and household objects, which were then carted off to the Reich. During the same months a Dutch equivalent of the Nuremberg laws, prohibiting marriage between Jews and non-Jews, became mandatory.

All this still remained less important for Etty Hillesum than her intense love affair with a German Jewish refugee, Hans Spier, a spiritual guide of sorts and a highly idiosyncratic psychotherapist. The German measures did not spare her of course. "Yesterday Lippmann and Rosenthal [to hand over assets]," she noted on April 15, 1942, "Robbed and hunted."[29] Yet she perceived most of the measures through the prism of her emotions: "I am so glad that he [Spier] is a Jew and I am a Jewess," she wrote on April 29. "And I shall do what I can to remain with him so that we get through these times together. And I shall tell him this evening: I am not really frightened of anything, I feel so strong; it matters little whether you have to sleep on a hard floor, or whether you are only allowed to walk through certain specified streets, and so on—these are only minor vexations, so insignificant compared with the infinite riches and possibilities we carry within us."[30]

On Saturday June 20, less than a month before the beginning of the deportations from Amsterdam to Westerbork and from Westerbork to Auschwitz, Etty directed her thoughts to Jewish attitudes and responses: "Humiliation always involves two. The one who does the humiliating and the one who allows himself to be humiliated. If the second is missing, that is if the passive party is immune to humiliation, then the humiliation vanishes into thin air. . . . We Jews should remember that . . . they can't do anything to us. . . . They can harass us, they can rob us of our material goods, of our freedom of movement, but we ourselves forfeit our greatest assets by our misguided compliance. By our feelings of being persecuted, humiliated and oppressed. . . . Our greatest injury is one we inflict upon ourselves."[31]

On March 27 a transport with one thousand Jews detained in Compiègne left France for Auschwitz. The early deportations from France did not encounter any difficulties, either in the occupied zone or in Vichy. In the occupied zone French authorities were far more worried about the increasing number of attacks against Wehrmacht personnel. The execution of hostages did not have the desired effect. On June 1 SS Gen. Karl Oberg, previously posted in Radom in the General Government, arrived in France as higher SS and police leader. Before taking office Oberg had paid a visit to the French capital on May 7, in the company of Heydrich. The atmosphere was favorable for closer collaboration between France and the Reich, as, since the end of April, Laval was back at the head of the Vichy government. Vallat had been replaced at the head of the CGQJ by a much fiercer Jew hater, Louis Darquier de Pellepoix, and the French police in the occupied zone were now headed by an ambitious newcomer, René Bousquet, all too ready to play his part in the German-French *rapprochement*. During Heydrich's visit, Bousquet requested the further deportation of some five thousand Jews from Drancy to the East. Although Heydrich made his agreement conditional upon the availability of transportation, four trains with approximately a thousand Jews each left for Auschwitz in the course of June.

Two major points of contention between the Germans and Vichy remained unresolved: the inclusion of French Jews in the deportations, and the use of French police in the roundups. Finally Bousquet gave in to the Germans, and on July 4 he conveyed Vichy's official stand: As a first step all "stateless" Jews from the occupied and unoccupied zones (that is, formerly German, Polish, Czechoslovak, Russian, Lithuanian, Latvian, or Estonian Jews) would be deported. French police forces would arrest the Jews in both zones. Moreover Laval suggested, on his own initiative, the deportation of children under age sixteen from the unoccupied zone. As for children in the occupied zone, Laval declared that their fate was of no interest to him.

In early June the Jewish star had been introduced in France. The measure caused momentary indignation in part of the population and expressions of sympathy for the "decorated" Jews, as had been the case in Germany. Vichy refused to enforce the decree on its territory in order to avoid the accusation that a French government stigmatized Jews of French citizenship. Among Catholic intellectuals, communists, and many students, reactions to the German measure were particularly negative. The Jews themselves quickly recognized the mood of part of the population and, at the outset at least, the star was carried with a measure of pride and defiance. Individual manifestations of sympathy, however, were not indicative of any basic shifts in public opinion regarding the anti-Jewish measures. Despite the negative response to the introduction of the star and soon thereafter to the deportations, an undercurrent of traditional anti-Semitism persisted in both zones.

"I hate the Jews," Pierre Drieu La Rochelle confided in his diary on November 8, 1942. "I always knew that I hated them."[32] In this case Drieu's outburst remained hidden in his diary. On the eve of the war, however, he had been less discreet in *Gilles*, an autobiographical novel that became both a bestseller and a classic of French literature. Compared with some of his literary peers, Drieu was in fact relatively moderate. In *Les Décombres*, a runaway bestseller published in the spring of 1942, Lucien Rebatet showed more of Nazi-like anti-Jewish rage: "Jewish spirit is in the intellectual life of France a poisonous weed that must be pulled out right to its most minuscule roots." Rebatet's stand regarding the Jews was part and parcel of an unconditional allegiance to Hitler's Reich: "I wish for the victory of Germany because the war it is waging is my war, our war. . . . I don't admire Germany for being Germany but for having produced Hitler. . . . I think that Hitler has conceived of a magnificent future for our continent, and I passionately want him to realize it."[33] Céline, possibly the most significant writer of this anti-Semitic phalanx, took up the same themes in an even more vitriolic form; however, his manic style and his insane outbursts marginalized him to a point. In December 1941 the German novelist Ernst Jünger encountered Céline at the German Institute in Paris: "He says," Jünger noted, "how surprised and stupefied he is that we soldiers do not shoot, hang, exterminate the Jews—he is stupefied that someone availed of a bayonet should not make unrestricted use of it."[34] Robert Brasillach was outwardly more polished, but his anti-Jewish hatred was no less extreme and persistent than that of Céline or Rebatet. He applauded the French and German policies regarding the Jews but, as French measures went, they appeared to him at times too feeble and too incomplete: "Don't forget the [Jewish] children,"[35] he called upon Vichy in a *Je Suis Partout* article.

From the beginning of 1942 mass killings of Jews were spreading throughout the Warthegau and the General Government, as the days of total annihilation were rapidly approaching. In the early spring Elisheva from Stanisławów, a young woman in her early twenties, had inserted the notes of an anonymous friend in her own chronicle: "We are utterly exhausted," the "guest diarist" recorded. "We only have illusions that something will change; this hope keeps us alive. But how long can we live on the power of the spirit that is also fading? . . . Yesterday, Elsa [Elisheva] told me that a man who had died of starvation couldn't fit into the coffin, so his legs had to be broken. Unbelievable!"[36]

On May 14 Elisheva reminisced that the situation in Stanisławów had suddenly changed: "It started in March. All the handicapped on the Aryan side were killed. It was a signal that something ominous was coming. And it was a disaster. On March 31, they started searching for the handicapped and old people, and later several thousand young and healthy people were taken. We were hiding in the attic and through the window I saw the transports of Hungarian Jews [who had been expelled from Hungary to Galicia in the late summer of 1941] leaving Rudolfsmühle [an improvised German prison]. I saw children from the orphanage wrapped in bed sheets. The houses around the ghetto were on fire. I heard some shooting, children crying, mothers calling, and Germans breaking into the neighboring houses. We survived."[37]

On June 9 Elisheva recognized that her own survival had been but a short reprieve: "Well, this whole scribbling does not make any sense. It is a fact we are not going to survive. The world will know about everything even without my wise notes. The members of the Jewish Council have been imprisoned. The hell with them—the thieves. But what does it mean to us? Rudolfsmühle has finally been liquidated. Eight hundred people have been taken to the cemetery [the killing site of Stanisławów. . . . The situation is hopeless but some people say it is going to be better. Let us hope so! Is being alive after the war worth so much suffering and pain? I doubt it. But I don't want to die like an animal."[38] Ten days later Elisheva's diary ended. Her diary was discovered in a ditch, along the road leading to the Stanisławów cemetery.

In Lodz, Sierakowiak's chronicling resumed in mid-March. In his saddlers' workshop, the food, it seems, was sufficient for "workshop workers" like him (category A). "The deportations are in progress, while the workshops are receiving huge orders and there is enough work for several months," he noted on March 26.[39] The deportations were temporarily halted on April 3. On that day the diarist recorded: "The deportations have been halted again, but nobody knows for how long. Meanwhile winter has returned with thick snow. Rumkowski has posted an announcement that there will be a cleaning of the ghetto on Monday. From eight in the morning to three in the afternoon, all inhabitants from the ages of fifteen to fifty will have to clean apartments and courtyards. There won't be any other work anywhere. All I care about, however, is that there is soup in my workshop."[40]

By mid-May 1942 the number of deportees from Lodz had reached 55,000. The last wave included exclusively 10,600 "Western Jews" from a total of 17,000 still alive in the ghetto at that time. It remains unclear why none of the "Western Jews" were included in the earlier deportations and why in early May they were the only deportees. The earlier reprieve may have been the result of German orders, in an attempt to avoid the spreading of any rumors about Lodz and ensure the orderly pace of deportations from the Reich. Whether Rumkowski was involved in the decision is not known, although he did not hide his growing hostility toward the "newcomers."

During the first half of 1942 the rapidly expanding deportations to the extermination centers had yet to reach the Jews of Warsaw. Information about the systematic extermination campaign was nonetheless spreading, mainly among activists of the various clandestine political movements. In mid-March, Zuckerman as representative of He-Halutz and other members of left-wing Zionist parties invited leaders of the Bund to attend a meeting to discuss the setting up of a common defense organization. After summing up the available information about the expanding extermination, Zuckerman came up with his proposal for a common Jewish defense organization that would also act in common in its relation with the Polish military underground. These suggestions were rejected by the Bund representatives. Their main argument seems to have been that the Bund was bound by its relations with the Polish Socialist Party (PPS) and that, as far as the PPS was concerned, the time for rebellion had not yet come. Once the Bund had stated his position, the representative of the "Poalei Zion left," decided that given the situation they would not participate either. Evidently the traditional hostility between Bundists and Zionists exacerbated their contrary interpretations of the events even on the brink of annihilation.

On April 17 fifty-two Jews, some members of the Bund, some of those working for the underground press, were pulled out of their apartments and shot in the back of the neck. The Germans were probably becoming aware of the first attempts to organize a Jewish underground in the Polish capital and mainly of the growing influence carried by the clandestine press. According to Zuckerman's memoirs the Gestapo had his name and address, but otherwise it did not have much precise information. The main aim of the executions was therefore, as Zuckerman surmises, "to instill terror."[41] An additional aim may have been to paralyze any underground plans ahead of the forthcoming *Aktion*. Indeed, as a result of the April massacres, the Council attempted to persuade the clandestine groups to put an end to their meetings.

A week before the beginning of the deportations, on July 15, 1942, Janusz Korczak invited the ghetto's who's who to a performance of Rabindranath Tagore's *Post Office*, staged and enacted by the staff and children of his orphanage. Korczak (Dr. Henryk Goldszmit) was a widely known educator and writer—mainly of highly prized children's books; for three decades he had been the director of the Jewish orphanage in Warsaw. After the establishment of the ghetto the "old doctor," as he was affectionately nicknamed, had to move his two hundred small charges within the walls. The play, the story of a sick boy confined to his dark room in a hut, expressed the boy's yearning to wander among trees and flowers, to hear the birds singing. In the play a supernatural being enables Amal (the hero's name) to walk an invisible path to the paradise he dreamed about. "Perhaps illusions would be a good subject for the Wednesday dormitory talk," Korczak wrote in his diary on July 18. "Illusions, their role in the life of mankind."[42]

CHAPTER 12

Total Extermination

July 1942–March 1943

WILHELM CORNIDES, a Wehrmacht noncommissioned officer, was stationed in Galicia in the summer of 1942. According to his diary entry of August 31, while he had been waiting for a train at the railway station in Rawa Ruska, another train entered the station: It carried Jews in some thirty-eight cattle cars. Cornides asked a policeman where the Jews came from: "'Those are probably the last ones from Lwów,' the policeman answered. 'That has been going on now for five weeks. . . . In Jaroslav, they let only 8 remain, no one knows why.' I asked: 'How far are they going?' Then he replied, 'To Belzec.' And then? 'Poison.' I asked: Gas? He shrugged his shoulders. Then he said only: 'At the beginning, they always shot them, I believe.'"

Later, in his compartment, Cornides struck up a conversation with a woman passenger, a railway policeman's wife, who told him that such transports "'were passing through daily, sometimes also with German Jews.' I asked: 'Do the Jews know then what is happening with them?' The woman answered: 'Those who come from far won't know anything, but here in the vicinity they know already.' . . . Camp Belzec is supposed to be located right on the railway line and the woman promised to show it to me when we pass it.'"

"At 6:20 p.m.," Cornides recorded, the train passed Belzec: "Before then, we had traveled for some time through a tall pine forest. When the woman called 'Now it comes,' one could see a high hedge of fir trees. A strong sweetish odor could be made out distinctly. 'But they are stinking already,' says the woman. 'Oh nonsense, that is only the gas,' the railway policeman [who had joined them] said, laughing. Meanwhile we had gone on about 200 yards—the sweetish odor was transformed into a strong smell of something burning. 'That is from the crematory,' says the policeman. A short distance further the fence stopped. In front of it, one could see a guard-house with an SS post."[1]

By late August 1942 the German armies on the eastern front had reached the oil fields and the (destroyed) refineries of Maikop and, further south, the slopes of the Caucasus; soon the German army flag would be hoisted on Mount Elbrus, Europe's highest peak. At the same time, Paulus' Sixth Army was approaching Stalingrad's outer defenses; it reached the Volga, north of the city, on August 23. In the north a new attack to break through the defenses of Leningrad was planned for early September. Yet, notwithstanding such impressive advances, the German military situation on the eastern front was becoming increasingly precarious. In the center and the south the armies were spread over considerable distances, and their supply lines were dangerously overstretched. Instead of heeding the warnings of his generals, however, Hitler obstinately insisted on forging ahead.

The fateful about-face came suddenly, in the course of a few weeks. On October 23, 1942, the British army attacked at El Alamein; within days, Rommel was in full retreat. The Germans were ousted from Egypt, then from Libya. The debacle of the Afrika Korps would halt, albeit for a short time, only at the Tunisian border. On November 7 American and British forces landed in Morocco and Algeria. On November 11, in response to the Allied landings, the Germans occupied the Vichy zone and sent forces to Tunisia, while the Italians slightly enlarged their own occupation area in the southeast of France. The major drama, however, unfolded on the eastern front.

The battle for Stalingrad had started in the last days of August, after a devastating German bombing of the city that left some forty thousand civilians dead. Stalin had sent his most brilliant strategist, Marshal Georgy Zhukov, to command the Stalingrad front. By October the battle had turned into house-to-house combat among the hulks of buildings, the ruins of factories, the remnants of grain silos. And, as Paulus was desperately attempting to take the city center and reach the Volga, undetected Soviet divisions were gathering on both flanks of the Sixth Army. On November 19 the Red Army counterattacked, and soon the Soviet pincer movement shattered the German rearguard at its weakest point, the area held by Romanian forces. Paulus's army was cut off. A second Soviet offensive destroyed a mixture of Italian and Hungarian units: The encirclement was complete.

While ordering a hasty retreat from the Caucasus, Hitler adamantly refused to abandon Stalingrad. The battle for the city soon became, in the eyes of millions the world over, a portent of ultimate victory or defeat. By the end of the year the Sixth Army was doomed. Nonetheless the Nazi leader still rejected Paulus's entreaty to allow him to surrender: Soldiers and commanders, the newly promoted field marshal was told, had to resist to the last and die a heroic death. On February 2, 1943, the Sixth Army stopped fighting. It had lost two hundred thousand men; ninety thousand soldiers, including Paulus and his generals, were led into captivity.

The German defeats in North Africa and on the eastern front were compounded by the rapid expansion of the Anglo-American bombing campaign: German industrial production did not slow down but the toll in lives, homes, and entire city areas began to undermine the population's faith in victory. Simultaneously partisan warfare turned into a growing threat in the occupied territories of Eastern Europe and in the Balkans, while resistance networks multiplied and got bolder in the West.

In the meantime Hitler's diatribes against the Jews went on with the same fanatical obsessiveness. The themes were the same as before. The "prophecy" reappeared again and again as a mantra, with minute nuances surfacing here and there. Thus in his Sportpalast speech of September 30 for the launching of the "winter relief" campaign, Hitler brandished his extermination threat with a particularly sadistic twist. "The Jews have once laughed at my prophecies, also in Germany. I don't know whether they are still laughing today, or if they have stopped laughing. But I can guarantee now as well: Everywhere they will stop laughing. And I shall also be vindicated in this prophecy."[2]

Some Jews understood what the crazed German messiah was proclaiming. "'The Jews will be exterminated,' Hitler said in his speech yesterday. He hardly said anything else," Sebastian commented on October 1.[3] The next day Klemperer recorded: "'Hitler's speech. . . . The same old song mercilessly exaggerated. . . . The shocking thing is not that a crazy man raves in ever greater frenzy, but that Germany accepts it, for the tenth year now and in the fourth year of the war, and that it [Germany] continues to allow itself to be bled."[4]

During his visit to Auschwitz on July 17, 1942, Himmler watched the extermination of a transport of Jews from Holland. A few days later an order came from the Reichsführer:

"All mass graves were to be opened and the corpses burnt. In addition the ashes were to be disposed of in such a way that it would be impossible at some future time to calculate the number of corpses burnt."[5]

During these same days of July, the German onslaught against the Jews of Europe reached its full scale. Throughout the spring and early summer, the extermination process—after decimating part of the Jewish population of the Warthegau, of Lodz, and of the occupied territories of the Soviet Union—had expanded to Jews from the Reich, from Slovakia and, district after district, from the General Government, except for Warsaw. In the second half of July the deportations from Holland and France began, followed by Warsaw, all within days of one another. In August the Jews of Belgium were included. In the General Government while the Warsaw Jews were being killed, a large part of the Jewish population of Lwów was carted away. In the first days of September, major roundups struck again at the Jews of Lodz, and, throughout, deportations from the West continued. It seems that notwithstanding all unforeseen political, technical, and logistical problems, the "Final Solution" had turned into a smoothly running organization of mass murder on an extraordinary scale. Whatever the feuds between various agencies and personalities within the SS or between the SS and party officials may have been in regard to control over various aspects of the extermination, nothing indicates that those tensions had any impact on the overall progress of the campaign.

In Holland the meticulous registration work accomplished by the Dutch census office, the German Zentralstelle, and the Jewish Council allowed for summonses to be sent on July 4 to four thousand Jews (mainly refugees), chosen from the updated lists. To fill the quota the Germans organized a sudden police raid in Amsterdam on July 14; it netted seven hundred more Jews. The Dutch police outdid German expectations, with Sybren Tulp personally participating in every roundup. Moreover, in May 1942, a unit of Voluntary Auxiliary Police had been created, comprising some two thousand men. These local police collaborators vied with the Germans in sheer sadism and brutality; most of the spies who garnered handsome profits from denouncing Jews in hiding came from their ranks.

Apparently the Germans had informed the Jewish Council in early March 1942 that Jews would be sent to labor camps in the East. But the Council believed that the deportees would be German Jews only and hence took no action. It was shocked in late June when informed that Dutch Jews would be included in the deportations. Ferdinand Aus der Fünten, commander of the German Special Police in Amsterdam, then chose the usual method: Some Dutch Jews would not be sent away, and the council would be allowed to distribute a given number of exemption certificates. The Germans knew that they could rely upon the docility of the people not immediately threatened. The council compiled the list of the 17,500 privileged ones whom it could exempt: These Jews had special stamps affixed to their identity cards. According to Gertrud van Tijn, "When the first [exemption] stamps were issued, the scenes at the Jewish Council were quite indescribable. Doors were broken, the staff of the council was attacked, and the police had often to be called in. . . . The stamps quickly became an obsession with every Jew."[6] More often than not, the decisions of the "exemptions' committee" were influenced by favoritism and corruption.

"The Jews here are telling each other lovely stories: They say that the Germans are burying us alive or exterminating us with gas. But what is the point of repeating such things, even if they should be true?"[7] This July 11 entry in Etty Hillesum's diary shows that ominous rumors about "Poland" were circu-lating in Amsterdam as the deportations started; it also shows that neither Hillesum nor most of the other Jews really believed them.

Immediate deportation threatened foreign refugees such as the Franks. On July 5 Margot, Anne's elder sister, received the summons to report to the assembly center. On the next day, assisted by the faithful Dutch couple Miep and Jan Gies, the Franks were on their way to a carefully prepared hiding place, an attic in the building where Otto Frank's office was located. Margot and Miep left first. Anne made sure that her cat would be taken in by neighbors, and, on July 6, at 7:30 in the morning, the Franks left their home. "So there we were," Anne noted on July 9, "Father, Mother, and I, walking in the pouring rain, each of us with a schoolbag and a shopping bag filled to the brim with the most varied assortment of items. The people on their way to work at that early hour gave us sympathetic looks; you could tell by their faces that they were sorry they couldn't offer us some kind of transportation; the conspicuous yellow star spoke for itself."[8]

Much of the initial outrage expressed by the Dutch population against the German persecution of the Jews had turned into passivity by 1942. The Dutch government-in-exile did not exhort its countrymen to help the Jews when the deportations started, although on two occasions, at the end of June and in July 1942, "Radio Oranje" did broadcast information previously aired by the BBC about the exterminations in Poland. These reports did not make any deep impression either on the population or even on the Jews. The fate of Polish Jews was one thing, the fate of the Jews of Holland quite another.

Some protests against the deportations nonetheless did take place. On July 11 all the major church leaders signed a letter addressed to Seyss-Inquart. The Germans tried "conciliation" first: They promised exemptions for some baptized Jews. Initially the churches did not give in: The main Reformed Church

(Herformde Kerk) proposed to have the letter publicly read on Sunday, July 26. The Catholic and Calvinist Church leaders agreed. When the German threatened retaliation, the Reformed Church leadership wavered, while the Catholic bishops decided to proceed nonetheless. In retaliation, during the night of August 1–2, the Germans arrested most Catholic Jews and sent them to Westerbork. Ninety-two Catholic Jews were ultimately deported to Auschwitz, among them the philosopher, Carmelite nun, and future Catholic saint, Edith Stein.

Soon after the beginning of the deportations, children were moved from the main assembly and processing hall, the Hollandsche Schouwburg (renamed Joodsche Schouwburg), to an annex on the opposite side of the street (the Crèche), a child-care center for working-class families. At that point two members of the Jewish Council succeeded in gaining access to some of the children's files and destroying them. Thus bereft of administrative identity, children were sporadically smuggled out of the Crèche with the help of the Dutch woman director, Henriette Rodriguez-Pimental; they were passed on to various clandestine networks that usually succeeded in finding safe places with Dutch families. Hundreds of children were thus saved.

Jewish adults encountered much greater difficulties in hiding among the population. The refusals they met could have resulted from fear, traditional anti-Semitism, and "civic obedience." From the outset, however, small networks of people who knew and trusted each other—and mostly shared a common religious background (Calvinist or Catholic)—did actively help Jews, despite the risks. The limited scope of the grassroots actions has been attributed to the absence of hands-on leadership from the hierarchy of all Dutch Christian churches, notwithstanding some of the courageous protests.

At the beginning of 1943 the Germans started rounding up the approximately eight thousand Jewish patients in various

hospitals, and among them the psychiatric inmates of Het Apel-
doornse Bos. The patients were ferociously beaten and pushed
into trucks. "I saw them place a row of patients," an eyewitness declared, "many of them older women on mattresses at
the bottom of one lorry and then load another load of human
bodies on top of them. So crammed were these lorries that the
Germans had a hard job to put up the tail-boards."[9] The trucks
carried the patients to the cordoned-off Apeldoorn railway
station.

A Dutch Jew described the arrival of the transport in Auschwitz: "It was one of the most horrible transports from Holland
that I saw. Many of the patients tried to break through the bar-
rier and were shot dead. The remainders were gassed immediately."[10] There are diverging accounts of the fate of the fifty
(Jewish) nurses who accompanied the transport. Some declare
that they were sent to the camp; others that they were gassed;
according to another witness, "some of them were thrown into
a pit, doused with petrol and burnt alive."[11] Aus der Fünten
had promised them that they could return immediately after
the trip or work in the East in a thoroughly modern mental
institution.

In early 1943 the Germans established the Vught labor
camp, which supposedly would allow Jews to remain as forced
laborers in Holland. It was a sophisticated "legal" option to
avoid deportation; the council strongly encouraged it, and the
obedient Dutch Jews went along. Of course, it was one further German scam, and the Vught inmates were systematically
transferred to Westerbork or, on several occasions, directly deported to the East.

"The papers announce new measures against the Jews,"
Jacques Biélinky recorded in Paris on July 15, 1942: "They are
forbidden access to restaurants, coffeehouses, movie theaters,
theaters, concert halls, music halls, pools, beaches, museums,

libraries, exhibitions, castles, historical monuments, sports events, races, parks, camping sites and even phone booths, fairs, etc. Rumor has it that Jewish men and women between ages eighteen and forty-five will be sent to forced labor in Germany."[12] On that same day the roundups of "stateless" Jews started in the provinces of the occupied zone, on the eve of the operation in Paris.

On July 16, at 4:00 a.m., the German-French roundup of 27,000 "stateless" Jews living in the capital and its suburbs began. Fifty municipal buses were ready, and so were 4,500 French policemen. No German units participated in the arrests. As rumors about the forthcoming raids had spread, many potential victims (mostly men) had gone into hiding. By July 17 in the afternoon 3,031 Jewish men, 5,802 women, and 4,051 children had been arrested; the number of Jews caught finally totaled 13,152. Unmarried people or childless couples were sent directly to Drancy; the others—8,160 men, women, and children—were assembled in a large indoor sports arena known mainly for its bicycle races, the Vélodrome d'Hiver (Vel d'Hiv). At the Vel d'Hiv nothing was ready, neither food nor water nor toilets nor beds or bedding of any sort. For three to six days thousands of hapless beings received one to two portions of soup per day. Two Jewish physicians and one Red Cross physician were in attendance. The temperature never fell below one hundred degrees Fahrenheit. Finally group after group of the Vel d'Hiv Jews were temporarily sent to Pithiviers and Beaune-la-Rolande, camps just vacated by the inmates deported in June.

The roundup had not achieved the expected results. In order to keep Drancy stocked with Jews ready for deportation, the arrests of stateless Jews had to extend to the Vichy zone, as agreed by the French government. The major operation, again exclusively implemented by French forces, took place from August 26 to 28; some 7,100 Jews were seized. By the end of the year 42,500 Jews had been deported from France to Auschwitz.

Until mid-1943 Drancy remained under French authority. For the camp administration filling the quotas imposed by the Germans for each departing transport remained the main goal. "Under our current obligation to come up with one thousand deportees on Monday," a French police officer noted on September 12, 1942, "we must include in these departures, at least in reserve, the parents of sick [children] and advise them that they could be deported without their children remaining in the infirmary."[13]

On August 11 Untersturmführer Horst Ahnert from Dannecker's office informed the RSHA that, due to the temporary halt in the roundups, he planned to send the children assembled in Beaune-la-Rolande and Pithiviers to Drancy, and asked for Berlin's authorization. On the thirteenth Günther gave his approval but warned Ahnert not to send transports filled with children only.

It was probably the arrival of these children, aged two to twelve, that the Drancy inmate George Wellers described after the war: "They were disembarked from the buses in the midst of the courtyard like small animals. . . . The elder children held the younger ones and did not let go of them until they reached their allocated places. On the stairs the bigger children carried the smaller ones, panting, to the fourth floor. There, they remained fearfully huddled together. . . . Once the luggage had been unloaded the children returned to the courtyard, but most of the younger ones could not find their belongings; when, after their unsuccessful search they wished to get back to their rooms, they could not remember where they had been assigned."[14]

In early 1943 the number of foreign Jews in France was rapidly dwindling and the weekly quotas of deportees were no longer being met; the Germans then decided to move to the next step: Pétain and Laval were now prodded to cancel naturalizations of Jews that had taken place after 1927. It was at this point, as we shall see, that, unexpectedly, after first agreeing, Laval changed his mind.

The immediate reaction of the majority of ordinary French people to the roundups was unmistakably negative in both zones. Although it did not lead to any organized protest, it did enhance readiness to help Jews on the run. Feelings of pity at the sight of the unfortunate victims, particularly women and children, spread, albeit briefly; but, as already mentioned, basic prejudice toward the Jews did not disappear. "The persecution of the Jews," a February 1943 report from a Resistance agent stated, "has profoundly wounded the French in their humane principles; it has even, at times, made the Jews almost sympathetic. One cannot deny, however, that there is a Jewish question: . . . The Blum ministry, which was overflowing with Jewish elements and the penetration of tens of thousands of foreign Jews into France provoked a defensive mechanism in France. People would pay any price not to see a similar invasion repeated."[15] Several other reports from similar sources dwelt on almost identical points.

The assembly of French cardinals and archbishops met in Paris on July 21, 1942, less than a week after the raid. On the following day Emmanuel Cardinal Suhard, in the name of the assembly, sent a letter of protest to the maréchal. It was the first official protest of the Catholic Church of France regarding the persecution of the Jews: "Deeply moved by the information . . . about the massive arrests of Israelites that took place last week. . . . It is in the name of humanity and of Christian principles that our voice is raised to protest in favor of the nonalienable rights of human beings."[16]

The papal nuncio in Vichy, Valerio Valeri, considered the letter as being rather "platonic." Helbronner thought so as well and beseeched his friend Jules-Marie Gerlier to intervene personally with Pétain. After obfuscating for a while the Lyons cardinal agreed to send a letter to the maréchal, and did so on

August 19. But, like Suhard before him, Gerlier wrote in circum-voluted terms that could only indicate to Pétain and to Laval that the church of France would ultimately abstain from any forceful confrontation. The cardinal did not ask for a meeting with Pétain, notwithstanding his promise to Helbronner. A few months beforehand, however, Gerlier had allowed the establishment in his diocese of an association to help Jews (Amitiés Judeo-Chrétiennes), led by Abbé Alexandre Glasberg (of Jewish background) and the Jesuit Pierre Chaillet; in August 1942 he intervened in favor of the same Father Chaillet, arrested for having hidden eighty-four Jewish children.

It was in this context that, on August 30, 1942, Jules-Gérard Saliège, archbishop of Toulouse, issued a pastoral letter denouncing the roundups and deportations, to be read in all churches of his diocese: "It had been reserved to our time to witness the sad spectacle of children, of women, of fathers and mothers being treated like a herd of animals; to see members of the same family separated from one another and shipped away to an unknown destination. . . . Jews are men. Jewesses are women. Foreigners are men, foreign women are women. They cannot be mistreated at will, these men, these women, these fathers and mothers of families. They are part of the human race."[17]

Saliège's pastoral letter has to be set in its context: While the letter undoubtedly expressed the archbishop's immediate moral reaction to the roundups of foreign Jews in the Vichy zone, it also served a tactical purpose. Apparently the letter was suggested to the Toulouse prelate by emissaries from Lyons. In other words, as the assembly of French cardinals and archbishops was paralyzed, Saliège became its voice; so, shortly afterward, did the bishop of Montauban. The episcopal assembly probably knew that these individual protests would be considered too marginal to cause official retaliation, yet they would allow face to be saved: The church of France had not remained silent.

Occasionally assistance was collective, remarkable in its scope, and no less remarkable in the absence of any proselytizing aims. Such was the case in the French Protestant community Le Chambon-sur-Lignon, a village in the mountainous Cévennes region, guided by its pastor, André Trocmé, and his family. The entire village took part in this extraordinary venture and ultimately did hide hundreds, possibly thousands of Jews at one moment or another throughout the entire period. It took a Protestant police officer sent by Vichy to uncover part of the hiding operation and to ensure the deportation of all the young Jewish charges of the children's home, Maison des Roches, and that of their director, Daniel Trocmé.

The usual German decrees had been applied in Belgium as they had been in France and in Holland, and approximately at the same time. Yet the commander in chief, General Falkenhausen, and the military administration were concerned lest the deportations, also scheduled for July, cause unrest among the population.

A report sent to the Wilhelmstrasse on July 9, by Minister Werner von Bargen, the Foreign Ministry representative with the military high command in Brussels, gave a generally faithful picture of the situation: "Considerations against the measure could stem, first, from the fact that understanding for the Jewish question is not yet very widespread here and that Jews of Belgian nationality are considered by the population as Belgians. Therefore the measure could be interpreted as the beginning of general forced evacuations [for labor in Germany]. Moreover the Jews here are integrated in the economic life, so that one could be worried about difficulties in the labor market. The military administration expects however to overcome these considerations, if the deportation of Belgian Jews is avoided. Thus, to start with, Polish, Czech, Russian and other Jews will be chosen, which should allow, theoretically, to reach the due number."[18]

Himmler had no qualms in agreeing to postpone the deportation of Belgian Jewish nationals, as he knew that they represented barely 6 percent of the 57,000 Jews registered by the Security Police. On August 4, 1942, the first transport of foreign Jews left Mechelen for Auschwitz. Yet the events in Belgium would, paradoxically, take a somewhat different course from those in neighboring Holland, for example. The beginning of the German onslaught caught Jews and non-Jews by surprise, and it was during the first two months of the operation that one-third of Belgian Jewry was sent to its death. However, while approximately 15,000 Jews were deported by November 1942, the German roundups became rapidly less successful during the following months: Some further 10,000 Jews were deported before the liberation of the country. About half of the Jewish population survived the war.

Notwithstanding strong prejudice against Jews, particularly against the vast number of foreign Jews, two factors led to a far higher rescue percentage in Belgium than in neighboring, relatively non-anti-Semitic Holland, home to a vast majority of native Dutch Jews: the spontaneous reaction of the population and the involvement of Belgian resistance organizations. There is no question that large-scale rescue operations initiated by "ordinary Belgians" took place at all levels of society. The issue that remains unanswered—and probably unanswerable—is the degree of influence of the Catholic Church on this surge of compassion and charity. That Catholic institutions did hide Jews, particularly Jewish children, is well documented; whether these institutions, and mainly the rank-and-file Catholic population, responded to the encouragements and instructions of the church hierarchy or merely to their own feelings remains unclear, as does the influence of the memory of German brutality in World War I.

Active cooperation between a rapidly established underground (Comité de Défense des Juifs, or CDJ) and the Belgian resistance organizations led to the hiding of about 25,000 Jews. This cooperation was facilitated by the fact that, from the outset, a significant number of foreign Jewish refugees were affiliated with the Belgian Communist Party or with left-wing Zionist organizations, particularly with the Communist organization for foreign workers (MOI), which was highly influential in the Belgian resistance.

In the East in the meantime, deportations and mass killings were growing apace. In mid-July, Hermann Höfle, Globocnik's main deportation and extermination expert, arrived in Warsaw from Lublin with a group of "specialists." On July 20 Czerniaków, aware of widespread rumors about pending deportations, decided to get some information from his longtime German "interlocutors" but was repeatedly told that the rumors were *Quatsch* and *Unsinn* [utter nonsense]. On July 21 several members of the Council were arrested as hostages, and so were other prominent Jews in the ghetto administration. The next morning, July 22, the entrance to the Council building was blocked by a few SS cars; the Council members and the heads of all departments assembled in Czerniaków's office; Höfle arrived with a small retinue. Höfle announced that the deportations would start within a few hours. Czerniaków tried to negotiate some exemptions but received no assurances whatsoever. On the twenty-third he noted in his diary: "In the morning at the Community. SS 1st Lieut. Worthoff from the deportation staff came and we discussed several problems. . . . When I asked for the number of days per week in which the operation would be carried on, the answer was seven days a week. . . . Throughout the town a great rush to start new workshops. A sewing machine can save a life. It is 3 o'clock. So far 4,000 are ready to go. The orders are that there must be 9,000 by 4 o'clock."[19] In the afternoon, as the Jewish police was unable to fill the quota, Polish and Lithuanian auxiliary police units launched their own roundup.

On that same evening the SS called Czerniaków back from home; he was told that on the next day 10,000 Jews had to be sent to the Umschlagplatz (transfer square). The chairman returned to his office, closed the door, wrote one farewell note to the council informing it of the new German demands, another to his wife, and took poison. Kaplan, no friend of Czerniaków, noted on July 26: "The first victim of the deportation decree was the President . . . who committed suicide by poison in the Judenrat building. . . . There are those who earn immortality in a single hour. The President, Adam Czerniakow, earned his immortality in a single instant."[20]

On July 22 Treblinka had opened its gates. Every day thousands of terrified ghetto inhabitants were driven to the Umschlagplatz, and from there a freight train carried five thousand of them to Treblinka. At first most of the Jews of Warsaw did not know what fate awaited them. On July 30 Kaplan mentioned "expulsion" and "exile." On August 5 the deportations engulfed all institutions for children, including orphanages. Korczak's orphanage, like all Jewish orphanages of the ghetto, was ordered to proceed to the Umschlagplatz. Korczak walked at the head of the column of children marching to their death. By September 21, the great *Aktion* was over: 10,380 Jews had been killed in the ghetto during the deportations; 265,040 had been deported to Treblinka and gassed.

Treblinka, the last and deadliest of the "Aktion Reinhard" camps, had been built to the northeast of Warsaw, close to the Warsaw-Białystok railway line. The "lower" or first camp extended over the larger area; it included the assembly and "undressing" squares, and, farther on, workshops and barracks. The second or "upper" camp was isolated from the first by barbed wire and thick foliage fences that hindered unwelcome observation. A heavy brick building concealed the three gas chambers linked to an engine by a system of pipes (a larger building with ten gas chambers would be added in October

1942). As in Chelmno, Belzec, and Sobibor, on arrival the deportees had to undress and leave all clothes or valuables for the sorting squads. From the "undressing" square the victims were driven to the gas chambers through "the road to heaven" (*Himmelstrasse*), a narrow corridor also hidden from the surroundings by thick branches. A sign pointed "to the showers."

Euthanasia physician Dr. Irmfried Eberl was appointed as the first commandant and, on July 23, 1942, the extermination began. According to SS-Unterscharführer Hingst's testimony, "Dr. Eberl's ambition was to reach the highest possible numbers and exceed all the other camps. So many transports arrived that the disembarkation and gassing of the people could no longer be handled." Within days Eberl completely lost control of the situation. His "incompetence" was compounded by widespread corruption: the money and valuables carried by the victims found their way into the camp staff's pockets and also into those of the commandant's euthanasia colleagues in Berlin. When Globocnik became aware of the situation in Treblinka, Eberl was immediately relieved of his position. In early September, Stangl, the Sobibor commandant, took over.

In Lodz, in the fall of 1942, as had been the case in Warsaw, the Germans established priority rules of their own. On September 1, the deportations started. The patients of the ghetto's five hospitals were "evacuated" within two hours; whoever protested was shot on the spot. In all, two thousand patients, including four hundred children, were carted away. Once the Germans had arrested most of the patients, they checked the hospital registry and if anybody was missing, family members were taken instead.

The deportation of the sick was immediately followed by an order to evacuate some further twenty thousand Jews, including all children under ten and all the elderly above sixty-five. As these categories totaled only seventeen thousand people, three thousand unemployed or unemployable inhabitants were added. On September 5 Sierakowiak's mother was taken away. "My most sacred, beloved, worn-out, blessed, cherished Mother has fallen victim to the bloodthirsty German Nazi beast!!! . . ." Two doctors, Czech Jews, suddenly arrived in the Sierakowiaks' apartment and declared the mother unfit for work; throughout the doctors' visit the father continued to eat the soup left by relatives in hiding and was also "taking sugar out of their bag." The mother left, with some bread in her bag and some potatoes. "I couldn't muster the willpower to look through the windows after her or to cry," Sierakowiak went on. "I walked around, talked and finally sat as though I had turned to stone. . . . I thought my heart was breaking. . . . It didn't break, though, and it let me eat, think, speak and go to sleep."[21]

On September 4, Rumkowski addressed a crowd of some fifteen hundred terrified inhabitants assembled on "Fireman Square": "The ghetto has been dealt a grievous blow. They ask that we give them that which is most precious—the children and old people. . . . In my old age I am compelled to stretch out my hand and beg: My brothers and my sisters, give them to me! Fathers and mothers, give me your children! . . . I must carry out the grim bloody surgery, I must amputate limbs to save the body! I must take away children and if I do not, others too may be taken. . . . We have in the ghetto many tuberculosis patients; their days . . . are numbered. I do not know—maybe it is a satanic plot, maybe it is not—but I cannot refrain from presenting it: Give me these patients and it may be possible to save healthy people in their stead."[22] "The president cries like a little boy," Josef Zelkowicz, one of the ghetto's chroniclers, added in his private diary.[23]

Between August 10 and 23, 1942, many of the Jews of Lwów were deported to the Janowska Road slave-labor camp and after a further selection, from there to Belzec. Some forty thousand of the victims arrested during the August roundup were exterminated. The remaining Jews of the city were driven into a ghetto, soon surrounded by a wooden fence. The *Judenrat* office was relocated to the ghetto area, but the *Judenrat* officials, among them the chairman, Henryk Landesberg, were not to resume their functions. According to the Germans, Landesberg had been in touch with the Polish underground. The chairman and twelve other Jewish officials were to be publicly hanged from the roof of the building and from lampposts.

The executions took some time, as the ropes used for the hangings broke; the victims who fell to the pavement were compelled to climb the stairs leading to the roof and were hanged again. The highest spot was kept for Landesberg, as chairman. He fell three times to the pavement and three times was brought back to his balcony. The bodies were left on display for two days. The Germans sent the bill for the ropes to the new *Judenrat*. As for the Jews of the Lwów ghetto, they did not survive for long: Most were liquidated in sporadic *Aktionen* and the remnant transferred to the Janowski camp in early 1943. When Lwów was liberated at the end of July 1944, out of a community of some 160,000 Jews in June 1941, some 3,400 were still alive.

In July 1942 the chief of the Vilna Jewish police, Jacob Gens, became the sole head of the ghetto. Among community leaders he was in many ways atypical. Born in Kovno, he fought as a volunteer in the Lithuanian war of independence in the aftermath of World War I and was promoted to officer rank. He married a Christian and was well regarded by Lithuanian nationalists (he himself was a right-wing Zionist). His wife and daughter remained on the Aryan side of the city. He possibly felt a moral obligation to take the position offered by the Germans. In the first letter from the ghetto that Gens sent to his wife, he wrote: "This is the first time in my life that I have to engage in such duties. My heart is broken. But

I shall always do what is necessary for the sake of the Jews in the ghetto."[24]

During the selections of late November 1941, Gens succeeded in saving some lives in particularly difficult circumstances; his standing among the inhabitants rose, and the Germans also kept adding to his tasks. But in mid-October 1942 the almost legendary *Kommandant* was confronted with a dire challenge: the order to kill Jews. Gens and his policemen were sent to a nearby town, Oszmiana, where about fourteen hundred Jews had been assembled for extermination. The police chief negotiated with the Germans who finally agreed that only four hundred Jews were to be murdered. Gens's men and some Lithuanians carried out the executions. Somehow news of the oncoming operation had spread in the ghetto as the policemen got on their way. Rudashevski was outraged by the very idea of such a participation: "How great is our shame, our humiliation!" he recorded on October 19. "Jews help the Germans in their organized, terrible work of extermination!"[25] But in fact the ghetto was not in uproar, contrary to what Rudashevski intensely hoped for and reported. It seems rather that the inhabitants accepted Gens's reasoning and his justifications: Save some by sacrificing others. "The tragedy is that the . . . public mostly approves of Gens's attitude," Kruk wrote on October 28. "The public figures that perhaps this may really help."[26]

A few weeks later a briefly oblivious community celebrated a significant achievement: "100,000 books in the ghetto." Kruk was in charge: "Because of this, the library is organizing a big cultural morning event, which will take place in the Ghetto theater on Sunday . . . [December 13], at noon. On the program: opening by G. Yashunski, welcome from the ghetto chief, writers, scientific circles, teachers and the Youth Club. Dr. Ts. Feldstein will speak on 'The Book and Martyrdom,' then a lecture by H. Kruk '100,000 Books in the Ghetto.' The second part will be a concert of words and music. The *finale*: Distribution of gift books to the first reader in the ghetto and the youngest reader of the library."[27]

No sooner had the Germans launched their major extermination campaign in the General Government and in Western Europe than pressure to deliver the Jews of southeastern, southern, and northern Europe had started.

The Germans did score an initial success in Romania when Antonescu authorized the deportation of Romanian Jews living in Germany or in German-occupied countries. In principle Bucharest had promised that the deportation of the approximately 300,000 Jews still living in Romania as such would follow. Soon after, however, the Romanians changed their mind. Repeated interventions by Jewish personalities, by the papal nuncio, Andrea Cassulo, and the Swiss minister, René de Weck; the bribing of officials and of Ion Antonescu's family by wealthy Romanian Jews and, also, Antonescu's resentment of German interference in an essentially internal matter—all contributed to the about-face in Bucharest. On October 11 Antonescu ordered the postponement of the deportations to the spring, and on November 11 the Romanian vice-prime minister Mihai Antonescu told Himmler's delegate in Bucharest, Gustav Richter, to his face that the Germans were behaving barbarically toward the Jews.

In early 1943 the situation in Hungary looked similar to that in Romania. A year beforehand, in the spring of 1942, the deportation of Hungarian Jews, first of one hundred thousand of them, was discussed with the Germans. In the fall of 1942 the change in policy started, obviously as a result of the shift in the global strategic balance. In October, when the Germans required that the Jews of Hungary be compelled to wear the yellow star, Kallay's government refused, and on October 5 the Germans' demand that the deportation of Hungary's eight hundred thousand Jews should start, was rejected.

In Bulgaria, Jewish policy also moved from cooperation with Germany to an increasingly independent stance. In June 1942 the Bulgarian parliament had authorized the government "to implement a solution to the Jewish problem." The first victims of King Boris's policies of collaboration were the Jews of Thracia (a former Greek province) and Macedonia (a former Yugoslav province)—areas Bulgaria had received as a reward for joining the German campaign against its two neighbors in April 1941. These eleven thousand foreign Jews (from Sofia's standpoint) were rounded up by the Bulgarian police, delivered to the Germans, and shipped to their death in Treblinka. The deportation of native Bulgarian Jews would, as we shall see, become a different matter altogether.

To these countries of southeastern Europe, Italy was certainly not setting the right example. With the implicit support of the highest levels of the state, wherever they could, in Croatia, in Greece, and in France, Italian officials were protecting the Jews. The Germans were fuming, but there was little they could do. Spain too continued to allow the mainly Jewish refugees who had visas for a further destination to cross its borders. However, once the deportations from France started, Spanish border guards began sending the fleeing Jews back to France. It took a direct threat from Churchill, in April 1943, to persuade Franco that, at that stage of the war, Spain's frontiers could not be fully closed.

In Scandinavia, Himmler's attempt, during his visit to Helsinki in July 1942, to convince the Finns to deliver the foreign Jews living in the country to Germany (about 150 to 200 people) brought mixed results. The Finnish secret police did start establishing lists of foreign Jews who could be deported (35 persons, according to some estimates) and delivered to the Germans in Estonia. But when rumor spread, protests erupted in the government and in public opinion. Finally the number of deportees was reduced to 8. On November 6, 1942, they were deported to Tallinn: One survived the war.

In Norway the German anti-Jewish campaign had started in the fall of 1942. The usual decrees turned the small Jewish population into a group of pariahs. On November 20 the deportations began by ship from Oslo to Stettin, then by train to Auschwitz. By the end of February 1943 the Jewish community of Norway had ceased to exist: More than seven hundred Jews had been murdered, and some nine hundred had fled to neutral Sweden. Up to this point the Swedes were quite restrictive in terms of their refugee policies; yet as information about the exterminations accumulated in Stockholm and once the deportations reached Scandinavia, the attitude of the Swedish Foreign Ministry changed: Jews who managed to flee to Sweden were given asylum. From then on Swedish help to Jews was extended not only to the whole of Scandinavia, but also to other rescue operations on the Continent.

The Germans did not have to concern themselves with Jews fleeing to neutral Switzerland. Authority over the foreigners living in Switzerland and over immigration was in the hands of the Federal Department of Justice and Police. During 1942 Swiss border police and customs officials were steadily reinforced by army units whose main task became to hunt down Jewish refugees. Notwithstanding some exceptions, Swiss policy of sending Jews back remained unchanged until late 1943 and, more selectively, even beyond that date.

In the summer of 1942 three German sources confirmed the most horrendous information available until then about the systematic and all-encompassing aspect of the exterminations. The impact of the first two reports remained limited, as their addressees did not forward them to London or Washington;

the third report would have major consequences within a few months.

Kurt Gerstein, a deeply religious Protestant, was head of the Technical Disinfection Service of the Waffen SS when, in late July 1942, he was ordered to obtain some 100 kg of prussic acid (Zyklon B) and deliver it to Lublin. After meeting with Globocnik, Gerstein proceeded to Belzec on August 2. In the camp Gerstein witnessed the arrival of a transport from Lemberg (Lwów). He saw how Ukrainian auxiliaries drove the Jews out of the freight cars, how the deportees were forced to strip naked and, told they would undergo disinfection, were pushed into the gas chambers. Gerstein timed the asphyxiation: The engine did not work at first. The Jews wept and wailed. After two and a half hours the engine started; thirty-two minutes later all the Jews were dead.

On the train journey from Warsaw back to Berlin, Gerstein started a conversation with a Swedish diplomat, Göran von Otter, attaché at the embassy in Berlin. Gerstein identified himself and told Otter what he had witnessed. Back in the capital the diplomat checked the SS officer's credentials and, convinced of his reliability, sent a report to Stockholm. The Swedish Foreign Ministry did not respond and did not inform the Allies. During the weeks that followed his return to Berlin, Gerstein attempted to inform the nuncio and the Swiss legation. He also informed Bishop Preysing's coadjutor, a Dr. Winter, as well as Bishop Dibelius and others—to no avail. Gerstein continued to play his double role to the end. He delivered Zyklon B shipments to the camps and unsuccessfully attempted to arouse German and foreign awareness of the events. At the end of the war he wrote three reports on what he had seen and otherwise knew, and handed them to the Americans, to whom he had given himself up. He was transferred to the French occupying forces and jailed in Paris as a possible war criminal. On July 25, 1945, he hanged himself in his cell.

Almost exactly at the date on which Otter's report reached Stockholm, a similar report was forwarded by the Swedish consul in Stettin, Karl Ingve Vendel. Vendel was in fact a Swedish intelligence agent monitoring German troop movements under the guise of consular activities and thus was also secretly in touch with some members of the German military opposition to the regime. After visiting a friend on an estate in East Prussia, Vendel, on August 9, 1942, filed a lengthy report on the situation in the General Government, which included a section on the extermination of the Jews: "In the city, all the Jews were assembled to what was officially announced as 'delousing.' At the entrance they were forced to take off their clothes . . . ; the delousing procedure, however, consisted of gassing and, afterward, all of them would be stuffed into a mass grave. . . . The source from which I obtained all this information on the conditions in the General Government is such that not the slightest shade of disbelief exists concerning the truthfulness of my informant's descriptions."[28] Vendel's report was not forwarded to the Allies either. After the war the Swedes admitted receiving the reports and not sending the information to the Allies.

At approximately the same time a third German source conveyed information that, in due time, put an end to Allied disbelief. In the last days of July 1942, a German industrialist, Eduard Schulte, well connected to high Nazi officials, traveled to Zurich and informed a Jewish business friend of a plan "prepared at Hitler's headquarters" for the total extermination of the Jews of Europe by the end of the year. The information was conveyed to Benjamin Sagalowitz, the press attaché of the Jewish community in Switzerland who, in turn, alerted Gerhart Riegner, the director of the Geneva office of the World Jewish Congress. Riegner asked to send a cable to World Jewish Congress headquarters in New York and London via the American and British legations in Bern. Both the American and the British diplomats agreed.

The identically worded text sent to Washington and to London read as follows: "Received alarming report that in Führer's headquarters plan discussed and under consideration according to which all Jews in countries occupied or controlled by Germany numbering three and a half four million should after deportation and concentration in East be exterminated at one blow to resolve once and for all the Jewish question in Europe stop Action reported planned for autumn methods under discussion including prussic acid stop We transmit information with all necessary reservation as exactitude cannot be confirmed stop Informant stated to have close connections with highest German authorities and his reports generally speaking reliable."[29]

The State Department and the Foreign Office remained skeptical, and Washington did not forward the cable to Stephen Wise, its main addressee. However, as the same cable had been received by the head of the British section of the World Jewish Congress, it was transmitted to Stephen Wise from London. On September 2, Undersecretary of State Sumner Welles phoned Wise and asked him to avoid publicizing the contents of the report before it could be independently confirmed. Wise agreed.

The International Committee of the Red Cross (ICRC), with headquarters in Geneva, included Swiss members only, and the Bern government's directives regarding major decisions went generally unchallenged. In August or September of 1942, Riegner had informed key members of the committee of the information that had been imparted to him. Notwithstanding the information at his disposal, Carl Burckhardt, a senior member of the ICRC, was opposed to any form of public protest, even very mildly formulated. Yet Burckhardt's confirmation to the American consul in Geneva of the information sent by Riegner probably contributed to the steps that followed in Washington and in London.

By November 1942, as further information about the German extermination campaign was accumulating in Washington, Welles had no choice but to tell Wise: "The reports received from Europe confirm and justify your deepest fears."[30] Within days the news became public in the United States, in England, in neutral countries, and in Palestine.

In fact, since October 1942 information about the extermination had been spreading in Great Britain and, on October 29, a protest meeting chaired by the archbishop of Canterbury, with the participation of British, Jewish, and Polish representatives, took place at Albert Hall. A month later, on November 27, the Polish government-in-exile officially recognized the murder of the country's Jews "along with Jews from other occupied countries who have been brought to Poland for this purpose."[31] On December 10 a detailed report about the mass exterminations in Poland was submitted to the Foreign Office by the Polish ambassador to London, Count Raczynski. The total and systematic eradication of the Jewish population of Poland was once again confirmed. The information reached Churchill, who demanded additional details. At this point the diplomatic obfuscation both in London and in Washington finally stopped. On December 17 all the Allied governments and the Free French National Committee solemnly announced that the Jews of Europe were being exterminated; they vowed that "those responsible for these crimes would not escape retribution."[32]

Although the Vatican too was well informed about the mass deportations and executions of Jews throughout Europe, the pope did not utter a single word addressing the Jewish issue. In the Vatican's view the pope *did* speak up in his Christmas Eve message of 1942. On page 24 of the twenty-six-page-long text, broadcast on Radio Vatican, the pontiff declared: "Humanity owes this vow to lead humanity back to divine law to hundreds of thousands of people who, through no fault of their own and solely because of their nation or their race, have been condemned to death or progressive extinction, . . . to the thousands upon thousands of noncombatants—women, children, the sick and the aged."[33]

Mussolini scoffed at the speech's platitudes; the Polish ambassador expressed his disappointment to the pope and even the French ambassador to the Vatican was apparently perplexed. It seems that most German officials also missed the portent of the papal address: Ambassador Diego von Bergen who, at the Vatican, followed every detail of Pius's policy, did not refer to the speech at all. As for Goebbels, that master interpreter of any propaganda move, his opinion of the papal speech was entirely dismissive: "The Christmas speech of the Pope is without any deep significance," he noted on December 26. "It carries on in generalities that are received with complete lack of interest among the countries at war."[34] The pope was convinced that he had been well understood. According to the January 5, 1943, report to London by the British ambassador to the Vatican, Sir D'Arcy Osborne, the pontiff believed that his message "had satisfied all demands recently made upon him to speak out."[35]

CHAPTER 13

Total Extermination

March 1943—October 1943

"Mᴙ ᴅᴇᴀʀ ʟɪᴛᴛʟᴇ ᴅᴀᴅᴅʏ, bad news: After my aunt, it's my turn to leave." Thus began the hastily penciled card sent on February 12, 1943, from Drancy by seventeen-year-old Louise Jacobson to her father in Paris. Both Louise's parents—divorced in 1939—were French Jews who had emigrated from Russia to Paris before World War I. Louise and her siblings were born in France and all were French citizens. Louise's father was a master cabinetmaker; his small business had been Aryanized, and, like all French Jews, he was waiting.

Louise and her mother had been arrested in the fall of 1942, following an anonymous denunciation: They were not wearing their stars and supposedly were active communists. Upon a demand from the SD, French police officers searched their home and, indeed, discovered communist pamphlets (belonging to Louise's brother and brother-in-law, both prisoners of war). A neighbor must have seen Louise's sister hiding the subversive literature under a stack of coal in the cellar. While her mother remained in a Paris jail, Louise was transferred to Drancy in late 1942 and, in February 1943, slated for deportation.

"Never mind," Louise went on. "I am in excellent spirits. . . .

You should not worry, Daddy. First, I am leaving in very good shape. This last week, I have eaten very, very well. I got two packages by proxy, one from a friend who was just deported, the other from my aunt. Now, your package arrived, exactly at the right moment. I can see your face, my dear daddy, and, that's precisely why I would like you to have as much courage as I do. . . . As for mother, it would probably be better if she knew nothing. . . . We leave tomorrow morning. I am with my friends, as many are leaving. I entrusted my watch and all my other belongings to decent people from my room. My daddy, I kiss you a hundred thousand times. . . . Be courageous and see you soon, your daughter Louise."[1]

On February 13, 1943, Louise left for Auschwitz in transport number 48 with one thousand other French Jews. A surviving female friend, a chemical engineer, went through the selection with her. "Tell them that you are a chemist," her friend whispered. When Louise's turn arrived and she was asked about her profession, she declared: "student"; she was sent to the left, to the gas chamber.[2]

From July 1943, the Soviet offensives determined the evolution of the war on the eastern front. Kiev was liberated on November 6, and in mid-January 1944 the German siege of Leningrad was definitively broken. At the same time the remnants of the Afrika Korps had surrendered in Tunisia, and in July 1943 British and American forces landed in Sicily.

Before the month was over military disasters swept the Duce away. On July 24, 1943, a majority of the Fascist Grand Council voted a motion of nonconfidence in their own leader. On the twenty-fifth King Victor Emmanuel III briefly received Mussolini and informed him of his dismissal and his replacement by Marshal Pietro Badoglio as the new head of the Italian government. As he left the king's residence the Italian dictator was arrested. Without a single shot being fired, the Fascist regime had collapsed. The former Duce was moved from Rome to the island of Ponza and finally imprisoned at the Gran Sasso, in the Appenines. Although German paratroopers succeeded in liberating Hitler's ally on September 12 and the Führer appointed him as the head of a fascist puppet state in northern Italy, a broken and sick Mussolini regained neither popular acceptance nor power.

English and American troops landed in southern Italy on September 3, and, on the eighth the Allies announced the armistice, secretly signed by Badoglio on the day of the landing. The German reaction was immediate: On the ninth and the tenth the Wehrmacht occupied the northern and central parts of the country and seized all Italian-controlled areas in the Balkans and in France. The Allies remained entrenched in the south of the peninsula; over the coming months their advance northward would be slow. The Allied successes on land were compounded by the steadily fiercer bombing campaign both against German military targets and cities. The July 1943 British bombing of Hamburg and the resulting firestorm caused the death of some thirty to forty thousand civilians. The night-time raids were British, the daytime operations American.

Notwithstanding the uninterrupted series of military disasters and the increasing vacillation of "allies" such as Hungary and Finland, Hitler was far from considering the war lost in the fall of 1943. New fighter planes would put an end to the Anglo-American bombing campaign, long-range rockets would destroy London and play havoc with any Allied invasion plans, newly formed divisions equipped with the heaviest tanks ever built would stem the Soviet advance. And if a military stalemate was achieved for some time, the Grand Alliance would crumble due to its inherent political-military tensions.

In Hitler's fantasizing, whipping up the anti-Jewish frenzy was one of the best ways to hasten the falling apart of the enemy alliance. If the Jews were the hidden link that held capitalism

and bolshevism together, a deluge of anti-Jewish attacks endlessly repeating that the war was a Jewish war launched only
for the sake of Jewish interests could influence foreign opinion
and add momentum to the antagonism between the West and
the Soviet Union.

A few days after the surrender of the Sixth Army, Goebbels
opened the floodgates of German rage: The minister's "total
war" speech, delivered at the Sportpalast on February 18, was
in many ways the epitome of the regime's propaganda style.
The huge crowd packing the hall had been carefully selected
to represent all parts of the *Volk*, to be ideologically reliable,
and thus ready to deliver the expected response. The event was
broadcast on all German radio channels to the nation and the
world. And, as Goebbels's speech was meant to mobilize every
last spark of energy, it had to brandish the mobilizing myth
of the regime: "Behind the onrushing Soviet divisions we can
see the Jewish liquidation squads. . . . The aim of Bolshevism is
the world revolution of the Jews. . . . Germany in any case has
no intention of bowing to this threat, but means to counter it
in time and if necessary with the most complete and radical
extermi—[correcting himself]—elimination [Applause. Shouts
of 'out with the Jews.' Laughter.]."[3]

In Bucharest, Sebastian had also heard the Goebbels speech:
"Goebbels' speech last night," he noted, "sounded unexpectedly dramatic. . . . The Jews are once more threatened with
extermination."[4] The next day Klemperer got the text of the
speech at the Jewish cemetery where he was then working:
"The speech contains a threat to proceed against the Jews, who
are guilty of everything, 'with the most draconian and radical
measures' if the foreign powers do not stop threatening the
Hitler government because of the Jews."[5]

In the meantime Goebbels continued to mobilize all German
media outlets for the most systematic anti-Jewish campaign
ever. On May 3, 1943, the minister issued a detailed circular,

labeled "confidential," to the press. After berating journalists for still lagging in this domain, the minister offered his own suggestions: "For example, countless sensational stories can be used, in which the Jew is the culprit. . . . The Jews must now be used in the German press as a political target: the Jews are to blame; the Jews wanted the war; the Jews are making the war worse; and, again and again, the Jews are to blame."[6]

To keep the extermination progressing at full pace, the Germans had to impose their will on increasingly reluctant allies. In the case of Romania, Hitler gave up. He did not want to confront Antonescu, whom he considered a trustworthy ally. In Hungary the situation was different. The Nazi leader believed that Horthy and Kallay were under Jewish influence and he (rightly) suspected them of hoping to switch sides. Moreover, for Hitler, the eight hundred thousand Jews of Hungary were a huge prize, almost within his grasp. On April 17 and 18, 1943, the Nazi leader met with Horthy at Klessheim and berated him about the mildness of Hungary's anti-Jewish measures, providing a "historical" example to prove his point: "People who did not defend themselves against the Jew," he went on, "perished. One of the best-known examples was the downfall of the once so proud Persian people, who now lived a miserable life as Armenians."[7] Hitler's exhortation did not suffice to change Horthy's policies—increasingly aimed at an understanding with the Allies. Clearly the moment of confrontation with Germany was rapidly approaching; it did not bode well for Hungary—nor, mainly, for its large Jewish community.

In the meantime the Bulgarian attitude regarding the country's further deportations of Jews still looked promising to Berlin. As we saw, in March and April 1943 Sofia had given the Germans all necessary assistance in deporting the Jews of occupied Thracia and Macedonia to Treblinka. Simultaneously, in March 1943, thousands of Bulgarian Jews had already been concentrated at assembly points, and the transports from the "old kingdom" were about to start. King Boris had promised it to the Germans. When it came to the deportation of native Bulgarian Jews, however, public protest erupted. The opposition found its strongest expression in parliament and among the leaders of the Bulgarian Orthodox Church. The monarch backed down.

Even in Slovakia hesitation about further deportations persisted. Merely twenty thousand mostly baptized Jews remained in the country after the last three transports to Auschwitz had departed in September 1942, following a three month lull. In the meantime, rumors about the fate of the deportees had seeped back. Thus, when Tuka mentioned the possibility of resuming the deportations, in early April 1943, protests from Slovak clergy and also from the population put an end to his initiative. On March 21 a pastoral letter condemning any further deportations had been read in most churches.

The German pressure on the Slovaks was relatively mild, possibly due to a bottleneck at Auschwitz resulting from the ongoing deportations from the West, the final transports from the Reich and the General Government, and the transports from Salonica, followed by the typhus epidemic in the camp that diverted transports to Sobibor. The fate of the remnants of Slovak Jewry would be sealed on the very eve of Germany's collapse.

In contrast the deportation of Salonica's Jews was carried out quickly and smoothly. The first train, with some 2,800 Jews, left the northern Greek city for Auschwitz on March 15, 1943; within a few weeks, 45,000 out of the 50,000 Jews of Salonica had been deported and mostly killed on arrival. A host of factors may explain the flawless implementation of the German assault upon the Jews of Salonica: The efficiency of the German officials and like-minded Salonicans; the periodic tension between the Greek inhabitants of the city and the still incompletely assimilated post–World War I Jewish refugees; the immediate compliance of Chief Rabbi Zwi Koretz, the spiritual head of the community, with all German orders; the absence of any information among the local Jews about the fate that awaited them once they boarded the trains, and also the absence of a Greek resistance movement that would play a major role a year later, during the deportation of the remaining Jews of the country.

For the Germans transporting the deportees to their death remained a logistical headache to the very end. In Holland, Belgium, and France the Jews were mostly assembled in Westerbork, Mechelen, or Drancy; in these assembly centers special trains arrived at regular weekly intervals. In the Reich itself, however, where no such central assembly camp existed, a *Russenzug* ("Russian train") arriving from the East with laborers had to be readied at one of the main departure cities and scheduled so as to allow for the timely arrival of connecting trains from smaller towns with their own loads of Jews. This demanded complex scheduling in and of itself, also due to the irregular arrivals of the trains from the East. Periodically, the Reichsbahn had to be paid for its services. Although most of the transports were easily funded by the RSHA from the victims' assets, at times the payments were not readily available or the moving of the trains through several currency zones created complex accounting problems for all involved.

The major challenge, however, was the availability of trains as such. Wehrmacht trains, military supply trains carrying armaments, and coal trains—were all given priority by the Reichsbahn over the "special trains." Moreover these trains were assigned old, worn-out locomotives and old cars, explaining their slow speed when moving and frequent stops for repairs.

But as the "special trains" represented such a minute fraction of the overall traffic, timely planning ultimately allowed almost any problem to be solved. On September 26–28, 1942, a conference of Transportation Ministry officials rose to the challenge in a highly positive spirit. After a listing of the number of trains required for the deportation of the Jewish population of the General Government to the extermination camps (district by district), the protocol expressed the overall confidence of the participants: "With the reduction of the transport of potatoes, it is expected that it will be possible for the special train service to be able to place . . . the necessary number of freight cars."

As for the "cargo" itself, it did not cause any major problems. Of course there were the usual suicides and some attempts to flee before boarding the trains, sometimes during the transports. Deaths during the transports were frequent, from exhaustion, thirst, suffocation, and the like.

Generally, the voyage from Western Europe, Italy, or even from Germany appears to have been less lethal than the transports within Eastern Europe. The Italian writer Primo Levi described his journey from the assembly camp at Fossoli di Carpi, near Modena, to Auschwitz, in early 1944: "Our restless sleep was often interrupted by noisy and futile disputes, by curses, by kicks and blows blindly delivered to ward off some encroaching and inevitable contact. Then someone would light a candle, and its mournful flicker would reveal an obscure agitation, a human mass, extended across the floor, confused and continuous, sluggish and aching, rising here and there in sudden convulsions and immediately collapsing again in exhaustion." Levi evokes the changing landscape, the successive names of cities, Austrian first, then Czech, and finally Polish: "The convoy stopped for the last time, in the dead of night, in the middle of a dark silent plain."[8] They had arrived.

For most deportees Levi's journey would have been considered a luxury trip. Usually freight cars had insufficient openings for fresh air and an entirely insufficient supply of water. According to surviving deportees from the Starachowice labor camp to Auschwitz, in July 1944 (a very short trip of 140 miles) the train was brutally overloaded, as the Red Army was approaching. Around seventy-five women were packed into each freight car and, separately, 150 men were crammed into each wagon. The journey lasted thirty-six hours. The struggle for water and mainly for air soon started in the men's cars. "Nineteen-year old Ruben Z. was 'very lucky' to find a place beside the small window for fresh air at the beginning of the trip. He got several beatings from people who were desperate to get near the window, and was finally pushed away and lost his place. He became so dizzy and weak that he could not remember what happened thereafter, other than that fifteen people had died in his car by the time they reached Birkenau."[9]

Looting, on a small or grand scale, was another main feature of the extermination years. On the spot, at the local murder sites, the procedure was simple. The victims would hand over any valuables to the SD man in command of the operation; after the killing their belongings would be searched again by members of the commando, and any object of value had to be handed over to the officer in charge, under penalty of death. Major operations were centralized in the Reich capital. In Berlin, all gold (including gold dental crowns torn from corpses) was usually smelted right away and turned into ingots of the Reichsbank. Other metals were mostly smelted as well, except if the value of the item as such was greater than its value as smelted metal. The most valuable items were turned over to a few jewelers trusted by the Finance Ministry or the SS, and were exchanged in occupied or neutral countries for industrial diamonds essential to the German war industry. The activities of one such longtime intermediary, working mainly with Swiss dealers, have been pieced together, and it seems that the authorities in Bern were well aware of the ongoing transactions and of the steady supply of industrial diamonds to the Reich, notwith-standing Allied economic warfare measures.

From mid-1942 on, most of the victims' belongings piled up in the major killing centers of "Aktion Reinhard" and in Auschwitz-Birkenau. In early August negotiations between the SS Main Office for Economic Administration (WVHA), formed in March 1942 under the command of Oswald Pohl to manage the finances and maintain the supply system for the SS, and all central Reich finance and economic agencies led to an agreement according to which Pohl's main office would centralize and itemize the booty. Within a few weeks Pohl's office issued a first set of guidelines, regulating all use and distribution of Jewish spoils from the camps, from precious stones to "blankets, umbrellas, baby carriages," to "glasses with gold frames," to "women's underwear," to "shaving utensils, pocket knives, scissors," and the like. Prices were set by the WVHA: "a pair of used pants—3 marks; a woolen blanket—6 marks." The final admonition was essential: "Check that all Jewish stars have been removed from all clothing before transfer. Carefully check whether all hidden and sewn-in valuables have been removed from all articles to be transferred."[10]

Throughout the Continent, Jewish furniture and house-hold goods were the domain of Rosenberg's agency. Part of the furniture was allocated to Rosenberg ministry's offices in the eastern territories, while most of the spoils were handed out or auctioned off to the Reich population. Vast amounts of goods, coming mainly from the camps, had to be mended before being shipped on to German agencies or markets; clothing was processed with particular care: Stars had to be taken off, as we saw; blood and other bodily stains washed away, and the usual wear and tear dealt with as thoroughly as possible in SS clothing workshops. Who decided what items could or could not be repaired remained unclear. One could not send tens of thousands of torn socks to the outlets in the Reich. The issue arose—but wasn't resolved—in an incident described by Filip Müller, sometime in the late spring of 1942, in one of the Auschwitz crematoria.

Müller, himself a Slovak Jew, arrived in Auschwitz in April 1942. He had just been transferred to the *Sonderkommando:* This was his initiation under the supervision of SS-Unterscharführer Stark. As was still common during these months, a group of Slovak Jews had been gassed with their clothes on. "Strip the stiffs!" Stark yelled, and gave Müller a blow. "Before me," Müller remembered, "lay the corpse of a woman. With trembling hands and shaking all over I began to remove her stockings. It was the first time in my life that I touched a dead body. She was not yet quite cold. As I pulled the stocking down her leg, it tore. Stark who had been watching, struck me again, bellowing: 'What the hell d'you think you're doing? Mind out, and get a move on! These things are to be used again! To show us the correct way he began to remove the stockings from another female corpse. But he, too, did not manage to take them off without at least a small tear."[11]

There can be no precise overview of the plunder and expropriation of Europe's Jewish victims. Orchestrated and implemented throughout the Continent first and foremost by the Germans, it spread to local officials, police, neighbors, or just any passerby in Amsterdam or Kovno, in Warsaw or Paris. It included "feeding" extortionists, distributing bribes, or paying "fines," individually but mainly on a huge collective scale. It comprised the grabbing of homes, the looting of household objects, furniture, art collections, libraries, clothes, underclothes, bedding; it meant the impounding of bank accounts and of insurance policies, the stealing of stores, or of industrial or commercial enterprises, the plundering of corpses—in short the pouncing upon anything usable, exchangeable or salable. It comprised slave labor, deadly medical experiments, enforced prostitution, loss of salaries, pensions, rents, any imaginable income—and, for the millions—loss of life.

From the early summer of 1942, Auschwitz II (Birkenau) gradually changed from a slave-labor camp where sporadic exterminations had taken place to an extermination center where the regular flow of deportees allowed for the selection of constantly expendable slave laborers. Throughout 1943 the Auschwitz complex of main and satellite camps vastly grew: The number of inmates rose from thirty to about eighty thousand in early 1944, and simultaneously tens of satellite camps were established next to plants and mines, even on the sites of agricultural stations. In Birkenau, a women's camp, a Gypsies' "family camp," and a "family camp" for Jews from Theresienstadt were set up in 1943. As we saw, the first gassing had taken place at Auschwitz Main Camp (Auschwitz I) in the reconverted morgue. Then, provisional gas chambers were set up in Birkenau. After some delay a technically much improved "crematorium II" was set up in Birkenau. Crematoria III, IV, and V followed; all the gas chambers became operational in the course of 1943.

Apart from the hall for undressing and the gas chamber, the basements of the crematoria, built on two levels, included a hall for the handling of the corpses (for the pulling out of gold teeth, cutting women's hair, detaching prosthetic limbs, collecting any valuables) by Jewish *Sonderkommando* members, after they had dragged the bodies out of the gas chamber. Then elevators carried the corpses to the ground floor, where several ovens reduced them to ashes. After the grinding of bones in special mills, the ashes were used as fertilizer in the nearby fields, dumped in local forests, or tossed into the river, close by. As for the members of the *Sonderkommandos*, they were periodically killed and replaced by a new batch.

Primo Levi, whose journey to Auschwitz we described, was

a twenty-four-year-old chemist from Turin who had joined a small group of Jews hiding in the mountains above the city, within the loose framework of the Resistance organization *Giustizia e Libertà* (Justice and Liberty). On December 13, 1943, Levi and his companions were arrested by the Fascist militia and, a few weeks later, transported to the Fossoli assembly camp. By the end of February 1944 the Germans took over. On February 22 the 650 Jews of the camp were deported northward. "The climax [of the four-day journey] came suddenly," Levi later wrote: "The door opened with a crash, and the dark echoed with outlandish orders in that curt, barbaric barking of Germans in command which seems to give vent to millennial anger. . . . In less than ten minutes all the fit men had been collected together in a group. What happened to the others, to the women, to the children, to the old men, we could establish neither then nor later: The night swallowed them up, purely and simply. Today, however, we know . . . that of our convoy no more than ninety-six men and twenty-nine women entered the respective camps of Monowitz-Buna and Birkenau, and that of all the others, more than five hundred in number, not one was living two days later."[12]

Of her arrival in Auschwitz from Theresienstadt, Ruth Kluger remembered that when the doors of the freight car were unsealed, the twelve-year-old girl, unaware that one had to jump, fell on the ramp: "I got up and wanted to cry," she reminisced, "or at least sniffle, but the tears didn't come. They dried up in the palpable creepiness of the place. We should have been relieved . . . to be breathing fresh air at last. But the air wasn't fresh. It smelled like nothing on earth, and I knew instinctively and immediately that this was no place for crying, that the last thing I needed was to attract attention." Kluger then noted the same welcoming party as Levi: "We were surrounded by the odious, bullying noise of the men who had hauled us out of the train with the monosyllables *'raus, raus'* (get out), and who simply didn't stop shouting as they were driving us along, like mad, barking dogs. I was glad to be walking safely in the middle of our heap of humanity."[13]

The first selection took place upon arrival, on the spot. As SS physician Friedrich Entress explained in his postwar statement, "the young people under sixteen, all the mothers in charge of children, and all the sick or frail people were loaded into trucks and taken to the gas chambers. The others were handed over to the head of the labor allocation and taken to the camp."[14] In fact Entress should have remembered one more category of Jews selected on arrival: interesting specimens for some of the medical or anthropological experiments. Thus Entress's notorious colleague, Joseph Mengele, who very often took part in the initial selections, was also present at arrivals to search for his special material. "Scouting incoming transports for twins with the order *Zwillinge heraus!* (Twins forward!), he also looked for individuals with physical abnormalities who might be used for interesting postmortems. After their measurements were taken, they were shot by an SS noncom and their bodies dissected."[15]

The deportees selected for slave labor were usually identified with a serial number, tattooed on their lower left arm; the category to which they belonged was indicated on their striped inmate "uniform" by a colored triangle (with different colors for political prisoners, criminals, homosexuals, Gypsies), which for all Jews was turned into a six-pointed star by the addition of a reversed yellow triangle. The results of the initial selections aimed at filling the ranks of the labor pool were at times truly disappointing. For example, in a transport from Theresienstadt at the end of January 1943, fewer than one thousand out of some five thousand deportees could be of some use at the I.G. Farben works. The others were immediately gassed.

The march or transportation to the crematoria of those selected for immediate gassing usually took place without incidents, as, according to a well-honed routine, the victims were told they would undergo disinfection. At the entrance to the crematorium, the new arrivals were taken in charge by a few SS men and by Jewish *Sonderkommando* members. These *Sonderkommando* men mixed with the unsuspecting victims in the undressing hall and, if necessary, like the SS guards, offered a few soothing comments. Once the undressing was completed and the belongings carefully hung on numbered hooks (shoes tied together), to prove that there was no ground for fear the party of SS men and *Sonderkommando* inmates accompanied the throng of candidates for "disinfection" into the gas chamber, fitted with the shower contraptions. A member of the *Sonderkommando* usually stayed to the very last moment; often an SS man also remained standing at the door sill until the last victim had crossed it. Then the door was shut and the gas pellets poured in.

Much has been written about the members of the *Sonderkommando*, these few hundreds of inmates, almost all Jews, who lived at the very bottom of hell, so to speak, before being killed and replaced by others. As we just saw, at times they helped the SS in soothing the fears of the prisoners entering the gas chambers; they pulled out the bodies, plundered the corpses, burned the remains, and disposed of the ashes; sorted and dispatched the belongings of the victims to *"Kanada"* (the derisive appellation of the hall where the belongings were stored and processed). An inmate of the women's camp that adjoined the crematoria, Krystina Zywulska, asked one of the *Sonderkommando* members how he could bear to do this work, day in and day out. His explanations—the will to live, witnessing, revenge—ended with what probably was the gist of it all: "You think that those working in *Sonderkommandos* are monsters? I'm telling you, they're like the rest, just much more unhappy."[16]

In many ways Auschwitz illustrated the difference between the Nazi concentration camp system in general and the exter-

mination system in its specific anti-Jewish dimension. In this
multipurpose camp with a mixed population of inmates, the
non-Jewish inmates soon became aware of the fundamental
difference between their own fate and that of the Jews. The
non-Jewish inmate could survive, given some luck and some
support from his national or political group. The Jew, on the
other hand, had ultimately no recourse from death and, as
a norm, remained utterly defenseless. For many a Polish or
Ukrainian inmate, or for many a German "criminal" inmate,
this was but one more opportunity to exercise their own anti-
Jewish terror within the generalized system of terror or just to
assert their own power against this entirely powerless group.

As Auschwitz was turning into the main murdering center
of the regime, the Jewish inmates soon considerably outnum-
bered all the other groups added together. According to the
historian Peter Hayes, "From the opening of the camp in May
1940 to its evacuation in January 1945, some 1.3 million people
were transported to the site, of whom only about 200,000 ever
left alive, only 125,000 of these surviving the Third Reich. Of
these captives, 1.1 million were Jews, about eighty percent of
whom succumbed upon arrival or shortly thereafter."[17]

"The Jews arrive here, that is to Auschwitz, at a weekly rate
of 7 to 8,000," Pvt. SM wrote home on December 7, 1942, on his
way to the front. "Shortly thereafter they die a 'hero's death.'"
And he added: "It is really good to see the world."[18] SM was
not alone in enjoying Auschwitz. For the approximately 7,000
members of the SS who at one time or another were assigned
to the camp and served there first under Höss until November
1943, then under Arthur Liebehenschel and Richard Baer, life
was definitely not unpleasant. All the usual amenities were
available: decent housing, good food, medical care, long stays
of spouses or companions, and regular furloughs to the *Heimat*
or to special vacation spots. In the camp itself, to relieve the
stress generated by their work, the SS could enjoy music played

especially for them by the female inmates' orchestra, which performed from April 1943 to October 1944. And, outside the camp, cultural life comprised an array of performances, once every two or three weeks at least, with a preference for comedies, *A Bride in Flight, Disturbed Wedding Night,* or *Merry Varieties,* and soirees under the motto "Attack of the Comics." There was no shortage of classics either: In February 1943 the Dresden State Theater presented *Goethe Then and Now.*

Within the Reich details about the extermination spread through any number of channels. Thus, as just mentioned, every summer hundreds of women visited their husbands who were guards in Auschwitz and other camps. The German population of the town of Auschwitz itself frequently complained about the odor produced by the overloaded crematoria. This particular problem was confirmed by Höss: "During bad weather or when a strong wind was blowing, the stench of burning flesh was carried for many miles and caused the whole neighborhood to talk about the burning of Jews, despite official counter-propaganda. It is true that all members of the SS detailed for the extermination were bound to strict secrecy, but as later SS legal proceedings showed, this was not always observed. Even the most severe punishment was not able to stop their love of gossip."[19]

What German civilians living in eastern Upper Silesia gathered about Auschwitz, what railway men, policemen, soldiers, and anybody traveling through the eastern reaches of the empire could easily hear or witness, Reich Germans who settled in the Warthegau learned by comparing what they had seen in 1940 or 1941 and what could not be missed one or two years later. A former woman settler, Elisabeth Grabe, spoke in an interview of her own experience in the Warthegau: "The Jews who had lived in the ghetto in Zychlin and Kutno disappeared one day (I can't remember when that was, perhaps

1942). People whispered to each other that they had been loaded into lorries and gassed. These rumors affected me even more painfully than the notion that I was using confiscated [Polish] furniture. By early 1943 the information about mass extermination of the Jews was so widespread in the Reich as to have probably reached a majority of the population."[20]

Opposition leaders were particularly well informed. The historian Hans Mommsen has shown that in 1942 the gassing of Jews was known to the Jesuit priest Alfred Delp, to the Prussian finance minister Johannes Popitz, and to Moltke, among others. As noted in part 1, members of the clandestine "Freiburg Circle" too acknowledged in late 1942 the mass extermination of European Jewry. This acknowledgment, however, did not induce the Freiburg group to consider the Jews in post–Nazi Germany as individuals and citizens like all others. Espousing notions garnered from traditional anti-Semitism and from Nazism, the group's "Great Memorandum" contemplated a series of measures for dealing with the surviving Jews in post–Nazi Germany.

Another illustration of the mixture of knowledge regarding the exterminations and the permanence of anti-Semitism among German opposition groups and in much of the population appeared in the second clandestine leaflet distributed in early July 1942 by the essentially Catholic White Rose resistance group based at the University of Munich. In this leaflet the murder of Jews in Poland was mentioned. Yet the Munich students presented the issue in a strangely convoluted way and added an immediate disclaimer: "We do not intend to say anything about the Jewish question in the broadsheet; nor do we want to enter a plea in their defense. No, we simply want to cite as an example the fact that since the conquest of Poland 300,000 Jews have been murdered in that country in the most bestial fashion. In this we see the most fearful crime against human dignity, a crime with which no other in the whole his-

tory of mankind can be compared. For whatever one thinks of
the Jewish question, the Jews too are human beings. . . . Perhaps someone may say the Jews deserved such a fate; . . . as-
suming somebody did say this, how would he deal with the
fact that the whole of the younger generation of Polish nobility
has been annihilated?"[21] In other words these militant enemies
of the regime were well aware that the mass killing of Jews
would not impress most readers of the leaflet and that crimes
committed against Polish Catholics had to be added. Whether
this addition also expressed the attitude of the White Rose
group itself is hard to tell, but it certainly indicates their assessment of Catholic middle-class public opinion in Germany
sometime in mid-1942.

In both Christian confessions, as we saw, prelates and many
ordinary priests knew that the trains transporting the Jews
from the Reich and from all over Europe to "Poland" were not
carrying them to labor camps but to their death. As beforehand, Catholic dignitaries remained divided about the appropriate way to react: The leading advocates of a public protest
were Bishop Preysing and a group of Munich Jesuits, while the
majority wished to avoid any confrontation with the authorities and favored various degrees of accommodation.

Not unexpectedly the most "accommodating" prelate of
all was Cardinal Bertram. Matters came to a head when, in
August 1943, upon Preysing's request, a "Draft for a Petition Favoring the Jews" was prepared, to be signed by all the country's
bishops and sent to Hitler and to other members of the party
elite. The bishops' conference rejected the idea of submitting
the petition and merely issued a pastoral letter admonishing
German Catholics to respect the right of others to life, also
that of "human beings of alien races and origin."[22] Preysing
still hoped to sway his fellow bishops by trying to muster encouragement and guidance from the Vatican. No encouragement was provided by Orsenigo: "Charity is well and good,"

the nuncio told the bishop, "but the greatest charity is not to make problems for the Church."[23]

The only private letter of protest addressed to Hitler by a church dignitary was sent on July 16, 1943, by Bishop Theophil Wurm, the leading personality of the Confessing Church. After affirming his own love of the fatherland and alluding to the heavy sacrifices that had become his own lot (he had lost his son and his son-in-law on the eastern front), Wurm turned to the core issue of the letter: "In the name of God and for the sake of the German people we give expression to the urgent request that the responsible leadership of the Reich will check the persecution and annihilation to which many men and women under German domination are being subjected, and without judicial trial. Now that the non-Aryans who have been the victims of the German onslaught have been largely eliminated, it is to be feared . . . that the so-called 'privileged' non-Aryans who have so far been spared are in renewed danger of being subjected to the same treatment." Wurm then protested against the threat that mixed marriages would be dissolved. Indirectly, he returned to the measures that had been taken against the Jews as such: "Such intentions like the measures taken against the other non-Aryans are in the sharpest contrast to Divine Law and an outrage against the very foundation of Western thought and life and against the very God-given right of human existence and human dignity."[24]

Wurm's letter received no response, and although it was not a declaration ex cathedra, as Galen's sermon against euthanasia had been, it was widely circulated. A few months later, on December 20, 1943, Wurm sent a letter to Lammers, pleading again for the safety of *Mischlinge*. This time, he received a handwritten warning from the head of Hitler's Chancellery: "I hereby warn you emphatically," Lammers wrote, "and request that in the future you scrupulously stay within the boundaries established by your profession and abstain from statements on general political matters."[25] This warning of dire retribution silenced Wurm and the Confessing Church.

Following the failed attempts to establish a unified resistance group in the spring of 1942, the Jewish Fighting Organization (Zydowska Organizacia Bojowa, or ZOB) was created in Warsaw on July 28, 1942, a few days after the beginning of the *Aktion*. The initial group of some two hundred members mostly succeeded in dodging the deportations, but beyond this there was little that the ZOB could do. In August some pistols and hand grenades were purchased from the Polish communist underground. A first and minor operation—an attempt to kill the chief of the Jewish police, Jozef Szerynski—failed. Much worse occurred a few days later: The Germans arrested a group of ZOB members on their way from Warsaw to Hrubieszów, and tortured and killed them; soon afterward, on September 3, the Gestapo caught some leading members of the organization in Warsaw and also murdered them: The arms were discovered and seized. This catastrophic series of events seemed at first to put an end to a courageous venture that had hardly begun.

An eerie period of apparent respite descended on the surviving inhabitants of the ghetto after mid-September. The approximately sixty thousand Jews left in an area of drastically reduced size either worked in the remaining workshops or in sorting the mounds of belongings abandoned by the victims. The German administrators had been replaced by Gestapo officials, mainly of low rank. None of the remaining Jews knew when the next German move would take place. By then much had transpired about Treblinka: "The women go naked into the bath-house to their death," Abraham Lewin quoted the report of an escapee, on September 27: "Death comes after seven or eight minutes. On their arrival they take away the shoes of the unfortunates. The proclamation in the square: 'Emigrants from Warsaw. . . .'"[26] He noted again, on October 5: "No one knows what tomorrow will bring and we live in perpetual fear and terror."[27] On November 17 Lewin mentioned the final liquidation of all the Jews of Lublin. News reports about mass exterminations in the Polish provinces soon replaced a spate of reports about protests in England and the United States regarding the murder of the Jews: "Departing this life is a matter of 10 or 15 minutes in Treblinka or in Oswiecim [Auschwitz]."[28] On January 15, 1943, Lewin wrote of renewed anxiety as the ghetto expected a forthcoming Aktion. The following day he recorded his last entry.

In the meantime the Jewish fighting organization had overcome the crisis triggered by the events of September 1942. Yet even under the dire new circumstances, unification of all political forces in support of armed resistance occurred only stagewise and not in full. A Jewish National Committee was first established in October 1942, uniting all left-wing and centrist Zionist youth movements together with the communists. The Bund, however, again refused to join, and only after further and lengthy discussions did it agree to "coordinate" its activities with the National Committee. A Jewish Coordinating Committee was set up. As for the right-wing Zionists (the Revisionists and their youth movement, Betar), they had already established an independent armed organization, the Jewish Military Union (ZZW), prior to and without any link with the Jewish Coordinating Committee. Whether the Revisionists did not want to cooperate with the "leftists" of the ZOB or whether the ZOB kept them at arms' length remains unclear. Ideological divisiveness persisted to the end.

On January 18, 1943, following a brief visit by Himmler, the Germans launched a new (albeit a limited) Aktion; their plan was partly foiled. Resistance members—Mordechai Anielewicz, the commander of the ZOB, among them—attacked the German escort of the front column and the Jews dispersed. Some five to six thousand Jews were ultimately caught during the January operation, including Lewin and his daughter; they were deported to Treblinka and murdered. This first sign of armed resistance probably led Himmler to issue an order to Krüger on February 16 to liquidate the ghetto entirely, "for security reasons."[29]

The January events considerably bolstered the authority of the fighting organization among the ghetto population and garnered praise from various Polish circles. During the weeks that followed the ZOB executed a few Jewish traitors; it collected— at times "extorted"—money from some wealthy ghetto inhabitants, acquired a few weapons from the communist AL (*Armia Ludowa*) and also from private dealers, and mainly organized its "combat groups" in expectation of the forthcoming German operation. In the meantime the inhabitants, increasingly ready to face an armed struggle in the ghetto, were hoarding whatever food they could get and preparing underground shelters for a lengthy standoff. The council, now chaired by a nonentity, Marc Lichtenbaum, and reduced to utter passivity, did nonetheless contact Polish resistance groups, mainly the *Armia Krajowa* (the Home Army, or AK), the dominant Polish resistance movement, to denounce the ZOB as a group of reckless adventurers without any backing in the ghetto.

The council's denunciations were not at the origin of the AK's reticence to provide help for the ZOB, although after the January events it agreed to sell some weapons. General Stefan Grot-Rowezki, the commander in chief of the Home Army, remained evasive when asked for stronger support. The traditional anti-Semitism of nationalist conservative Poles may have played a role, but there was more to this basically negative stance. The AK was suspicious of the leftist and pro-Soviet leanings of part of the ZOB (while it was ready to supply some weapons to the Revisionists); furthermore—and mainly, so it seems—the Polish command was worried that fighting could spread from the ghetto to the city while its own plans for an uprising and its own forces were not yet ready. As a result AK even offered its help to transfer the Jewish fighters from the ghetto to partisan groups in the forests. The offer was turned down.

As for the leaders and members of the ZOB, they had no illusion about the outcome of the approaching struggle. "I remember a conversation I had with Mordechai Anielewicz," Ringelblum wrote. "He gave an accurate appraisal of the uneven struggle, he foresaw the destruction of the ghetto and he was sure that neither he nor his combatants would survive the liquidation of the ghetto. He was sure that they would die like stray dogs and no one would even know their last resting-place."[30]

When the final liquidation of the Warsaw ghetto started on April 19, 1943, the eve of Passover, the Jews were not caught by surprise: The streets were empty, and as soon as German units entered the area, firing started. Street battles lasted for several days until the Jewish combatants were compelled to retreat into the underground bunkers. Each bunker became a small fortress, and only the systematic burning down of the buildings and the massive use of flame throwers, tear gas, and hand grenades finally drove the remaining fighters and inhabitants into the streets. On May 8 Anielewicz was killed in the command bunker at 18 Mila Street. Combat continued sporadically while some groups of fighters succeeded in reaching the Aryan side of the city by way of the sewers. Days later some of the fighters again took to the sewers and returned to the ghetto ruins to try and save some remnants: They did not find anybody alive.

On May 16 SS general Jürgen Stroop proclaimed the end of the *Grossaktion*. Symbolically the Germans concluded the operations by blowing up the Warsaw (Great) Synagogue. According to Stroop fifteen Germans and auxiliaries had been killed and some ninety wounded during the fighting. "Of the total of 56,065 Jews caught," the SS general reported further, "about 7,000 were exterminated within the former Ghetto in the course of the action, and 6,929 by transporting them to T.II [Treblinka], which means 14,000 Jews were exterminated altogether. Beyond the number of 56,065 Jews an estimated number of 5,000 to 6,000 were killed by explosions or in fires."[31]

It is against this overall background that an outstanding initiative, taken already in 1942 by a group of Polish Catholics, should be mentioned. Under the impulse of a well-known female writer, Zofia Kossak-Szezucka, a declaration (titled "Protest"), written by Kossak in August 1942, during the deportation of the ghetto inhabitants to Treblinka, stated that, notwithstanding the fact that the Jews were and remained the enemies of Poland, the general silence in the face of the murder of millions of innocent people was unacceptable and Polish Catholics had the obligation to raise their voice: In late 1942 the group established the Council to Aid Jews, or Zegota. Over the ensuing months and until the occupation of Poland by the Soviet army, its members saved and assisted thousands of hidden Jews mainly on the Aryan side of Warsaw. Over time the political-ideological composition of the Zegota leadership changed, and the Catholic movement that had initiated the establishment of the council left it in July 1943. The withdrawal of these conservative Catholics from the rescue operations tallied with the positions taken by much of the Polish Catholic Church, and of course with those of the majority of the population and of the underground movements.

The life of Jews in former Poland was coming to an end. On March 31, 1943, the Kraków ghetto was liquidated and those of its inhabitants who were selected for work were sent to the Plaszow slave-labor camp; their liquidation was to follow later on. And so it went from ghetto to ghetto, then from work camp to work camp. In some ghettos the situation appeared different, albeit for a short while. Thus the forty thousand Jews who, in the fall of 1942, were still alive in Białystok, had good reasons for hope. As in Lodz, the ghetto was particularly active in manufacturing goods and performing services for the Wehrmacht. Barash's relations with the military and even with some of the civilian authorities seemed good. A local resistance movement was getting organized under the leadership of Mordechai Tenenbaum, although the German threat did not appear immediate.

The first warning signals came in late 1942–early 1943 with the deportation of all Jews from the Białystok district to Treblinka. During the first days of February, 1943, the Germans struck again, but as had previously happened in Lodz, only part of the population (ten thousand Jews) was deported and approximately thirty thousand inhabitants remained. Moreover, in a meeting on February 19, a representative of the Białystok Security Police commander promised Barash that no further resettlement of Jews was expected for the time being. The continued presence of thirty thousand Jews in the ghetto was likely to last until "the end of the war."

Life returned to "normal" for the remaining population of the ghetto: Barash was confident that the new stability would last; Tenenbaum, however, was convinced that the liquidation of the ghetto was approaching. Indeed, under Globocnik's personal command, the Germans prepared to liquidate the ghetto in utter secrecy, to avoid a repeat performance of the Warsaw events. On August 16, 1943, when the operation started, Barash and Tenenbaum were both taken by complete surprise. While the mass of the population followed the orders and moved helplessly to the assembly sites, sporadic fighting flared up in various parts of the ghetto, with only minimal impact on the "evacuation" operation. Within days the ghetto was emptied and the fighters had either been killed or had committed suicide.

In July 1943, the Germans massacred 26,000 inhabitants of

the Minsk ghetto; some 9,000 Jewish laborers remained alive
for a few months, but at the end of 1943 no Jews were mentioned anymore in the Reichskommissar's report about the
capital of Belorussia. Small groups of Jews fled to nearby forests to join partisan units. A number of armed rebellions took
place but were easily quelled as the Germans now expected
some sporadic resistance.

In some ghettos, on the other hand, where determined resistance could have been expected, as in Vilna, events took an
unexpected turn. "Here in the ghetto, the mood is cheerful,"
Kruk recorded on June 16, 1943. "All rumors about liquidation have disappeared for the time being. A rapid building and
expansion of the ghetto industry has been going on in recent
weeks. . . . Yesterday, District Commissar Hingst and [Hingst's
deputy] Murer visited the ghetto. Both left very satisfied and
'amused' themselves with the ghetto representatives. The
ghetto breathed in relief. We ask—for how long?"[32] During the
first days of April, though, the ghetto population's optimism
was sharply challenged. The Germans assembled several thousand Jews from the smaller ghettos of the Vilna district under
the pretext of sending them to Kovno; instead, they were dispatched to Ponar and massacred.

On June 21, 1943, Himmler ordered the liquidation of all
ghettos in the *Ostland*. Working Jews were to be kept in concentration camps and "the unnecessary inhabitants of the Jewish
ghettos were to be evacuated to the East." Of course the members of the FPO were not aware of the liquidation decision but,
nonetheless, they perceived the April killings as an omen. For
them the question now arose: Should armed resistance be organized in the ghetto, or should the FPO leave for the forests
and eventually join Soviet partisan units before the Germans
struck? Gens himself, aware of the debate, was determined to
have the FPO stay in the ghetto, together with the population
that it would help to defend and, eventually, allow to flee. Yet,

by the end of June, as the Germans were systematically liqui-
dating the remaining small communities in the Vilna region,
an increasing number of FPO members moved to the forests
against Gens's will: A confrontation within the ghetto was
barely avoided.

It seems that at this point in time (June/July 1943), the communist members of the FPO were hiding from Kovner and his
left-wing Zionist comrades (Hashomer Hatzair) that they were
actually under the orders of a far larger communist organization and that their delegate, Itzik Wittenberg, had been elected
head of the FPO without Kovner and his people being aware
of the dimension and secretive nature of the communist penetration. Gens had apparently decided that Wittenberg represented a danger to his own plans and, on July 15, late at night,
as the communist leader was conferring with the ghetto chief
(on Gens' invitation), police forces arrested him. Freed by FPO
members, Wittenberg went into hiding. The German reaction
was foreseeable: If Wittenberg was not delivered, the ghetto
population would be exterminated. Whether under pressure from his comrades or because he sensed the fear of the
ghetto populace, Wittenberg agreed to give himself up; once
in German hands, he committed suicide.

On September 14 the Germans ordered Gens to report
to the headquarters of the Security Police. Although he had
been warned of danger and told to flee, the ghetto chief went
nonetheless to avoid reprisals against the population. At six
o'clock that same afternoon, the Germans shot him. Part of
the remaining twenty thousand inhabitants were murdered in
Ponar, part were deported to Sobibor, while able-bodied men
(including Kruk) were shipped to labor camps in Estonia. The
Jews left in the ghetto were murdered just before the arrival of
the Red Army.

On April 6, 1943, on the day he had recorded the massacre
in Ponar, Rudashevski's diary ended. The last line read: "We

may be fated for the worst." In Lodz, Sierakowiak broke off his own diary entries a week or so after Rudashevski; the last line was recorded on April 15: "There is really no way out of this for us." In the summer he died of tuberculosis and starvation.

On March 2, 1943, following a lengthy conversation with Göring, Goebbels noted in his diary: "Göring is completely aware of what would threaten us all if we were to weaken in this war. He has no illusions in this regard. In the Jewish question in particular, we are so fully tied in, that for us there is no escape anymore. And it is good that way. Experience shows us that a movement and a people that have burned their bridges fight by far more unconditionally than those who still have a way back."[33]

CHAPTER 14

Total Extermination

Fall 1943–Spring 1944

I AM TAKING advantage of a lonely Sunday evening to write you a letter that I have owed you for a long time." Thus began the plea that Kurt Gerstein—the deeply religious Protestant, Waffen-SS officer, and haunted witness of extermination who in vain had tried to inform the world—addressed on March 5, 1944, to his father, a retired judge and a firm supporter of the regime:

> I do not know what goes [on] inside you, and would not presume to claim the smallest right to know. But when a man has spent his professional life in the service of the law, something must have happened inside him during these last few years. I was deeply perturbed by one thing you said to me. . . . You said:
>
> "Hard times demand tough methods!" No, no maxim of that kind is adequate to justify what has happened. I cannot believe that this is the last word my father has to say on such unparalleled happenings: my old father cannot depart from this place with such words and thoughts. It seems to me that all of us with some time left to live have more than enough cause to reflect on the

practical possibilities and limits, as well as on the consequences of this casting away of all restraint.[1]

Gerstein was exceptional and lonely in his way as a morally tormented and "treasonous" member of the extermination system. There is no doubt, nonetheless, that the religious
source of his attitude did also play a role for other Germans
and Europeans, some of whom we mentioned and thousands
of whom we know nothing about. Their oppositional stand,
whatever form it may have taken, should be part of any reflections on the role of Christianity in the years of extermination.
Generally speaking their path was not the one chosen either
by the Christian churches or institutions and even less so, as
we shall primarily see in this chapter, by their most exalted
leaders.

In strictly military terms the last months of 1943 and early
1944 were dominated by steady Soviet progress in all sectors
of the eastern front, whereas the Western allies edged only
very slowly up the Italian peninsula and actually stalled at the
German "Gustav line." Yet in terms of the Grand Alliance the
defining event of these months took place at the Roosevelt-
Churchill-Stalin meeting in Tehran, between November 28 and
December 1. Notwithstanding British fears and hesitations, the
American strategy was accepted: American and British forces
would land on the coast of Normandy sometime in May 1944.
Simultaneously the Soviet Union would launch a major of-
fensive, thus precluding the shift of any German forces to the
West.

Hitler anticipated the Allied landing with much confidence.
The German defenses along the Atlantic and North Sea coasts,
and the Wehrmacht forces in the West would turn the Anglo-
American operation into a catastrophic defeat for the invaders.
Then, immune for a long time to the further threat of a landing,

the entire German might would turn against the Soviet army, recapture the lost territories, and eventually force Stalin to sue for peace. In the meantime, unable to effectively counter the Allied bombing offensive, the führer was, in Speer's words, "in the habit of raging against the British government and the Jews, who were to blame for the air raids."[2] Apparently the bombings added an element of blind fury and even stronger thirst for murderous vengeance to Hitler's anti-Jewish obsession: The Jews were guilty! Indeed, throughout this last phase of the war, his murderous fury exploded in an unlimited urge for destruction and death.

When no hope of survival remained, psychological conditions were ready for a Jewish uprising: Such had been the situation in Warsaw after the January 1943 *Aktion*, and such it was in the summer and fall of 1943 for the Jewish workers' teams left alive in Treblinka and Sobibor. As the deportations to both camps were tapering off, these Jews understood that their own liquidation could not be far off.

According to Shmuel Wilenberg, one of the survivors of the Treblinka uprising, by May 1943, after the extermination of the remaining Warsaw ghetto population, not much doubt remained about their own fate. In late July 1943 the decision was finalized: the uprising had to take place as soon as possible. The date and time were set for August 2 at 4:30 in the afternoon. The head of the main organizing committee in the lower camp, Marceli Galewski, an engineer from Lodz and a former "camp elder," could in principle coordinate the exact time for the beginning of the operation with the upper camp, given the fact that master carpenter Jacob Wiernik was allowed by the Germans to move freely throughout both areas.

At the decisive moment, however, nothing went according to plan. The first shot was fired half an hour ahead of the time set for the beginning of the revolt, due to unforeseen circumstances, and soon coordination between the different combat teams broke down. Nonetheless, as chaos was spreading and part of the camp was set on fire, hundreds of inmates, either in groups or on their own, succeeded in breaking through the fences and escaping. Various estimates indicate that of the 850 inmates living in the camp on the day of the uprising, about 100 were caught at the outset, 350 to 400 perished during the fighting, some 400 fled but half of them were caught within hours; of the remaining 200, approximately 100 succeeded in escaping the German dragnet and the hostile population; the number of those who ultimately survived is unknown. After fleeing the immediate surroundings of the camp, Galewski was unable to go on and poisoned himself. Wiernik survived and became an essential witness.

The immediate reason for the uprising in Sobibor was the same as in Treblinka, and from early 1943 on, a small group of the camp's working Jews started planning the operation. Yet only in late September, when a young Jewish Red Army lieutenant, Alexander Pechersky, who had arrived from Minsk with a group of Soviet POWs, joined the planning group, were concrete steps rapidly taken. The date of the uprising was set for October 14. The plan foresaw the luring of key SS members to various workshops under some fictitious pretext and killing them. The first phase of the plan, the liquidation of the SS personnel, succeeded almost without a hitch; although the second phase, the collective moving through the main gate, soon turned into uncontrolled fleeing, more than 300 inmates succeeded in escaping to the surrounding forests. Pechersky and his group crossed the Bug River and joined the partisans.

The cooperation of Jewish inmates and Soviet POWs in the breakout was a unique aspect of the Sobibor uprising. Yet it added a further dimension to the security scare in Berlin. Coming after the Warsaw rebellion, the uprisings of Treblinka and Sobibor convinced Himmler that the murder of most Jewish workers, even in the Lublin district, should be completed as rapidly as possible. On November 3, 1943, the SS killed 18,400 inmates in Majdanek while music was played over loudspeakers to cover the sounds of shooting and the cries of the dying prisoners. This was Operation "Harvest Festival."

In September 1942, irked by King Christian X's laconic response to the birthday congratulations he had sent him, Hitler recalled the Reich plenipotentiary to Denmark, Cecil von Renthe-Fink. In his stead the German leader appointed Werner Best, who had left his position in Paris a few months beforehand, and demanded harsher policies against the Danes and their Jews. During the first months of his tenure in Denmark, Best nonetheless pursued his predecessor's policy, and even the persecution of Denmark's eight thousand Jews remained minimal. In late July 1943 the situation began to change. Mussolini's fall, the Allied landing in Sicily, and the massive bombing of Hamburg convinced most Danes that Germany's defeat was approaching. Sabotage, limited until then, grew, and strikes erupted in several cities. The Danish government was losing its grip. For Best, a change of policy appeared unavoidable.

On August 29 the Germans imposed martial law. A few days later, in a cable to Berlin, Best demanded that the Jewish question be solved. On September 17 Hitler gave his authorization. On the same day Best ordered the seizure of the membership lists from the Jewish community office and a date for a general roundup of Denmark's Jews was set for October 2, although both the army and the navy commanders made it clear that their units would not participate. Sometime at the end of September, the embassy adviser on shipping matters, Georg F. Duckwitz, disclosed the date of the raid to one of his Danish friends. Thereupon the Swedish government, informed of the forthcoming operation by its ambassador in Copenhagen, offered to take in all of Denmark's Jews. Moreover Stockholm broadcast its offer, thus informing the endangered Jews that they could find asylum in Sweden. On the eve of the German move, around 7,000 Jews were ferried over to Sweden in a coordinated operation supported by the vast majority of the Danish population. Some 485 Jews were seized and, upon Best's intervention with Eichmann, deported to Theresienstadt, where most of them survived the war.

At the same time, in the summer of 1943, transports were bringing more Jews into Westerbork from all parts of Holland and from the labor camps. Then, with absolute regularity, every Tuesday, another transport loaded its cargo of between 1,000 and 3,000 Jews and departed for "Poland." By the end of the war, more than 100,000 Jews had transited through Westerbork alone, mostly on their way to extermination. "It will be my parents' turn to leave soon," Etty Hillesum recorded on July 10, 1943. "If by some miracle not this week, then certainly one of the next. Mischa [Etty's brother] insists on going along with them, and it seems to me that he probably should; if he had to watch our parents leave this place, it [would] totally unhinge him. I shan't go. I just can't. It is easier to pray for someone from a distance than to see him suffer by your side. It is not fear of Poland that keeps me from going along with my parents, but fear of seeing them suffer. And that, too, is cowardice."[3]

In order to increase the number of deportees from France, the Germans were now pushing Vichy to adopt a law revoking the citizenship of Jews naturalized since 1927. But after seemingly going along with the German scheme in the early summer of 1943, Laval rejected the new demand in August. Reports from the prefects had convinced the head of the Vichy government that public opinion would resent the handing over of French citizens (even recently naturalized ones) to the Germans. The Germans were not deterred: They would start the deportation of French Jews on their own. To that effect Dannecker's successor, Obersturmbannführer Heinz Röthke got reinforcement: Eichmann's special delegate, Aloïs Brunner, arrived directly from Salonica, where, as we saw, the deportation of almost the entire Jewish population had just been successfully completed. Brunner immediately replaced the French officials in charge of Drancy with his own men and ordered UGIF-North to take over the internal administration of the camp.

In the face of the unremitting German determination, both UGIF-North and South were helpless. André Baur, the head of UGIF-North, refused to go along with Brunner's plan to entice Jews who had not been arrested to join their families in Drancy. When, in desperation, Baur demanded a meeting with Laval, Eichmann's delegate had him arrested (under the pretext that two Drancy detainees, one of whom was Baur's relative, had escaped). Brunner's intention to decapitate UGIF-North in order to have an entirely submissive Jewish leadership in hand became even clearer when, after Baur's arrest, the Germans raided various UGIF offices and, using the flimsiest pretexts, sent further UGIF leaders, including Baur, Lambert, as well as the most thoroughly French of all French Jews, the president of the Consistoire, Jacques Helbronner, to Drancy, eventually to Auschwitz, to their death. UGIF-North continued to exist, but its new leaders were now the subservient Georges Edinger and someone later never fully cleared of the suspicion of having played a murky role, Juliette Stern.

In the meantime, however, still under Baur's stewardship and more actively so later on, UGIF-North was ready to cooperate in a German scheme whose intention must have been obvious from the start. Some Jewish children would be released from Drancy and, together with others already in UGIF's care, kept out of the camp, on condition that all be sent to designated homes, under the responsibility of the organization. It meant, in other words, that the children were a captive group whom the Germans could seize whenever they wished so. To foil the German plan became an increasingly urgent task for some members of UGIF itself, as well as for the semiclandestine Children's Relief Committee (OSE), the officially disbanded Jewish Scouts organization, and the communist "Solidarity" welfare association. All attempted to transfer children from the UGIF homes to foster families, Christian institutions, and to OSE safe havens. Yet, as we shall see, when shortly before the liberation of Paris the Germans pounced on the UGIF homes, many of the young charges were still there.

In the southern zone the German-French roundups continued to encounter Italian obstruction during the last months of Mussolini's regime, and during Badoglio's brief rule. On February 25, 1943, Ribbentrop had traveled to Rome to confront Mussolini personally. The Duce tried to avoid a clash by declaring that his men were arresting the Jews in their zone, a statement that both he and Ribbentrop knew to be false. In fact, in early March, the Italian military commander in France ordered the local French authorities to release immediately the Jews they had arrested in cities under Italian control. As news about the Italian attitude spread, Jews in ever greater numbers fled to this paradoxical safe haven, and by March 1943 some thirty thousand of them were living under Fascist protection in southeastern France.

No sooner had the Germans moved into Rome, and into Nice and its surroundings, than the hunt for the Jews residing in the former Italian zone started. The Germans were ready to pay one hundred, one thousand, and at times five thousand francs per individual to professional informers who specialized in identifying Jews on the streets. They also received other well-remunerated help, that of a "society lady," for example, who delivered seventeen of her clients to the Gestapo. The overall results were disappointing nonetheless. By mid-December 1943 barely 1,819 Jews had been caught and deported. The partial German failure may have been the result of the nonparticipation of the French police in the operations, and of the greater readiness now shown by the population and by religious institutions to hide the mostly French Jews. And, as the Wehrmacht also refused to take part in the roundups, the Gestapo was essentially left to its own devices. In other regions of France, the German anti-Jewish drive also ended in mixed results during the last months of 1943.

Barely two weeks after the German occupation of Rome, the main leaders of the community, Ugo Foà and Dante Almansi, were summoned by Herbert Kappler, the SD chief in the Italian capital. They were ordered to deliver fifty kilograms of gold within thirty-six hours. If the ransom was paid on time, no harm would befall the city's Jews. Although Kappler had been secretly instructed by Himmler to prepare the deportation from Rome, it now appears (from declassified OSS documents) that the extortion was Kappler's own idea, meant to avoid the deportation and eventually help instead in sending the Jews of Rome to work at local fortifications. The gold was collected in time from members of the community and shipped to the RSHA on October 7. The Jewish leaders believed in Kappler's assurances and, when warned by Chief Rabbi Israel Zolli and others that further German steps could be expected, they chose to ignore the warnings: What had happened elsewhere could not happen in Rome.

And indeed, during the following days, the Germans appeared more interested in looting than in anything else. The priceless treasures of the Biblioteca della Comunità Israelitica (the Library of the Israelite Community) became a special target. On October 14 Rosenberg's men loaded the library books into two railroad cars and shipped them off to Germany. And, although some of the Jews of Rome argued that "crimes against books were not crimes against people,"[14] panic started spreading. Frantically Jews looked for hiding places; the richer among them were soon gone.

On October 6 Dannecker arrived in Rome at the head of a small unit of Waffen-SS officers and men. A few days later, on October 16, Dannecker's unit, with small Wehrmacht reinforcements, arrested 1,259 Jews in the Italian capital. After *Mischlinge*, partners in mixed marriages, and some foreigners had been released, 1,030 Jews, including a majority of women and some two hundred children under the age of ten, remained imprisoned at the military college. Two days later these Jews were transported to the Tiburtina railway station and from there to Auschwitz. Most of the deportees were gassed immediately, 196 were selected for labor; 15 survived the war. Throughout the country the roundups continued until the end of 1944: The Jews were usually transferred to an assembly camp at Fossoli di Carpi in northern Italy and from there sent to Auschwitz. Thousands managed to hide among a generally friendly population or in religious institutions; some managed to flee across the Swiss border or to the areas liberated by the Allies. Nonetheless throughout Italy about 7,000 Jews, some 20 percent of the Jewish population, were caught and murdered.

Since the end of the war the arrests and deportations of the Jews of Rome (and of Italy) have been the object of particular scholarly attention and of a number of fictional renditions, given their direct relevance to the attitude of Pope Pius XII.

On October 16 in the morning, the day of the roundup, the pope was informed of the events. The raid went on despite threats about the possibility of a papal protest; the pope kept silent. On October 25, after the deportees' train had left Italy on its way to Auschwitz, an article in the Vatican's official newspaper, *L'Osservatore Romano,* sang the praises of the Holy Father's compassion: "With the [enhancement] of so much evil, the universal and paternal charity of the Pontiff has become, it could be said, ever more active; it knows neither boundaries nor nationality, neither religion nor race. This manifold and ceaseless activity on the part of Pius XII has intensified even more in recent times in regard for the increased suffering of so many unfortunate people."[5]

The German ambassador to the Holy See, Ernst von Weizsäcker, sent a translation of the article to the Wilhelmstrasse, with a notorious cover letter: "The Pope, although under intense pressure from various sides, has not allowed himself to be pushed into a demonstrative comment against the deportation of the Jews of Rome, although he must know that such an attitude will be used against him by our adversaries. . . . As there apparently will be no further German action taken on the Jewish question here, it may be expected that this matter, so unpleasant in regard to German-Vatican relations, is liquidated." Referring then to the article in *L'Osservatore Romano*, Weizsäcker added: "No objections need be raised against this statement, insofar as its text will be understood by very few people only as a special allusion to the Jewish question."[6]

As we saw, Ruth Kluger and her mother arrived from Theresienstadt in Auschwitz in May 1944, and for a short while they were shoved into the "family camp" (to which we shall return). Then both were transferred to the women's camp, where the decisive selection took place: Healthy women aged fifteen to forty-five would be sent to a labor camp; the others would be gassed. Ruth was twelve. When her turn arrived she declared her age. Her fate would have been sealed had her mother not taken a daring initiative: In a moment of inattention among the guards, she rushed her daughter to another line. Ruth promised her to declare that she was thirteen. "The line moved," Kluger recalled, "towards an SS man who, unlike the first one, was in a good mood. His clerk was perhaps nineteen or twenty. When she saw me, she left her post, and almost within the hearing of her boss, she asked me quickly and quietly and with an unforgettable smile of her irregular teeth: 'How old are you?' 'Thirteen,' I said as planned. Fixing me intently, she whispered, 'Tell him you are fifteen.' Two minutes later it was my turn. When asked for my age I gave the decisive answer. 'I am fifteen.' 'She seems small,' the master over life and death remarked. He sounded almost friendly, as if he was evaluating cows and calves. 'But she is strong,' the woman said, 'look at the muscles in her legs. She can work.' He agreed, 'why not?' She made a note of my number, and I had won an extension on life."[7] "Neither psychology nor biology explains it," Kluger later wrote about the young German woman's initiative. "Only free will does. The good is incomparable and inexplicable, because it doesn't have a proper cause outside itself, and because it doesn't reach for anything beyond itself."[8]

While Ruth was still in Theresienstadt, throughout 1943, some changes took place in the ghetto-camp. At the beginning of the year the heads of the Reichsvereinigung arrived from Berlin, and so did the remaining leaders of Austrian and Czech communities. For reasons not entirely clear, Eichmann decided on a change in the leadership of the camp: Edelstein remained on the Council, but a German and an Austrian Jew were put ahead of him in the new hierarchy. Paul Eppstein, the former de facto leader of the Reichsvereinigung and Benjamin Murmelstein, a Viennese rabbi, took over the (Jewish) reins of the ghetto. In the meantime a German *Mischling* converted to Protestantism, an ex-officer of the Imperial Army and Prussian to the marrow of his bones, Karl Löwenstein, had been transferred from the Minsk ghetto and appointed chief of the Theresienstadt Jewish police. The changes did not stop at that: for no clear reason again, the first commandant, Siegfried Seidl, was replaced by a brutal Austrian SS captain, Tony Burger.

In August 1943 a mysterious transport of more than one

thousand children arrived from Białystok. Rumor had it that they would be exchanged for Germans and possibly sent to Palestine. Two months later, well dressed and without wearing the yellow patch, they were sent on their way, accompanied by a few counselors, including Franz Kafka's sister Ottla, straight to Auschwitz.

Shortly before the departure of the Białystok children, another transport, an unusually massive one with some five thousand people, had also left Theresienstadt for Auschwitz. The prehistory of this particular transport started several months earlier when the International Committee of the Red Cross demanded to visit Theresienstadt and also a "Jewish labor camp." By late 1942, as we saw, the Geneva organization was aware of the extermination and throughout early 1943, information about the mass murder of Europe's Jews kept accumulating at ICRC's headquarters. On April 15, 1943, the Red Cross chief delegate in Berlin, Roland Marti, reported that the Jewish population of the Reich capital had dwindled to fourteen hundred persons and that they too were slated for deportation to camps in the East. He then added: "There is no news or trace of the 10,000 Jews who left Berlin between 28.2.43 and 3.3.43 and who are now presumed dead (if they were presumed dead less than six weeks after deportation they had obviously been murdered)."[9]

Before sending his report to Geneva, Marti had inquired at the German Red Cross whether packages could be sent to the deportees; the answer had been negative. Eichmann and his acolytes could have no doubts by then that a demand from Geneva to allow ICRC representatives to visit a Jewish camp would be forthcoming. This was precisely the kind of situation Theresienstadt had been established for. But what should be done if the Red Cross delegates insisted on visiting the ultimate reception place for deportees leaving Theresienstadt? As Theresienstadt was meant to be a hoax from the outset, some kind of sham complement had to be set up in Auschwitz, just in case. This was the rationale behind the establishment of a "family camp."

No selection took place upon the arrival of the five thousand deportees' transport, and the entire group was settled in a special subcamp, BIIb, in which most of the draconian rules of life and death in Birkenau did not apply. The inmates could wear their civilian clothes, families were kept together, and every day some five hundred children were sent to a special area, block 31, where they attended some classes, sang in a chorus, played games, were told stories—in short were kept as unaware as possible of what Auschwitz-Birkenau was really all about. In December 1943, another five thousand Jews from Theresienstadt joined the first batch. Six months exactly after their arrival, on March 7, 1944, on the night of the Jewish festival of Purim, the 3,792 survivors of the September transport (the others had died in the meantime, notwithstanding their "favorable" living conditions) were sent to crematorium III and gassed. Other transports from Theresienstadt arrived in May 1944. In July, when it became obvious to Eichmann that the Red Cross commission would not ask to see Auschwitz, the entire "family camp," with a few exceptions (such as Ruth Kluger and her mother), was sent to the gas chambers.

Why the Red Cross delegate, Maurice Rossel, did not demand to proceed to Birkenau after the visit to Theresienstadt is not clear. He was told by his SS hosts that the Czech ghetto was the "final camp"; yet Rossel could hardly have believed, in June 1944, that Theresienstadt was all there was to see regarding the deportation of the Jews of Europe. Be it as it may, on July 1, the ICRC representative sent an effusive thank-you note to Eberhard von Thadden, his counterpart at the Wilhelmstrasse. He even enclosed photos taken by the delegation during the visit of the camp as mementos of the pleasant excursion. After expressing his gratitude, also in the name of the ICRC, for all the help extended to the delegation during its visit, Rossel added: "The voyage to Prague will remain an excellent memory for us and it pleases us to assure you, once again, that the report about our visit in Theresienstadt will be reassuring for many, as the living conditions [in the camp] are satisfactory."[10]

Throughout 1943 and most of 1944 the Germans were trying to complete the deportations from every corner of the Continent and hasten the pace of extermination. At the end of October 1943 the Kovno ghetto became a concentration camp. A few days beforehand batches of young Jews had been deported to the Estonian labor camps, while the children and the elderly were sent to Auschwitz. In late December the pits at the ninth fort were opened and tens of thousands of corpses dug out: These remnants of most of the Kovno community and of the transports of Jews from the Reich and the Protectorate were then burned on a number of huge pyres, restacked day after day. Abraham Tory, the Kovno diarist, escaped from the city at the end of March 1944 and survived the war. Three months later, as the Soviet army was approaching, the remaining eight thousand inhabitants of the ghetto-camp were deported (including the members of the council and its chairman, Elchanan Elkes). The men were sent to Dachau, the women to Stutthof, near Danzig. By the end of the war three-quarters of these last Kovno Jews had perished. Elkes himself died in Dachau, shortly after his arrival.

On October 19, 1943, Elkes had written a "last testament." It was a letter to his son and daughter who lived in London; it was given to Tory and retrieved with the diary, after the liberation of Kovno. The very last words of the letter were filled with fatherly love, but they could not erase the sense of utter despair carried by the lines that just preceded: "I am writing this in an hour when many desperate souls—widows and orphans, threadbare and hungry—are camping on my doorstep, imploring us [the council] for help. My strength is ebbing. There is a desert inside me. My soul is scorched. I am naked and empty. There are no words in my mouth."[11]

In the fall of 1943 Lodz remained the last large-scale ghetto in German-dominated Europe (except for Theresienstadt). As their fate was being sealed, the unsuspecting inhabitants of the ghetto went on with the misery of their daily life plagued by hunger, cold, endless hours spent in workshops, exhaustion, and ongoing despair. And yet, mood also changed on occasion, as on December 25, 1943, for example, the first day of Hanukkah: "There are gatherings in larger apartments. Everyone brings a small appropriate gift: a toy, a piece of *babka* (cake), a hair ribbon, a couple of brightly colored empty cigarette packages, a plate with a flower pattern, a pair of stockings, a warm cap. Then comes the drawing of lots; and chance decides. After the candles are lighted, the presents are handed out. Ghetto presents are not valuable, but they are received with deep gratitude. Finally, songs are sung in Yiddish, Hebrew, and Polish, as long as they are suitable for enhancing the holiday mood. A few hours of merrymaking, a few hours of forgetting, a few hours of reverie."[12]

Although, as we have seen, the Allies had publicly recognized the extermination of the Jews, London and Washington obstinately shied away from any concrete rescue steps. In all fairness it remains difficult to this day to assess whether some of the rescue plans initiated by Germany's satellites or by some subordinate German officials were genuinely meant as exchanges of some sort or were no more than extortionist ploys. Thus in late 1942 and during the first months of 1943, the Romanian authorities informed the Jewish Agency that they were ready to release seventy thousand Jews from Transnistria for two hundred thousand lei per person. The offer could have been an early Romanian feeler for contacts with the Allies but, in a hardly subtle maneuver to keep in the good graces of both sides, Radu Lecca, general secretary for Jewish affairs in Antonescu's government, who traveled to Istanbul to negotiate with Jewish Agency representatives, soon thereafter informed the German ambassador in Bucharest of the initiative. From that moment on the initiative was doomed.

The *Yishuv* leadership was divided in its estimate of the proposal and was well aware of the fact that the Allies would not allow the transfer of seventy thousand Jews to Palestine. Indeed the British position, shared by the State Department, was one of adamant rejection. In February 1943 the Romanian offer was reported in Swiss newspapers and in the *New York Times*, leading to some public outcry about Allied passivity, to no avail. Over the coming weeks the plan was reduced to the transfer of five thousand Jewish orphans from Transnistria to Palestine. Eichmann agreed to this latter proposal provided the Allies allowed the transfer to Germany of twenty thousand able-bodied German POWs, in exchange for the children.

Sporadic negotiations with the Romanians continued nonetheless throughout 1943, and the possibility of bribing whoever had to be bribed in Bucharest seemed to keep the rescue option alive. The operation was definitively scuttled by the obstruction of the U.S. State Department and the British Ministry of Economic Warfare regarding the transfer by the World Jewish Congress of the money needed to Switzerland. (The Treasury Department had given its authorization.) In December 1943 the Foreign Office delivered a note to the American ambassador in London, John Winant, indicating that the British authorities were "concerned with the difficulty of disposing of any considerable number of Jews should they be rescued from enemy-occupied territories."[13]

The publicity given the absence of rescue operations from early 1943 on had convinced both the Foreign Office and the

State Department that some gesture was necessary: A conference on the "refugee situation" was decided upon. The conference, attended by high-ranking British and American officials, opened in Bermuda on April 19, 1943, under the chairmanship of the president of Princeton University, Harold W. Dodds. After twelve days of deliberations the meeting ended with the release of a statement to the press declaring that "concrete recommendations" would be submitted to both governments; however, due to the war situation, the nature of these recommendations could not be revealed.

American Jewish leaders were themselves anxious to achieve results and well aware of the demand for more forceful initiatives that arose from growing segments of the country's Jewish population, mainly from a small but vocal group of right-wing Zionists (Revisionists) led by Peter Bergson. Yet, for Stephen Wise, embarrassing the president by public manifestations against American inaction was unacceptable. Wise did not hesitate to air his views publicly. At the American Jewish Conference held in August 1943, one month after the meeting of Bergson's "Emergency Conference to Save the Jewish People in Europe," Wise told his audience: "We are Americans, first, last, and at all times. Nothing else that we are, whether by faith or race or fate, qualifies our Americanism. We and our fathers chose to be, and now choose to abide, as Americans. Our first and sternest task, in common with all other citizens of our beloved country is to win the anti-Fascist war. Unless that war be won, all else is lost."[14]

Wise's view was echoed by most of the participants at the conference and, all in all, by most American Jewish organizations and their publications. Rare were the mainstream leaders ready to admit that not enough had been or was being done; one of those was Rabbi Israel Goldstein, who, at the same American Jewish Conference, did not hide his feelings: "Let us forthrightly admit that we American Jews, as a community of

five millions, have not been stirred deeply enough, have not exercised ourselves passionately enough, have not risked enough
of our convenience and our social and civic relations, have not
been ready enough to shake the bond of so-called amicability
in order to lay our troubles upon the conscience of our Christian neighbors and fellow citizens."[15]

To the dismay of the administration and that of mainstream American Jewish leadership, the Bergsonites did
not let go. At the end of 1943 they succeeded in convincing
Senator Guy Gillette of Iowa and Representative Will Rogers
of California to introduce a rescue resolution into Congress.
During the debates Assistant Secretary of State Breckenridge
Long, who for years spared no effort to limit Jewish immigration to the utmost, demanded to testify and presented the
House Committee on Foreign Affairs with misleading data
about the number of Jewish refugees the State Department
had allowed to enter the United States. When Long's testimony became known, officials at the Treasury Department
brought up evidence about the State Department's ongoing
efforts to hide information about the extermination and
hinder rescue efforts. This evidence was submitted to the
president by Secretary of the Treasury Henry Morgenthau.
This time Roosevelt considered it politically wise to react,
and in January 1944 he announced the establishment of the
War Refugee Board to be headed by Assistant Secretary of
the Treasury John Pehle. The WRB received the mandate
to coordinate and lead any rescue operations that its officials
would have examined and recommended.

The confirmation of the news about the ongoing extermination of European Jewry led to mass protests in the streets of Tel
Aviv, to the proclamation by the *Yishuv*'s chief rabbis of days of
fasting and other manifestations of collective mourning. Soon,
however, everyday concerns and even traditional celebrations
resurfaced; throughout 1943 major festivals were organized by

the kibbutz movement, and Hebrew University students celebrated Purim in the usual carnival procession. In the words
of the historian Dina Porat, "Agony was a part of daily life and,
when the news was particularly bitter, expressions of pain multiplied. But public attention was not sustained, and life would
return to normal for weeks or months, until the next shocking
event."[16]

Unlike her brother Mischa, Etty Hillesum had decided to stay
in Westerbork when her parents' deportation date arrived. But,
on September 6, 1943, the order came: She was to board the
same transport. In a letter of September 7 a friend, Jopie Vlee-
schouwer, described the events of that day: "Her parents and
Mischa went to the train first. Then I trundled a well packed
rucksack and a small hamper with a bowl and mug dangling
from it to the train. And there she stepped on to the platform,
talking gaily, smiling, a kind word for everyone she met on
the way, every inch the Etty you all know so well. Then I lost
sight of her for a bit and wandered along the platform. I saw
Mother, Father H. and Mischa board wagon No. 1. Etty finished up in wagon No. 12, having first stopped to look for a
friend in wagon No. 14 who was pulled out again at the last
moment. Then a shrill whistle and the 1000 'transport cases'
were moving out. Another flourish from Mischa who waved
through a crack in wagon No. 1, a cheerful 'bye' from Etty in
No. 12 and they were gone."[17]

On that same day Etty still managed to throw a postcard
out of the train; it was addressed to a friend in Amsterdam:
"Opening the Bible at random I find this: 'The Lord is my
high tower.' I am sitting on my rucksack in the middle of a full
freight car. Father, Mother and Mischa are a few cars away. In
the end, the departure came without warning, on sudden special orders from The Hague. We left the camp singing, Father
and Mother firmly and calmly, Mischa too. We shall be trav-

eling for three days. Thank you for all your kindness and care. Goodbye for now from the four of us."[18]

According to a Red Cross report, Etty was murdered in Auschwitz on November 30, 1943; her parents and brother Mischa shared the same fate. Her brother Jaap survived the camp but died on his way back to Holland at the end of the war.

CHAPTER 15

The End

March 1944–May 1945

ON APRIL 6, 1944, Klaus Barbie, chief of the Gestapo in Lyons, informed Röthke of a particularly successful catch: "This morning, the Jewish children's home *Colonie d'Enfants* in Izieu (Ain) has been taken away. A total of 41 children, ages 3–13, have been caught. Moreover all the Jewish staff was captured: 10 people, including 5 women. We have not seized any cash or valuables. The transport to Drancy will take place on April 7."[1] Most of the children and staff of Izieu were deported from Drancy to Auschwitz on April 13 in transport 71; the remaining ones were deported on May 30 and June 30: None survived.

The murder of the children and staff of Izieu was but a minute event in the routine of German mass extermination, but it demonstrated, as the war entered its last year, that notwithstanding the rapidly deteriorating situation of the Reich, no effort would be spared, no roundup deemed too insignificant in the final drive toward the complete extermination of the European Jews.

The Wehrmacht managed to stem the Allied advance on Rome until early June 1944 and, in mid-March, it had occu-

pied Hungary. Although the Allied landing in Normandy on
June 6 succeeded, and although in the summer and autumn
the Soviet forces occupied Poland and the Baltic countries,
while simultaneously toppling the Romanian regime, taking
over Bulgaria, and establishing a front line on the outskirts
of Budapest, the Germans still launched dangerous counter-
offensives, both east and west. By the end of the year, however, the Reich's military might was spent: East Prussia had
already partly fallen into Soviet hands and huge Allied forces
were poised on the borders of the Reich; moreover the industrial capacity of the country was rapidly sinking under the
relentless Anglo-American bombing attacks.

On April 27, 1944, the propaganda minister recorded a
conversation that must have taken place on the previous day
in Berlin. The most recent bombing of Munich had caused
heavy damage. Hitler was filled with intense desire for vengeance against England. Then, without transition, Goebbels
noted: "The *Führer's* hatred against the Jews has intensified
even further rather than declined. The Jews must be punished for their crimes against the European nations and in
general against the entire cultured world. Wherever we can
get hold of them, they should not escape retribution. The
advantages of anti-Semitism do offset its disadvantages, as I
always said."

Anti-Semitism did indeed spread throughout the Continent.
It was as tangible in France as in the Ukraine, as real in Poland
as in Germany itself, and also in Holland.

In the early spring of 1944 Anne Frank's chronicle of everyday life in hiding and of the ebb and flow of intimate feelings
became more widely open to reflections on the fate of her
people and on anti-Semitism. On April 11, after describing a
brief alarm, during which she believed that the police had discovered their hiding place, she went on with a declaration of
overflowing love for the Dutch nation. Barely a month later,

on May 22, she was less assured of her place in postwar Dutch society:

> To our great sorrow and dismay, we have heard that many people have changed their attitude towards us Jews. We've been told that anti-Semitism has cropped up in circles where once it would have been unthinkable. This fact has affected us all very, very deeply. The reason for the hatred is understandable, maybe even human, but that doesn't make it right. According to the Christians, the Jews are babbling their secrets to the Germans, denouncing their helpers and causing them to suffer the dreadful fate and punishments that have already been meted out to so many. All this is true. But, as with everything, they should look at the matter from both sides: Would Christians act differently if they were in our place? Could anyone, regardless of whether they are Jews or Christians, remain silent in the face of German pressure? Everyone knows it's practically impossible, so why do they ask the impossible from the Jews? . . . Oh, it's sad, very sad that the old adage has been confirmed for the umpteenth time: "What one Christian does is his own responsibility, what one Jew does, reflects on all the Jews."[2]

Anne had also heard that after the war foreign Jews would be sent back to the countries they had fled from. Thus, the young girl who, a few weeks earlier had proclaimed her intense wish to become Dutch, now assessed her chances of being accepted with some wariness after she heard about the change in the public mood: "I have only one hope," she wrote on that same day. "That this anti-Semitism is just a passing thing, that the Dutch will show their true colors, that they will never waver from what they know in their hearts to be just, for this is unjust!"[3]

Somebody denounced the Jews hidden at 263 Prinsen-gracht. On August 4, 1944, they were arrested, transferred to a prison in Amsterdam, then deported to Auschwitz. Margo and Anne were later taken to Bergen-Belsen, where they both died of typhus a few weeks before the liberation of the camp. They were probably buried in a mass grave. Except for Otto Frank, none of the eight residents of the Annex survived. Miep and Jan found Anne's diary pages scattered all over the hiding place.

In France collaborationist extremism surged in early 1944 with the appointment of the man of the Gestapo, Joseph Dar-nand as secretary-general for the maintenance of order, and, a few months later, as secretary of state of the interior, and that of Philippe Henriot, a militant Catholic and extreme rightist from the prewar years, as secretary of state for propaganda and information; their views and their fanaticism were on a par with those of their models and allies, the SS. While Henriot spewed the vilest anti-Semitic propaganda in his twice-daily broadcasts, Darnand's men denounced, arrested, tortured, and killed Resistance fighters and Jews. They killed Victor Basch, the former chairman of the League of Human Rights and his wife, both in their eighties; they killed Blum's former minister of education, Jean Zay; they killed Reynaud's minister of the interior, Georges Mandel, to name but their best-known Jewish victims. Undeterred by the landing in Normandy and by the approaching Allied forces, the Paris Gestapo forged ahead. On July 20 and 24 the Germans raided the children's homes of UGIF-North, where some 650 children were still kept as-sembled by the organization's leadership. At first 233 children were caught and transported to Drancy. Edinger's immediate reaction was to order the dispersal of the remaining children, but shortly thereafter he canceled the order. The remaining children were taken away. To the very end the leaders of UGIF-North were afraid of German retaliation—probably against themselves.

On August 17 and 22 the last transports of Jews left France for Auschwitz. On August 25 Gen. Philippe Leclerc's Free French division, attached to the U.S. forces in the West, liberated Paris.

In Italy and in the formerly Italian-occupied areas the roundups of Jews had not encountered much success, as the Jews found hiding places in small villages. The means at the disposal of the Germans did not allow for thorough searches either in small or even in midsize communities. The Germans thus set some hopes upon a new ordinance issued by the Fascist government that all Jews should be sent to concentration camps.They hoped that the Fascist police would take matters in hand and allow the small Gestapo task force to spread its men as advisers to the local police units.

In some areas the order issued by Mussolini's government was indeed followed, even without German participation. Thus in Venice, on December 5–6, 1943, the local police arrested 163 Jews either in their houses or at the Old Peoples' Home. A repeat performance, this time with German participation, took place at the Old People's Home on August 17, and finally, on October 6, 1944, twenty-nine Jewish patients were seized in three Venetian hospitals. In the old rice factory, La Riseria di San Sabba, which replaced the Fossoli camp since August 1944, the oldest and weakest inmates were murdered on the spot; the rest, the majority, were deported to Auschwitz and exterminated. And, in Milan, a gang of Italian Fascists outperformed the Germans in feats of bestiality. Pietro Koch's men had established their headquarters in a villa soon known as *Villa Triste* ("sad villa"), where they tortured and executed their victims, Jews and non-Jews.

Simultaneously with the roundups in Italy (and in southeastern France), the Germans turned to mainland Greece and to the Greek islands. Two weeks before Passover, on March 23, 1944, some 800 Jews had assembled at the main Athens synagogue for a distribution of matzoth promised by the Germans. All were arrested, driven to the Haideri transit camp, and, in early April, deported to Auschwitz. No Jewish community in the Aegean was forgotten, not even the smallest. Most of the Jews of the Greek islands were arrested in the course of July 1944. On July 23, the 1750 Jews of Rhodes and the 96 Jews of the tiny island of Kos were rounded up and crammed into three barges, on their way to the mainland. Those who had survived the sea voyage and the mishandling on arrival were herded into the usual freight cars and, on August 16, they reached Auschwitz. One hundred fifty-one deportees from Rhodes survived the war, as did twelve Jews from Kos.

The Wehrmacht occupied Hungary on March 19, 1944. Under threat of unilateral military action, the Nazi leader compelled Horthy to set up a pro-German government. Döme Sztójay, the former ambassador to Berlin, was appointed prime minister. Hitler also demanded that some one hundred thousand Jews be delivered "for labor" in Germany. Horthy submitted. On that same day Edmund Veesenmayer was appointed as Hitler's special delegate to the new Hungarian government; Eichmann too arrived in the Hungarian capital, soon followed by the members of his "special intervention unit Hungary."

The anti-Jewish measures were indeed immediately launched. On April 7 the roundups started in the Hungarian provinces, with the enthusiastic cooperation of the Hungarian gendarmerie. Within less than a month, ghettos or camps for hundreds of thousands of Jews sprung up in Carpatho-Ruthenia, in Transylvania, and later in the southern part of the country. According to German plans Budapest would be "evacuated" last, approximately from late June on.

One may wonder whether the attitude adopted by the Jewish Council (appointed on March 12) did not, more than in most other places, add to the passivity and subservience of the

Jewish masses. The council was well informed, and so were many Hungarian Jews, essentially in Budapest. Returning members of the labor battalions, Hungarian soldiers back from the eastern front and Jewish refugees from Poland and Slovakia did spread the information they had gathered about the mass extermination of Jews, as did the Hungarian services of the BBC. Moreover, on April 7 two Slovak Jews, Rudolf Vrba and Alfred Wetzler, escaped from Auschwitz, and on the twenty-first they reached Slovakia. Within days they had written a detailed report about the extermination process in the Upper Silesian camp and delivered it to the "Working Group" in Bratislava. These "Auschwitz Protocols" reached Switzerland and the Allied countries; large excerpts were soon published in the Swiss and the American press. To this day, however, it is not clear how long it took for the report to reach the Jewish Council in Budapest. The Budapest council, headed by Samu (Samuel) Stern, may have assumed that any warning to Jews of the provinces would be useless.

Mass deportations to Auschwitz started on May 15. The crematoria of Birkenau could not keep up with the gassing pace, and open-air cremation pits had to be added. According to SS officer Perry Broad's testimony at the Auschwitz trial in Frankfurt: "Soon the ovens were burnt out as a result of the continuous heavy use and only crematorium no. III was still smoking. . . . The special commandos had been increased and worked feverishly to keep emptying the gas chambers. . . . The last body had hardly been pulled from the gas chambers and dragged across the yard behind the crematorium, which was covered in corpses, to the burning pit, when the next lot were already undressing in the hall ready for gassing."[4] Höss himself described the cremation in the open pits: "The fires in the pits had to be stoked, the surplus fat drained off, and the mountain of burning corpses constantly turned over so that the draft might fan the flames."[5]

Soon after the beginning of the deportations, pressure from within the country, particularly from Horthy's long-time conservative political allies and from his closest circle of advisers, started building up to bring a halt to cooperation with the German deportations. Toward the end of June, international intervention strengthened the internal Hungarian opposition: The king of Sweden, the pope, the American president, all intervened with the regent. On July 2 a heavy American raid on Budapest emphasized Roosevelt's message. Horthy vacillated, ready to comply with these demands yet unable for several weeks to impose his will upon the pro-Nazi members of his government. When, on July 8, the deportations from Hungary finally stopped, 438,000 Jews had been sent to Auschwitz and approximately 394,000 immediately exterminated. Of those selected for work, very few were alive at the end of the war. In Budapest about 250,000 Jews were still awaiting their fate.

The main institutions that to a certain degree could have stemmed the anti-Jewish drive were the churches. Pius XII did join other leaders in interceding with Horthy to stop the German operation. This first public intervention of the pope in favor of the Jews was sent on June 25, 1944; but even this message was worded in rather hazy terms, without explicitly mentioning the Jews; neither was there any mention of extermination.

The heads of the Catholic and Protestant churches in Hungary knew too what the deportations to Germany meant; none, however, could be swayed to take a public stand against the policies of the Sztójay government. Both churches sought first and foremost to obtain exemptions for converted Jews, and in this they were partly successful, precisely because they abstained from any public protest against the deportations in general. As for the deportation of the Jews as such, the head of the Hungarian Catholic hierarchy, Justinian Cardinal Seredi,

finally drafted a short pastoral note that was read on July 16, a
week after Horthy had stopped the transports.

As the events in Hungary unfolded with extraordinary rapidity, two related issues arose that remain highly contentious
to this very day: The attempt of some members of the Jewish
"Relief and Rescue Committee" (*Vaadah*, in Hebrew) to negotiate with the Germans; and the Allied decision concerning the
bombing of the railway line from Budapest to Auschwitz or of
the Auschwitz killing installations as such.

The *Vaadah* was established in the Hungarian capital at the
beginning of 1943 to help Jewish refugees, mainly from Slovakia and Poland, who had fled to Hungary. Rudolf Kastner, a
Zionist journalist from Cluj, Joel Brand, another native from
Transylvania and something of an adventurer in politics and
otherwise, and an engineer from Budapest, Otto Komoly,
became the leading personalities of the *Vaadah*, whose executive committee had been joined by several other Hungarian
Jews. In late March 1944 Kastner and Brand met in Budapest
with Dieter Wisliceny. Eichmann's envoy was offered a substantial amount of money (two million dollars) to avoid deportation of the Jews of Hungary. But as it became clear that the
Vaadah could not come up with such an amount, Eichmann
summoned Brand sometime in mid- or late-April and offered
to exchange the lives of eight hundred thousand Hungarian
Jews for the delivery by the Western Allies of ten thousand
winterized trucks, to be used solely on the eastern front. The
SS would allow Brand to travel to Istanbul, in the company
of Bandi Grosz, a multiple agent and a shady figure by all accounts, on whom Himmler's men were relying to establish
contacts with the West.

Of course there was no intention to free any substantial
number of Hungarian Jews. The unparalleled rapidity and
scale of the deportations and of the extermination is the best
indication of what the Germans really had in mind. The intent

of the contacts was grossly simple: If the Allies rejected the German offer, they could be saddled with the responsibility for contributing to the extermination of the Hungarian Jews; as after the Evian conference of July 1938, the Germans could proclaim once again: "Nobody wants them!" If by chance, however, due to Jewish pressure the Allies were to start any kind of negotiations, Stalin would surely oppose it and the rift in the Grand Alliance, which Hitler impatiently awaited, would follow. The rationale behind Grosz's mission was most probably identical: If the West accepted the idea of separate negotiations, the Soviets would be informed and the end result would be the same.

On May 19, 1944, Brand and Grosz landed in Istanbul. While Grosz went on his separate "mission," Brand conveyed the SS proposal to the *Yishuv*'s delegates in Istanbul. A series of rapidly unfolding events followed. The Jewish Agency Executive, convened in Jerusalem by Ben-Gurion, decided to intervene immediately with the Allies, even if the chances of a deal with the Germans were seen as slim. The British high commissioner in Palestine, informed by Ben-Gurion, agreed that Moshe Shertok, secretary of the Jewish Agency's Political Department, be allowed to travel to Istanbul to meet with Brand. While Shertok's departure was delayed, Brand himself had to leave Turkey. Thus it was in Aleppo (Syria), where he was kept under British arrest, that the envoy from Budapest met with Shertok on June 11. Brand repeated the gist of the German message to Shertok.

Although the leadership of the *Yishuv* soon understood that Grosz's mission was the main German ploy and Brand's a mere accessory and additional bait, Shertok and Chaim Weizmann, president of the World Zionist Organization (WZO), nonetheless interceded with foreign minister Anthony Eden in London for some gesture that would allow to gain time and eventually save part of Hungarian Jewry. On July 15 they were told that the German "offer" was rejected. In the meantime Brand had been transferred from Aleppo to Cairo, where he remained under British interrogation. At that point his mission had come to an abrupt end.

It remains hard to believe that the shrewd Kastner had high hopes regarding the success of Brand's mission. But he must soon have understood that SS officers in Budapest were ready for more limited deals that could be explained away as ransoming operations for the Reich, as well as be highly lucrative for some of the SS participants. Thus, in a series of negotiations that lasted from April to June 1944, Kastner persuaded Wisliceny, Eichmann, and another Himmler underling, Kurt Becher, to allow a train with (ultimately) 1,684 Jews to leave Budapest for Switzerland, as a sign of German goodwill, in the framework of the wider "exchange negotiations." The price was a thousand dollars per Jew, and Becher, who negotiated the final arrangement, managed to have some of the lucky passengers pay twice. On June 30 the train left, first—and unexpectedly—for Bergen-Belsen: The "Kastner Jews" nonetheless reached Switzerland in two transports, one in the early fall, the second several weeks later. Although Kastner was not alone in choosing the passengers, his influence on the selection committee was considerable; it led to postwar accusations of nepotism, to two court cases in Israel, and eventually it did cost Kastner his life.

During the same months another rescue project of a very different kind also collapsed: the Allied bombing of the railway line from Hungary to Auschwitz and possibly of the extermination sites in Auschwitz-Birkenau.

On May 25, 1944, a representative of the War Refugee Board in Bern, Roswell McClelland, passed on to Washington a message he had received from Isaac Sternbuch, the representative of the American Union of Orthodox Rabbis in Switzerland; the message was addressed to the Union of

Orthodox Rabbis in New York: "We received news from Slovakia," Sternbuch wrote, "according to which they ask prompt air raids should be made over the two towns Kaschau (Kosice) . . . and . . . Presov . . . and also the whole railroad line between them. . . . It is the single near route from Hungary to Poland. . . . Do the necessary that bombing should be repeated at short intervals to prevent rebuilding."[6]

The "Working Group" was the source of the information from Slovakia received by Sternbuch. A first letter sent by Weissmandel sometime in early May 1944 had not been acknowledged, so that on May 31 the Slovak rabbi repeated his entreaty and again gave details about the deportations: These details were extraordinarily precise, as was the description of the killing installations. Weissmandel's letter ended with an agonized plea: "Now we ask: how can you eat, sleep, live? How guilty will you feel in your hearts if you fail to move heaven and earth to help us in the only ways that are available to our own people and as quickly as possible? . . . For God's sake, do something now and quickly."[7]

Intense consultations and contacts followed in late June, after Jewish organizations and the WRB in Washington received Sternbuch's message. Pehle transmitted the message to the assistant secretary of war, John J. McCloy, but with reservations: ". . . I made it very clear to Mr. McCloy that I was not, at this point at least, requesting the War Department to take any action on this proposal other than to appropriately explore it."[8] A few days later, Leon Kubowitzki, the head of the Rescue Department of the World Jewish Congress, addressed a letter to Pehle, this time suggesting not the bombing of the railway line from Hungary to Auschwitz but rather the destruction of the death installations at the camp by Soviet paratroopers or Polish underground units. The idea of bombing the installations from the air came at the same time from another Jewish representative, Benjamin Akzin.

On July 4, 1944, Assistant Secretary of War McCloy dismissed this flurry of projects and entreaties in a letter to Pehle: "The War Department is of the opinion that the suggested air operation is impracticable. It could be executed only by the diversion of considerable air support essential to the success of our forces now engaged in decisive operations and would in any case be of such very doubtful efficacy that it would not amount to a practical project."[9] Although Churchill was briefly involved and appeared to be in favor of some action, by mid-July London was as negative as Washington.

In the meantime Höss had been recalled to Auschwitz to supervise the extermination of the Hungarian Jews. For the flawless implementation of his task he was awarded the Iron Cross first and second class.

As Germany was swaying under Allied military pressure on all fronts in the summer of 1944, an event of major importance took place in the Reich itself: the attempt on Hitler's life. A growing number of officers, many of whom had previously been unquestioning, even enthusiastic devotees of the regime and its leader, were ready in 1944 to support the small circle of determined opponents of Nazism who were conspiring to kill the Nazi leader and save Germany from total catastrophe. The plot failed due to sheer bad luck. It brought frightful retribution in its wake. Over the following months and up to the last weeks of the war, reprisals did not stop, not only against the main plotters but against most of the members of opposition groups uncovered by the Gestapo.

In late July 1944 the Red Army liberated Majdanek. On August 23 Antonescu's regime collapsed, and on the thirty-first the Soviet army occupied Bucharest. A few days later it was Bulgaria's turn. In the meantime, on August 1, after the Soviet forces had reached the eastern bank of the Vistula in the Warsaw area, the Home Army gave the signal for an uprising

in the city. A fierce urban battle unfolded between the insur-
gents and German reinforcements, while the Soviets at first
could not, then did not intervene in any forceful way. On October 2 the remaining Polish forces finally surrendered, while
their capital had been reduced to rubble. Soon thereafter the
Soviet army occupied Warsaw. At the outset the Soviet divisions had been pushed back by German counterattacks along
the Vistula; later on Stalin, in his own way, solved the problem
of a nationalist opposition to the communist rule he meant to
impose on Poland: He let the Germans decimate it.

Emanuel Ringelblum and his son were caught by the Germans before the Polish uprising, in March 1944, and shot. Many
other Jews, who had also found refuge on the Aryan side of the
city, perished during the battle for Warsaw.

As the Red Army was approaching Lodz, the Germans decided to dismantle the Chelmno killing site. The brief respite
in the deportations triggered hope and joy in the ghetto, as
Rosenfeld noted on July 28: "We are facing either apocalypse
or redemption. The chest dares breathe more freely already.
People look at each other as if to say: 'We understand each
other, right!' . . . After so much suffering and terror, after so
many disappointments, it is hardly surprising that they are not
willing to give themselves over to anticipatory rejoicing. . . .
And if at long last, the day of the 'redemption' should be at the
doorstep, it is better to let oneself be surprised than to experience yet another disappointment. That's human nature, this
is the human mentality of Ghetto Litzmannstadt at the end of
July 1944."[10] It was Rosenfeld's last diary entry.

On August 2 the Germans announced "the relocation of
the ghetto." Beginning on August 3 five thousand Jews a day
had to assemble at the railway station. Some of the inhabitants tried to hide. As the Jewish police was unable to deal with
the situation, German police and firemen units from the city
moved into the ghetto and started dragging out the rapidly

dwindling number of Jews. On August 28 the ghetto's end had come. Rumkowski, his wife, the son they had adopted, and his brother and his wife were on the last transport that left that day for Auschwitz-Birkenau. Neither Rumkowski nor any member of his family survived. When the Red Army occupied the city in January 1945, 877 ghetto Jews were still alive.

Poland was liberated. Of the 3.3 million Jews who had lived in Poland in 1939, some 300,000 survived the war, of whom 40,000 had been hidden in Poland as such.

In early July 1944, as the Red Army reached the eastern borders of Lithuania, 33,000 Jews were still alive in the German-occupied Baltic countries, mainly in the Kovno and Shavli ghettos and in the labor camps of Estonia. In mid-July, as we saw, the Kovno ghetto was liquidated: Some 2,000 of its inhabitants were killed on the spot and 7,000 to 8,000 deported to camps in Germany. Between July 15 and 22 some 8,000 Jews were deported from Shavli to the Stutthof camp near Danzig.

Kruk, in the meantime, was an inmate of Klooga, the main Estonian slave-labor camp. He had resumed his chronicling, although less systematically so than in Vilna. At the end of August 1944, he was transferred again, this time to neighboring Lagedi. "So far I have slept on the bare ground," he wrote on August 29. "Today I built a lair for myself, boarded up the holes in the barrack—an achievement for Lagedi. . . . If possible, I shall continue to record."[11] He did so for a few more days. The last entry in Kruk's diary was dated September 17, 1944. He recorded the hiding of his manuscripts in the presence of witnesses: "Today, the eve of Rosh Hashanah, a year after we arrived in Estonia, I bury the manuscripts in Lagedi, in a barrack of Mrs. Shulma[?], right across from the guard's house. Six persons are present at the burial."[12] The next day, according to Benjamin Harshav, the editor of the English translation of Kruk's diary, "All Jews from Klooga and Lagedi, including Herman Kruk, were hastily exterminated. The inmates were ordered to carry logs and spread them in a layer, and then they were forced to undress and lie down naked on the logs, where they were shot in the neck. Layer was piled on top of layer, and the entire pyre was burned. The next morning, the first Red Army units reached the area. One of the six witnesses mentioned by Kruk in his final entry survived. He returned to Lagedi, dug up the diary, and brought it to Vilna."[13]

The final year of the war had brought a rapid deterioration in the condition of Theresienstadt's inmates. Already in the fall of 1943, Jakob Edelstein had been arrested for having helped some inmates to escape the camp and was sent to Auschwitz with his wife, Miriam, his son, Aryeh, and old Mrs. Olliner, Miriam's mother. While Edelstein was kept in block 11 of the main camp, his family was kept detained in the "family camp" in Birkenau. On June 20, 1944, they were all reunited in front of crematorium III and shot. Jakob was shot last, after he had to witness the killing of his son, his wife, and his mother-in-law. On September 27, 1944, Paul Eppstein was arrested on the trumped-up charge of attempting to escape. He was brought to the small fortress and executed. The inmates of Theresienstadt were now led by the last of the three elders, the Viennese Benjamin Murmelstein.

In the autumn of 1944 a second film was shot in Theresienstadt, this time by Kurt Gerron, a well-known Jewish actor, director, and overall Weimar star performer. It presented Theresienstadt as a happy resort town, complete with parks, swimming pools, soccer tournaments, schools, and endless cultural activities (concerts, theater, etc.); it featured "happy faces" all around. Completed in November 1944, this second hoax on a grand scale, titled *Theresienstadt: A Documentary from the Jewish Settlement Area*—and not, as is often mentioned, "The *Führer* Gives a Town to the Jews" (an ironic title made up by

the inmates themselves)—was never shown in public. Gerron
left Theresienstadt on the last transport to Auschwitz and was
gassed on arrival.

In April 1945, after some further improvement work, a
second ICRC delegation visited the camp, once more in the
company of a vast SS retinue that included Adolf Eichmann, no
less. Once again the Geneva delegates were satisfied: In their
report Theresienstadt became a "small Jewish state." Incidentally, they were the only audience to see Gerron's film; even
they found it "slightly too propagandistic."[14]

There was no armed uprising in Theresienstadt, although
it seems that the Germans took such a possibility into account
in the fall of 1944, after the events in Treblinka and Sobibor,
and the desperate and immediately beaten down rebellion of
the Auschwitz *Sonderkommando* Jews, in October. Thus mainly
young people boarded the transports to Auschwitz during the
deportations of those months. In February 1945 the Germans
ordered the building of two sites, a vast hall with doors closing
hermetically and a covered pit of huge proportions: Both sites
could have been used to exterminate the entire Jewish population on the spot, had the decision been taken to liquidate
the camp before the arrival of the Soviet forces. The detainees
were ultimately spared: 141,184 Jews had at one time or another been sent to Theresienstadt; at the end of the war, 16,832
were still alive.

The final entry in Redlich's diary, dated October 6, 1944,
was part of the "Diary of Dan" [the name of his newborn son],
in which he commented on events by addressing his infant
child: "Tomorrow, we travel my son. We will travel on a transport like thousands before us. As usual, we did not register
for this transport. They put us in without a reason. But never
mind, my son, it is nothing. All of our family already left in the
last weeks. Your uncle went, your aunt, and also your beloved
grandmother. . . . Tomorrow, we go too, my son. Hopefully,

the time of our redemption is near."[15] Redlich and his infant son were murdered on arrival.

In Slovakia the uprising of the underground was premature, notwithstanding the rapid progress of the Red Army: The Germans and their auxiliaries rapidly overcame the local partisans. The Jews who had joined the armed rebellion were usually shot whenever caught, and so were three of the four parachutists sent by the *Yishuv*; the remnants of the community were mainly deported to Auschwitz, also to some other camps, including Theresienstadt, during the last months of 1944 and in early 1945. The Vatican tried to intervene to halt the deportations, at least those of converted Jews, but without success. Tiso who, previously, had been less extreme than his closest aides, now defended the deportations in a letter to Pius XII: "The rumors about cruelties are but an exaggeration of hostile enemy propaganda. . . . The deportations were undertaken in order to defend the nation from its foe. . . . We owe this as [an expression] of gratitude and loyalty to the Germans for our national sovereignty."[16]

In the meantime the events in neighboring Hungary took a sharp turn for the worse. On October 15 Horthy announced his country's withdrawal from the war. On the same day the Germans took control of Budapest, arrested the regent and his son and appointed an "Arrow Cross" (Niylas) government led by Ferenc Szálasi, leader of the Hungarian Fascist movement, and backed by most of the Hungarian army. On October 18 Eichmann returned to Budapest. Over the following days and weeks, the Germans sent some 50,000 Jews on a trek from the Hungarian capital to the Austrian border, under the escort of Hungarian gendarmerie first, then of German guards. The aim was to march these Jews to the vicinity of Vienna, where they would build fortifications to defend the Austrian capital. Thousands of marchers perished from exhaustion and mistreatment or were shot by the guards. Another 35,000 Jews were orga-

nized into labor battalions to build fortifications around Budapest: They became prime targets for Niylas thugs whose fury
increased as the Soviet forces approached the capital. When
compelled to retreat into the city with the fleeing army units,
the members of the Jewish labor battalions were killed on the
bridges or on the banks of the Danube and thrown into the
river. The carnage took such proportions that "special police
units had to be called out to protect the Jews from the raging
Niylas."[17]

As Soviet troops were already fighting in the city, the
killings went on, including mostly Jews but also other "enemies." A Hungarian lieutenant described events that probably occurred in mid-January 1945: "I peeped round the
corner of the Vigadó Concert Hall and saw victims standing
on the track of the number 2 streetcar line in a long row,
completely resigned to their fate. Those close to the Danube
were already naked; the others were slowly walking down
and undressing. It all happened in total silence, with only
the occasional sound of a gunshot or machine-gun salvo. In
the afternoon, when there was nobody left, we took another
look. The dead were lying in their blood on the ice slabs or
floating in the Danube. Among them were women, children,
Jews, Gentiles, soldiers, and officers."[18]

In February 1945 the Soviet army occupied the whole of Budapest.

The disintegration of the Reich accelerated as weeks went by
and as, between January and March 1945, the command and
control system increasingly broke down. In the West, Belgium
and Holland were liberated, the Rhineland and the Ruhr fell
into Allied hands, and, on March 7, a U.S. armored division
crossed the Rhine at Remagen. On the eastern front in the
meantime, after taking control of Budapest, Soviet forces were
moving toward Vienna; to the northeast, the Baltic countries

were again in Stalin's grip; most East Prussian strongholds fell one after the other, and millions of German civilians were fleeing westward in an increasingly chaotic panic as news of Soviet savagery spread. In March, Soviet units crossed the river Oder: The road to Berlin was open. A few weeks beforehand Stalin, Roosevelt, and Churchill had met at Yalta, redrawn the borders of Eastern Europe, and divided Germany into occupation zones. And, in those same days of February 1945, Dresden, filled with refugees fleeing the Russians, was turned into a burning inferno by two successive air raids: a British, then an American one.

While one German city after another suffered catastrophic damages, while transportation was becoming increasingly chaotic, the Gestapo sent out new deportation summonses. In January 1945 many of the two hundred *Mischlinge* or partners in mixed marriages who still lived in Stuttgart were ordered to be ready for deportation to Theresienstadt. Similar summonses were being sent out throughout the entire Reich. On February 13 in the afternoon Klemperer recorded: "Today at eight o'clock [in the morning] I was at Neumark's. Frau Jährig came out of his room weeping. Then she told me: Evacuation of those capable of work, it's called outside work duty; as I myself [Klemperer] am released from duty, I remain here. So, the end is more likely for me than for those who are leaving. She: That is not the case; on the contrary, remaining here is a privilege. . . . The circular to be delivered stated that one had to present oneself at 3 Zeughausstrasse early on Friday morning, wearing working clothes and with hand luggage, which would have to be carried for a considerable distance, and with provisions for two to three days travel. . . . The whole thing is explicitly no more than outside work duty—but is without exception regarded as a death march."[19]

A few hours later, the bombing of Dresden started. At first Victor and Eva lost contact with each other in the pandemo-

nium. . . . By chance they met again on the Elbe riverbank.
They took off Victor's star and, as non-Jews now, they hid
with other refugees at the house of acquaintances, outside the
burning city, before moving westward.

The Nazi leader, living in an increasingly delusional world,
never stopped mulling over the Jewish issue: "Jesus was certainly not a Jew," he explained to Bormann on November 30,
1944. "The Jews would never have delivered one of their own to
the Romans and to a Roman court; they would have convicted
him themselves. It seems that many descendants of Roman legionaries lived in Galilee and Jesus was one of them. It could
be that his mother was Jewish."[20] The usual themes followed:
Jewish materialism, the perversion of Jesus' ideals by Paul, the
link between Jews and communism, and the like. Nothing
seemed to have changed in Hitler's innermost ideological landscape from his earliest forays into political propaganda in 1919
to the last months of his crusade against "the Jew."

Notwithstanding the continuous fury of the anti-Jewish
propaganda, German policies regarding the remaining Jews
became increasingly inconsistent. On the one hand, Hitler and
part of the SS apparatus directly involved in the implementation of the "Final Solution" did not waver to the very end on
the policy of extermination. On the other hand extermination
was delayed at times, with the Nazi leader's "blessing" by last-
minute need for slave labor. In fact by early 1944 Hitler had
been ready to compromise regarding the presence of Jewish
slave laborers on German soil. Speer confirmed, in a memorandum dated April 1944, that Hitler authorized the use of one
hundred thousand Hungarian Jews in urgent building projects
for armament factories to be located in the Protectorate. Soon
thereafter Jewish camp inmates would be brought back to the
Reich.

Thus, already in the late summer of 1944, some forty thousand Jews selected in Auschwitz and Stutthof had been shipped

to two major satellite camps of Dachau, Kaufering, and Mühl-dorf, where Organization Todt (OT) used them to build the heavily protected, semiunderground halls needed for air-craft construction (the *Jägerplan*). Somewhat later, mainly in the wake of the Auschwitz evacuation, other Jewish workers would be marched to the Harz mountains, to slave in the tun-nels of Dora-Mittelbau where, some Germans still believed, the ongoing production of V-2 rockets would save the Reich. The Jewish workers shipped to the Dachau satellite camps were joined by thousands of Hungarian Jews marched directly from Budapest to the Bavarian construction sites. The OT rap-idly proved itself equal to the SS in its mistreatment of the slave laborers, and by the fall of 1944 hundreds had been killed or were too weak to continue working. At this point the Dachau commandant decided to send these Jews back to Auschwitz for gassing.

It seems that although at some stage the Reichsführer did countermand the steps taken by his underlings to pursue the "Final Solution," he was unable to sustain this alternative, afraid as he was of Hitler's reaction. Nonetheless, from early 1945 on, in order to find an opening to the West, Himmler was ready to give up small groups of Jews to prove his goodwill. Thus in early January the Reichsführer negotiated the release of thousands of Jews with an old friend of his, the Swiss federal councillor Jean-Marie Musy, as an opening to negotiations with the Western powers. A first train carrying twelve hundred Jews from Theresienstadt arrived in Switzerland in January 1945. In-formed of the deal, Hitler put an immediate end to it.

At this point another channel appeared more promising: ne-gotiations by way of Sweden. The Swedes informed Himmler in February 1945 that they were ready to undertake a series of humanitarian missions which, if agreed to by the Germans, could possibly lead to wider contacts. To that effect Count Folke Bernadotte was dispatched to Germany. Bernadotte's mission, ostensibly under the banner of the Swedish Red Cross but backed in fact by the Swedish government, aimed first at liberating Scandinavian internees from Neuengamme (near Hamburg) and transferring them to Sweden. Himmler agreed. The Swedes then pushed for the release of Jews from Theresienstadt and Bergen-Belsen. During March and April 1945 initiatives to save Jews still alive in the camps multiplied, and groups of internees were indeed released as chaos spread throughout Germany.

The infamous "death marches" started in early 1945. Sometime in January, Himmler gave the order for the complete evacuation of all the camps in the East with, according to some testimonies, an ominous warning to the camp commanders: "The *Führer* holds you personally responsible for . . . making sure that not a single prisoner from the concentration camps falls alive into the hands of the enemy."[21] Other testimonies indicate that the decision about the fate of the inmates was left to the camp commanders. Moreover, in a basic directive that had already been issued in July 1944, Richard Glücks, head of the concentration camps division of the WVHA, had stated clearly that in an "emergency situation" (evacuation) the camp commanders were to follow the directives of the regional HSSPFs. In other words nobody seemed to know who was in charge of the evacuations. But, in the rapidly increasing chaos, the marches westward started.

Not all the seven to eight hundred thousand camp inmates lurching along the roads or stranded in open railroad cars during these last months of the war were Jews. Yet, as a reflection of the camps' population, the Jews ultimately represented a majority of these final victims of the monstrous Reich. During the marches, approximately 250,000 of these Jewish prisoners perished from exhaustion, freezing, shootings, or being burned alive.

In early 1945 Ruth Kluger and her mother started marching in the mass of inmates from the small Christianstadt labor camp (to which they had been transferred from Auschwitz sometime in the second half of 1944), a satellite camp of Gross-Rosen, also in Upper Silesia. But after a few days they escaped from the march and survived by moving from farm to farm, then by blending into the stream of German refugees fleeing westward, until they reached Straubing, in Bavaria. Soon thereafter the Americans arrived.

As for Filip Müller, his chances of survival were slim: Members of the *Sonderkommando* were not to be left alive. Müller nonetheless did escape, marching, then ferried, then marching again to Mauthausen, then to Melk and further to Gusen 1, and by early April 1945, out of Gusen again. Finally he reached some small camp near Wels: Starving prisoners lay there, on the floors of the barracks: The guards were gone. Müller settled on a rafter and waited. A few days later shouting inmates spread the news: "We are free!"[22]

None of the major camps was entirely emptied of inmates in the evacuations. In Auschwitz, for example, sick inmates remained in each of the three camps after the January 19 mass evacuation. And SS units, still sporadically battling the Soviets in the area, also remained for a full week. Although the Breslau HSSPF had given the order to murder all the remaining inmates, the SS units rather concentrated on the destruction of what remained of the gas chambers and the crematoria and the burning of archives.

"We all said to each other that the Russians would arrive soon, at once," Primo Levi, who in those days was an inmate in the Monowitz infirmary block, reminisced. "We all proclaimed it, we were all sure of it, but at bottom nobody believed it, because one loses the habit of hoping in the Lager [the camp], and even of believing in one's own reason. In the Lager it is useless to think, because events happen for the most part in an unforeseeable manner; and it is harmful, because it keeps alive a sensitivity which is a source of pain, and which some providential natural law dulls when suffering passes a limit."[23] The Soviet troops liberated Auschwitz on January 29. Primo Levi was a free man.

After part of the Reich Chancellery had been destroyed by massive American bombings in early February 1945, Hitler retreated to the vast underground bunker spreading two stories deep under the building and its garden. It was there that, a few weeks later, he decided to stay as the Red Army was closing in on Berlin. It was there in his subterranean abode that he heard extraordinary tidings: On April 13 Roosevelt died. Great expectations surged again, and Hitler shared them with the troops on the eastern front in his April 16 proclamation: "At the moment when fate has taken away the greatest war criminal of all times [Roosevelt], the turn of this war will be decided."[24]

On April 20, as somewhat subdued toasts were raised in Hitler's bunker to celebrate the führer's fifty-sixth birthday, Dr. Alfred Trzebinski, senior physician at the Neuengamme concentration camp, received the order to dispose of twenty Jewish children who had been used as guinea pigs for SS doctor Kurt Heissmeyer's experiments on tuberculosis. The twenty Jewish children, ten boys and ten girls, aged five to twelve, had arrived in Birkenau with their families from France, Holland, Poland, and Yugoslavia. The families disappeared in the gas chambers and, in the fall of 1944, the twenty children were sent to Neuengamme. During the following months the children, injected with Heissmeyer's preparations, became seriously ill. On April 20, as British forces were approaching the camp, the order came. The killing would not take place in Neuengamme but at the Bullenhuser Damm school in Rothenburgsort, near Hamburg, a subcamp of Neuengamme.

At his postwar trial Trzebinski described the course of the

events. The SS personnel arrived at Bullenhuser Damm with six Russian prisoners, two French doctors, two Dutch inmates, and the children. The children were put in a separate room, an air-raid shelter: "They had all their things with them—some food, some toys they had made themselves, etc. They sat on the benches and were happy that they had gotten out. They didn't suspect a thing." Trzebinski gave sedatives to the children, while, in the boiler room all the adult inmates were put to death. "I must say," Trzebinski went on, "that in general the children's condition was very good, except for one twelve-year-old boy who was in bad shape; he therefore fell asleep very quickly. Six or eight of the children were still awake—the others were already sleeping. . . . Frahm [an orderly] lifted the twelve-year-old boy and said to the others that he was taking him to bed. He took him to a room that was maybe six or eight yards away, and there I saw a rope already attached to a hook. Frahm put the sleeping boy into the noose and with all his weight pulled down on the body of the boy so that the noose would tighten."[25] The other children followed, one by one.

On April 21, 1945, in the evening, as Soviet shells started falling near the former buildings of the Reich Chancellery, the Nazi chief let his entourage know that he would stay in the bunker and kill himself; everybody else could leave if they wished so. His mistress, Eva Braun, whom Hitler would marry on the eve of their suicide, was determined to die with him. Faithful Goebbels, his wife, Magda, and their six children were also in the bunker: They would share their leader's fate. On April 29 the time had come: The führer dictated his "Private Testament" and then his message to future generations, his "Political Testament."

In the first half of the document, the Nazi leader addressed the German people, the world, and history. "It is untrue," he declared, "that I or anybody else in Germany had wanted the war in 1939." And immediately, at the very outset of the message, he turned to his main obsession: "It [the war] was exclusively willed and triggered by the international statesmen, who were either of Jewish descent or worked for Jewish interests." Full-scale raving followed. Hitler then settled accounts with Göring and Himmler, whom he demoted and expelled from the party for their dealings with the Western powers, nominated Grand Adm. Karl Doenitz as the new head of state and chief of the armed forces, appointed Goebbels as chancellor, and designated the new ministers. Hitler then reached the unavoidable final exhortation: "Most of all, I engage the leadership of the nation and its followers to the strictest keeping of the race laws and the merciless struggle against the universal poisoner of all people, international Jewry."[26]

Beside such foreseeable reactions, one aspect of the testament was utterly unexpected: In Hitler's final message, of bolshevism there was no trace. The Nazi leader had probably decided to concentrate his entire apologia on demonstrating that neither Germany's catastrophic end nor the murder of the Jews were his responsibility. The responsibility was squarely laid upon those who in September 1939 had pushed for war: the Western plutocrats and the warmongering Jews. Stalin, his ally at the time, was better left unmentioned, as the partition of Poland within days of the invasion showed that the Reich and the Soviet Union had decided to share the Polish spoils in a pact that considerably facilitated the German attack and proved that Hitler was intent on launching the war.

On April 30, shortly after 3:00 p.m.,[27] Hitler and his close entourage committed suicide. Seven days later Germany surrendered.

In early April the Klemperers, now ordinary German refugees, reached Upper Bavaria; their identity had not been discovered: They were saved. So were, also, the dazed survivors who had been left behind in the camps, those who remained alive during the death marches, those who emerged from their hiding places in Christian institutions, in "Aryan" families, in mountains or forests, among partisans or in resistance movements, those who lived in the open under false identities, those who had fled in time from German-dominated areas, those who kept their new identities, and those, known or unknown, who had betrayed and collaborated for the sake of survival.

Between five and six million Jews had been killed, among them almost a million and a half under the age of fourteen. They comprised the immense mass of silent victims and also most of the diarists and authors of letters whose voices we heard in these pages. From among the few hundreds of thousands of Jews who had survived, most struck roots in new surroundings, either by necessity or by choice; they built their lives, resolutely hid their scars, and experienced the common share of joys and sorrows dealt by everyday existence. For several decades many evoked the past mainly among themselves, behind closed doors, so to speak; some became occasional witnesses, others opted for silence. Yet whatever the path they chose, for all of them those years remained the most significant period of their lives. They were entrapped in it: Recurrently it pulled them back into overwhelming terror and, throughout, notwithstanding the passage of time, it carried along with it the indelible memory of the dead.

NOTES

CHAPTER 1: INTO THE THIRD REICH

1. Alan E. Steinweis, "Hans Hinkel and German Jewry, 1933–1941," *Leo Baeck Institute Yearbook* [hereafter *LBIY*] 38 (1993): p. 212.

2. Joseph Wulf, ed., *Die bildenden Künste im Dritten Reich: Eine Dokumentation* (Gütersloh, 1963), pp. 36, 81ff.

3. Wolfgang Benz, ed., *Das Exil der kleinen Leute: Alltagserfahrung deutscher Juden in der Emigration* (Munich, 1991), p. 16.

4. Ibid., p. 17.

5. For the petition and the other details, see *Akten der Reichskanzlei: Die Regierung Hitler, 1933–1938*, part 1, *1933–1934*, ed. Karl-Heinz Minuth, vol. 1 (Boppard am Rhein, 1983), pp. 296–98, 298n.

6. Wolfgang Benz, ed., *Die Juden in Deutschland 1933–1945: Leben unter nationalsozialistischer Herrschaft* (Munich, 1988), p. 18.

7. Klaus Drobisch, "Die Judenreferate des Geheimen Staatspolizeiamtes und des Sicherheitsdienstes der SS 1933 bis 1939," *Jahrbuch für Antisemitismusforschung* 2 (1993): p. 231.

8. Martin Broszat, Elke Fröhlich, and Falk Wiesemann, eds., *Bayern in der NS-Zeit: Soziale Lage und politisches Verhalten der Bevölkerung im Spiegel vertraulicher Berichte* (Munich, 1977), p. 432.

9. Heinz Höhne, *Die Zeit der Illusionen: Hitler und die Anfänge des Dritten Reiches 1933–1936* (Düsseldorf, 1991), p. 76.

10. Henry Friedlander and Sybil Milton, eds., *Archives of the Holocaust*, vol. 17, *American Jewish Committee New York*, ed. Frederick D. Bogin (New York, 1993), p. 4.

11. Joseph Goebbels, *Die Tagebücher von Joseph Goebbels*, ed. Elke Fröhlich, part 1, *1924–1941*, vol. 2, *1.1.1931–31.12.1936* (Munich, 1987), pp. 398–99.

12. Ibid., p. 400.

13. Peter Hanke, *Zur Geschichte der Juden in München zwischen 1933 und 1945* (Munich, 1967), p. 85.

14. Joseph Walk, ed., *Das Sonderrecht für die Juden im NS-Staat* (Heidelberg, 1981), pp. 12–13.

15. Deborah Dwork, *Children with a Star: Jewish Youth in Nazi Europe* (New Haven, 1991), p. 22.

16. Harold James, "Die Deutsche Bank und die Diktatur 1933–1945," in *Die Deutsche Bank 1870–1995*, ed. Lothar Gall et al. (Munich, 1995), p. 337.

17. Klaus Scholder, *Die Kirchen und das Dritte Reich*, vol. 1, *Vorgeschichte und Zeit der Illusionen 1918–1934* (Frankfurt am Main, 1977), pp. 338ff.

18. Ibid.

19. Wolfgang Gerlach, *Als die Zeugen schwiegen: Bekennende Kirche und die Juden* (Berlin, 1987), p. 42.

20. Doris L. Bergen, *Twisted Cross: The German Christian Movement in the Third Reich* (Chapel Hill, NC, 1996), p. 23.

21. Scholder, *Die Kirchen und das Dritte Reich*, pp. 612ff.

22. Guenter Lewy, *The Catholic Church and Nazi Germany* (New York, 1964), p. 271.

23. Klee to Foreign Ministry, September 12, 1933, *Documents on German Foreign Policy, Series C (1933–1937)*, vol. 1 (Washington, DC, 1957), pp. 793–94.

24. His Eminence Cardinal Faulhaber, *Judaism, Christianity and Germany: Advent Sermons Preached in St. Michael's, Munich, in 1933* (London, 1934), pp. 5–6.

25. Gerhard Sauder, ed., *Die Bücherverbrennung* (Munich, 1983), p. 89.

26. Jacob Boas, "German-Jewish Internal Politics under Hitler 1933–1938," *LBIY* 29 (1984): p. 3.

27. Abraham Margalioth, "The Problem of the Rescue of German Jewry During the Years 1933–1939: The Reasons for the Delay in Their Emigration from the Third Reich," in Yisrael Guttman and Ephraim Zuroff, eds., *Rescue Attempts During the Holocaust* (Jerusalem, 1977), pp. 249ff.

28. Yehuda Bauer, *My Brother's Keeper: A History of the American Jewish Joint Distribution Committee 1929–1939* (Philadelphia, 1974), p. 111.

29. Free Association for the Interests of Orthodox Jewry to the Reich Chancellor, Frankfurt, October 4, 1933, *Akten der Reichskanzlei*, vol. 2, *12/9/33–27/8/34*, pp. 884ff.

30. Robert Weltsch, "Vorbemerkung zur zweiten Ausgabe" (1959), in Siegmund Kaznelson, ed., *Juden im Deutschen Kulturbereich: Ein Sammelwerk* (Berlin, 1962), pp. xvff.

31. Steinweis, "Hans Hinkel," p. 215.

32. Sir Horace Rumbold to Sir John Simon, May 11, 1933, *Documents on British Foreign Policy 1919–1939*, 2nd series, vol. 5: *1933*, London, 1956, pp. 233–35.

33. Consul General at Berlin to the Secretary of State, November 1, 1933, *Foreign Relations of the United States, 1933*, vol. 2 (Washington, DC, 1948), p. 362 (italics added).

34. *Akten der Reichskanzlei: Die Regierung Hitler*, part 1, vol. 1, p. 631.

35. Wolfgang Michalka, ed., *Das Dritte Reich*, vol. 1 (Munich, 1985), p. 137.

CHAPTER 2: THE SPIRIT OF THE LAWS

1. Martin Broszat and Elke Fröhlich, *Alltag und Widerstand: Bayern im Nationalsozialismus* (Munich, 1987), p. 434.

2. Ian Kershaw, *The "Hitler Myth": Image and Reality in the Third Reich* (Oxford, 1987), p. 71.

3. Ian Kershaw, "'Working Towards the Führer': Reflections on the Nature of the Hitler Dictatorship," *Contemporary European History 2*, no. 2 (1993): p. 116.

4. Ingo Müller, *Hitler's Justice: The Courts of the Third Reich* (Cambridge, MA, 1991), pp. 91–92.

5. Ibid., p. 93.

6. For the cable to Müller see Eberhard Röhm and Jörg Thierfelder, *Juden-Christen-Deutsche, 1933–1945*, 3 vols. (Stuttgart, 1990), vol. 1, p. 268.

7. Baltic Sea Resort Management, Binz, 17.5.38, SD Main Office, microfilm MA–554, IfZ, Munich.

8. Werner T. Angress, "Die 'Judenfrage' im Spiegel amtlicher Berichte 1935," in *Das Unrechtsregime: Internationale Forschung über den Nationalsozialismus*, vol. 2, *Verfolgung, Exil, belasteter Neubeginn*, ed. Ursula Büttner et al. (Hamburg, 1986), p. 29.

9. Commander of SD main region Rhine to SS Gruppenführer Heissmeyer, Koblenz, 3.4.1935, SD-Oberabschnitt Rhein, microfilm MA–392, IfZ, Munich.

10. Robert Weltsch, "A Goebbels Speech and a Goebbels Letter," *LBIY* 10 (1965), p. 281.

11. Ibid., pp. 282–83.

12. Ibid., p. 285.

13. Ibid. (Misprinted as "West-end" in Weltsch's text).

14. Michael H. Kater, *Different Drummers: Jazz in the Culture of Nazi Germany* (New York, 1992), p. 43.

15. Steinweis, "Hans Hinkel," p. 215.

16. Report of the Police Directorate Munich, April/Mai 1935 (Geheimes Staatsarchiv, Munich, MA 104990); Fa 427/2, IfZ, Munich, pp. 24ff.

17. Jochen Klepper, *Unter dem Schatten deiner Flügel: Aus den Tagebüchern der Jahre 1932–1942* (Stuttgart, 1983), p. 269.

18. Ibid., p. 270.

19. Albert Fischer, *Hjalmar Schacht und Deutschlands "Judenfrage": Der "Wirtschaftsdiktator" und die Vertreibung der Juden aus der deutschen Wirtschaft* (Cologne, 1995), pp. 154–55.

20. Adolf Hitler, *Speeches and Proclamations, 1932–1945*, ed. Max Domarus, trans. Chris Wilcox and Mary Fran Gilbert, vol. 2, *The Chronicle of a Dictatorship, 1935–1938* (Wauconda, IL, 1992), pp. 706–7.

21. Jeremy Noakes and Geoffrey Pridham, eds., *Nazism 1919–1945: A Documentary Reader.* 3 vols. (Exeter, England, 1983), vol. 2, p. 463.

22. Robert L. Koehl, *The Black Corps: The Structure and Power Struggles of the Nazi SS* (Madison, WI, 1983), p. 102.

23. Bernhard Lösener, "Als Rassereferent im Reichsministerium des Innern," *VfZ* 3 (1961): p. 276.

24. Führer's Deputy Circular No 228/35, 2.12.1935, Stellvertreter des Führers (Anordnungen . . .), Db 15.02, IfZ, Munich.

25. Michael R. Burleigh and Wolfgang Wippermann; *The Racial State* (Cambridge, MA, 1991), p. 49.

26. Ibid.

27. David Bankier, *The Germans and the Final Solution: Public Opinion under Nazism* (Oxford, 1992), p. 78.

28. Ibid., p. 79.

29. Gestapa to all State police offices, 24.11.35, Ortspolizeibehörde Göttingen, microfilm MA–172, IfZ, Munich.

30. Gestapa to all State police offices, 4.4.1936, ibid.

31. Some Gestapo reports reported greater pessimism among the Jews and an urge to emigrate, also to Palestine. See Franz Josef Heyen,

*Nationalsozialismus im Alltag: Quellen zur Geschichte des Nationalsozi-
alismus vornehmlich im Raum Mainz-Koblenz-Trier* (Boppard am Rhein,
1967), pp. 138–39.

32. Margarete T. Edelheim-Mühsam, "Die Haltung der jüdischen Presse ge-
genüber der nationalsozialistischen Bedrohung," in *Deutsches Judentum:
Aufstieg und Krise,* ed. Robert Weltsch (Stuttgart, 1963), pp. 376–77.

33. Claudia Koonz, *Mothers in the Fatherland: Women, the Family and Nazi
Politics* (New York, 1987), p. 358.

34. Lucy S. Dawidowicz, *The War Against the Jews, 1933–1945* (New York,
1975), p. 178.

35. Charlotte Beradt, *Das Dritte Reich des Traums* (Frankfurt am Main,
1981), p. 98.

36. Ibid.

37. Ibid., p. 104.

38. Lion Feuchtwanger and Arnold Zweig, *Briefwechsel 1933–1958,* vol. 1
(Frankfurt am Main, 1986), p. 97.

39. C. G. Jung, "Civilization in Transition," in *Collected Works,* vol. 10
(New York, 1964), p. 166.

40. Ernst L. Freud, ed., *The Letters of Sigmund Freud and Arnold Zweig*
(New York, 1970), p. 110.

41. Kurt Tucholsky, *Politische Briefe* (Reinbek/Hamburg, 1969), pp.
117–23.

CHAPTER 3: IDEOLOGY AND CARD INDEX

1. Goebbels, *Tagebücher,* part 1, vol. 3, p. 55.

2. Ibid., p. 351.

3. Deborah E. Lipstadt, *Beyond Belief: The American Press and the Coming of
the Holocaust 1933–1945* (New York, 1986), p. 80.

4. Gulie Ne'eman Arad, "The American Jewish Leadership's Response"
(Ph.D. diss., Tel Aviv University, 1994), pp. 418–19.

5. *Der Parteitag der Arbeit vom 6 bis 13 September 1937: Offizieller Bericht über
den Verlauf des Reichsparteitages mit sämtlichen Kongressreden* (Munich,
1938), p. 157.

6. Hitler, *Speeches and Proclamations,* p. 938.

7. Richard Gutteridge, "German Protestantism and the Jews in the
Third Reich," in *Judaism and Christianity under the Impact of National*

Socialism, ed. Dov Kulka and Paul R. Mendes-Flohr (Jerusalem, 1987), p. 238. See also Gutteridge, *Open Thy Mouth for the Dumb! The German Evangelical Church and the Jews 1879–1950* (Oxford, 1976), pp. 158ff.

8. Gutteridge, *Open thy Mouth for the Dumb!*, pp. 159–60.

9. II.112 to II.11, 15.6.37, Sicherheitsdienst des Reichsführers SS, SD Hauptamt, Abt. II 112, microfilm MA–554, IfZ, Munich.

10. Michael Wildt, *Die Judenpolitik des SD 1935 bis 1938* (Munich, 1995), pp. 66–67.

11. For the most complete investigation of this subject, see Reiner Pommerin, *Sterilisierung der "Rheinlandbastarde": Das Schicksal einer farbigen deutschen Minderheit 1918–1937* (Düsseldorf, 1979).

12. Helma Kaden et al., eds., *Dokumente des Verbrechens: Aus Akten des Dritten Reiches, 1933–1945* (Berlin, 1993), vol. 1, pp. 83ff.

13. Ernst Klee, *"Euthanasie" im NS-Staat: Die Vernichtung "lebensunwerten Lebens"* (Frankfurt am Main, 1985), p. 61.

14. Hans Mommsen and Susanne Willems, eds., *Herrschaftsalltag im Dritten Reich: Studien und Texte* (Düsseldorf, 1988), p. 446.

15. Friedlander and Milton, *Archives of the Holocaust*, vol. 20, pp. 85–87, and *Akten der Parteikanzlei der NSDAP* (abstracts), part 1, vol. 1, p. 245.

16. Reich Minister of Education . . . 25.11.1936, Reichsministerium für Wissenschaft . . . , microfilm MA 103/1, IfZ, Munich.

17. Ibid., 19.4.1937.

18. Wilhelm Grau to State Secretary Kunisch, Reich Ministry of Education . . . , ibid., 18.2.1936.

19. Deputy Führer to the Reich Minister of the Interior, ibid., 15.10.1936.

20. Hanke, *Zur Geschichte der Juden in München*, pp. 139–40.

21. Kommission zur Erforschung der Geschichte der Frankfurter Juden, ed., *Dokumente zur Geschichte der Frankfurter Juden 1933–1945* (Frankfurt am Main, 1963), p. 163.

22. *Chronik der Stadt Stuttgart 1933–1945* (Stuttgart, 1982), vol. 3, p. 354.

23. Ibid., p. 368.

24. Peter Hayes, "Big Business and Aryanisation in Germany 1933–1939," in *Jahrbuch für Antisemitismusforschung* 3 (1994): pp. 260–61.

25. Wilhelm Treue, "Hitlers Denkschrift zum Vierjahresplan," *VfZ* 3 (1955).

26. Hitler, *Speeches and Proclamations*, p. 1057.

CHAPTER 4: RADICALIZATION

1. Peter Gay, *Freud: A Life for Our Time* (New York, 1988), p. 628.

2. F. L. Carstens, *Faschismus in Österreich: Von Schönerer zu Hitler* (Munich, 1978), p. 233.

3. Wildt, *Die Judenpolitik des SD*, pp. 52–53.

4. Götz Aly and Susanne Heim, *Vordenker der Vernichtung: Auschwitz und die deutschen Pläne für eine neue europäische Ordnung* (Hamburg, 1991), p. 33.

5. The State Commissary for Private Business (Walter Rafelsberger) to Heinrich Himmler, 14.8.1939, Persönlicher Stab des Reichsführers SS, microfilm MA–290, IfZ, Munich.

6. Heinz Höhne, *The Order of the Death's Head: The Story of Hitler's SS* (New York, 1970), p. 337.

7. Gordon J. Horwitz, *In the Shadow of Death: Living Outside the Gates of Mauthausen* (London, 1991), pp. 13–14.

8. Henry L. Feingold, *Bearing Witness: How America and Its Jews Responded to the Holocaust* (Syracuse, NY, 1995), p. 75.

9. *Foreign Relations of the United States, 1938*, vol. 1 (Washington, DC, 1950), pp. 740–41.

10. Shlomo Z. Katz, "Public Opinion in Western Europe and the Evian Conference of July 1938," *Yad Vashem Studies 9* (1973): p. 106.

11. Ibid., p. 108.

12. Ibid., p. 111.

13. Ibid., p. 113.

14. Ibid., p. 114.

15. Heinz Boberach, ed., *Meldungen aus dem Reich: Die geheimen Lageberichte des Sicherheitsdienstes der SS 1938–1945*, vol. 2 (Herrsching, 1984), p. 23.

16. David S. Wyman, *Paper Walls: America and the Refugee Crisis 1938–1941* (New York, 1985), p. 50.

17. Eliahu Ben-Elissar, *La Diplomatie du IIIe Reich et les Juifs, 1933–1939* (Paris, 1969), p. 251.

18. Adolf Hitler, *Reden und Proklamationen, 1932–1945: Kommentiert von einem deutschen Zeitgenossen*, ed. Max Domarus. 4 vols. (Munich 1965), vol. 2, p. 899.

19. Meir Michaelis, *Mussolini and the Jews: German-Italian Relations and the Jewish Question in Italy 1922–1945* (London, 1978), p. 191.

20. Georges Passelecq and Bernard Suchecky, *L'Encyclique cachée de Pie XI: Une occasion manquée de l'Église face à l'antisémitisme* (Paris, 1995), pp. 180–81.

21. Sam H. Shirakawa, *The Devil's Music Master. The Controversial Life and Career of Wilhelm Furtwängler* (New York, 1992), p. 221.

22. Raul Hilberg, *The Destruction of the European Jews* (Chicago, 1961), p. 82.

23. Walk, *Das Sonderrecht*, p. 234.

24. Reich Chamber of Physicians to Ministry of Education, 3.10.38, Reichsministerium für Wissenschaft . . . , microfilm MA 103/1, IfZ, Munich.

25. Avraham Barkai, *From Boycott to Annihilation: The Economic Struggle of German Jews 1933–1943* (Hanover, NH, 1989), p. 129.

26. Ibid., p. 118.

27. Hugh R. Wilson to Secretary of State, June 22, 1938, in *The Holocaust: Selected Documents*, 18 vols., ed. John Mendelsohn (New York, 1982), vol. 1, pp. 139–40.

28. Bella Fromm, *Blood and Banquets: A Berlin Social Diary* (London, 1943; reprint, New York, 1990), p. 274.

29. Goebbels, *Tagebücher*, part 1, vol. 3, p. 490.

30. Conseil Fédéral, "Procès-verbal de la séance du 28 mars 1938," *Documents Diplomatiques Suisses*, vol. 12 (1.1.1937–31.12.1938), ed. under the direction of Oscar Gauye, Gabriel Imboden and Daniel Bourgeois (Bern, 1994).

31. For these details see Carl Ludwig, *Die Flüchtlingspolitik der Schweiz in den Jahren 1933 bis 1945: Bericht an den Bundesrat zuhanden der eidgenössischen Räte* (Bern, 1957), pp. 124ff.

32. Ben-Elissar, *La Diplomatie*, p. 286.

33. Michael R. Marrus, "The Strange Story of Herschel Grynszpan," *American Scholar* 57, no.1 (Winter 1987–88): pp. 70–71.

34. Ibid., pp. 71–72.

CHAPTER 5: A BROKEN REMNANT

1. Paul Sauer, ed., *Dokumente über die Verfolgung der jüdischen Bürger in Baden-Württemberg durch das Nationalsozialistische Regime 1933–1945*, vol. 2 (Stuttgart, 1966), pp. 25–28.

2. "50, dann 75 Synagogen brennen: Tagebuchschreiber Goebbels über die Reichskristallnacht," *Der Spiegel*, July 13, 1992, p. 126.

3. Walter Buch to Göring, 13.2.1939, Herbert Michaelis and Ernst Schraepler, eds., *Ursachen und Folgen: Vom deutschen Zusammenbruch 1918 und 1945 bis zur staatlichen Neuordnung Deutschlands in der Gegenwart: Eine Urkunden- und Dokumentsammlung zur Zeitgeschichte*, vol. 12 (Berlin, n.d.), p. 582.

4. Goebbels, "50, dann 75 Synagogen brennen," pp. 126–28.

5. Hermann Graml, *Anti-Semitism in the Third Reich* (Cambridge, MA, 1992), p. 13.

6. Goebbels, "50, dann 75 Synagogen brennen," pp. 126–28.

7. *Nazi Conspiracy and Aggression* (Washington, DC, 1946), vol. 5, doc. no. 3051–PS, pp. 799–800.

8. Michalka, *Das Dritte Reich*, vol. 1, p. 165.

9. Mayor of Ingolstadt to the Government of Upper Bavaria, Munich, 1.12.1938, Monatsberichte des Stadtrats Ingolstadt, 1929–1939 (Stadtarchiv Ingolstadt No. A XVI/142), IfZ, Fa 411.

10. Gauye, Imboden, and Bourgeois, *Documents Diplomatiques Suisses*, p. 1020.

11. Alfons Heck, *The Burden of Hitler's Legacy* (Frederick, CO, 1988), p. 62.

12. Ulrich von Hassell, *Die Hassell-Tagebücher 1938–1944: Aufzeichnungen vom Andern Deutschland*, ed. Klaus Peter Reiss and Freiherr Friedrich Hiller von Gaertringen (Berlin, 1988), p. 70.

13. Michaelis and Schraepler, *Ursachen*, vol. 12, p. 581.

14. Ibid., p. 600.

15. Walk, *Das Sonderrecht*, pp. 254–55.

16. Ibid., p. 254.

17. *Trial of Major War Criminals Before the International Military Tribunal* [*IMT*], 42 vols. (Nuremberg, 1948), vol. 28, pp. 509–10.

18. Ibid., pp. 536–39.

19. Ibid.

20. Herbert Freeden, "Das Ende der jüdischen Presse in Nazideutschland." *Bulletin des Leo Baeck Instituts* 65 (1983), p. 8.

21. Ibid., p. 9.

22. Lynn H. Nicholas, *The Rape of Europa: The Fate of Europe's Treasures in the Third Reich and the Second World War* (New York, 1994), p. 43.

23. Susanne Heim and Götz Aly, "Staatliche Ordnung und 'Organische Lösung': Die Rede Hermann Görings 'über die Judenfrage' vom 6 Dezember 1938," *Jahrbuch für Antisemitismusforschung* 2 (1993): pp. 393ff.

24. Detlev J. K. Peukert, *Inside Nazi Germany: Conformity, Opposition and Racism in Everyday Life* (New Haven, 1987), p. 59.

25. Saul Friedländer, *Pius XII und das Dritte Reich* (Hamburg, 1965), p. 70.

26. Klaus Schwabe, Rolf Reichardt, and Reinhard Hauf, eds., *Gerhard Ritter: Ein politischer Historiker in seinen Briefen* (Boppard am Rhein, 1984), p. 339.

27. Ibid., pp. 769ff.

28. Bertram to Rust, 16.11.1938, *Akten deutscher Bischöfe*, vol. 4, *1936–1939*, ed. Ludwig Volk (Mainz, 1981), pp. 592–93.

29. Goebbels, *Tagebücher*, part 1, vol. 3, p. 532.

30. Lipstadt, *Beyond Belief*, p. 99.

31. Arthur Morse, *While Six Million Died: A Chronicle of American Apathy* (New York, 1968), pp. 270ff.

32. Vicki Caron, "Prelude to Vichy: France and the Jewish Refugees in the Era of Appeasement," *Journal of Contemporary History* 20 (1985), p. 163.

33. George F. Kennan, *From Prague after Munich: Diplomatic Papers 1938–1940* (Princeton, 1968), p. 86.

34. Hitler, *Reden und Proklamationen*, part 1, vol. 2, p. 1055.

35. Ibid., pp. 1056–58.

36. Philippe Burrin, *Hitler and the Jews: The Genesis of the Holocaust* (New York, 1994), pp. 60–61.

37. Pätzold, *Verfolgung*, p. 222.

38. Arad, Gutman, and Margalioth, *Documents on the Holocaust*, p. 140.

39. Konrad Kwiet, "Forced Labor of German Jews in Nazi Germany," *LBIY* 36 (1991): p. 392.

40. Norbert Frei, *Der Führerstaat: Nationalsozialistische Herrschaft 1933 bis 1945* (Munich, 1987), p. 86.

CHAPTER 6: POLAND UNDER GERMAN RULE

1. Victor Klemperer, *I Will Bear Witness: A Diary of the Nazi Years, 1933–41*, vol. 1 (New York, 1998), p. 306.

2. Ibid.

3. Chaim Aron Kaplan, *Scroll of Agony: The Warsaw Diary of Chaim A. Kaplan*, ed. Abraham I. Katsh (Bloomington, IN, 1999), p. 19.

4. Dawid Sierakowiak, *The Diary of Dawid Sierakowiak* (New York, 1996), p. 36.

5. Adam Czerniaków, *The Warsaw Diary of Adam Czerniaków*, ed. Raul Hilberg, Stanislaw Staron, and Josef Kermisz (New York, 1979), p. 74.

6. Noakes and Pridham, *Nazism*, vol. 3 (Exeter, England, 1997), p. 319.

7. Franz Halder, *Kriegstagebuch: Tägliche Aufzeichnungen des Chefs des Generalstabes des Heeres, 1939–1942*, ed. Hans Adolf Jacobsen (Stuttgart, 1962–64), vol. 1, p. 107.

8. Richard Breitman, *The Architect of Genocide: Himmler and the Final Solution* (New York, 1991), p. 73.

9. Pätzold, *Verfolgung*, p. 234.

10. Hitler, *Reden und Proklamationen* (Leonberg, 1987–88), part 1, vol. 2, p. 1340.

11. Ibid., p. 1342.

12. Ibid., vol. 3, pp. 1442 and 1443.

13. Shimon Huberband, "The Destruction of the Synagogues in Lodz," in *Lodz Ghetto: Inside a Community under Siege*, eds. Alan Adelson and Robert Lapides (New York, 1983), p. 70.

14. Alexander B. Rossino, "Destructive Impulses: German Soldiers and the Conquest of Poland," *Holocaust and Genocide Studies* 7, no. 3 (1997): p. 356.

15. Sierakowiak, *Diary*, p. 54.

16. Zygmunt Klukowski, *Diary from the Years of Occupation, 1939–44*, edited by Andrew Klukowski and Helen Klukowski May (Urbana, 1993), p. 40.

17. Pätzold, *Verfolgung*, pp. 236ff.

18. Dieter Pohl, *Von der "Judenpolitik" zum Judenmord: Der Distrikt Lublin des Generalgouvernements, 1939–1944* (Frankfurt am Main, 1993), p. 52.

19. Kaden et al., eds., *Dokumente des Verbrechens: Aus Akten des Dritten Reiches, 1933–1945*, pp. 176–77.

20. Kaplan, *Scroll of Agony*, p. 57.

21. Isaiah Trunk, *Judenrat: The Jewish Councils in Eastern Europe under Nazi Occupation* (New York, 1972), p. 244.

22. Antony Polonsky and Norman Davies, eds., *Jews in Eastern Poland and the USSR, 1939–46* (New York, 1991), p. 28.

23. David Engel, "An Early Account of Polish Jewry under Nazi and Soviet Occupation Presented to the Polish Government-In-Exile, February 1940," *Jewish Social Studies* 45 (1983): p. 11.

24. Anna Landau-Czajka, "The Jewish Question in Poland: Views Expressed in the Catholic Press between the Two World Wars," *Polin: Studies in Polish Jewry* 11 (1998): p. 263.

25. Ibid., p. 265.

26. Walk, *Das Sonderrecht*, p. 305.

27. Pätzold, *Verfolgung*, p. 235.

28. Walk, *Das Sonderrecht*, p. 307.

29. Klemperer, *I Will Bear Witness*, vol. 1, p. 321.

30. Philip Friedman, *Roads to Extinction: Essays on the Holocaust*, ed. Ada June Friedman (New York, 1980), p. 336.

31. Emanuel Ringelblum, *Notes from the Warsaw Ghetto: The Journal of Emanuel Ringelblum*, ed. Jacob Sloan (New York, 1974), pp. 47–48.

32. Raul Hilberg and Stanislaw Staron, introduction to Czerniaków, *Warsaw Diary* , p. 152.

33. Apolinary Hartglas, "How Did Czerniaków Become Head of the Warsaw Judenrat?," *Yad Vashem Bulletin* 15 (1964), pp. 4–7.

CHAPTER 7: A NEW EUROPEAN ORDER

1. Otto Dov Kulka and Eberhard Jäckel, *Die Juden in den geheimen NS-Stimmungsberichten 1933–1945* (Düsseldorf, 2004), p. 439.

2. John Lukacs, *The Duel: Hitler vs. Churchill: 10 May–31 July 1940* (Oxford, 1992), pp. 206ff.

3. Mihail Sebastian, *Journal, 1935–1944* (Chicago, 2000), p. 297.

4. Kaplan, *Scroll of Agony*, p. 162.

5. Ibid., pp. 163–64.

6. Klemperer, *I Will Bear Witness*, vol.1, p.349.

7. Helmut Krausnick, ed., "Einige Gedanken über die Behandlung der Fremdvölkischen im Osten," *Vierteljahrshefte für Zeitgeschichte (VfZ)* 5, no. 2 (1957): pp. 194ff.

8. *DGFP* Series D, vol. X, p. 113.

9. Röhm and Thierfelder, *Juden*, vol. 3, part 2, p. 193.

10. Walk, *Das Sonderrecht*. p. 325.

11. Ibid., p. 327.

12. Ibid., p. 330.

13. Pätzold, *Verfolgung*, p. 324.

14. Klemperer, *I Will Bear Witness*, vol. 1, pp. 345–46.

15. Rebecca Rovit and Alvin Goldfarb, eds., *Theatrical Performance during the Holocaust: Texts, Documents, Memoirs* (Baltimore, 1999), p. 76.

16. Eric Rentschler, *The Ministry of Illusion: Nazi Cinema and Its Afterlife* (Cambridge, MA, 1996), pp. 153–54.

17. Josef Wulf, ed., *Teater und Film im Dritten Reich: Eine Dokumentation* (Frankfurt am Main, 1989), p. 410.

18. Hermann Glaser, "Film," in Wolfgang Benz, Hermann Graml, and Hermann Weiss, eds., *Enzyklopädie des Nationalsozialismus* (Stuttgart, 1997), p. 175.

19. Adelson and Lapides, *Lodz Ghetto*, p. 36.

20. Philippe Burrin, *France under the Germans: Collaboration and Compromise* (New York, 1996), p. 56.

21. Jeannine Verdés-Leroux, *Refus et violences: politique et littérature à l'extréme droite des années trente aux retombées de la Libération* (Paris, 1996), p. 164.

22. Jean-Marie Mayeur, "Les églises devant la Persécution des Juifs en France," in *La France et la question juive: 1940–1944*, Georges Wellers, André Kaspi, and Serge Klarsfeld (Paris, 1981), p. 151ff.

23. Renée Poznanski, *Jews in France during World War II* (Waltham, MA, 2001).

24. Röhm and Thierfelder, *Juden*, vol. 3, part 2, p. 270.

25. Benjamin Leo Wessels, *Ben's Story: Holocaust Letters with Selections from the Dutch Underground Press*, ed. Kees W. Bolle (Carbondale, IL, 2001), p. 21.

CHAPTER 8: A TIGHTENING NOOSE

1. Joseph Goebbels, *Die Tagebücher von Joseph Goebbels: Sämtliche Fragmente*, ed. Elke Fröhlich (Munich, 1998), part 1, vol. 9 (December 1940—July 1941), pp. 377–79.

2. Halder, *Kriegstagebuch*, vol. 2, pp. 21, 31, 32, 34, 36, mainly 49ff.

3. Saul Friedländer, *Prelude to Downfall: Hitler and the United States, 1939–41* (New York, 1967), pp. 165ff.

4. Ibid., p. 171.

5. Hitler, *Reden*, part 2, pp. 1663–64.

6. Jürgen Förster, "Operation Barbarossa as a War of Conquest and Annihilation," in *The Attack on the Soviet Union: Germany and the Second World War*, ed. Horst Boog (Oxford, 1998), p. 185.

7. Götz Aly, *"Final Solution": Nazi Population Policy and the Murder of the European Jews* (London, 1999), p. 172.

8. Andreas Hillgruber, *Staatsmänner und Diplomaten bei Hitler: Vertrauliche Aufzeichnungen über Unterredungen mit Vertretern des Auslandes* (Frankfurt am Main, 1967–70), vol. 1, pp. 573–74.

9. This measure was probably taken to allow for a maximum of emigration possibilities for Jews from the Reich and the Protectorate. As for the reference to the forthcoming "Final Solution," it was, at this stage, a vague and widely used formula referring to any range of possibilities.

10. Christopher R. Browning, *The Path to Genocide: Essays on Launching the Final Solution* (Cambridge, 1992), pp. 44–46.

11. Donald L. Niewyk, ed., *Fresh Wounds: Early Narratives of Holocaust Survival* (Chapel Hill, 1998), p. 174.

12. Sierakowiak, *Diary*, p. 89.

13. Lucjan Dobroszycki, ed., *The Chronicle of the Lodz Ghetto, 1941–1944* (New Haven, 1984), p. 6.

14. Władysław Bartoszewski, "The Martyrdom and Struggle of the Jews in Warsaw Under German Occupation 1939–1943," in *The Jews in Warsaw: A History*, ed. Władysław T. Bartoszewski and Antony Polonsky (Oxford, 1991), p. 314.

15. Kaplan, *Scroll of Agony*, p. 245.

16. Israel Gutman, *The Jews of Warsaw, 1939–1943: Ghetto, Underground, Revolt* (Bloomington, IN, 1982), p. 71.

17. Ringelblum, *Notes*, pp. 204–5.

18. Marcel Reich-Ranicki, *The Author of Himself: The Life of Marcel Reich-Ranicki* (London, 2001), p. 153.

19. Ibid., p. 159.

20. Lucjan Dobroszycki, ed., *The Chronicle of the Lódz Ghetto, 1941–1944* (New Haven, 1984) , 25ff. and 35.

21. Sierakowiak, *Diary*, p. 88.

22. Ibid., p. 89.

23. Arad et al, *Documents on the Holocaust*, p. 230.

24. Czerniaków, *Warsaw Diary*, p. 233.

25. Hersch Wasser, "Daily Entries of Hersch Wasser," ed. Joseph Kermish, in *Yad Vashem Studies* 15 (1983): p. 266.

26. Trunk, *Judenrat*, pp. 499–500.

27. Mary Berg, *Warsaw Ghetto, A Diary*, ed. Sh. L. Shnayderman (New York, 1945), pp. 45–46.

28. Hitler, *Reden*, part 2, pp. 1663–64.

29. Sebastian, *Journal*, p. 316.

30. Renée Poznanski, *Etre juif en France pendant la Seconde Guerre mondiale* (Paris, 1994), p. 103.

31. Simon Schwarzfuchs, *Aux prises avec Vichy: Histoire politique des Juifs de France, 1940–1944* (Paris, 1998), pp. 90ff.

32. Bob Moore, *Victims and Survivors: The Nazi Persecution of the Jews in the Netherlands, 1940–1945* (London, 1997), p. 70.

33. Gordon J. Horwitz, *In the Shadow of Death: Living Outside the Gates of Mauthausen* (New York, 1990), pp. 52–53.

34. Ibid., p. 53.

35. Etty Hillesum, *An Interrupted Life: The Diaries of Etty Hillesum, 1941–1943* (New York, 1983), pp. 23–24.

36. Melissa Müller, *Anne Frank: The Biography* (New York, 1998), p. 174.

37. Quoted in Burkhart Schneider, Pierre Blet, and Angelo Martini, eds., *Die Briefe Pius' XII. An die deutschen Bischöfe 1939–1944* (Mainz, 1966), p. 134 n 4.

38. Hillel Levine, *In Search of Sugihara: The Elusive Japanese Diplomat Who Risked His Life to Rescue 10,000 Jews from the Holocaust* (New York, 1996), p. 253.

CHAPTER 9: THE EASTERN ONSLAUGHT

1. Karel C. Berkhoff, *Harvest of Despair: Life and Death in Ukraine under Nazi Rule* (Cambridge, MA, 2004), pp. 75–76.

2. Ibid., p. 77.

3. Dobroszycki, *Chronicle*, p. 62.

4. Sierakowiak, *Diary*, p. 105.

5. Ibid.

6. Sebastian, *Journal*, p. 370.

7. Herman Kruk, *The Last Days of the Jerusalem of Lithuania: Chronicles from the Vilna Ghetto and the Camps, 1939–1944*, ed. Benjamin Harshav (New Haven, 2002), pp. 46–47.

8. Czerniaków, *Warsaw Diary* , p. 251.

9. Ibid., p. 256.

10. Klemperer, *I Will Bear Witness*, vol. 1, pp. 390–91.

11. Nuremberg doc. L–221, International Military Tribunal, *Trial of the Major War Criminals Before the International Military Tribunal, Nuremberg, 14 November 1945–1 October 1946* (New York, 1971), vol. 38, pp. 68–94.

12. Bianka Pietrow-Ennker, "Die Sowjetunion in der Propaganda des Dritten Reiches: Das Beispiel der Wochenschau," *Militärgeschichtliche Mitteilungen* 46, no. 2 (1989): pp. 79ff. and 108–9.

13. Joseph Goebbels, *Die Zeit ohne Beispiel: Reden und Aufsätze aus den Jahren 1939/40/41* (Munich, 1941), pp. 526–31.

14. Ortwin Buchbender and Reinhold Sterz, eds., *Das Andere Gesicht Des Krieges: Deutsche Feldpostbriefe 1939–1945* (Munich, 1982), p. 73.

15. Walter Manoschek, ed., *"Es gibt nur eines für das Judentum—Vernichtung: Das Judenbild in deutschen Soldatenbriefen, 1939–1944* (Hamburg, 1997), p. 32.

16. Ibid., p 33.

17. Shimon Redlich, *Together and Apart in Brzezany: Poles, Jews, and Ukrainians, 1919–1945* (Bloomington, IN, 2002), pp. 114ff.

18. Isaac Rudashevski, *The Diary of the Vilna Ghetto, June 1941–April 1943*, ed. Percy Matenko (Tel Aviv, 1973), pp. 35–36.

19. Jean Ancel, "The Romanian Way of Solving the Jewish Problem in Bessarabia and Bukovina, June-July 1941," *Yad Vashem Studies* 19 (1988): p. 190.

20. Jonathan Steinberg, *All or Nothing: The Axis and the Holocaust, 1941–1943* (London, 1990), p. 30.

21. Ibid.

22. John Cornwell, *Hitler's Pope: The Secret History of Pius XII* (New York, 1999), p. 255.

23. Eugen Kogon, Hermann Langbein, and Adalbert Rückerl, eds., *Nazi Mass Murder: A Documentary History of the Use of Poison Gas* (New Haven, 1993), pp. 54ff and 60ff.

24. Klemperer, *I Will Bear Witness*, vol. 1, p. 434.

25. Ibid., p. 445.

26. David Bankier, *The Germans and the Final Solution: Public Opinion under Nazism* (Oxford, 1992), p. 129.

27. Lieven Saerens, "Antwerp's Attitude Toward the Jews from 1918 to 1940 and Its Implications for the Period of Occupation," in *Belgium and the Holocaust: Jews, Belgians, Germans*, edited by Dan Michman (Jerusalem, 1998), pp. 192–93.

CHAPTER 10: THE "FINAL SOLUTION"

1. *Ostland* was the name given to the German-occupied territories of the Baltic states (Estonia, Latvia, and Lithuania), Belarus, and parts of Ukraine and Russia.

2. Sophie Dubnov-Erlich, *The Life and World of S. M. Dubnov: Diaspora Nationalism and Jewish History* (New York, 1991), pp. 246–47.

3. Friedländer, *Prelude to Downfall*, pp. 290ff.

4. Christopher R. Browning, *Nazi Policy, Jewish Workers, German Killers* (Cambridge, 2000), p. 38.

5. Sierakowiak, *Diary*, p. 136.

6. Ibid., p. 138.

7. Kaplan, *Scroll of Agony*, p. 272.

8. Jacques Biélinky, *Journal, 1940–1942: Un journaliste juif à Paris sous l'Occupation*, ed. Renée Poznanski (Paris, 1992), p. 156.

9. A. Scott Berg, *Lindbergh* (New York, 1998), pp. 426–27.

10. Ibid., p. 427.

11. Goebbels, *Tagebücher*, part 2, vol. 1, p. 417.

12. Hitler, *Reden*, part 2, vol. 4, pp. 1756–57.

13. Ibid., p. 1759.

14. Goebbels, *Tagebücher*, part 2, vol. 2, pp. 498ff.

15. Heinrich Himmler. *Der Dienstkalender Heinrich Himmlers 1941/42*, edited by Peter Witte et al (Hamburg, 1999), p. 194.

16. Bernd Rother, "Franco und die deutsche Judenverfolgung," *Vierteljahrshefte für Zeitgeschichte (VfZ)* 46, no. 2 (1998), pp. 189ff and particularly 195.

17. Peter Longerich, *Politik der Vernichtung: Eine Gesamtdarstellung der nationalsozialistischen Judenverfolgung* (Munich, 1998), p. 443.

18. Manoschek, *"Es gibt nur eines für das Judentum—Vernichtung,"* p. 45.

19. Ibid., p. 49.

20. Helmuth James von Moltke, *Letters to Freya: 1939–1945,* ed. Beate Ruhm von Oppen (New York, 1990), pp. 155–56.

21. Ibid., p. 175.

22. Ibid., p. 183.

23. Hassell, *Die Hassell-Tagebücher 1938–1944: Aufzeichnungen vom Andern Deutschland* (Berlin, 1988), p. 277.

24. Horwitz, *In the Shadow of Death,* p. 35.

25. Klee, *"Euthanasie" im NS-Staat,* p. 349.

26. Uwe Dietrich Adam, *Judenpolitik im Dritten Reich* (Düsseldorf, 1972), pp. 292ff and 299–301.

27. Ludwig Volk, ed., *Akten deutscher Bischöfe über die Lage der Kirche, 1933–1945,* vol. 5 (Mainz, 1983), pp. 555ff.

28. Ursula Büttner, " 'The Jewish Problem Becomes a Christian Problem': German Protestants and the Persecution of the Jews in the Third Reich," in *Probing the Depths of German Antisemitism: German Society and the Persecution of the Jews, 1933–1941,* ed. David Bankier (New York, 2000), pp. 454ff.

29. Tuvia Friling, *Arrow in the Dark: David Ben-Gurion, the Yishuv's Leadership and Rescue Efforts during the Holocaust,* 2 vols. (Tel Aviv, 1998), vol. 1, p. 45.

30. Sierakowiak, *Diary*, p. 141.

31. Ibid., p. 144.

32. Ibid., p. 142.

33. Dobroszycki, *Chronicle,* pp. 80–81.

34. Ibid., p. 109.

35. Ibid., p. 113.

36. Oskar Rosenfeld, *In the Beginning Was the Ghetto: Notebooks from Lodz,* ed. Von Hanno Loewy (Evanston, IL, 2002), p. 32.

37. Walter Laqueur, *The Terrible Secret: Suppression of the Truth about Hitler's "Final Solution"* (Boston, 1981), p. 130.

38. Yitzhak Zuckerman, *A Surplus of Memory. Chronicle of the Warsaw Ghetto Uprising,* ed. Barbara Harshav (Berkeley, 1993), pp. 156ff.

39. Rudashevski, *Diary*, p. 46.

40. Israel Gutman, *Resistance: The Warsaw Ghetto Uprising* (Boston, 1994), p. 103.

41. Zuckerman, *A Surplus of Memory*, pp. 153–54.

42 Sebastian, *Journal*, p. 458.

43. Klemperer, *I Will Bear Witness*, vol. 1, p. 456.

CHAPTER 11: TOTAL EXTERMINATION

1. Dalia Ofer, *Escaping the Holocaust: Illegal Immigration to the Land of Israel, 1939–1944* (New York, 1990), p. 158.

2. Bernard Wasserstein, *Britain and the Jews of Europe, 1939–1945* (London, 1979), pp. 145–46.

3. Sebastian, *Journal*, pp. 476–77.

4. Hitler, *Reden*, pp. 1828–29.

5. Kaplan, *Scroll of Agony*, p. 297.

6. David Bankier, "The Use of Antisemitism in Nazi Wartime Propaganda," in *The Holocaust and History: The Known, the Unknown, the Disputed and the Reexamined*, edited by Michael Berenbaum and Abraham J. Peck (Bloomington, IN, 1998), p. 45.

7. Ibid., pp. 45–46.

8. Ibid., p. 46.

9. For the full text of the conference, see Kurt Pätzold and Erika Schwarz, eds., *Tagesordnung Judenmord: Die Wannsee-Konferenz am 20. Januar 1942. Eine Dokumentation zur Organisation der "Endlösung"* (Berlin, 1992), pp. 102–12.

10. Sierakowiak, *Diary*, p. 148.

11. Browning, *Nazi Policy*, p. 74.

12. Goebbels, *Tagebücher*, part 2, vol. 4, p. 350.

13. Ibid., p. 351.

14. Ibid., p. 405.

15. Heinrich Himmler, *Heinrich Himmler: Geheimreden, 1933 bis 1945, und andere Ansprachen*, ed. Bradley F. Smith and Agnes F. Peterson (Frankfurt am Main, 1974), p. 159.

16. Nuremberg Doc. NO- 5574, reproduced in Tatiana Berenstein, ed., *Faschismus, Getto, Massenmord: Dokumentation über Ausrottung und*

Widerstand der Juden in Polen während des zweiten Weltkrieges (East Berlin, Rütten & Leoning, 1961), p. 303.

17. Egon Redlich, *The Terezin Diary of Gonda Redlich*, ed. Saul S. Friedman (Lexington, KY, 1992), pp. 3ff.

18. Ibid., p. 53.

19. Ibid., p. 61.

20. Ruth Kluger, *Still Alive: A Holocaust Girlhood Remembered* (New York, 2001), pp. 78–79.

21. Redlich, *Terezin Diary*, p. 61.

22. Gitta Sereny, *Into that Darkness: From Mercy Killing to Mass Murder* (London, 1974), p. 111.

23. Helmut Heiber, ed., *Akten der Partei-Kanzlei der NSDAP*, vol. 1, part 2, abstract no. 26106.

24. Klemperer, *I Will Bear Witness, 1942–1945*, vol. 2, p. 58.

25. Ibid., p. 52.

26. Ibid., p. 9.

27. Ibid., p. 28.

28. Ruth Andreas-Friedrich and June Barrows Mussey, *Berlin Underground, 1938–1945* (New York, 1947), pp. 77–78.

29. Hillesum, *Interrupted Life*, p. 93.

30. Ibid., p. 107.

31. Ibid., p. 122.

32. Pierre Drieu La Rochelle, *Journal, 1939–1945*, ed. Julien Hervier (Paris, 1992), p. 302.

33. Lucien Rebatet, *Les Décombres* (Paris, 1942), p. 605.

34. Frédéric Vitoux, *Céline: A Biography* (New York, 1992), p. 378.

35. David Carroll, *French Literary Fascism: Nationalism, Anti-Semitism, and the Ideology of Culture* (Princeton, 1995), p. 275.

36. Alexandra Zapruder, *Salvaged Pages: Young Writers' Diaries of the Holocaust* (New Haven, 2002), pp. 322–23.

37. Ibid., p. 325.

38. Ibid., p. 327.

39. Sierakowiak, *Diary*, p. 149.

40. Ibid., p. 151.

41. Zuckerman, *A Surplus of Memory*, pp. 177ff.

42. Janusz Korczak, *Ghetto Diary*, ed. Aaron Zeitlin (New York, 1978), p. 192.

CHAPTER 12: TOTAL EXTERMINATION

1. Raul Hilberg, ed., *Documents of Destruction: Germany and Jewry, 1933–1945* (Chicago, 1971), pp. 208ff.

2. Hitler, *Reden*, vol. 2, part 1, p. 1920.

3. Sebastian, *Journal*, p. 511.

4. Klemperer, *I Will Bear Witness*, vol. 2, p. 150.

5. Rudolf Höss, *Kommandant in Auschwitz: Autobiographische Aufzeichnungen*, edited by Martin Broszat (Stuttgart, 1958), p. 188.

6. J. Presser, *Ashes in the Wind: The Destruction of Dutch Jewry* (Detroit, 1988), p. 167.

7. Hillesum, *Interrupted Life*, p. 147.

8. Anne Frank, *The Diary of a Young Girl: The Definitive Edition*. ed. Otto Frank and Mirjam Pressler (New York, 1995), pp. 18ff and 21.

9. Presser, *Ashes in the Wind*, p. 182.

10. Ibid., p. 184.

11. Ibid.

12. Biélinky, *Journal*, pp. 232–33.

13. Michael R. Marrus and Robert O. Paxton, *Vichy France and the Jews* (New York, 1981), p. 255.

14. Georges Wellers, *De Drancy à Auschwitz* (Paris, 1946), pp. 55ff.

15. Renée Poznanski, "Jews and non-Jews in France during World War II: A Daily Life Perspective," in *Lessons and Legacies V: The Holocaust and Justice*, ed. Ronald Smeltser (Evanston, IL, 2002), p. 306.

16. Serge Klarsfeld, *Vichy-Auschwitz. Le rôle de Vichy dans la solution finale de la question juive en France*, vol. 1 (Paris, 1983), p. 280.

17. Friedländer, *Pius XII*, p. 115.

18. Krüger-Bulcke and Lehmann, *Akten*, series E, vol. 3, p. 125.

19. Ibid., p. 385.

20. Kaplan, *Scroll of Agony*, pp. 324–25.

21. Sierakowiak, *Diary*, pp. 219–20.

22. Jozef Zelkowicz, *In Those Terrible Days: Writings from the Lodz Ghetto*, ed. Michael Unger (Jerusalem, 2002), pp. 280–83.

23. Ibid., p. 280.

24. Friedman, *Roads to Extinction*, pp. 365–66.

25. Rudashevski, *Diary*, pp. 70–71.

26. Kruk, *The Last Days*, p. 389.

27. Ibid., pp. 421–22.

28. For the translation of Vendel's report, see Steven Kublik, *The Stones Cry Out* (New York, 1987).

29. David S. Wyman, *The Abandonment of the Jews: America and the Holocaust, 1941–1945* (New York, 1998), pp. 42ff.

30. Ibid., p. 51.

31. Wasserstein, *Britain and the Jews*, p. 172.

32. Ibid., p. 173.

33. Friedländer, *Pius XII*, p. 131.

34. Goebbels, *Tagebücher*, part 2, vol. 6, p. 508.

35. Martin Gilbert, *Auschwitz and the Allies* (New York, 1981), p. 105.

CHAPTER 13: TOTAL EXTERMINATION

1. Louise Jacobson and Nadia Kaluski-Jacobson, *Les Lettres de Louise Jacobson et de ses proches: Fresnes, Drancy, 1942–1943* (Paris, 1997), p. 141.

2. Ibid., pp. 41–42.

3. Noakes and Pridham, *Nazism*, vol. 4, pp. 490ff.

4. Sebastian, *Journal*, p. 546.

5. Klemperer, *I Will Bear Witness*, vol. 2, p. 202.

6. Noakes and Pridham, *Nazism*, vol. 4, p. 497.

7. Hillgruber, *Staatsmänner und Diplomaten bei Hitler*, vol. 2, pp. 256–57.

8. Primo Levi, *Survival in Auschwitz: The Nazi Assault on Humanity* (New York, 1996), p. 18.

9. Christopher R. Browning, *Collected Memories: Holocaust History and Postwar Testimony* (Madison, WI, 2003), p. 75.

10. Adalbert Rückerl, ed., *NS-Prozesse. Nach 25 Jahren Strafverfolgung: Möglichkeiten, Grenzen, Ergebnisse* (Karlsruhe, 1971), pp. 109–11.

11. Filip Müller, *Eyewitness Auschwitz: Three Years in the Gas Chambers* (Chicago, 1999), p. 12.

12. Levi, *Survival in Auschwitz*, pp. 19–20.

13. Kluger, *Still Alive*, p. 94.

14. Kogon, Langbein, and Rückerl, *Nazi Mass Murder*, p. 133.

15. Robert Jay Lifton and Amy Hackett, "Nazi Doctors," in *Anatomy of the Auschwitz Death Camp*, ed. Yisrael Gutman and Michael Berenbaum (Bloomington, IN, 1994), p. 313.

16. Danuta Czech, "The Auschwitz Prisoner Administration," in *Anatomy of the Auschwitz Death Camp*, ed. Yisrael Gutman and Michael Berenbaum (Bloomington, IN, 1994), p. 374.

17. Peter Hayes, "Auschwitz, Capital of the Holocaust," *Holocaust and Genocide Studies* 17, no. 2 (2003): p. 330.

18. Manoschek, *"Es gibt nur eines für das Judentum—Vernichtung,"* p. 63.

19. Höss, *Kommandant in Auschwitz*, p. 190.

20. Ibid., pp. 216–17.

21. Inge Scholl, *The White Rose: Munich, 1942–1943* (Middletown, CT, 1983), p. 78.

22. Ibid., p. 75.

23. Ibid., p. 76.

24. Richard Gutteridge, *Open Thy Mouth for the Dumb!*, pp. 353ff.

25. Gerlach, *And the Witnesses Were Silent*, p. 204.

26. Abraham Lewin, *A Cup of Tears: A Diary of the Warsaw Ghetto*, ed. Antony Polonsky (Oxford, 1988), p. 186.

27. Ibid., p. 188.

28. Ibid., p. 240.

29. Arad et al., *Documents on the Holocaust*, p. 292.

30. Emanuel Ringelblum, "Little Stalingrad defends itself," in *To Live with Honor and Die with Honor!—: Selected Documents from the Warsaw Ghetto Underground Archives "O.S." ("Oneg Shabath")*, edited by Joseph Kermish (Jerusalem, 1986), pp. 599–600.

31. "The Jewish Quarter of Warsaw Is No More!" in *The Stroop Report*, ed. Sybil Milton (New York, 1979), May 24, 1943, entry.

32. Ibid., p. 566.

33. Goebbels, *Tagebücher*, part 2, vol. 7, p. 454.

CHAPTER 14: TOTAL EXTERMINATION

1. Saul Friedländer, *Kurt Gerstein: The Ambiguity of Good* (New York, 1969), pp. 201ff.

2. Albert Speer, *Inside the Third Reich: Memoirs* (New York, 1970), p. 299.

3. Etty Hillesum, *Letters from Westerbork* (New York, 1986), p. 97.

4. Stanislao G. Pugliese, "Bloodless Torture: The Books of the Roman Ghetto Under the Nazi Occupation," in *The Holocaust and the Book:*

Destruction and Preservation, ed. Jonathan Rose (Amherst, MA, 2001), p. 53.

5. Friedländer, *Pius XII*, p. 208.

6. Krüger-Bulcke and Lehmann, *ADAP, Series E*, vol. 7, pp. 130–31.

7. Kluger, *Still Alive*, pp. 107–8.

8. Ibid., p. 107.

9. Jean-Claude Favez, *The Red Cross and the Holocaust* (Cambridge, 1999), p. 41.

10. Krüger-Bulcke and Lehmann, *ADAP, Series E*, vol. 8, pp. 153–54.

11. Martin Gilbert, introduction, to Avraham Tory, *Surviving the Holocaust: The Kovno Ghetto Diary*, ed. Martin Gilbert and Dina Porat (Cambridge, 1990), pp. 506–7.

12. Dobroszycki, *Chronicle*, pp. 422–23.

13. Ariel Hurwitz, "The Struggle Over the Creation of the War Refugee Board (WRB)," *Holocaust and Genocide Studies* 6 (1991): p. 19.

14. Gulie Ne'eman Arad, *America, Its Jews, and the Rise of Nazism* (Bloomington, IN, 2000), pp. 220ff.

15. Ibid.

16. Dina Porat, *The Blue and the Yellow Stars: The Zionist Leadership in Palestine and the Holocaust, 1939–1945* (Cambridge, MA, 1990), pp. 62–63.

17. Hillesum, *Interrupted Life*, pp. 220ff.

18. Hillesum, *Letters from Westerbork*, p. 146.

CHAPTER 15: THE END

1. Translated in Serge Klarsfeld, *Vichy-Auschwitz: Le rôle de Vichy dans la solution finale de la question juive en France*, 2 vols. (Paris, 1983–85), vol. 2, p. 382.

2. Frank, *The Diary of a Young Girl*, pp. 297–98.

3. Ibid., p. 298.

4. Noakes and Pridham, *Nazism*, p. 592.

5. Höss, *Kommandant in Auschwitz*, p. 152.

6. Eugene Levai, *Black Book on the Martyrdom of Hungarian Jewry* (Zurich, 1948), p. 232.

7. Michael J. Neufeld and Michael Berenbaum, eds., *The Bombing of*

Auschwitz: Should the Allies Have Attempted It? (New York, 2000), p. 250.

8. Lucy S. Dawidowicz, ed., *A Holocaust Reader* (New York, 1976), pp. 321ff.

9. Neufeld and Berenbaum, *The Bombing of Auschwitz,* p. 256.

10. Ibid., pp. 258–59.

11. Rosenfeld, *In the Beginning Was the Ghetto*, p. 281.

12. Kruk, *The Last Days*, p. 703.

13. Ibid., p. 704.

14. Ibid., p. 705.

15. Vojtěch Blodig, "Die letzte Phase der Entwicklung des Ghettos Theresienstadt," in Miroslav Kárni, Vojtěch Blodig, and Margita Kárná, eds., *Theresienstadt in der "Endlösung der Judenfrage"* (Prague, 1992), p. 274.

16. Redlich, *Terezin Diary*, p. 161.

17. Livia Rothkirchen, "The Situation of the Jews in Slovakia between 1939 and 1945," *Jahrbuch für Antisemitismusforschung* 7 (1998): p. 63.

18. Randolph L. Braham, *The Politics of Genocide. The Holocaust in Hungary* (Detroit, 2000), p. 184.

19. Krisztián Ungváry, *The Siege of Budapest: One Hundred Days in World War II* (Munich, 2005), p. 302.

20. Klemperer, *I Will Bear Witness*, vol. 2, p. 404.

21. Adolf Hitler, *Monologe im Führer-Hauptquartier 1941–1944*. Eds., Werner Jochmann and Heinrich Heim (Munich, 2000), pp. 412–13.

22. Hitler, *Reden*, p. 2226.

23. Filip Müller, *Eyewitness Auschwitz*, p. 171.

24. Levi, *Survival in Auschwitz*, p. 171.

25. Hitler, *Reden*, pp. 2223–24.

26. Günther Schwarberg, *The Murders at Bullenhuser Damm* (Bloomington, IN, 1984), pp. 37–41.

27. Hitler, *Reden*, p. 2226.

SELECTED BIBLIOGRAPHY

LETTERS, DIARIES, AND OTHER PRE-1945 LITERATURE

Adelson, Alan, and Robert Lapides, eds. *Lodz Ghetto: Inside a Community Under Siege.* New York, 1989.

Czerniaków, Adam. *The Warsaw Diary of Adam Czerniaków.* Edited by Raul Hilberg, Stanislaw Staron, and Josef Kermisz. New York, 1979.

Dobroszycki, Lucjan, ed. *The Chronicle of the Lódz Ghetto, 1941–1944.* New Haven, 1984.

Flinker, Moses. *Young Moshe's Diary: The Spiritual Torment of a Jewish Boy in Nazi Europe.* Edited by Shaul Esh and Geoffrey Wigoder. Jerusalem, 1971.

Frank, Anne. *The Diary of a Young Girl: The Definitive Edition.* Edited by Otto Frank and Mirjam Pressler. New York, 1995.

Hillesum, Etty. *An Interrupted Life: The Diaries of Etty Hillesum, 1941–1943.* New York, 1983.

———. *Letters from Westerbork.* New York, 1986.

Kaplan, Chaim Aron. *Scroll of Agony: The Warsaw Diary of Chaim A. Kaplan.* Edited by Abraham I. Katsh. Bloomington, IN, 1999.

Klemperer, Victor. *I Will Bear Witness: A Diary of the Nazi Years, 1933–1941,* Vol. 1. New York, 1998.

———. *I Will Bear Witness: A Diary of the Nazi Years, 1942–1945,* Vol. 2. New York, 1999.

Korzak, Janusz. *Ghetto Diary.* Edited by Aaron Zeitlin. New York, 1978.

Kruk, Hermann. *The Last Days of the Jerusalem of Lithuania: Chronicles from the Vilna Ghetto and the Camps, 1939–1944.* Edited by Benjamin Harshav. New Haven, 2002.

Lewin, Abraham. *A Cup of Tears: A Diary of the Warsaw Ghetto.* Edited by Antony Polonsky. Oxford, 1988.

Redlich, Egon. *The Terezin Diary of Gonda Redlich*. Edited by Saul S. Friedman. Lexington, KY, 1992.

Ringelblum, Emanuel. *Notes from the Warsaw Ghetto: The Journal of Emanuel Ringelblum*. Edited by Jacob Sloan. New York, 1974.

Rosenfeld, Oskar. *In the Beginning Was the Ghetto: Notebooks from Lódz*. Edited by Von Hanno Loewy. Evanston, IL, 2002.

Rubinowicz, Dawid. *The Diary of Dawid Rubinowicz*. Edmonds, WA, 1982.

Rudashevski, Isaac. *The Diary of the Vilna Ghetto, June 1941–April 1943*. Edited by Percy Matenko. Tel Aviv, 1973.

Sebastian, Mihail. *Journal, 1935–1944*. Chicago, 2000.

Sierakowiak, Dawid. *The Diary of Dawid Sierakowiak*. Edited by Alan Adelson. New York, 1996.

Tory, Avraham. *Surviving the Holocaust: The Kovno Ghetto Diary*. Edited by Martin Gilbert and Dina Porat. Cambridge, 1990.

POST-1945 LITERATURE

Allen, Michael Thad. *The Business of Genocide: SS, Slave Labor and the Concentration Camp*. Chapel Hill, NC, 2002.

Aly, Götz, ed. *Cleansing the Fatherland: Nazi Medicine and Racial Hygiene*. Baltimore, 1994.

———. *"Final Solution": Nazi Population Policy and the Murder of the European Jews*. New York, 1999.

Aly, Götz, and Susanne Heim. *Architects of Annihilation: Auschwitz and the Logic of Destruction*. Princeton, 2002.

Arad, Yitzhak. *Ghetto in Flames: The Struggle and Destruction of the Jews in Vilna in the Holocaust*. Jerusalem, 1980.

———. *Belzec, Sobibor, Treblinka: The Operation Reinhard Death Camps*. Bloomington, IN, 1987.

Arendt, Hannah. *Eichmann in Jerusalem: A Report on the Banality of Evil*. New York, 1963.

Baldwin, Peter, ed., *Reworking the Past: Hitler, the Holocaust and the Historians*. Boston, 1990.

Bankier, David. *The Germans and the Final Solution: Public Opinion under Nazism*. Oxford, 1992.

———. ed. *Probing the Depths of German Antisemitism: German Society and the Persecution of the Jews, 1933–1941*. New York, 2000.

Barkai, Avraham. *From Boycott to Annihilation: The Economic Struggle of German Jews, 1933–1943*. Hanover, NH, 1989.

Bartov, Omer. *Hitler's Army: Soldiers, Nazis, and War in the Third Reich*. New York, 1991.

———. *Murder in our Midst: The Holocaust, Industrial Killing, and Representation*. New York, 1996.

Bauer, Yehuda. *My Brother's Keeper: A History of the American Joint Distribution Committee 1929–1939*. Philadelphia, 1974.

———. *Jews for Sale? Nazi-Jewish Negotiations, 1933–1945*. New Haven, 1994.

———. *Rethinking the Holocaust*. New Haven, 2001.

Bauman, Zygmunt. *Modernity and the Holocaust*. New Haven, 2001.

Bergen, Doris L. *Twisted Cross: The German Christian Movement in the Third Reich*. Chapel Hill, NC, 1996.

Berkhoff, Karel C. *Harvest of Despair: Life and Death in Ukraine under Nazi Rule*. Cambridge, MA, 2004.

Birnbaum, Pierre. *Anti-semitism in France: A Political History from Léon Blum to the Present*. Oxford, 1992.

Bondy, Ruth. *"Elder of the Jews": Jakob Edelstein of Theresienstadt*. New York, 1989.

Braham, Randolph L. *The Politics of Genocide: The Holocaust in Hungary*. Abridged ed. Detroit, 2000.

Breitman, Richard. *The Architect of Genocide: Himmler and the Final Solution*. New York, 1991.

Broszat, Martin, and Saul Friedländer. *"A Controversy about the Historicization of National Socialism."* In *Reworking the Past: Hitler, the Holocaust and the Historians*. Edited by Peter Baldwin. Boston, 1990.

Browning, Christopher R. *Ordinary Men: Reserve Police Battalion 101 and the Final Solution in Poland*. New York, 1992.

———. *Nazi Policy, Jewish Workers, German Killers*. Cambridge, 2000.

———. *The Origins of the Final Solution: The Evolution of Nazi Jewish Policy, September 1939–March 1942*. Lincoln, NE, 2004.

Burleigh, Michael. *Death and Deliverance: "Euthanasia" in Germany c. 1900–1945*. Cambridge, 1994.

———. *The Third Reich: A New History*. London, 2000.

Burrin, Philippe. *Hitler and the Jews: The Genesis of the Holocaust*. London, 1994.

————. *France under the Germans: Collaboration and Compromise*. New York, 1996.

Cesarani, David. *The Final Solution: Origins and Implementation*. New York, 1994.

————. *Becoming Eichmann: Rethinking the Life, Crimes, and Trial of a "Desk Murderer."* New York, 2006.

Cohen, Richard I. *The Burden of Conscience: French Jewish Leadership during the Holocaust*. Bloomington, IN, 1987.

Cornwell, John. *Hitler's Pope: The Secret History of Pius XII*. New York, 1999.

Davies, Norman. *Rising '44: The Battle for Warsaw*. London, 2003.

Dawidowicz, Lucy S. *The War Against the Jews, 1933–1945*. Toronto, 1986.

Dobroszycki, Lucjan, and Jeffrey S. Gurock. *The Holocaust in the Soviet Union*. Armonk, NY, 1993.

Dwork, Deborah. *Children with a Star: Jewish Youth in Nazi Europe*. New Haven, 1991.

Ezergailis, Andrew. *The Holocaust in Latvia, 1941–1944: The Missing Center*. Riga/Washington, DC, 1996.

Favez, Jean-Claude. *The Red Cross and the Holocaust*. Cambridge, 1999.

Feingold, Henry L. *Bearing Witness: How America and Its Jews Responded to the Holocaust*. Syracuse, NY, 1995.

Fest, Joachim C. *Hitler*. New York, 1974.

Friedlander, Henry. *The Origins of Nazi Genocide: From Euthanasia to the Final Solution*. Chapel Hill, NC, 1995.

Friedländer, Saul. *Pius XII and the Third Reich: A Documentation*. New York, 1966.

————. *Kurt Gerstein: The Ambiguity of Good*. New York, 1969.

————. *Nazi Germany and the Jews: The Years of Persecution, 1933–1939*. New York, 1997.

————. *The Years of Extermination: Nazi Germany and the Jews, 1939–1945*. New York, 2007.

Friedman, Philip. *Roads to Extinction: Essays on the Holocaust*. Edited by Ada June Friedman. New York, 1980.

Friling, Tuvia. *Arrows in the Dark: David Ben-Gurion, the Yishuv Leadership, and Rescue Attempts during the Holocaust*. Madison, WI, 2005.

Goldhagen, Daniel Jonah. *Hitler's Willing Executioners: Ordinary Germans and the Holocaust*. New York, 1996.

Gross, Jan T. *Neighbors: The Destruction of the Jewish Community in Jedwabne, Poland*. Princeton, 2001.

Gutman, Yisrael, and Cynthia J. Haft. *Patterns of Jewish leadership in Nazi Europe, 1933–1945*. Jerusalem, 1979.

Gutman, Yisrael. *The Jews of Warsaw, 1939–1943: Ghetto, Underground, Revolt*. Bloomington, IN, 1982.

———. *Resistance: The Warsaw Ghetto Uprising*. Boston, 1994.

Gutman, Yisrael, and Avital Saf, eds. *The Nazi Concentration Camps*. Jerusalem, 1984.

Gutman, Yisrael, and Michael Berenbaum. *Anatomy of the Auschwitz Death Camp*. Bloomington, IN, 1994.

Gutteridge, Richard. *Open Thy Mouth for the Dumb! The German Evangelical Church and the Jews 1879–1950*. Oxford, 1976.

Hayes, Peter. *Industry and Ideology: IG Farben in the Nazi Era*. New York, 1987.

———. *From Cooperation to Complicity: Degussa in the Third Reich*. Cambridge, 2004.

Herf, Jeffrey. *Reactionary Modernism: Technology, Culture, and Politics in Weimar and the Third Reich*. New York, 1986.

———. *The Jewish Enemy: Nazi Propaganda during World War II and the Holocaust*. Cambridge, MA, 2006.

Hilberg, Raul. *Perpetrators, Victims, Bystanders: The Jewish Catastrophe, 1933–1945*. New York, 1992.

———. *The Destruction of the European Jews*. 3 vols. New Haven, 2003.

Jäckel, Eberhard. *Hitler in History*. Hanover, NH, 1984.

Kaplan, Marion A. *Between Dignity and Despair: Jewish Life in Nazi Germany*. New York, 1998.

Kater, Michael H. *The Twisted Muse: Musicians and Their Music in the Third Reich*. New York, 1997.

Kershaw, Ian. *The Nazi Dictatorship: Problems and Perspectives of Interpretation*. London, 1993.

———. *Hitler, 1889–1936: Hubris*. London, 1998.

———. *Hitler, 1936–45: Nemesis*. New York, 2000.

Kertzer, David I. *The Popes Against the Jews: The Vatican's Role in the Rise of Modern Anti-Semitism*. New York, 2001.

Kluger, Ruth. *Still Alive: A Holocaust Girlhood Remembered*. New York, 2001.

Laqueur, Walter. *The Terrible Secret: An Investigation into the Suppression of Information about Hitler's "Final Solution."* London, 1980.

Laqueur, Walter, and Richard Breitman. *Breaking the Silence.* New York, 1986.

Laqueur, Walter, and Judith Tydor Baumel, eds. *The Holocaust Encyclopedia.* New Haven, 2001.

Levi, Erik. *Music in the Third Reich.* New York, 1994.

Levi, Primo. *Survival in Auschwitz: The Nazi Assault on Humanity.* 1958. Reprint, New York, 1996.

Lewy, Guenter. *The Nazi Persecution of the Gypsies.* New York, 2000.

Lifton, Robert Jay. *The Nazi Doctors: Medical Killing and the Psychology of Genocide.* New York, 1986.

Lipstadt, Deborah E. *Beyond Belief: The American Press and the Coming of the Holocaust, 1933–1945.* New York, 1986.

Lookstein, Haskel. *Were We Our Brothers' Keepers? The Public Response of American Jews to the Holocaust, 1938–1944.* New York, 1985.

Lower, Wendy. *Nazi Empire-Building and the Holocaust in Ukraine.* Chapel Hill, NC, 2005.

Marrus, Michael R., and Robert O. Paxton. *Vichy France and the Jews.* New York, 1981.

Marrus, Michael R. *The Holocaust in History.* Hanover, NH, 1987.

Mayer, Arno J. *Why Did the Heavens not Darken?: The "Final Solution" in History.* New York, 1988.

Mazower, Mark. *Inside Hitler's Greece: The Experience of Occupation, 1941–44.* New Haven, 1993.

———. *Salonica, City of Ghosts: Christians, Muslims and Jews, 1430–1950.* New York, 2004.

Mendelsohn, Ezra. *The Jews of East Central Europe Between the World Wars.* Bloomington, IN, 1983.

Morley, John F. *Vatican Diplomacy and the Jews during the Holocaust, 1939–1943.* New York, 1980.

Müller, Melissa. *Anne Frank: The Biography.* New York, 1998.

Müller, Filip. *Eyewitness Auschwitz: Three Years in the Gas Chambers.* Chicago, 1999.

Ne'eman Arad, Gulie. *America, Its Jews, and the Rise of Nazism.* Bloomington, IN, 2000.

Neufeld, Michael J., and Michael Berenbaum, eds. *The Bombing of Auschwitz: Should the Allies Have Attempted It?* New York, 2000.

Payne, Stanley G. *A History of Fascism, 1914–1945*. Madison, WI, 1995.

Paxton, Robert O. *Vichy France: Old Guard and New Order, 1940–1944*. New York, 2001.

Peukert, Detlev J. K. *Inside Nazi Germany: Conformity, Opposition and Racism in Everyday Life*. New Haven, 1987.

Phayer, Michael. *The Catholic Church and the Holocaust, 1930–1965*. Bloomington, IN, 2000.

Polonsky, Antony, and Norman Davies, eds. *Jews in Eastern Poland and the USSR, 1939–46*. New York, 1991.

Poznanski, Renée. *Jews in France during World War II*. Waltham, MA, 2001.

Presser, J. *Ashes in the Wind: The Destruction of Dutch Jewry*. Detroit, 1988.

Proctor, Robert N. *Racial Hygiene: Medicine under the Nazis*. Cambridge, MA, 1988.

Pulzer, Peter. *The Rise of Political Anti-Semitism in Germany and Austria*. Cambridge, MA, 1988.

Rentschler, Eric. *The Ministry of Illusion: Nazi Cinema and its Afterlife*. Cambridge, MA, 1996.

Roseman, Mark. *The Villa, the Lake, the Meeting: Wannsee and the Final Solution*. London; New York, 2002.

Segev, Tom. *The Seventh Million: The Israelis and the Holocaust*. New York, 1993.

Sereny, Gitta. *Into that Darkness: From Mercy Killing to Mass Murder*. London, 1974.

Sofsky, Wolfgang. *The Order of Terror: The Concentration Camp*. Princeton, 1997.

Speer, Albert. *Inside the Third Reich: Memoirs*. New York, 1970.

Steinbacher, Sybille. *Auschwitz, A History*. London, 2005.

Steinweis, Alan E. *Art, Ideology and Economics in Nazi Germany: The Reich Chamber of Culture and the Regulation of the Culture Professions in Nazi Germany*. Chapel Hill, NC, 1988.

Sternhell, Zeev. *Neither Right nor Left: Fascist Ideology in France*. Berkeley, 1986.

Tec, Nechama. *Defiance: The Bielski Partisans*. New York, 1993.

Trunk, Isaiah. *Judenrat: The Jewish Councils in Eastern Europe under Nazi Occupation*. New York, 1972.

————. *Jewish Responses to Nazi Persecution: Collective and Individual Behavior in Extremis.* New York, 1979.

Ungváry, Krisztián. *The Siege of Budapest: One Hundred Days in World War II.* New Haven, 2005.

Wyman, David S. *Paper Walls: America and the Refugee Crisis, 1938–1941.* New York, 1985.

————. *The Abandonment of the Jews: America and the Holocaust, 1941–1945.* New York, 1998.

Yahil, Leni. *The Holocaust: The Fate of European Jewry.* New York, 1990.

Zuccotti, Susan. *Under His Very Windows: The Vatican and the Holocaust in Italy.* New Haven, 2000.

Zuckerman, Yitzhak. *A Surplus of Memory: Chronicle of the Warsaw Ghetto Uprising.* Berkeley, 1993.

INDEX

Merchant of Venice, The (Shakespeare), 98

Messersmith, George S., 30

Mexico, 182

Meyerbeer, 42

midwifery, 122

migration, Jewish. *see* emigration

Mihajlović, Draža, 245

Ministry of Agriculture and Food Supply, 304

Ministry of the Economy, 75–76

Ministry of the Interior, 99–101, 167
    Advisory Committee for Population and Racial Policy, 73

Minsk ghetto, 262, 302, 370–371, 377

Minzberg, Leon, 169

Mischdorf, 107

Mischlinge (mixed breeds), 48–51, 57–58, 65, 69–70, 72–73, 124, 125, 262, 292, 383, 385, 414

Mit brennender Sorge, 68

Moldavia, 244

Molnár, Ferenc, 187

Molotov, Vyacheslav, 201–202

Moltke, Freya von, 270–271, 362

Moltke, Helmuth von, 270–271

Mommsen, Hans, 362

Monowitz-Buna, 357

Monroe Doctrine, 233

Moore, Bob, 221

Moravia, 139–140, 267

Morgenthau, Henry, 392

Morocco, 268–269, 318

Moscow, 263–264
    Jewish bolshevism in, 67

Moshkin, Ilya, 302

Mossad L'Aliyah Beth, 182–183

Mount Elbrus, 317

Moyne, Lord, 287–288

Mozart, Wolfgang Amadeus, 28, 42

Muehsam, Heinrich, 305

Mühldorf, 415–416

Müller, Filip, 355, 418

Müller, Heinrich, 137

Müller, Ludwig, 18, 37–38

Munich
    anti-Jewish measures, 10, 80–81, 83–84, 98–102, 114–115, 121
    bombing of, 396
    "Eternal Jew" exhibition (1937), 98
    Hitler in (1934), 34
    large-scale disturbances (1935), 43
    opposition groups in, 362–363
    synagogue destruction in, 114

Munich Jesuits, 363

Murmelstein, Benjamin, 385, 410

music, xv, 3, 28, 29, 41–42, 97–98, 210–211, 255

Mussolini, Benito, 95–96, 106–107, 172, 178, 179, 344, 381, 399
    fall of, 346–347, 378
    march on Rome (1940), 174

Musy, Jean-Marie, 416

Napoleon, 196, 200

National Association of Jews in Germany, 24

National Association of Physicians, 194

National Representation of German Jews (Reichsvertretung Deutscher Juden), 23–24, 37–38, 54

National Socialist Association of Teachers, 128

National Socialist German Workers Party (NSDAP), 6–7

National Socialist Party. *See also* Nazi Germany
    congress of 1935, 44–49
    in France, 192–197
    Hitler's accession to power, 3–6, 33–34
    Hitler's proclamations and, 151–152
    Nuremberg congress (1935), 44–49
    party rally of 1938, 94
    Weltanshauung of, 67–68

National Socialist Students Association, 22–23

Naumann, Max, 4

Nazi Germany. *See also* Hitler, Adolf; National Socialist Party; *specific cities*; Third Reich
    anti-Comintern pact with Japan, 62
    anti-Jewish measures. See anti-Jewish measures
    assault on the Soviet Union, 148, 200–205, 216, 231–233, 245, 263–264, 300, 302
    Austrian annexation, 64, 86, 87–92, 165–166
    Catholic Church in, 362–363
    deportations from, 108–110, 180–182, 184–185, 261–262, 264–265, 268, 272, 276, 304–305
    deportations in, 108–110, 180–182, 184–185, 261–262, 264–265, 268, 272, 276, 304–305, 386